Hedonic Methods in Housing Markets

Andrea Baranzini • José Ramirez
Caroline Schaerer • Philippe Thalmann
Editors

Hedonic Methods in Housing Markets

Pricing Environmental Amenities and Segregation

Springer

Editors
Andrea Baranzini
Geneva School of Business Administration (HEG Genève)
University of Applied Sciences Western Switzerland
Switzerland

José Ramirez
Geneva School of Business Administration (HEG Genève)
University of Applied Sciences Western Switzerland
Switzerland

Caroline Schaerer
Geneva School of Business Administration (HEG Genève)
University of Applied Sciences Western Switzerland
Switzerland

Philippe Thalmann
École Polytechnique Fédérale de Lausanne
Switzerland

ISBN 978-0-387-76814-4 ISBN 978-0-387-76815-1 (eBook)
DOI 10.1007/978-0-387-76815-1

Library of Congress Control Number: 2008931292

Printed on acid-free paper

springer.com

Acknowledgements

This book would not have been possible without the help, collaboration and support of many persons. All the contributions have been personally commissioned and we have tried to coordinate the contents, so as to avoid overlap and foster complementarities, in order to treat the most relevant questions related to the application of the hedonic approach to the valuation of environmental amenities and to segregation/discrimination issues. Our greatest gratitude is to the authors, who have participated with much enthusiasm to this project and spent a lot of time in writing and revising their chapters. Draft papers were presented and discussed during an intense workshop at the Geneva School of Business Administration on 29 and 30 June 2007. Each selected chapter was reviewed and revised several times, with particular attention to presenting the main results of the literature, to fostering intuition and to showing policy implications.

We are particularly indebted to Laurence Infanger, Eva Robinson and Bea Van Gessel for their help in the organization and management of the Geneva Workshop. Thanks to Professor Jacques Silber, Bar-Ilan University, Israel, for his help in revising some of the chapters. Many thanks to Pierre-Yves Odier for putting the book into form: this was not an easy task, with so many different chapter formats and short deadlines.

We gratefully acknowledge financial support for the Geneva workshop and our own research in the field of hedonics by the Geneva School of Business Administration (HEG Genève); the University of Applied Sciences Western Switzerland (HES-SO); the Research group on the Economics and Management of the Environment (REME) of the Swiss Federal Institute of Technology, Lausanne (EPFL); the Swiss Academy of Humanities and Social Sciences; and the Swiss National Science Foundation, National Research Program 54 "Sustainable development of the built environment".

Last but not least, we are very grateful to our managing editors at Springer, Barbara Fess and Gillian Greenough, for support, advice and their faith in our project.

A.B., J.R., C.S. & P.T.
Geneva, 1st February 2008

Contents

List of Contributors

Bajari, Patrick
Department of Economics, University of Minnesota
1035 Heller Hall, 271 19th Avenue South, Minneapolis, MN 55455
United States

Baranzini, Andrea
Geneva School of Business Administration (HEG Genève)
University of Applied Sciences Western Switzerland (HES-SO)
7 Route de Drize, CH – 1227 Carouge-Geneva
Switzerland

Bayer, Patrick
Department of Economics, Duke University
222 Social Sciences Building, Durham, NC 27708
United States

Brossard, Thierry
Centre National de Recherche Scientifique, Université de Franche-Comté
UFR Lettres SHS, 32 rue Megevand, 25030 Besançon Cedex
France

Cavailhès, Jean
Centre d'Économie et Sociologie appliquées à l'Agriculture
et aux Espaces Ruraux, Institut National de la Recherche Agronomique
26 Bd Dr Petitjean, BP 87999, 21079 Dijon Cedex
France

Geniaux, Ghislain
Unité Ecodéveloppement, Institut National de la Recherche Agronomique
Domaine St-Paul, Site Agroparc, 84914 Avignon cedex 9
France

Hilal, Mohamed
Centre d'Économie et Sociologie appliquées à l'Agriculture
et aux Espaces Ruraux, Institut National de la Recherche Agronomique
26 Bd Dr Petitjean, BP 87999, 21079 Dijon Cedex
France

Hite, Diane
Department of Agricultural Economics and Rural Sociology,
Auburn University
209-B Comer Hall, Auburn, AL 36849
United States

Joly, Daniel
Centre National de Recherche Scientifique, Université de Franche-Comté
Lettres SHS, 32 rue Megevand, 25030 Besançon Cedex
France

Kahn, Matthew E.
Institute of the Environment, University of California
La Kretz Hall, Suite 300, Box 951496, Los Angeles, CA 90095
United States

Knight, John R.
Finance and Real estate, Eberhardt School of Business,
University of the Pacific
4622 Pebble Beach Drive, Stockton, CA 95219
United States

Kriström, Bengt
Department of Forest Economics, SLU-Umeå
Skogsmarkgränd 1, 90183 Umeå
Sweden

McMillan, Robert
Department of Economics, University of Toronto
Room 4060, Sidney Smith Hall, 100 St. George Street, Toronto, ON M5S 3G3
Canada

Napoléone, Claude
Unité Ecodéveloppement, Institut National de la Recherche Agronomique
Domaine St-Paul, Site Agroparc, 84914 Avignon cedex 9
France

Nelson, Jon P.
Department of Economics, Pennsylvania State University
608 Kern Building, University Park, PA 16802
United States

Ramirez, José V.
Geneva School of Business Administration (HEG Genève)
University of Applied Sciences Western Switzerland (HES-SO)
7 Route de Drize, CH – 1227 Carouge-Geneva
Switzerland

Schaerer, Caroline
Geneva School of Business Administration (HEG Genève)
University of Applied Sciences Western Switzerland (HES-SO)
7 Route de Drize, CH – 1227 Carouge-Geneva
Switzerland

Thalmann, Philippe
Research lab on the economics and management of the environment (REME)
Swiss Institute of Technology Lausanne (EPFL)
Station 16, 1015 Lausanne
Switzerland

Taylor, Laura O.
Agricultural and Resource Economics, North Carolina State University
Campus Box 8109, Raleigh, NC 27695-8109
United States

Tourneux, François-Pierre
Centre National de Recherche Scientifique, Université de Franche-Comté
Lettres SHS, 32 rue Megevand, 25030 Besançon Cedex
France

Tritz, Céline
Centre National de Recherche Scientifique, Université de Franche-Comté
Lettres SHS, 32 rue Megevand, 25030 Besançon Cedex
France

Wavresky, Pierre
Centre National de Recherche Scientifique, Université de Franche-Comté
Lettres SHS, 32 rue Megevand, 25030 Besançon Cedex
France

Wong, David W.S.
School of Computational Sciences, George Mason University
MS 6A2, 4400 University Drive, Fairfax, VA 22030
United States

Zabel, Jeffrey E.
Departments of Economics, Tufts University
54 Oak Avenue, 8 Upper Campus Rd., Newton, MA 02465
United States

List of Abbreviations

AHS	American Housing Survey
AIC	Akaike Information Criteria
ARIP	Accidental Release Information Program
BDD	Black Boundary Discontinuity Design
BLS	U.S. Department of Labor, Bureau of Labor Statistics
CAR	Conditional Autoregressive Model
CBD	Central Business District
CBG	Census Block Group
CERCLIS	Comprehensive Environmental Response, Compensation and Liability Information System
CS	Compensating Surplus
CV	Contingent Valuation
DB	Decibel
DNL	Day-Night Average Sound Level
EDF	Estimated Degree Of Freedom
EJ	Environmental Justice
EPA	Environmental Protection Agency
EPNL	Effective Perceived Noise Level
EUR	Euro
FIML	Full Information Maximum Likelihood
GAM	General Additive Models
GCV	Generalize Cross Validation
GIS	Geographic Information Systems
GLM	Generalized Linear Model
GMM	Generalized Method of Moments
GWR	Geographically Weighted Regressions
HDMA	Home Mortgage Disclosure Act
HDR	Highest Density Region
HP	Hedonic Price
HPM	Hedonic Price Model
HRF	Hedonic Rent Function
IPUMS	Integrated Public Use Microdata Series
LISA	Local Indicators of Spatial Autocorrelation
MAUP	Modifiable Areal Unit Problem
MGWR	Mixed Geographically Weighted Regression
MLS	Multiple Listing Service
MSA	Metropolitan Statistical Area

MWTP	Marginal Willingness to pay
NDI	Noise Deprecation Index
NOx	Nitrogen Oxide level
OLS	Ordinary least Squares
OS	Open Space
P-IRLS	Penalized Iteratively Reweighted Least Square
PUMAs	Public Use Microdata Areas
RDU	Raleigh-Durham International Airport
RP	Revealed Preferences
RUM	Random Utility Model
RSS	Residuals Sum of Square
SAR	Spatial Auto Regressive Model
SED	Spatial Error Dependence Model
SEM	Spatial Error Model
SF3	Census Tract Summary Files
SLD	Spatial Lag Dependence Model
2SLS	Two-Stage Least Squares
SMA	Spatial Moving Average Process
SMSA	Standard Metropolitan Statistical Area
SO_2	Sulfur Dioxide
SP	Stated Preferences
TASSIM	Transportation and Air Shed Simulation
TOM	Time on the Market
TRI	Toxic Release Inventory
UBRE	Unbiased Risk Estimator
USD	United States Dollar
USEPA	United States Environmental Protection Agency
WLS	Weighted Least Squares
WTP	Willingness to Pay

List of Figures

List of Tables

Introduction

Andrea Baranzini[1], José V. Ramirez[1], Caroline Schaerer[1], Philippe Thalmann[2]

[1]Geneva School of Business Administration, Carouge Geneva, Switzerland

[2]Swiss Federal Institute of Technology, Lausanne, Switzerland

1. Basics of the Hedonic Price Model

In the 1920s, possibly even a decade earlier, agricultural economists started to explain unit land prices by regressing them on property attributes (Colwell and Dilmore 1999). Well known is Frederick Waugh's (1928) regression of the prices of different types of asparagus on their color, diameter and homogeneity, with a view to helping farmers produce the quality demanded by the market. He found that Bostonians wanted green asparagus. More influential was the study by Andrew Court (1939), who had been mandated by General Motors to defend the company against Congress' accusations of monopolistic price pushing, after the U.S. Department of Labor Bureau of Labor Statistics (BLS) price index for cars had grown by 45% between 1925 and 1935. Court was probably the first to estimate a quality-adjusted price index on the basis of the hedonic price (HP) model. He found that car prices had actually declined by 55% over that period for the same quality.

Quality-adjusted price indices is just one, albeit important and increasingly common application of the HP method for economic policy.[1] The principle is simple. The basic form of the HP model is a functional relationship between the price P of a heterogeneous good i and its quality characteristics represented by a vector $\mathbf{x}_i$:

$$P_i = \mathrm{f}(\mathbf{x}_i;\boldsymbol{\beta}) + u_i \tag{1}$$

---

[1] Recent surveys of the hedonic approach literature, in particular applied to housing markets, are provided by e.g. Bateman et al. (2001), Day (2001), Palmquist (1999; 2005), Sheppard (1999) and Taylor (this Volume). For application of hedonic methods to actual economic policy, see Palmquist and Smith (2002).

In the context of this book, the heterogeneous good i is a property with price P_i and $\boldsymbol{x}_i$ would include its structural attributes of size and quality, characteristics of the immediate neighborhood and indicators of its environment and accessibility. $\boldsymbol{\beta}$ stands for the vector of coefficients that are estimated for the characteristics. There is always a non-explained part of the price represented by u.

After the equation has been estimated, it can be used to predict the price of any property i with characteristics $\boldsymbol{x}_i$:

$$\hat{P}_i = \mathrm{f}(\mathbf{x}_i;\hat{\boldsymbol{\beta}}) \tag{2}$$

Depending on the functional form of f(.), $\boldsymbol{\beta}$ is more or less directly related to a concept of unit price for the characteristics, as though the heterogeneous good were a shopping cart and its characteristics were commodities purchased separately. For characteristics measured in discrete quantities, an implicit price for characteristic k (p_k) of any property i can be computed as follows, where $\boldsymbol{x}_{\{-k\}}$ is the vector of all characteristics but the kth:

$$\hat{p}_k = \mathrm{f}(x_k + 1, x_{\{-k\}};\hat{\boldsymbol{\beta}}) - \mathrm{f}(x_k, x_{\{-k\}};\hat{\boldsymbol{\beta}}) \tag{3}$$

For continuous characteristics, it is common to compute implicit marginal prices:

$$\hat{p}_k = \frac{\partial \mathrm{f}(\mathbf{x}_i;\hat{\boldsymbol{\beta}})}{\partial x_k} \tag{4}$$

Implicit prices generally depend on the level of the characteristic and sometimes even on that of the other characteristics. Intuitively, the implicit price of an open fire place in a house depends on how many fire places it already contains and the number of low-temperature days.

If the data span several periods, one could take that into account by adding a time dummy to the explanatory variables (for a detailed introduction, see Triplett 2006). Consider for instance a log-linear model:

$$\ln P_i = \boldsymbol{\beta}'\mathbf{x}_i + \beta_{Ti}T_i + u_i \tag{5}$$

where T_i is the time dummy for the period of transaction of property i and β_{Ti} the coefficient for that period. The adjusted price of a property i sold in period T_i satisfies:

$$\ln \hat{P}_i = \hat{\boldsymbol{\beta}}'\mathbf{x}_i + \hat{\beta}_{Ti}T_i \tag{6}$$

If the same property had been sold in the base period for which thus there is no time dummy ($T_i = 0$), its estimated price $\hat{P}_{i0}$ would satisfy:

$$\ln \hat{P}_{i0} = \hat{\boldsymbol{\beta}}'\mathbf{x}_i \tag{7}$$

This allows estimating the price index between the base period and period T_i as $\exp(\hat{\beta}_{Ti})$.

Alternatively, hedonic price indices are computed by allowing the coefficients of the characteristics (i.e. the implicit prices) change every period and aggregating those implicit price changes using a traditional index number formula (Laspeyres, Paasche, Fisher, etc.). In that case, weights must be chosen, which amounts to designing a typical or representative property. The aggregation of the implicit price changes can be done more easily and in an intuitively more appealing fashion by simply computing the adjusted price of the representative property over time. Indexing that property by i and periods by t, the price index is:

$$\frac{\hat{P}_{it+1}}{\hat{P}_{it}} = \frac{f(\mathbf{x}_i; \hat{\boldsymbol{\beta}}_{t+1})}{f(\mathbf{x}_i; \hat{\boldsymbol{\beta}}_t)} \tag{8}$$

This ratio amounts to estimating the price of the same bundle of characteristics at two different dates. It can of course also be used to compare prices across regions without interference of quality differences. More relevant for policy purposes is the use of this HP method for testing whether prices are "fair", i.e. compatible with the market instead of distorted by market imperfections, discrimination or segregation (e.g. Kiel and Zabel 1996; Zabel, Hite, this Volume). Thus, the price P_i of a property of characteristics $\boldsymbol{x}_i$ can be compared to the price paid on average for such a bundle of characteristics $\hat{P}_i = f(\mathbf{x}_i; \hat{\boldsymbol{\beta}})$. When the HP method is a regression of rents on their characteristics, it can even be used as a reference for rent regulation.

In the area of environmental economics, the HP method is used more frequently for estimating the impact of specific environmental amenities or nuisances on property prices, or to transfer the value of risks derived from wages differentials in the labor market (see e.g. Viscusi 1993) to assess environmental risks. Indeed, many environmental and land use characteristics are not traded in markets and are thus often undervalued. As a result, when assessing public projects and policies, environmental values are often not fully integrated in the discussions or not considered at the same level as e.g. the financial costs related to environmental protection.

Actually, the HP approach is not the only economic valuation technique and the literature proposes various methods for assessing the value of non-marketed goods such as environmental quality (for a survey, see e.g. Mäler and Vincent 2006; van den Bergh 1999). For instance, the "avoided cost" approach consists in the assessment of the defensive expenditures undertaken by the individuals to reduce impact of an environmental disamenity, e.g. in the case of noise, expenditures for double-glazing. This approach is relatively simple to implement, but it is not theoretically correct, since it does not refer to individual preferences and can thus hardly be interpreted as a proxy for welfare gains or losses. There are two classes of valuation methods, which are based on preferences.

On the one hand, "stated preferences" (SP) methods apply contingent valuation, conjoint analysis or choice experiments in order to directly infer individuals' preferences for given environmental features or landscape uses. Contingent valuation (CV) is the most popular approach among SP techniques. It is based on a structured survey that defines a hypothetical market from which to infer willingness-to-pay (WTP) measures for particular environmental amenities or landscape features.

On the other hand, "revealed preferences" (RP) approaches make use of market information in order to infer the value of environmental and landscape characteristics. For instance, the travel cost method is based on travel expenditures and on the opportunity cost of the time spent for travelling in order to infer the value of a given site, such as a park or a natural reserve. Such an approach is however generally limited to recreational uses (see e.g. Hanley et al. 2003, for a survey). The HP method belongs to the family of RP valuation approaches. Indeed, if characteristic x_k whose implicit price is computed in equation (3) or (4) is an environmental characteristic, the implicit price measures the impact of that characteristic on property prices. It answers questions such as: What is the loss of wealth for property owners exposed to airport-related noise? Or: What would rental income be absent a given nuisance?

The fundamental advantages of the hedonic approach with respect to the others valuation methods are the following:

- It is based on households' real WTP for the dwelling's characteristics as revealed on the market, rather than households' assessment of hypothetical alternatives from which their supposed WTP is deduced (see also Cropper and Oates 1992);
- It integrates and values environmental quality and the features of the urban neighborhood of the dwellings in a coherent framework, which also incorporates physical apartment and building quality characteristics;
- With the recent development of geographic information systems (GIS) (see Cavailhès et al., this Volume), statistical treatments and environmental quality measures, the hedonic approach allows to analyze a large portion of the housing/rental market, including thousands of observations, providing thus more reliable indications than, e.g. surveys confined to a few hundreds of households.

We should however note that the HP method, like all the valuation techniques proposed in the literature, is a partial equilibrium approach, as it assumes that the price of the property would be different without the environmental nuisance and nothing else. Consider a neighborhood close to a landfill. Comparing prices paid for properties in that neighborhood with prices paid in other neighborhood with a full HP method allows identifying the depressing impact on prices of the landfill. Depending on the size of the market, it might be risky, however, to assume that all those property prices would sell at the higher price if the landfill were closed. Indeed, that neighborhood might precisely be attracting a clientele with low purchasing power and might not find sufficient buyers willing to pay the higher prices. Therefore, as shown by Palmquist (1992), it is only when the externality is "localized" (like e.g. noise) that the hedonic price schedule does not change, and thus the WTP for an environmental change can be determined from the implicit price.

It is even trickier to interpret implicit prices as WTP for protection from the environmental nuisance or for the environmental amenity. To begin with, the marginal WTP is only equal to the marginal implicit price for an individual who is in equilibrium, i.e., who could choose among bundles of characteristics with the same implicit prices until she found the one that maximizes her welfare. The marginal implicit price changes with the level of the corresponding characteristic and, possibly, the levels of other characteristics. So does the individual's marginal WTP, but it unlikely changes in the same fashion as the marginal implicit price. As a result, drawing out the marginal implicit price and integrating does not yield total WTP. It is rather necessary to add structure to preferences, information on occupants and, possibly, the supply side of the market, to be able to estimate WTP in a second stage of the HP method, as shown first by Rosen (1974) and Freeman (1974) and applied by Bajari and Kahn in this Volume. The identification problem is much more severe than this brief presentation suggests and several contributions in this Volume address it. If it is still possible to extract preferences from the hedonic model, then consumer surpluses can be estimated. This can be used in cost-benefit analysis or for compensation payments.

Another identification problem plaguing the application of HP method to environmental valuation is that of poor or missing indicators. The size and even the quality and condition of a property are relatively easy to measure. It is much more difficult to measure environmental amenities. Even when technical measures are relatively easy to obtain, such as concentrations of some air pollutant or peak noise levels, it is very hard to be sure that those measures correspond to what tenants and buyers perceive (for a discussion, see Taylor, this Volume, Nelson, this Volume and Baranzini et al. 2006). Moreover, very often environmental indicators are only available at a relatively aggregate level, e.g. that of the census tract. This might bias estimated coefficients and, more importantly, amplify their standard errors. Spatial econometrics are increasingly used to address this problem, e.g. by Geniaux and Napoléone in this Volume.

In addition, the HP approach used for environmental assessment faces all the problems of standard HP method, such as the choice of functional form, for which theory provides very little guidance, multicolinearity, as many characteristics of properties often go together, non-standard residuals, segmentation of the data, as multiple housing markets may co-exist with imperfect information and arbitrage (Nelson, this Volume). Those problems have relatively little consequence when the goal is to predict quality-adjusted prices as in equation (2), except possibly the market imperfections problem. Thus, the fact that prices depend also on the conditions of the transaction (time on market, bargaining power of buyer and seller) may limit the ability of the HP method to predict prices (see Knight, this Volume). The econometric issues are much more problematic when one is interested in individual marginal prices and even more so when those marginal prices are extrapolated to determine WTP.

We emphasize that the HP model can be used not only to estimate the economic consequences of environmental nuisances or to assess the economic value of environmental amenities, but also to consider their distribution among the population. One could argue that local nuisances such as noise and air pollution are compensated by lower housing prices. In that case, a problem arises if that compensation is imperfect, in the sense that some households pay higher rents than other households exposed to similar nuisances. A form of "environmental injustice" can thus result, as discussed by Hite, this Volume. More in general, when socio-economic or demographic pattern of households are linked to such overpaying, that hints at discrimination, either by landlords or by some feature of housing policy (e.g. rent regulation). Prejudice could co-exist with discrimination and, indeed, are mutually reinforcing (Zabel, this Volume). Prejudice against groups is seen when housing prices are impacted by a change in the socio-demographic composition of the neighborhood.

Estimators of hedonic models are however very reluctant to include personal characteristics next to those of the dwellings in equation (1). Indeed, textbook economics and Rosen's (1974) theoretical foundations of the HP method show that competitive market prices are independent of individual buyers and sellers. Therefore, the race or any other characteristic of the buyer should not affect the price of houses. However, the rents and prices for housing contracts are obviously not always set on textbook competitive markets and thus, when there is widespread discrimination, some characteristics of the buyer, such as race, can affect the price of the house. The neighborhood socio-demographic characteristics can also be considered as a variable defining the quality of the neighborhood and thus also have an influence prices. It seems therefore important to take into account as much as possible indicators on the household and neighborhoods characteristics while controlling for the housing characteristics when estimating the hedonic locus related to housing prices or rents (see Kiel and Zabel, 1996; Zabel, this Volume).

However, the HP just depicts the equilibrium price locus and from it is thus difficult to infer why (if any) price differences are due to discrimination or segregation forces (see Bajari and Kahn, 2005 and this Volume). In addition, as discussed by Bayer and McMillan (2007 and this Volume) segregation measures used in HP studies are often correlated with unobserved neighborhood quality (e.g. schools quality) and thus the results on segregation are likely to be biased. Using the HP method to assess discrimination and segregation is therefore not an easy task and an important field for future research. In this context, it will be essential to also clarify the concept of segregation to be used in HP models. A starting point in this field is discussed by the contribution of Wong (this Volume), who evaluates how segregation measures can be incorporated into HP models.

2. The Contributions in this Volume

This book is composed of three parts: Part I on methods includes two chapters on the basics, problems and the literature related to the application of the HP method; the four chapters in Part II discuss applications of the HP method to urban environment issues, while the four chapters in Part III analyze its relevance and limits when dealing with segregation and discrimination issues. The book's Appendix explains how to implement a hedonic model, by making use of a free dataset and free software.

The first part of the book is devoted to the presentation of the theoretical bases, problems and recent developments in applying the hedonic model.

In her contribution, *Laura Taylor* reviews the general framework upon which hedonic analysis is built and provides an overview of some topical implementation issues and recent developments. The chapter takes up in turn such fundamental issues as those related to the possibility to recover unbiased parameter estimates from first-stage HP estimation, the endogeneity of regressors due to omitted variables and simultaneous determination of prices and observable characteristics, and market imperfections. She also addresses the policy-relevant issue of the second stage hedonic estimation, in order to attempt recovering preference parameters from the estimated implicit prices.

John Knight emphasizes the role of the conditions of transactions for predicting prices. Given that the housing market is quite distant from a perfectly competitive one, this chapter is an in-depth exploration on the inclusion of the buyer and owner characteristics in the HP method, in order to account for bargaining power. Contrary to most of existing HP studies, in this chapter Knight discusses in detail the opportunities to incorporate time on the market data in the HP framework, in order to analyze the impact of various market imperfections on house price. But the buyers' characteristics could also affect prices through preferences and WTP. On thin markets, where individual buyers matter, it might be difficult to disentangle this effect from the bargaining power effect. Knight's chapter is thus not just a paper on how selling conditions influence property prices but also a review of the literature on the marketing process, with interesting proposals on how it should be taken into account in hedonic estimation.

The second part of the book reviews the application of the hedonic approach to the valuation of natural land use preservation and noise abatement measures. The application of the HP method to assess and value urban environmental issues has a longstanding tradition in applied economics, in particular because the results of HP studies can contribute to a wide range of policy issues. Indeed, results of HP studies can feed three main policy areas. The first is in the context of formal or informal cost-benefit analyses, which are required by several countries, e.g. the USA, EU and Switzerland, in particular for major infrastructure or for assessing the economic efficiency of specific projects or policies (see e.g. US OMB, 1996; EC, 1999; DFE, 2000). A second application of the results of the HP method is in the context of evaluation of the full cost of specific economic activities, in order to implement corrective policies, e.g. environmental taxes (e.g. see Bickel and Friedrich 2004), or to correct the global measure of economic performance, e.g. green GDP (e.g. UN et al. 2003). Finally, HP studies can be used in litigation, for instance in helping determining the monetary compensation to exposure to environmental disamenities or catastrophes (e.g. compensation for aircraft noise).

Noise is a main challenge to environmental policy. Although noise policies were implemented in several countries in the last decades, the proportion of the population that is exposed to noise levels exceeding legal limits is still relatively important. For instance, it is estimated that in European OECD countries, about 30% of the population is exposed to road traffic noise levels above 55 decibels and about 15% above 65 decibels (OECD, 2001). In the urban context, noise is thus a major environmental disamenity which has an important impact on the quality of life and as such, it might have an impact on housing prices. Indeed, starting already in the 1960's, there emerged a relatively important literature on the impact of traffic and aircraft noise on property values (see Palmquist and Smith, 2002). The chapter by *Jon Nelson* provides an extensive review of HP noise studies, their potential and limitations. He critically discusses the most recent developments and comes out with a number of major issues of relevance to HP researchers. In particular, he points out the importance to account for the spatial nature of the housing market, a problem which is of particular relevance to the recent literature, given the larger sample of housing data. Market segmentation and spatial dependence are discussed at length, with the different approaches and applications in the literature. The chapter also presents the opportunity to take advantage of housing market adjustments in order to analyse the changes in noise evaluation over time and asymmetric information. The issue of noise measurement and annoyance is also discussed. Finally, the chapter present results from stated preferences (SP) techniques and compares them with the HP approach.

Jean Cavailhès, *Thierry Brossard*, *Mohamed Hilal*, *Daniel Joly*, *François-Pierre Tourneux*, *Céline Trit*, and *Pierre Wavresky* show how the HP method can fruitfully be used to understand periurbanisation, i.e. the move of urban dwellers to near-city locations. The expansion of the cities into the country-side is a fast growing characteristic of most developed countries. For instance, the authors mention that in France, about one-third of the land area is periurban, a proportion that has doubled in the last ten years. In this context, Jean Cavailhès and co-authors examine the role or magnitude of preferences for greenery and the view on different types of landscape. The authors firstly review the different strategies and results from the relatively recent literature on the economic valuation of landscape use. They show that the measures of landscape composition and diversity, as well as the measure of the view on them, have drastically changed in recent years, thanks to the advent of geographically information systems (GIS) data. In the second part of the chapter, the authors present an original application by using transaction prices data for detached houses in the region around Besançon (France). The view on plots of different types at different distances is the main location information entered into the HP model, next to distance to town hall (which turns out to be insignificant) and a dummy for the municipality. The view is measured with great detail, along 120 rays at eyes level, taking into account natural and built obstacles. They find that landscape contributes little to explaining house prices, possibly because it is quite homogenous. It is however interesting to highlight that landscape features have an impact on prices only when they are very close to houses and are visible, which seems to indicate that households are quite short-sighted.

With the increasing wealth of geographic descriptors, it has become both possible and necessary to better select the appropriate location variables for the hedonic price equation and to allow for spatial variability of the coefficients for the standard quality descriptors. *Ghislain Geniaux* and *Claude Napoléone* survey semi-parametric models that allow dealing systematically with geographic descriptors. They draw on advanced spatial econometric and smoothing methods, where geographic coordinates play a key role. To show how those methods can take into account the location of properties relative to several agglomerations, the authors estimate a hedonic price equation for house sales in the Vaucluse district in Southern France, for which they define seven potential central business districts (CBD). It is interesting to note how figures and maps play an important role with those econometric methods.

Patrick Bajari and *Matthew Kahn* also examine the incentives for suburbanization by comparing how home buyers value the attributes of urban and suburban houses respectively, including community attributes. They go through all the steps of Rosen's (1974) two-stage approach and beyond to determine home buyers' WTP for those attributes and for avoiding commutes. They estimate a local linear hedonic equation, use it to compute WTP for a change in the main housing attributes, and regress this on household characteristics. This empirical strategy provides interesting information on the joint distribution of tastes and demographic characteristics. Then, the authors use that information to estimate average WTP for two policy counterfactuals: a denser city and the concentration of all employment in the CBD. This allows estimating the incentives for urban sprawl and the gains of locating employment closer to suburban dwellings. The data used are a huge set of 173,000 property transactions and corresponding individual or census tract household characteristics in Los Angeles county, for the period 2000 to 2003.

The third part of the book extends the discussion by considering the role of the individual characteristics in the housing market and more specifically the fact that some categories of households might potentially be concentrated in neighborhoods of low environmental quality. After introducing traditional and more advanced measures of segregation, the chapters present and discuss recent findings on residential segregation and discrimination on the housing market.

David Wong introduces the problem of segregation and clarifies the legitimacy to consider it in a HP model. Since part of the procedure in hedonic modeling applied to the housing market is to identify the variables describing the neighborhood characteristics, Wong emphasizes that the degree of neighborhood segregation can be an influential characteristic in defining neighborhood quality. By carefully presenting and commenting aspatial and spatial measures of segregation, his chapter provides a solid understanding of residential segregation and describes how it can be taken into account when estimating a HP model. To date, few HP models have actually used segregation indices and therefore this chapter opens the door to promising research.

Jeffrey Zabel discusses how the HP method can be used to test for discrimination in the housing market. He introduces four models of prejudice and racial discrimination, including the Border and the Amenity models, two influential models in the literature on housing discrimination, and indicates how they could be tested with the HP method. He shows the practical difficulties that are typically met when performing such tests, which are mainly related to the neighborhood definition and to insufficient data. Finally, he uses this framework to review and evaluate the empirical literature on racial discrimination and segregation on the U.S. housing market produced over the last 25 years, observing that the vast majority of the classical discrimination literature was written in the 1970s, but that there is actually a renewed interest for these issues in the HP literature.

Indeed, *Diane Hite* shows how the HP approach can be useful in analyzing environmental justice. Her chapter begins by defining environmental justice, how it relates to discrimination and how it could possibly be tested using within the HP framework. In a nutshell, there is lack of environmental justice when the disadvantaged group has to locate in a less favorable environment and fails to get compensation through lower housing prices. Hite develops two approaches to test environmental discrimination. The first compares the implicit prices for environmental quality obtained when estimating separate hedonic price equations for different groups of the population. The second, based on the random utility model, tests whether the disadvantaged group would be more likely to choose the environmentally more favorable location if it had access to the consumption bundle (other housing characteristics and remaining income) of the advantaged group. Hite surveys the discrimination literature based on those two approaches but also on other indicators of discrimination. She carefully indicates the many difficulties faced by those approaches, which are all more or less strongly related to insufficient available data. Indeed, the advent of large datasets with housing and personal data at the household level and the corresponding information on exposure to environmental nuisances bear some promise for much finer tests of environmental injustice.

The chapter by *Patrick Bayer* and *Robert McMillan* starts with a discussion on how segregation preferences are accounted for in a HP framework. With the help of a basic but very interesting model of racial sorting, they show that the coefficient of a race composition indicator in a hedonic price equation is likely to underestimate the taste for segregation because of the heterogeneity of households' preferences. Moreover, they highlight that it is very difficult to distinguish empirically between self sorting and segregation because common measures of preference for segregated neighborhoods may be seriously tainted by unmeasured quality differences that are typically correlated with race. They maintain that this result applies to all hedonic models that include socio-demographic neighborhood data. After providing evidence of the high correlation between racial composition of neighborhoods and the school quality in the Francisco Bay Area, the authors describe and estimate a HP model emphasizing boundary areas between neighborhoods. The results seem indeed to suggest that HP models studying segregation issues should pay attention to the issues of unobserved neighborhood quality and heterogeneous preferences. Those interesting results are a promising avenue for future research, also outside the USA reality.

In the Appendix, *Bengt Kriström* provides a didactic approach to estimating a simple HP model using the freely available software R (see R Development Core Team 2007). The chapter makes use of the famous data for the Boston Standard Metropolitan Statistical Area (SMSA), 1970, used in the classic study of Harrison and Rubinfeld (1978) and then in a wide range of papers. Based on those data, he shows step-by-step how the HP model is specified and analyzed. To give an insight on the issues that need to be addressed in an empirical hedonic study, the chapter provides detailed results and comments on standard econometric problems, such as the choice of functional form, multicollinearity or heteroskedasticity. It should be noted that all the exact computer codes are provided so that all the results in this Appendix are entirely and directly replicable, which allows direct exploration of the analysis and a comparison with what has been found in the literature.

References

Baranzini A, Schaerer C, Ramirez JV, Thalmann P (2006) Feel it or measure it – perceived vs. measured noise in hedonic models. Available at SSRN: http://ssrn.com/abstract=937259

Bateman IJ, Day B, Lake IR, Lovett AA (2001) The effect of road traffic noise on residential property values: a literature review and hedonic pricing study. Scottish Executive Development Department, Edinburgh, UK

Bickel P, Friedrich R. (eds) (2004) ExternE. Externalities of Energy. Methodology 2005 Update. Office for Official Publications of the European Communities, Luxembourg

Colwell PF and Dilmore G (1999) Who was first? An examination of an early hedonic study. Land Economics 75(4): 620-626

Court AT (1939) Hedonic price indexes with automotive examples. In: The Dynamics of Automobile Demand. General Motors Company, New York, 99-117

Cropper ML, Oates WE (1992) Environmental Economics: A Survey. Journal of Economic Literature, 30(2): 675-740

Day B (2001) The theory of Hedonic Markets: Obtaining welfare measures for changes in environmental quality using hedonic market data. Economics for the Environment Consultancy

Département Fédéral de l'Économie (2000) Analyse d'impact de la réglementation. Direction de la politique économique, Analyse de la réglementation, version du 8 mars 2000 Secrétariat d'État à l'économie (seco), Berne

European Commission (EC) (1999) Economic Evaluation of a Directive on National Emission Ceilings for Certain Atmospheric Pollutants. E.C., Brussels
Freeman AM (1974) On Estimating Air Pollution Control Benefits from Land Value Studies. The Journal of Environmental Economics and Management, 1, 277-288.
Hanley N, Shaw WD, Wright RE (2003) The New Economics of Outdoor Recreation. Edward Elgar, Cheltenham
Harrison Jr D, Rubinfeld DL (1978) Hedonic housing prices and the demand for clean air. Journal of environmental economics and management 5: 81–102
Kiel KA, Zabel JE (1996) House price differentials in U.S. cities: household and neighborhood racial effects, Journal of housing economics 5: 143–165
Mäler, KG, Vincent J (eds.) (2006) Handbook of Environmental Economics. Vol 2, Valuing Environmental Changes. Elsevier, North-Holland
Organisation for Economic Co-Operation and Development (OECD) (2001), OECD Environmental Outlook. OECD, Paris
Palmquist RB (1992) Valuing Localized Externalities. Journal of Urban Economics 31: 59-68
Palmquist RB (1999) Hedonic Models. In van den Bergh JCJM (ed.) Handbook of Environmental and Resource Economics. Edward Elgar, Cheltenham, 765-776.
Palmquist RB (2005) Property Value Models. In: Mäler KG and Vincent J. (eds.) Handbook of Environmental Economics, Vol. 2. North Holland, Amsterdam
Palmquist RB, Smith VK (2002) The Use of Hedonic Property Value Techniques for Policy and Litigation. In: Tietenberg TH and Folmer H. (eds.) The International Yearbook of Environmental and Resource Economics 2002/2003. Edward Elgar, 115-164.
R Development Core Team (2007) R: A language and environment for statistical computing. R Foundation for statistical computing, Vienna, Austria, http://www.R-project.org
Rosen S (1974) Hedonic price and implicit markets: product differentiation in pure equilibrium. Journal of political economy 82: 34–55
Sheppard S (1999) Hedonic analysis of housing markets. In: Handbook of regional and urban economics. Volume 3. Applied urban economics. Elsevier science, North-Holland Amsterdam New York Oxford, pp 1595–1635
Triplett J (2006) Handbook on Hedonic Indexes and Quality Adjustments. Special Application to Information Technology Products. OECD, Paris
United States Office of Management and Budget (US OMB) (1996) Economic Analysis of Federal Regulations Under Executive Order 12866. Executive Office of the President, Washington DC
United Nations (UN), European Commission, International Monetary Fund, Organisation for Economic Co-operation and Development, World Bank (2003) Integrated Environmental and Economic Accounting. Studies in Methods, Series F, 61, Rev.1 (ST/ESA/STAT/SER.F/61/Rev.1)
van den Bergh JCJM (ed.) (1999) Handbook of Environmental and Resource Economics. Edward Elgar, Cheltenham
Viscusi WK (1993) The Value of Risks to Life and Health. Journal of Economic Literature 31: 1912-1946
Waugh FV (1928) Quality factors influencing vegetable prices. Journal of Farm Economics 10(2): 185-196

PART I
Methods

1 Theoretical Foundations and Empirical Developments in Hedonic Modeling

Laura O. Taylor[1]

North Carolina State University, Raleigh, United States

1.1 Introduction

Although hedonic analyses have been reported as far back as Waugh's (1928) analysis of agricultural markets, it was Rosen's (1974) seminal work that began a rich theoretical and empirical literature exploring the role of housing attributes in consumer decision making. Housing choice not only confers to the owner/renter consumption of property and structural housing characteristics, but consumption of all location characteristics of the property such as proximity to environmental amenities and disamenities. As such, observed choices over housing reveals to the researcher information about the underlying preferences for these amenities or other characteristics of interest. In this chapter, we review the hedonic model as developed by Rosen as well as recent theoretical and empirical developments in hedonic modeling.[2]

In the next section, we present Rosen's hedonic model describing consumer and firm decision making within a heterogeneous goods market. Implementation of Rosen's hedonic framework consists of two related steps often referred to as first-stage and second-stage analyses. In a first-stage analysis, the equilibrium hedonic price function is estimated using information about sales prices and housing characteristics. This analysis allows researchers to recover the implicit prices of housing characteristics. First-stage analyses are the most common application of the hedonic method because the data requirements are minimal and the needed economic insights often only require marginal price information. In Section 1.3, we consider estimation of the equilibrium hedonic price function. We focus on

[1] The author would like to thank the Editors of this Volume, Bengt Kriström, and Jon P. Nelson for helpful comments on an earlier draft of this chapter.

[2] Other reviews of the hedonic method, primarily for the purposes of nonmarket valuation, are found in Palmquist (2005), Taylor (2003), Freeman (2003), and Bockstael and McConnell (2007).

A. Baranzini et al. (eds.), *Hedonic Methods in Housing Markets*, doi: 10.1007/978-0-387-76815-1_1,

recent research concerned with recovering unbiased parameter estimates for the hedonic price function. In particular, concern over endogenous regressors due to omitted variables and simultaneous determination of prices and observable characteristics is discussed. In Section 1.4, we also review research which relaxes the assumption that the housing market is perfectly competitive with fully informed agents.

While most hedonic analyses only estimate a first stage hedonic price function, information from this first stage analysis may be used to complete a second stage analysis in which the underlying preferences for housing characteristics are estimated. Rosen (1974) described a two-step procedure in which implicit prices for housing characteristics recovered in the first stage analysis could be combined with observed quantities of characteristics chosen to estimate underlying demands for characteristics. In the thirty years since Rosen's first proposed this two-stage approach, much has been written about its potential and its limitations. We review the method and recent research which indicates the promise of the method has yet to be fully exploited. We also review alternative methods of recovering demand parameters including random utility models and locational equilibrium models. Section 1.5 offers concluding statements.

1.2 Theoretical Foundations

The behavioral process assumed to underlie the hedonic price equilibrium, as initially set forth by Rosen (1974) is presented in this section. The discussion below follows that of Taylor (2003). We initially assume a perfectly competitive market with many buyers and sellers, and that a continuum of house attributes are available. Following common notation, let Z represent a housing bundle with characteristics $\underline{z} = z_1, z_2, \ldots, z_n$. The competitive equilibrium establishes an equilibrium price schedule $P(\underline{z})$, which is taken as exogenous by each consumer and producer of housing.

Assume consumer utility is defined over two goods, Z and X, a composite numeraire. Consumer j with demographic characteristics α^j has utility defined as:

$$U^j(X, z_1, z_2, \ldots, z_n; \alpha^j). \tag{1.1}$$

If we assume the consumer only purchases one unit of housing, the budget constraint is given by $y^j = X + P(\underline{z})$. The consumer seeks to maximize utility by choosing X and each element of Z such that the following marginal condition is satisfied for each z_i:

$$\frac{\partial P}{\partial z_i} = \frac{\partial U / \partial z_i}{\partial U / \partial X}. \tag{1.2}$$

Equation 1.2 indicates that the consumer will choose levels of each z_i and X such that the marginal rate of substitution between any characteristic, z_i, and the composite numeraire commodity, X, is equal to the rate at which the consumer can trade z_i for X in the marketplace.

An alternative formulation of the consumer's problem is to describe the optimal bid a consumer will make for a house. The bid function, θ, describes the relationship between the dollar bid consumer j will make for house Z as one or more of its component characteristics are changed, while utility and income remain constant. Equation 1.1 can be used to define the bid function formally by recognizing that income less the bid a consumer makes for house Z is the amount of money left over to spend on the numeraire, X. Thus, the relationship:

$$U^j(y_0 - \theta, \underline{z}, \alpha^j) \equiv U_0 \tag{1.3}$$

indicates how a consumer's optimal bid must vary in response to changes in $\underline{Z}$ if utility and income are held constant. Solving equation 1.3 for θ indicates that $\theta^j = \theta(\underline{z}, y_0, U_0^j, \alpha^j)$, where y_0 is exogenous income and U_0^j is a fixed level of utility. Total differentiation of equation 1.3 yields the first-order condition for a consumer that the marginal bid for z_i, θ_{zi}, will equal the marginal rate of substitution between any characteristic, z_i, and X. Combining this last result with that in equation 1.2 indicates that for utility maximization, the marginal bid a consumer places for any house characteristic must equal the marginal price of that characteristic, or:

$$\theta_{zi} \equiv \frac{\partial \theta}{\partial z_i} = \frac{\partial P}{\partial z_i} \equiv P_{zi}. \tag{1.4}$$

Many environmental applications of the hedonic model focus on estimation of $P(\underline{z})$, and thus P_{zi}, relying on the condition in equation 1.4 to recover marginal willingness to pay for the environmental attribute.

Although the vast majority of hedonic housing applications implicitly or explicitly assume housing supply is fixed, supply is easily modeled in the perfectly competitive framework considered by Rosen. Allow a firm with characteristics δ^k to maximize profits:

$$\Pi = H * P(\underline{z}) - C(H, \underline{z}, \delta^k) \tag{1.5}$$

where H is the number of housing units of type Z that the firm produces and $C(\bullet)$ is a well-behaved cost function. Recall, the assumption is that firms face an exogenous price function $P(\underline{z})$. Thus, while the firm cannot affect $P(\underline{z})$, it can affect the price it receives for its product by choosing the bundle of attributes in Z it chooses to produce. We will assume the firm chooses a single type to produce, Z^k, and then chooses how many of that type to produce.[3] Maximizing profits through the choice of $\underline{z}$ and H indicates the following marginal condition:

$$\partial P(\underline{z}) \Big/ \partial z_i = \frac{\partial C(H,\underline{z},\delta^k)}{\partial z_i} \cdot \frac{1}{H} \tag{1.6}$$

which indicates that the firm's optimal choice of z_i must satisfy the condition that the marginal price of z_i is equated to the marginal cost of producing z_i per house. The firm also maximizes profits with respect to the number of housing units to produce. The first order condition related to this choice indicates that the total price of a house, $P(\underline{z})$, must equal the marginal cost of producing a housing unit, i.e., $\partial C(H,\underline{z},\delta^k)/\partial H$.

Similar to the consumer's problem, we can define an offer function for firms which describes the amount of money a firm is willing to accept for any particular house type, Z, holding constant the number of units produced and its level of profit, or $\varphi^k = \varphi(\underline{z}; H, \Pi_0, \delta^k)$. Substituting the offer function in for $P(\underline{z})$ and solving the optimal offers indicates that at the optimum the marginal offer for each characteristics will equal the marginal cost of producing that characteristic, or:

$$\varphi_{zi} \equiv \frac{\partial \varphi}{\partial z_i} = \frac{\partial C}{\partial z_i}\frac{1}{H}. \tag{1.7}$$

Combining equation 1.6 and equation 1.7 indicates that at the optimum, the marginal offer for each characteristic will just equal the marginal price for that characteristic.

The bid, offer, and hedonic price function are depicted in Figure 1.1, which first appears in Rosen (1974). $P(\underline{z})$ is shown to be a nonlinear function of z_1, a relationship we often expect to be the case. However, because $P(\underline{z})$ is an envelope function, it make take any form. Properties of the bid function are easily described using Figure 1.1, which depicts the bid functions for two consumers, θ^1 and θ^2. Bid functions are concave in $\underline{z}$ and higher levels of utility for the consumer are represented by bid function contours closer to the horizontal axis (i.e., $U_2^1 > U_1^1 > U_0^1$ in Figure 1.1). Similarly, offer functions for two firms, φ^1 and φ^2, are also depicted with higher levels of profits being indicated by offer functions which are further from the horizontal axis. As indicated in Figure 1.1, offer functions are convex in $\underline{z}$.

---

[3] This assumption is easily relaxed and the firm may produce multiple varieties if we assume the cost function is separable in product types.

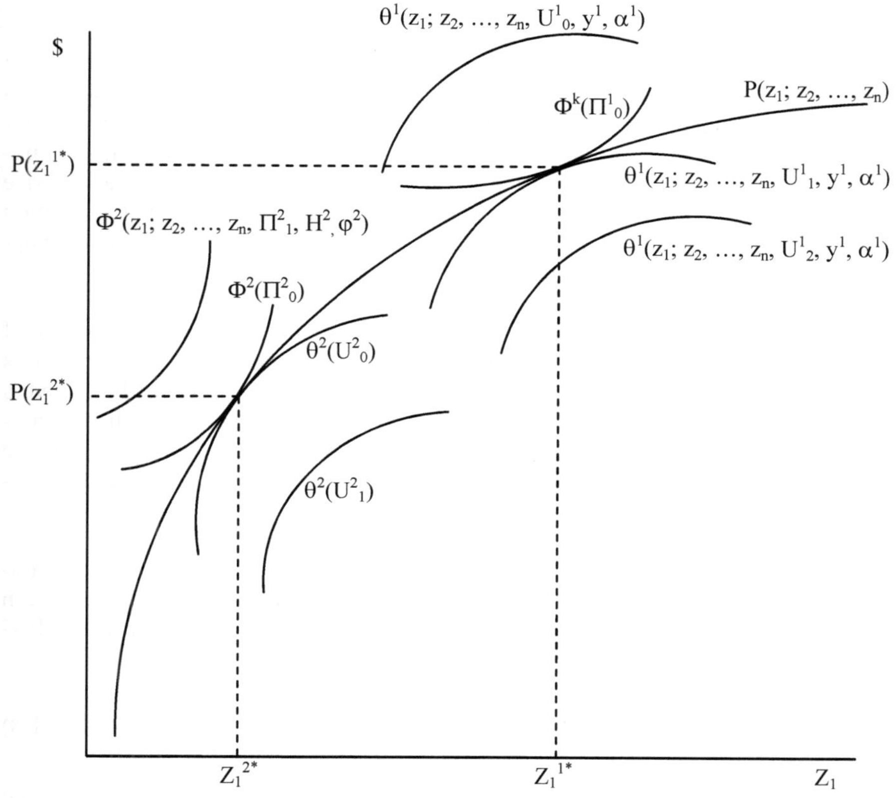

Fig. 1.1 Hedonic Equilibrium. Source: Taylor (2003)

As made clear by Figure 1.1, consumers and producers find their optimal consumption bundle of $\underline{z}$ by equating marginal bids and marginal offers to the marginal prices of $\underline{z}$. Figure 1.1 also highlights the envelope nature of the hedonic price function, $P(\underline{z})$. Most importantly, Figure 1.1 illustrates that with relatively small data requirements – just information on prices and product characteristics – we can recover the marginal valuation consumers place on those characteristics. However, Figure 1.1 is deceptively simple. As discussed in more detail in the next two sections, uncovering even marginal values for housing characteristics that are representative of the population can be a tricky affair because of data limitations, theoretical limitations of the Rosen model, or both. We explore these issues in the next two sections.

1.3 Estimation of the Hedonic Price Function

As indicated in the previous section, the implicit prices, $P_{zi}=\partial P(\underset{\sim}{z})/\partial z_i$, reveal the implicit marginal willingness to pay for an increment in a structural, neighborhood, or locational feature of interest, z_i.[4] As such, a great deal of empirical work in housing has as its focus the estimation of the hedonic price function as an "end-point" in the analysis. In this section, we consider estimation of the hedonic price function, focusing on recent advances and extensions to the traditional estimation approaches. More detailed reviews of common estimation concerns in hedonic applications can be found in Palmquist (2005) and Taylor (2003).

Before discussing estimation approaches, it is useful to remind the reader of two key assumptions underlying the hedonic model as presented in the previous section. It is assumed that the market is perfectly competitive and that both buyers and sellers are perfectly informed.[5] It is also assumed that there are no discontinuities in the product continuum available to consumers. In the discussion below, we first assume these assumptions apply to the data generating process and then discuss recent extensions which relax these assumptions.[6]

Because the hedonic price function is an envelope function, there is no theoretical guidance for its specification, except in limiting cases where the product can be costlessly repackaged, in which case the hedonic price function is linear. Perhaps the most commonly used specification is a semi-log:

$$ln(P_i) = \alpha + \sum_{j=1}^{J} \beta_j z_{ji} + \varepsilon_i \tag{1.8}$$

where the natural log of the ith house is a function of the J characteristics assumed to influence price, α and β are coefficients to be estimated, and ε is a normally distributed error term. Often, independent variables are also transformed with natural log or quadratic terms. The more general Box-Cox transformation is often estimated:

---

[4] As discussed in more detail in the next section, there are some conditions regarding the change in the characteristic that must be met for the hedonic price function to provide an ex-ante measure of the marginal willingness to pay for a marginal change in the characteristics.

[5] In this chapter, we only consider housing sales markets. Discussions of the housing rental markets are available in Jud et al. (1996) and Taylor (2003).

[6] It is not feasible to cover all possible extensions to the stylized model usually assumed to underlie the housing markets being considered. Other questions that arise, but which will not be addressed in this chapter are the importance of transactions costs in preventing optimal adjustments by households (Knight in this Volume), and the impacts of housing regulations on market equilibria. See Mäler (1977) for an early critique of the assumptions underlying the hedonic model as applied to environmental valuation, many of which are still applicable today and are being addressed in current research.

$$P_i^{(\theta)} = \alpha + \sum_{j=1}^{J} \beta_j z_{ji}^{(\lambda)} + \varepsilon_i \tag{1.9}$$

where $P^{(\theta)} = (P^{\theta} - 1)/\theta$ and $z^{(\lambda)} = (z^{\lambda} - 1)/\lambda$, and θ and λ are additional parameters to be estimated.[7] While the Box-Cox has linear and logarithmic transformations as special cases, it has several drawbacks. We are usually interested in the conditional mean of price, not the conditional mean of $P^{(\theta)}$. In addition, the Box-Cox estimators will be inconsistent if $P^{(\theta)} = (P^{\theta} - 1)/\theta$ does not follow a normal distribution. Wooldridge (1992) provides an alternative general transformation which does not require second moment or other distributional assumptions to obtain consistent estimates, although it is somewhat less accessible to the applied researcher as estimation requires nonlinear optimization. Examples of the Wooldridge transformation applied in a housing context are in Wooldridge (1992) and Gencay and Xian (1996).

Estimation of the price function proceeds in a variety of ways. Most common is OLS or maximum likelihood estimation of a function similar to that in equation 1.8 or in equation 1.9. More recently, semi-parametric and nonparametric estimators have been applied.[8] While a fully nonparametric regression model is likely intractable due to the dimensionality inherent in housing data, additive nonparametric regression models are better suited to housing applications as they involve only univariate smoothing, yet allow for multiple regressors. Results are also more easily interpreted with additive models, especially when the goal is to assess the impact of a particular characteristic on housing prices. Nonparametric and semiparametric applications of hedonic price estimation are seen in Anglin and Gencay (1996), Gencay and Xian (1996), Iwata et al. (2000), Bao and Wan (2004), Bin (2004), Bajari and Kahn (2005 and in this Volume), and Martins-Filho and Bin (2005).

Regardless of whether a parametric or nonparametric approach is taken to estimation, one must consider the choice of regressors carefully. There is no simple way to determine the complete set of relevant characteristics for price determination. Characteristics generally included fall into three categories: (1) characteristics of the house and the lot, (2) features of the neighborhood such as the quality of the school district or the level of crime in the area and (3) the property's locational characteristics such as proximity to employment centers or recreation areas.[9]

---

7 See Cropper et al. (1988) for a comparison across common functional form choices.

8 Quantile regression may be considered in addition to estimating models of the conditional mean (see, for example, Koenker and Hallock 2001).

9 Category (2) and (3) could be combined as location-specific amenities/disamenities. The division into two categories here is meant to represent spatial amenities that accrue to parcels as a group (e.g., all homes within a school district's boundaries receive the same level of school quality) versus those which are parcel specific (e.g., proximity to a feature of interest varies continuously in space across parcels).

The characteristics in these latter two categories are of most interest for research topics addressed by this Volume. Measuring these characteristics appropriately is not necessarily a straightforward task. For instance, measures of school quality could include teacher/student ratios, test scores, or percentage of children that receive financial assistance for lunches. Each of these statistics are typically available for schools in the U.S.[10] Which is the relevant measure? Often there is a high degree of correlation among measures relating to the same characteristic of interest such that including them all may lead to imprecisely estimated coefficients.[11] On the other hand, dropping a variable to avoid multicollinearity could very well introduce bias. These are classical econometric issues. Clearly, balanced judgment on the part of the researcher, as well as reporting of sensitivity analyses to the choices made, are all part of the well conducted hedonic study.

Related to the above, to avoid measurement error the researcher would ideally have a measure of characteristics that are consistent with perceptions of the characteristics by market participants. For structural and lot characteristics, data available to the researcher are likely to be measured in the same way that market participants measure the characteristics (i.e., square footage, presence of a fireplace, building material types). However, for neighborhood or location characteristics, market perceptions of characteristics such as exposure risks associated with proximity to a hazardous waste site may be very different, and possibly uncorrelated with, measures available to the researcher. Baranzini et al. (2006), Hartley et al. (2007) and Poor et al. (2001) represent the few studies that are able to directly examine objective and subjective measures of environmental quality in a hedonic housing framework. In these studies, the authors conducted surveys of homebuyers to elicit perceptions of the environmental variable of interest, thus allowing direct comparisons between subjective and objective measures of the variables in hedonic regressions. There have been many studies which consider how information changes or "events" may affect environmental perceptions by examining changes in hedonic prices in response to observed information changes or events (recent examples include Ash 2007; Loomis 2004; Ihlanfeldt and Taylor 2004; and Gayer et al. 2002). These studies do not have direct measures of homebuyer perceptions, but assume that changes in prices reflect changes in perceptions. Leggett (2002) develops a model for welfare measurement when subjective and objective measures of environmental quality differ. While his context is the random utility model (RUM), it could be extended to housing applications of the RUM (discussed in the next section).

[10] Cheshire and Sheppard (2004) conduct a detailed assessment of school quality capitalization into U.K. housing prices, highlighting the nuanced and often highly non-linear relationships between housing values and location-specific amenities.

[11] An often overlooked approach to examining the sources of multicollinearity is to examine the variance inflation factors, see Belsley et al. (2005) and Chatterjee et al. (2000) for a detailed discussion.

Omitted variables and concern over endogenous regressors has taken a prominent role in recent research. For instance, Chay and Greenstone (2005) and Greenstone and Ghallager (2006) argue that endogeneity due to omitted variables has been a problem of first-order importance in previous studies estimating the marginal values of spatial amenities, noting that it is likely that observed spatial features of interest such as proximity to hazardous waste sites will covary with unobserved spatial aspects of a housing market. If this is the case, parameter estimates will be both biased and inefficient. To address this issue, Greenstone and coauthors use quasi-experimental designs to identify the effects of environmental disamenities on house prices. While Chay and Greenstone (2005) find stronger relationships between housing prices and spatially varying environmental conditions (air quality) than in previous work based on cross-section hedonic analysis, Greenstone and Ghallager (2006) find the opposite to be the case when considering proximity to hazardous waste sites.

Endogeneity in hedonic price function estimation can also arise from simultaneous determination of sales price and a regressor. Perhaps the clearest example of this is the joint-determination of sales price and a property's time on the market (*TOM*). While a number of studies estimate the impact of various factors on *TOM* or sales price, the simultaneous determination of sale price and *TOM* has generally been overlooked (exceptions are seen in recent work by Knight 2002; and in this Volume; Huang and Palmquist 2001). Consider the following two equation system:

$$SP = \beta_0 + \beta_1 TOM + Z\beta + \varepsilon \tag{1.10}$$

$$TOM = \gamma_0 + \gamma_1 SP + \gamma X + \eta \tag{1.11}$$

where SP is sales price, Z is a vector of all relevant factors influencing sales price, X is a vector of all relevant factors influencing TOM (some elements of X may be contained in Z), ε and η are the structural model error terms so that $E(\varepsilon|Z)=0$ and $E(\eta|X)=0$. Examples of factors that influence *TOM* are those which capture seller motivation, such as commission paid to agents and the ratio of initial list price to expected sale price, and whether or not the house is vacant during the sale period. It is well known that estimation of equation 1.10 in absence of considering the endogeneity of *TOM* results in inconsistent parameter estimates.

Environmental hedonic applications typically ignore *TOM* altogether, with the exception being Huang and Palmquist (2001). Huang and Palmquist find endogeneity bias to be important in their hedonic estimation of housing prices in Seattle, Washington. To consistently estimate equation 1.10 and equation 1.11, they use full-information maximum likelihood (FIML) methods. Although results for *TOM* are dramatically different in the naïvely estimated *SP* equation as compared to the FIML model, the coefficient estimates for most housing and neighborhood characteristics (including noise externalities associated with highways) are quite similar across models. In a similar vein, Cavailhés et. al., this Volume, find that *TOM* endogeneity is not empirically important in their application using a Hausman test.

Unfortunately, these two studies give little comfort for hedonic applications which do not have *TOM* information available and thus cannot test the implicitaions of the simultaneous determination of TOM and sales price. If *TOM* is not available for empirical testing, then at best we know that we have only consistently estimate the reduced form equation that arises from substituting equation 1.11 into equation 1.10 if X and Z are orthogonal to each other. Uncovering the structural parameters of interest, β, is difficult as the reduced form parameters are likely to be complicated nonlinear functions of the structural parameters. For a more detailed discussion of TOM, see Knight in this volume.

Another important example of simultaneity bias in hedonic price function estimation relates to land use spillovers and is particularly important for studies assessing the value of open space. Following Irwin and Bockstael (2001), assume property i has only one neighbor, property j, and vice-versa. The value of property i and j in time t are given by:

$$P_{it} = \beta_0 + Z_{it}\beta + \delta\, OS_{it} + \varepsilon_{it} \qquad (1.12)$$

$$P_{jt} = \beta_0 + Z_{jt}\beta + \delta\, OS_{jt} + \varepsilon_{jt} \qquad (1.13)$$

where P_{it} (P_{jt}) is the market value of house i (j) in time t, Z is a vector of factors that affect residential property values, including the characteristics of improvements, OS is the amount of open space around each property (i.e., the degree to which the neighboring property is developed). Importantly, OS is privately held open space and thus is subject to being developed in any future period.[12] Now consider the economic forces which determine the degree to which any one property is developed:

$$OS_{it} = \alpha_0 + W_{jt}\alpha + \eta\, P_{jt} + \zeta_{jt} \qquad (1.14)$$

$$OS_{jt} = \alpha_0 + W_{it}\alpha + \eta\, P_{it} + \zeta_{it}. \qquad (1.15)$$

In the above, the amount of open space on property i is a function of factors that influence the cost of developing property i's neighbor (W_j) and the value of property i's neighbor in residential use (P_j). Solving this system makes clear that P_{it} will be a function of Z_{it}, Z_{jt}, W_{it}, W_{jt} and a weighted sum of all errors. Unlike previous studies estimating the value of open-space surrounding residential properties, Irwin and Bockstael (2001) and Irwin (2002) explicitely consider the endogeneity of open-space determination and use an instrumental variables approach to identify the effects of open space on residential property value.

In the above discussion, endogenous regressors arise from simultaneous determination of sales price and one of the regressors. Some confusion exists regarding what housing characteristics can reasonably be considered endogenous in a first

[12] If all open space is publicly provided and permanently it may be exogenous to the system if the factors determining which parcels are preserved are exogenous to the real estate market.

stage hedonic regression due to simultaneous determination. To clarify, it is important to note that simultaneity does not arise in a first stage regression because of households' location decisions along the hedonic price function. For instance, consider a commonly included characteristic, square footage of a home. Square footage is not endogenous in a first stage regression because of the fact that households who choose larger homes pay higher total prices, ceteris paribus. We are not estimating the underlying parameters of the bid or offer functions (i.e., we are not estimating the demand or supply of square footage) in the first stage regression, and as such, it is not endogenous. Of course, endogeneity of square footage could arise for other classical reasons. For example, square footage might be correlated with an important omitted variable (see also Nelson in this volume).

Perhaps the most common approach in hedonic analysis has been to assume that any omitted variables are independent of the regressors and to consider omitted variables as factors that only introduce spatial error correlation. Spatial processes may be important in housing markets for a variety of reasons, but concern over spatial error dependence has dominated the literature.[13] Following Anselin (1988), a general model of housing price determination including spatial effects is:

$$\begin{aligned} P &= \rho W_1 P + ZB + \varepsilon \\ \varepsilon &= \lambda W_2 \varepsilon + \mu \\ \mu &\sim N(0,\sigma^2 I) \end{aligned} \tag{1.16}$$

where Z is a NxK matrix of property characteristics, P is sales price, B is a Kx1 vector of coefficients, W_1 and W_2 are NxN spatial weight matrices, ε is a Nx1 spatial autoregressive error, μ is a Nx1 random error term with variance σ^2, and ρ and λ are coefficients on the spatially lagged variables, P and ε. In equation 1.16, ρ, B, and λ are estimated and W_1 and W_2 are arbitrarily chosen by the researcher. Data may be assumed to have spatial dependence (i.e., $\rho \neq 0$) or spatial autoregression (i.e., $\lambda \neq 0$) or both. The process by which one observation is related to another may be allowed to vary as well (i.e., $W_1 \neq W_2$).

The spatial weights matrices are similar to a lag operator in time series, but are multidimensional. The spatial weight matrix defines the sense in which properties are believed to be neighbors and determines the importance of any one observation to another. In housing hedonics, distance-decay matrices appear to be the most common specification of the weights matrix wherein the importance of each property on the current property decays as distance increases.[14] Alternative struc-

[13] A recent paper by Kim et al. (2003) focuses on spatial lags (i.e., non-zero ρ in equation 1.16) and suggests that welfare measurement must consider the "spatial multiplier" that results from the assumed spatial lag model. Small and Steimetz (2006) provide conditions under which this suggestion is correct.

[14] A sample of recent studies investigating the value of site-specific amenities which consider spatial dependence that are not cited elsewhere in this chapter are: Bell and Bockstael (2000); Brasington (1999); Boxall et al. (2005); Kim et al. (2003); Leggett and

tures, such as a lattice matrix in which elements of the spatial weight matrix, w_{ij}, equal one if a property shares a border with the observation of interest are also used.

Specification of the spatial weights matrix continues to be one of the more controversial aspects of spatial econometrics. Evidence exists that an inappropriate assumption of a first order spatial error process leads to substantially flawed inference (Walker and McGarvey 2006). With panel data, spatial error processes can be accounted for in the estimation of the variance/covariance matrix for the parameters, with no need to specify a weight matrix (Driscoll and Kraay 1998). Unfortunately, the asymptotic results that underlie these methods require that the time dimension of the panel be at least close to the width.

In addition to data limitations, consideration must be given to market conditions and whether or not there are likely to be violations in the assumptions underlying the hedonic equilibrium described in the previous section. Clearly, the assumption of perfect information can be violated in many hedonic applications. The manner in which information is assumed to be imperfect may also differ depending on the application. First, consider imperfect information on the part of some agents in the market. Seller disclosure laws represent a public policy response to asymmetric information in housing market. In a series of papers, Pope (2006, 2007a, 2007b) considers this asymmetric information context in housing markets, teasing out the impact of information using quasi-random natural experiments. Pope finds evidence that buyers do not appear to be fully-informed about housing characteristics, even when the underlying information is publicly available (e.g., boundaries for airport noise and flood zones). Pope finds that imperfect information results in significant attenuation of hedonic price estimates for disamenities when a fraction of the buyers are uninformed.

Munn and Palmquist (1997) consider a different type of imperfect information. In their analysis of the sales of unimproved parcels for the purposes of timber harvest, buyers and sellers are both imperfectly informed and thus use agents who reduce transactions costs within a stochastic frontier framework. In this framework, the role of agents who reduce uncertainties is explicitly modeled by allowing for an asymmetric error component. An interesting area for future research would be to apply the approach of Munn and Palmquist to residential property sales involving real estate agents versus those which do not. With detailed information, one could explore the role of agent "knowledge" on local property markets and hedonic estimates of neighborhood or locational characteristics.

Specification of the hedonic model, measurement error, omitted variables, endogenous regressors, and spatial error correlation are just a few of the potential

---

Bockstael (2000); Noonan (2007); Patterson and Boyle (2002); Petrie and Taylor (2007) and Theebe (2004).

issues to be considered when estimating a first stage hedonic regression. Once estimation is complete, the researcher should carefully report marginal prices or elasticities for structural characteristics as well as environmental variables of interest. The economic magnitude of these variables, not just their statistical significance, will provide an important validity check for the estimation results (for more on this point generally, see McCloskey 1985; Ziliak and McCloskey 2004; for a review of component characteristics' impact on housing prices, see Sirmans et al. 2005).

1.4 Nonmarket Valuation within the Hedonic Framework

As indicated earlier, the majority of hedonic studies rely on the following utility maximizing condition to connect implicit prices to welfare measures associated with changes in an environmental or other housing amenity:

$$\theta_{zi} \equiv \frac{\partial \theta}{\partial z_i} = \frac{\partial P}{\partial z_i} \equiv P_{zi} \,. \tag{1.17}$$

However, caution must be taken in interpreting P_{zi} as a correct measure of the benefits of a marginal increase in z_i. P_{zi} is only a measure of the net benefits of a change in z_i if the change in z_i is both marginal and localized. The latter condition indicates that the change in z_i should occur for a relatively small portion of the overall market, so as to not shift the market supply of z_i which would result in a shift in the hedonic price function (). In this case, the improvement in z_i is simply capitalized into the price of the homes affected. This capitalization reflects the net benefits of the change in z_i if there are no transactions costs associated with moving (so that the owners/renters of the homes which receive the improvements can relocate and obtain their original level of utility). For non-marginal but localized changes in z_i, the net benefits are analogously derived when there are no transactions costs associated with changing location for the occupant, and are given by $\{ P(z_i^1; z_2 ... z_n) - P(z_i^0; z_2 ... z_n) \}$ where z_i^1 represents an improved condition and z_i^0 represents the initial condition.[15]

If there are transactions costs associated with moving households, then the net benefits estimated from the hedonic price function represent an upper-bound of the true net benefits. The hedonic price function can only be used to forecast an upper-bound on the net benefits of improvements in z_i if transactions costs are prohibitively high so as to keep households from relocating in response to changes in z_i or if households can move, but homes identical to their existing housing

[15] Note, predicting the house price based on an estimated hedonic price function with a transformed dependent variable and obtaining standard errors for the predicted price can be complicated (see Wooldridge 2000 for an example when the dependent variable is a logarithmic transformation of sales price).

(prior to a change in z_i) are not available (see also Taylor 2003; Sheppard 1999; Ohsfeldt and Smith 1990; and Bartik 1988).

Non-local changes in characteristics will affect the hedonic equilibrium in an unknown way that cannot be forecast with ex-ante information alone. Thus, implicit prices estimated from hedonic price function alone will not represent benefit estimates from a change in the amenity. For this, and other reasons, it is often desirable to estimate the underlying preferences for the attribute of interest. To do so, a "second stage" analysis is required which uses price information from the first stage estimation of the hedonic price function in conjunction with observed quantities of characteristics purchased and demographic information to identify the underlying preferences. There are several approaches available to recover preference parameters. A key concern in each approach is ensuring identification of the demand parameters. Before describing the empirical approaches, we first review the economic concepts being measured.

The marginal bid function for characteristic z_i is equivalent to an inverse compensated demand function for z_i.[16] The marginal bid function describes the change in WTP for z_i as the level of z_i changes, holding utility and all other characteristics and goods constant. Figure 1.2 indicates two marginal bid functions for two consumers, and two marginal price functions for characteristic z_i. Initially consider only the solid-line which indicates the marginal bid function for consumer 1, θ^{1}_{zi} and the marginal price function given by P^{A}_{zi} . The marginal bid function is equivalent to the marginal hedonic price function at the consumer's optimal consumption bundle (point "A" in Figure 1.2).

[16] The intuition for this relationship is described in Taylor (2003) and is as follows. The bid function describes the maximum WTP for a specific bundle of characteristics, holding utility and income constant. Because $\partial\theta/\partial y=1$, the marginal bid function, θ_{zi}, only depends on $\underline{z}$, utility, and exogenous consumer characteristics, α^{j}, and as such is equivalent to an inverse compensated demand function for z_i.

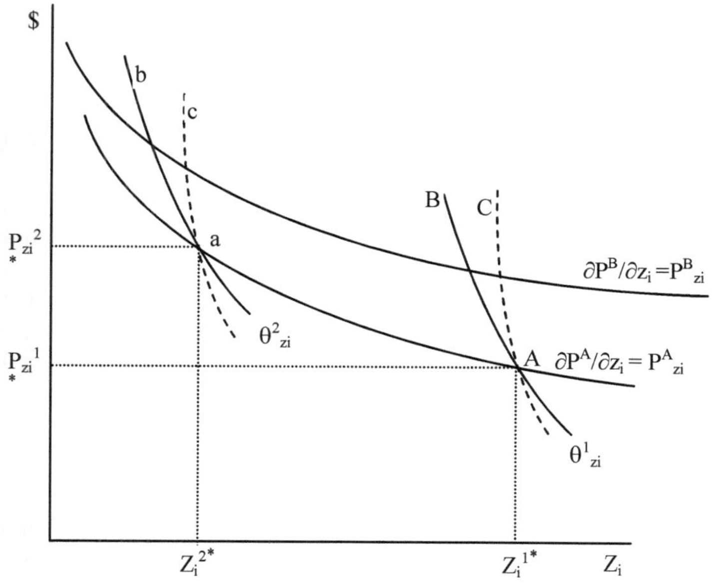

Fig.1.2 Second Stage Marginal Bid Identification. Source: Taylor (2003)

Measures of welfare change associated with a change in z_i from z_i^0 to z_i^1 are given by:

$$W(\Delta z_i) = \int_{z_i^0}^{z_i^1} \frac{\partial \theta(z_i; \underline{z}, U^j)}{\partial z_i} dz_i, \tag{1.18}$$

where $W(\Delta z_i)$ is compensating or equivalent surplus for a change in z_i, depending on whether U^j is the initial level of utility or the level after the change in z_i, respectively.

One approach to recovering preference information is to estimate inverse *un*-compensated demands and then duality results may be used to recover estimates of compensating or equivalent surplus. Uncompensated demands can be derived analytically if the hedonic price function is linear. If the hedonic price function is non-linear, then the budget constraint is non-linear and traditional optimization methods are inappropriate to use in this case. However, as Palmquist (1988) indicates, the choices a consumer makes when facing a budget constraint that is linearized around the optimal consumption bundle will be identical to those when the individual faces the original non-linear budget constraint (see also Blomquist 1989). The linear budget constraint is of the form:

$$y_a^j = X + \sum_{i=1}^{n} p_i^* z_i, \tag{1.19}$$

where p_i^* represents the marginal price of characteristics z_i evaluated at the quantity of z_i which the consumer actually chooses, and y_a^j is consumer j's income adjusted as follows:

$$y_a^j = y - P(Z^*) + \sum_{i=1}^{n} p_i^* z_i^* . \tag{1.20}$$

The linear budget constraint in equation 1.19 is exogenous as the implicit prices faced by the consumer, p_i^*, are held constant at the level associated with this consumer's actual purchase. Income is adjusted as indicated in equation 1.20 since the linear budget constraint implies a larger consumption set than is affordable for the consumer with income y facing a non-linear budget constraint in which marginal prices for z_i are decreasing as amounts of z_i are increased. The linear budget constraint in equation 1.19 can be used with the first order conditions in equation 1.2 to solve for the inverse uncompensated demands:

$$p_1^j = f(z_1, z_2, \ldots, z_n, x, y_a, \alpha^j). \tag{1.21}$$

To recover welfare estimates, one may specify the form of utility, derive and estimate a system of uncompensated demands and then use duality to analytically recover estimates of compensating or equivalent variation by solving for indirect utility or expenditure functions (see, for example, Palmquist and Israngkura 1999; Parsons 1986). Alternatively, one can estimate a single demand for a characteristic of interest and use differential equation methods to recover an associated utility or indirect utility function as demonstrated by Hausman (1981) and Vartia (1983).[17] Following the discussion in Palmquist (2005), suppose a log-linear uncompensated demand of the following form is estimated:

$$\partial P / \partial z_1 = e^{\alpha} z_1^{\beta_1} z_2^{\beta_2} X^{\gamma} . \tag{1.22}$$

Using the fact that $\partial P / \partial z_1 = \partial \theta / \partial z_1$ and that X can be written in terms of the (y-θ), equation 1.12 becomes a differential equation in θ:

$$\partial \theta / \partial z_1 = e^{\alpha} z_1^{\beta_1} z_2^{\beta_2} (y - \theta)^{\gamma} , \tag{1.23}$$

which is separable and can then be solved analytically for θ. As Palmquist (2005) then shows, measures of welfare change are simply computed using the analytical form for θ. For example, compensating surplus (CS) for an improvement in z_1 is defined as $\theta(z_1^1, z_2, u_0) - \theta(z_1^0, z_2, u_0)$ and given equations 1.22 and 1.23, it would be:

[17] Boyle et al. (1999) take a single-equation approach to estimating the demand for water quality within a hedonic housing context, however they do not use duality results to recover exact welfare estimates and instead report quasi-consumer surplus measures.

$$CS = y - \left[-\frac{1-\gamma}{\beta_1 + 1}\left(e^{\alpha} z_{11}^{\beta_1+1} z_2^{\beta_2} - e^{\alpha} z_{10}^{\beta_1+1} z_2^{\beta_2}\right) + (y - P_0)^{1-\gamma} \right]^{1/_{1-\gamma}} - P_0 . \qquad (1.24)$$

Given estimates of α_1, β_1, β_2, and γ, equation 1.24 is computed in a straightforward manner.

A second approach to recovering preference parameters is to assume a form of utility and then analytically derive and estimate the equilibrium condition given in equation 1.2 above. This approach is taken in Chattopadhyay (1999) and Cropper et al. (1993). While welfare measures are not directly computed from the estimating equation, the demand parameters are recovered and welfare measures are computed analytically using the assumed form for utility. To see this, recall that at the optimal level of consumption the marginal bid for z_i is equal to the marginal rate of substitution of z_i for the numeraire, X, or: $\theta_{zi}(z_i, \underline{z}, U) = MRS_{zi,X}(z_i, \underline{z}, X)$. Solving the utility function for X and substituting into the MRS function that is estimated, we can compute welfare effects using equation 1.18 above since:

$$W(\Delta z_i) = \int_{zi0}^{zi1} \frac{\partial \theta(z_i; \underline{z}, U^j)}{\partial z_i} dz_i \equiv \int_{zi0}^{zi1} MRS(z_i; \underline{z}, X(z_i; \underline{z}, U^j))\, dz_i . \qquad (1.25)$$

Since utility parameters have been estimated, utility in equation 1.25 can be computed at either the original level of z_i or the altered level depending on the desired welfare measure.

Regardless of the analytical approach used to recover preference information, identification strategies must be considered carefully. One approach to identification is to use data from separate, geographically distinct housing markets. In this approach, it is assumed the consumers have homogeneous preferences across markets, but differences in supply conditions result in different marginal prices across markets. If this is the case, estimating separate hedonic price functions in each market will identify demand as illustrated in Figure 1.2, where P_{zi}^A and P_{zi}^B represent the marginal price functions estimated in two separate markets. Given this additional information, we can now determine if it is point "*b*" or "*c*" that is the optimal choice for consumer type θ^2, and whether the marginal bid function is represented by the solid or dashed line. Examples of recent studies which have used multiple markets as an identification strategy include Sheppard (1999); Boyle et al. (1999); Palmquist and Israngkura (1999) and Zabel and Kiel (2000).

Identification in single markets relies on functional form restrictions to achieve identification of the preference function. The functional forms chosen for utility and the hedonic price function must differ and imply the rank conditions for identification are met (see Quigley 1982; Chattopadhyay 1999). Historically the multiple-market approach has been viewed as a more palatable approach to identification. Single-market approaches have been criticized because the tight parameterization required, however recent research is 'resurrecting' the single-market approach.

Eckland et al. (2004, 2002a, 2002b) indicate that if marginal prices, $P_{zi} = \partial P / \partial z_i$, are nonlinear functions of z then the variation in estimated marginal prices, P_{zi} , adds information which helps to identify preference parameters. Eckland et al. (2004, 2002b) show that nonlinearity in marginal prices is a generic property of the hedonic equilibrium, and not an arbitrary assumption used for empirical convenience. As such, the hedonic model is generically nonparametrically identified within a single market and nonlinear instrumental variables or transformation model methods (Horowitz 1998) can identify preference parameters without exclusion restrictions.

In contrast to multiple-market approaches to estimating demand parameters which assume consumers are homogeneous within and across markets, recent work by Bajari and Benkard (2005), Bajari and Kahn (2005 and this Volume) presents a framework for estimating demand parameters within a single-market context that allows for consumer heterogeneity.[18] In this approach, marginal prices and utility parameters are allowed to vary by household, and the distributions of preference parameters are estimated non-parametrically. This approach is described in detail by Bajari and Khan in this Volume, and thus will not be reiterated here.

In contrast to the two-stage hedonic approach to estimating demand parameters (using either multiple or single markets), an alternative approach is to directly estimate utility parameters using a random utility model (RUM). In this framework consumers are assumed to make a discrete choice between house bundles, rather than a continuous choice over attribute levels as in the Rosen model. The utility of the consumer's chosen house is known to the consumer, but is measured with error by the researcher. Thus, utility (U) is assumed to be the sum of a systematic portion (V) and a random component. This can be written as follows for consumer j who is observed choosing house k:

$$U^j(X^k, \underline{z}^k; \alpha^j) = V^j(X^k, \underline{z}^k; \alpha^j) + \varepsilon_k \tag{1.26}$$

where $U(\bullet)$ is the true, but unobservable utility given in equation 1.1 and ε is the error term introduced because the researcher cannot observe all relevant aspects of the individual. The individual maximizes utility by selecting the house which yields the highest level of utility from among the set of all possible alternatives, A. The probability that consumer j selects house k is given by:

$$Pr(k|A) = Pr[U_k > U_l)] = Pr\{V(X^k, \underline{z}^k; \alpha^j) + \varepsilon_k > V(X^l, \underline{z}^l; \alpha^j) + \varepsilon_l], \ \forall\ k,l \ni A;\ k \neq l. \tag{1.27}$$

[18] Eckland et al. (2004) also assume homogeneity in consumer preferences within a single market.

The assumption about the distribution of the random error term implies which probabilistic model is estimated. A common assumption is that the error terms are independently and identically distributed following a Type 1 extreme value distribution, leading to the well known conditional logit model. To relax the independence of irrelevant alternatives assumption inherent in the conditional logit model, McFadden's (1981) nested logit model or random parameters logit may be used.

In a recent application of the above approach, Chattopadhyay (2000) estimates welfare changes using a nested logit approach and considers several alternative nesting hierarchies. He compares these results to those obtained using a two-stage single-market approach described above and used in Chattopadhyay (1999). Chattopadhyay finds that estimates of the values for neighborhood amenities are sensitive to the choice of nesting structure assumed and that benefit estimates for the environmental amenity studied (air quality in the Chicago area) are consistently lower in the nested logit model than in the hedonic model. These results, taken together with earlier simulation studies by Quigley (1986), Quigley and Mason (1990) and Cropper et al. (1993) present inconsistent evidence regarding the relative performance of the RUM approach to the traditional hedonic approach, thus leaving open the question as to which method is preferred.

1.5 Conclusions

While a comprehensive review of the theoretical and empirical issues that might arise in a hedonic housing context would be prohibitively long, this chapter has attempted to provides a review of the general framework upon which hedonic analysis is built and provide an overview of some topical implementation issues. In particular, in Section 1.3, we focused on recent research concerned with the ability of traditional first-stage data and estimation procedures to recover unbiased parameter estimates. Concerns over endogenous regressors due to omitted variables and simultaneous determination of prices and observable characteristics are playing a prominent role in recent research. In addition, the traditional interpretation of the hedonic price function relies on Rosen's (1974) characterization of a perfectly competitive market with perfectly informed agents. In section 1.3, we reviewed some recent research which relaxes these assumptions in housing markets.

While estimation of the hedonic price function to determine the implicit prices of housing characteristics dominates the literature, uncovering underlying preferences for housing characteristics is an important aspect of hedonic housing research. In Section 1.4, we reviewed a number of different methods that have been used to recover preference estimates, as well as newer approaches which show substantial promise for broadening the use of second-stage hedonic estimation. Using housing markets to uncover the links between demographics and preferences for site-specific amenities is essential for effective policy-making. The combination of improved data availability and new (or revisited) methods for estimating preference parameters makes this a promising area for future applied researchers.

References

Anselin, L (1988) Spatial Econometrics: Methods and Models. Dordrecht: Kluwer Academic Press

Anglin P, Gencay R (1996) Semiparametric estimation of hedonic price functions. Journal of applied econometrics 11: 633–648

Ash M (2007) The impact of hurricane Ivan on expected flood losses, perceived flood risk, and property values. Journal of housing research 16: 47–60

Bajari P, Benkard CL (2005) Demand estimation with heterogeneous consumers and unobserved product characteristics: a hedonic approach. Journal of political economy 113: 1239–1276

Bajari P, Kahn ME (2005) Estimating housing demand with an application to explaining racial segregation in cities. Journal of business and economic statistics 23: 20–33

Bartik T (1988) Measuring the benefits of amenity improvements in hedonic price models. Land economics 64: 72–83

Baranzini A, Schaerer C, Ramirez JV, Thalmann P (2006) Feel it or measure it – perceived vs. measured noise in hedonic models. Available at SSRN: http://ssrn.com/abstract=937259

Bao HXH, Wan ATK (2004) On the use of spline smoothing in estimating hedonic housing price models: empirical evidence using Hong Kong data. Real estate economics 32: 487–507

Bell KP, Bockstael NE (2000) Applying the generalized-moments estimation approach to spatial problems involving microlevel data. Review of Economics and Statistics 82:72-82

Belsley DA, Kuh E, Welsch RE (2005) Regression diagnostics: identifying influential data and sources of collinearity. Wiley-IEEE, New Jersey

Bin O (2004) A prediction comparison of housing sales prices by parametric versus semiparametric regressions. Journal of housing economics 13: 68–84

Blomquist S (1989) Comparative statics for utility maximization models with nonlinear budget constraints. International economic review 30: 275–296

Boyle KJ, Poor J, Taylor LO (1999) Estimating the demand for protecting freshwater lakes from eutrophication. American journal of agricultural economics 85: 1118–1122

Boxall PC, Chan WH, McMillan ML (2005) The Impact of oil and natural gas facilities on rural residential property values: a spatial hedonic analysis. Resource and energy economics 27: 248–269

Brasington DM (1999) Which measures of school quality does the housing market value? Journal of real estate research 18: 395–413

Chatterjee S, Hadi AS, Price B (2000) Regression analysis by example. John Wiley & Sons, 3rd edn, New York

Chattopadhyay S (1999) Estimating the demand for air quality: new evidence based on the Chicago housing market. Land economics 75: 22–38

Chattopadhyay S (2000) The effectiveness of McFaddens's nested logit model in valuing amenity improvement. Regional science and urban economics 30: 23–43

Chay K, Greenstone M (2005) Does air quality matter? Evidence from the housing market. Journal of political economy, April: 376–424

Cheshire P, Sheppard S (2004) Capitalising the value of free schools: The impact of supply characteristics and uncertainty. economic journal 114: 397–424
Cropper M, Deck L, McConnell KE (1988) On the choice of functional form for hedonic price functions. Review of economics and statistics 70: 668–675
Cropper M, Deck L, Kishor N, McConnell KE (1993) Valuing product attributes using single market data: a comparison of hedonic and discrete choice approaches. Review of economics and statistics 70: 668–675
Driscoll JC, Kraay A (1998) Consistent covariance matrix estimation with spatially dependent panel data. Review of economics and statistics 80: 549–560
Eckland I, Heckman JJ, Nesheim L (2002a) Identifying hedonic models. American economic review 92: 304–309
Eckland I, Heckman JJ, Nesheim L (2002b) Identification and estimation of hedonic models. Working paper CWP07/02, Centre for microdata methods and practice, available at http://ideas.repec.org/s/ifs/cemmap.html
Eckland I, Heckman JJ, Nesheim, L (2004) Identification and estimation of hedonic models. Journal of Political Economy, Part 2 Supplement 112(1): S60-109
Gayer T, Hamilton JJ, Viscusi WK (2002) The market value of reducing cancer risk: hedonic housing prices with changing information. Southern economic journal 69: 266–289
Gencay R, Xian Y (1996) A forecast comparison of residential housing prices by parametric versus semiparametric conditional mean estimators. Economics letters 52: 129–135
Greenstone M, Gallagher J (2006) Does hazardous waste matter? Evidence from the housing market and the superfund program. Working paper No. 05-27, Department of economics, MIT, available at SSRN: http://ssrn.com/abstract=840207
Hartley P, Hendrix ME, Osherson DN (2007) Real estate values and air pollution: measured levels and subjective expectations. Available at www.ruf.rice.edu/~econ/faculty/Hartley/HoustonOzone.pdf
Hausman JA (1981) Exact consumer's surplus and deadweight loss. American Economic Review 71:662-676
Horowitz JL (1998) Semiparametric methods in econometrics. Springer-Verlag, New York
Huang JC, Palmquist RB (2001) Environmental conditions, reservation prices, and time on the market for housing. Journal of real estate finance and economics 22: 203–219
Ihlanfeldt KR, Taylor LO (2004) Externality effects of small-scale hazardous waste sites: evidence from urban commercial property markets. Journal of environmental economics and management 47: 117–139
Irwin EG (2002) The effects of open space on residential property values. Land economics 78: 465–480
Irwin EG, Bockstael NE (2001) The problem of identifying land use spillovers: measuring the effects of open space on residential property values. American journal of agricultural economics 83: 698–704
Iwata S, Murao H, Wang Q (2000) Nonparametric assessment of the effects of neighborhood land uses on the residential house values. In: Fomby T, Carter Hill R (eds) Advances in econonometrics: Applying kernel and nonparametric estimation to economic topics. JAI Press,New York, pp 229–257
Jud GD, Benjamin JD, Sirmans SG (1996) What do we know about apartments and their markets? Journal of real estate research 11: 243–257
Kim CW, Phipps TT, Anselin L (2003) Measuring the benefits of air quality improvement: a spatial hedonic approach. Journal of environmental economics and management 45: 24–39
Knight JR (2002) Listing price, time on market, and ultimate selling price: causes and effects of listing price changes. Real estate economics 30: 213–237

Koenker R, Hallock K (2001) Quantile regression. Journal of economic perspectives 15: 143–156
Leggett CG (2002) Environmental valuation with imperfect information - The case of the random utility model. Environmental and resource economics 23: 343–355
Leggett CG, Bockstael NE (2000) Evidence of the effects of water quality on residential land prices. Journal of Environmental Economics and Management 39(2):121-144
Loomis JB (2004) Do nearby forest fires cause a reduction in residential property values? Journal of forest economics 10: 149–157
Mäler KG (1977) A note on the use of property values in estimating marginal willingness to pay for environmental quality. Journal of Environmental Economics and Management 4(4):355-369.
Martins-Filho C, Bin O (2005) Estimation of hedonic price functions via additive nonparametric regression. Empirical economics 30: 93–114
Mason C, Quigley JM (1990) Comparing the performance of discrete choice and hedonic models. In: Fisher, Nijkamp, Papageorgiou (eds) Spatial choices and processes. North Holland, Amsterdam
McCloskey DN (1985) The loss function has been mislaid: the rhetoric of significance tests. American economic review 75: 201–205
McFadden D (1981) Econometric models of probabilistic choice. In: Manski, C.F. and McFadden, D., Editors, Structural Analysis of Discrete Data with Econometric Applications, MIT Press, Cambridge, MA, 198–272
Munn IA, Palmquist RB (1997) Estimating hedonic price equations for a timber stumpage market using stochastic frontier estimation procedures. Canadian journal of forestry resources 27: 1276–1280
Noonan DS (2007) Finding an impact of preservation policies: price effects of historic landmarks on attached homes in Chicago, 1990–1999. Economic development quarterly 21: 17–33
Ohsfeldt R, Smith B (1990) Calculating elasticities from structural parameters in implicit markets. Journal of urban economics 27: 212–221
Palmquist RB (1988) Welfare measurement for environmental improvements using the hedonic model: the case of nonparametric marginal prices. Journal of Environmental Economics and Management 15:297-312
Palmquist RB (2005) Property value methods. In: Mäler KG, Vincent J (eds) Handbook of environmental economics, Elsevier, North Holland, Amsterdam
Palmquist RB, Israngkura A (1999) Valuing air quality with hedonic and discrete choice models. American journal of agricultural economics 81: 1128–1133
Parsons GR (1986) An almost ideal demand system for housing attributes. Southern Economic Journal 53(2):347-363
Patterson RW, Boyle KJ (2002) Out of sight, out of mind? Using GIS to incorporate visibility in hedonic property value models. Land economics 78: 417–425
Petrie R, Taylor LO (2007) Estimating the value of water use permits: a hedonic approach applied to farmland in the southeastern United States. Land economics 83: 302–318
Poor J, Boyle KJ, Taylor LO, Bouchard R (2001) Objective versus subjective measures of water clarity in hedonic property value models. Land economics 77: 482–493
Pope JC (2006) Do scarlet letters lead to scarlet homes? Household reactions to public information from sex offender registries. Working paper, Department of agricultural and applied economics, Virginia Polytechnic University
Pope JC (2007a) Buyer information and the hedonic: The impact of a seller disclosure on the implicit price for airport noise. Working paper, Department of agricultural and applied economics, Virginia Polytechnic University

Pope JC (2007b) Do seller disclosures affect property values? Buyer information and the hedonic model. Working paper, Department of agricultural and applied economics, Virginia Polytechnic University

Quigley JM (1982) Nonlinear budget constraints and consumer demand: an application to public programs for residential housing. Journal of urban economics 12: 177–201

Quigley JM (1986) The evaluation of complex urban policies: simulating the willingness to pay for the benefits of subsidy programs. Regional science and urban economics 16: 31–42

Rosen S (1974) Hedonic prices and implicit markets: product differentiation in pure competition. Journal of political economy 82: 666–677

Sheppard S (1999) Hedonic analysis of housing markets. In: Handbook of regional and urban economics. Volume 3. Applied urban economics. Elsevier science, North-Holland Amsterdam New York Oxford, pp 1595–1635

Small KA, Steimetz S (2006) Spatial hedonics and the willingness to pay for residential amenities. Working paper no 05-06-31, UC irvine economics, available at: www.socsci.uci.edu/~ksmall/Spatial%20Hedonics%20Paper.pdf

Sirmans SG, Macpherson DA, Zietz EN (2005) The composition of hedonic pricing models. Journal of real estate literature 13: 3–43

Taylor LO (2003) The hedonic method. In: Champ B, Boyle KJ, Brown T (eds) A primer on nonmarket valuation. Kluwer academic publishers, Dordrecht, pp 331–393

Theebe MAJ (2004) Planes, trains, and automobiles: the impact of traffic noise on house prices. Journal of real estate finance and economics 28: 209–234

Vartia Y (1983) Efficient methods of measuring welfare change and compensated income in terms of ordinary demand functions. Econometrica 51(1):79-98

Walker MB, McGarvey M (2006) Robust covariance estimators for spatially correlated errors in a fixed effects models: finite sample performance. Working paper, Andrew young school of policy studies, Georgia State University

Waugh FV (1928) Quality factors influencing vegetable prices. Journal of farm economics 10: 185–196

Wooldridge JM (1992) Some alternatives to the Box-Cox regression model. International economic review 33: 935–955

Wooldridge JM (2000) Introductory econometrics: a modern approach. Thompson learning, South western college publishing

Zabel JE, Kiel KA (2000) Estimating the demand for air quality in four U.S. cities. Land Economics 76(2): 174-194

Ziliak ST, McCloskey DN (2004) Size matters: the standard error of regressions in the American Economic Review. Journal of socio-economics 33: 527–546

2 Hedonic Modeling of the Home Selling Process

John R. Knight

University of the Pacific, Stockton, United States

2.1 Introduction

Many aspects of the housing market distinguish it from a perfectly competitive market. In a perfectly competitive market, a large number of buyers and sellers, together with ease of entry and exit, ensure that all participants are price takers. The marketplace is clearly defined and products in such markets are perfectly homogeneous. Moreover, information about price is easily obtained and instantly known.

Housing markets are quite different. Products in housing markets are differentiated to varying degrees, and information about the quantity and quality of the amenities that compose the price is difficult and costly to obtain. Transactions ultimately involve one buyer and one seller who bargain over an unknown price. Entry and exit are severely constrained by the large capital sums involved as well as by the relatively high transactions costs.

These aspects of housing markets make the selling transaction a process rather than an event. The process begins on the seller side with the choice of a selling strategy that includes setting an initial listing price. The second phase of the process involves the contemporaneous searches of the seller and the prospective buyers. During this phase, the buyer gathers information and makes comparisons among comparable available homes that meet the buyer's housing needs. Inspection of these homes reveals the quantity and quality of amenities of importance to the buyer. At the same time, the seller is gathering information about the market's valuation of his property from the arrival rate and presence or absence of bids from prospective buyers. The seller may use this information to alter the selling strategy, perhaps by revising the listing price. The search phase ends when a prospective buyer finds a match for his housing needs and initiates the next phase of the process, bargaining, by making an offer for the home. The selling process concludes when buyer and seller agree on a selling price and complete the transaction.

A. Baranzini et al. (eds.), *Hedonic Methods in Housing Markets*, doi: 10.1007/978-0-387-76815-1_2,

A considerable literature has developed over the last several years regarding the selling process sketched above. To date however, hedonic studies of environmental amenities and disamenities have largely ignored the impact of the selling process on selling price and attribute values. This chapter provides a review of the relevant theories that have been offered to explain buyer and seller behavior in this process, describes an econometric model that may be employed to test these theories within the hedonic framework, and highlights some of the important empirical results.

2.2 Hedonic Pricing Framework

The standard hedonic pricing model proposed by Rosen (1974) does not incorporate the many market imperfections associated with a home sale. The composite price of the house reflects not just the quantity and quality of the house attributes, but also differences in buyer and seller characteristics and search strategies. The spatial and temporal contexts of the sale are also important. In other words, the same house could sell at a different price given shifting markets, a different seller, and/or a different set of potential buyers.

The hedonic model must be modified to incorporate the impacts of the various market imperfections on house price. The customary method of accounting for the impact of the search process on home selling price is to incorporate a measure of time on market[1], together with variables thought to affect time on market, into the standard hedonic pricing model. In general, the model regresses the log of selling price on time-on-market, marketing choices of the seller, physical characteristics of the house, location, and time of sale.

$$log(SP) = f(TOM , P, B, L, T)$$

Where :

- TOM: A measure of the time-on-market of the property from its initial listing until its ultimate sale.
- P: A set of physical characteristics of the home. For example, square feet of living area, the number of bedrooms and bathrooms, the age of the home, whether the home has a pool and/or fireplace, and the number of stories of the house.
- B: Vectors of buyer and seller characteristics that relate to the relative bargaining strength of the market participants.
- L: A variable or vector of variables to control for the location of the home. In many cases the spatial aspect of the home is modeled in the error term.

[1] The terms 'time-on-market', 'selling time', 'marketing time', 'time to sale', and 'days on market' are used interchangeably throughout this chapter to refer to the amount of time elapsing between the initial offer for sale and the sales transaction.

- T: A time-of-sale variable to capture the influences of the market as a whole. This may take the form of a time trend or a set of dummy variables for the individual time periods.

The statistical model relating ultimate selling price to these factors is:

$$SP = X_1\beta_1 + \varepsilon_1 . \tag{2.1}$$

SP is usually the natural log of selling price, X_1 a matrix of the explanatory variables described above, β_1 the vector of parameters, and ε_1 an error term.

Because the time-on-market variable is endogenous, the error term in the selling price equation is correlated with this explanatory variable. Therefore, time-on-market is separately specified and estimated. Such a specification would ideally include signals of the seller's motivation for a quick sale, aspects of the house that affect its marketability, and characteristics of the market within which the house is sold.

$$TOM = f(S, H, M)$$

Where:

- S: A vector of variables denoting the selling strategy. For example, the amount of the markup of list price over expected selling price, whether owner financing is offered, the size of commission offered by the seller, and the size and type of brokerage to engage.
- H : A vector of particular physical attributes of the home thought to affect its marketability. For example, the home's heterogeneity, and whether or not the home is vacant.
- M : A vector of market characteristics to control for the spatial and temporal contexts of the sale.

The resulting statistical model is:

$$TOM = X_2\beta_2 + \varepsilon_2 . \tag{2.2}$$

Where *TOM* is the natural log of the number of days a home remains on the market prior to sale, X_2 a matrix of variables thought to explain marketing time, β_2 a vector of parameters, and ε_2 an error term correlated with time-on-market through the endogeneity of selling price. Many of the same factors thought to influence a seller to accomplish a quick sale would likely also influence a seller to accept a lower offer, so disentangling the contemporaneous impacts is difficult. By using heterogeneity as a composite representation of the principal attributes, it is at least possible to employ the individual house physical characteristics to identify the time-on-market equation and perform two-stage least squares estimation.

In the first stage, the estimate predicted values of the two endogenous variables, $\hat{SP}$ and $\hat{TOM}$ are estimated, and in the second stage these predicted values are substituted as explanatory variables in each of the individual structural equations. The second stage estimators are:

$$SP = \hat{Z}_1\delta_1 + \overline{e}_1 \tag{2.3}$$

where $\hat{Z}_1$ contains $\hat{TOM}$ and the explanatory variables in X_1, and

$$TOM = \hat{Z}_2\delta_2 + \overline{e}_2 \tag{2.4}$$

where $\hat{Z}_2$ contains $\hat{SP}$ and the exogenous variables in X_2.

In large samples the correlations of $\overline{e}_1$ and $\overline{e}_2$ with their respective explanatory variables disappear, and because each equation is over-identified, two-stage least squares provides consistent estimates of the model parameters.

2.3 Survey of the Theoretical Literature

Most of the selling process literature, both theoretical and empirical, involves one-period models, and deals with strategic decisions made by the seller at the initiation of the process. This branch of the literature investigates the determinants of selling price and/or time-on-market and the influence of the strategic decisions on seller and buyer search behavior. A second, much smaller, branch of the literature, both in terms of theoretical development and empirical testing, deals with changes that occur between the initial listing and the initial match between buyer and seller. This branch studies the revisions in strategy as buyers and sellers become better informed about house value and the market within which a sale is to be made. Another branch, well developed theoretically but extremely scant empirically, involves the bargaining between seller and prospective buyer once a match has occurred.

2.3.1 Search Theory and Single-Period Models of Search

The preponderance of work in house selling literature has used as a starting point search theory borrowed from the job search literature in the field of labor economics (see Lippman and McCall 1978 for a review of the job search literature). Search theory is especially appropriate in the case of housing because of the heterogeneity of the product, because of the need to match buyer and seller, and because of the cost and time involved in gathering information relative to the product and its price. In housing markets, search theory has been developed from both viewpoints, that of the seller (Yavas 1992; Yavas and Yang 1995; Arnold 1999; Sirmans et al. 1995; Horowitz 1992), and that of the buyer (Horowitz 1986; Anglin 1997; Knight et al. 1994). Arnott (1989) and Wheaton (1990) develop search and matching models for clearing the market as a whole.

A general description of the search model as applied to housing is as follows. The seller wishes to maximize the selling price of the property in the shortest possible time, but is constrained by the cost of the search and uncertainty about the market's valuation of the property. The seller adopts a stopping rule where the marginal benefit of continuing to search for a buyer is just equal to the marginal cost of additional search. The stopping rule r^* satisfies the condition:

$$\int_r^{\bar{p}} (p-r) f(p) dp = c_s \text{ , for } r = r^*$$

where c_s is the marginal cost of seller search, p the selling price and r the seller's reservation price. The density $f(p)$ represents the seller's distribution of possible selling prices for the home, the relevant portion of which is contained in $[r, \bar{p}]$.

The buyer wishes to purchase the best set of amenities for the lowest possible price, and because of search costs would also like to minimize the duration of search. Likewise, the buyer has a stopping rule w^* that satisfies the condition:

$$\int_w^{\bar{\phi}} (\phi - w) g(\phi) d\phi = c_B \text{ , for } w = w^*$$

where w represents the buyer's reservation search value, $\bar{\phi}$ the upper limit of value for a particular property, and c_B the buyer's cost of continued search.

Perhaps the most important strategic decision of the seller is the determination of a listing price. Yavas and Yang (1995) provide a model that includes buyer, seller and broker in analyzing the seller's choice of listing price. In addition to search costs, the listing price depends on the seller's valuation of the property, his perceived bargaining power, and broker commission rates. Higher listing prices increase the price received, provided that a match is found, but decrease the probability of a match. The listing price provides a formal connection between seller and buyer searches, and also influences the search intensity of a broker if a broker is employed. Knight et al. (1994) focus on buyer behavior and find similarly that lower listing prices increase the proportion of buyers who will make an offer, but reduce the size of the offer from any given buyer. In contrast, Horowitz (1992) models buyer behavior and treats the listing price as a parameter, controlled by the seller, of the distribution from which bids are sampled. Arnold (1999) is interested in the impact of the seller's listing price on the arrival rate of prospective buyers.

2.3.2 Pricing with Demand Uncertainty and Multi-period Models of Search

The theoretical literature discussed above treats the selling process as a one-period event. The seller sets an initial strategy hoping to sell for the highest possible price in the shortest period of time. In fact, there are many discrete events that occur during the selling process. For example, a seller may change listing prices, switch brokers, withdraw the property temporarily, or cancel the listing altogether. Buyers inspect properties, make offers, and respond to counteroffers. Learning takes place as a result of these discrete events, as the seller gathers information from the arrival rate of prospective buyers and the presence or absence of bids. That information can be used to revise strategy based on the new information set.

A combination of product heterogeneity and thin markets creates uncertainty with regard to property valuation. Because time elapses during the selling period of a home, a seller has an opportunity to revise pricing strategy as information arrives about the market's valuation. Lazear (1986) provides the underlying theory of pricing behavior when demand for a product is uncertain and price changes are permitted over time. He shows that the initial price chosen and the size of incremental price reductions are a function of the number of periods over which the seller can learn about the buyer's valuation, as well as how much learning can take place in each period. The amount of learning, in turn, depends on initial pricing and on the nature of the market for the asset to be sold.

The choice of initial listing price is important in this multi-period model, as it influences not only the number of prospective buyers choosing to inspect the home, but also the proportion of prospective buyers who enter the bargaining stage after inspection. While the seller may influence buyer behavior through the choice of a list price, the size of the pool and the success in attracting bids are also strongly influenced by the characteristics of the property. Some properties will trade in very thin markets because of their unusual nature and these properties will be relatively insensitive to the efforts of the seller to expand the pool of buyers. For example, high-priced homes and homes with unusual structural characteristics are likely to fall outside the search parameters of all but a few buyers.

Lazear's theory suggests that houses trading in especially thin markets should start with a relatively lower price and not change price, while houses in a more actively traded category should start with a relatively higher listing price, and revise the price as more is learned about the distribution of buyer valuations of the property.

While Lazear focuses on seller learning associated with prospective buyer arrival rates, Taylor (1999) offers a multi-period theory of initial list price strategy based on buyer learning that takes place over the selling period of a home. When a buyer encounters a home that has been on the market for an extended period, there are two reasonable explanations: 1) the house is priced too high to attract bids, or 2) there is something wrong with the house. Taylor's theory exposes opposing incentives for setting the initial listing price. Setting a low initial price increases the probability of an early sale, avoiding the stigmatizing effect of a failure to sell. On the other hand, setting a high initial price leads buyers to believe that the reason for failure to sell is the high price, rather than property flaws.

2.4 Survey of the Empirical Literature

The empirical literature surrounding the home selling process is extensive. The process influences selling price as manifested by the significance of the time-on-market variable when included in the hedonic pricing equation. Other elements of the process affecting selling price are the relative bargaining strength of seller and buyer and the spatial and temporal contexts of the sale.

2.4.1 Explaining Time-on-Market

A number of studies have attempted to explain the difference in the time required to sell a home, either separately or as the first stage in a selling price model. The common element among these studies is the notoriously low explanatory power of the models. Two basic approaches are employed in these studies: duration models and least squares regressions. Both typically use log of time on market as the dependent variable.

Duration models are arguably more appropriate for the purpose. In addition to measuring the significance of the explanatory variables and providing a prediction of time-on-market for a house with a given set of characteristics, they provide survival probabilities (the probability that a home will sell over a given period of time) and hazard probabilities (the probability that a home will sell at a particular time, given that it has not yet sold). Least squares regressions are restricted versions of duration models for which a normal underlying distribution and a constant hazard function are assumed. Duration models allow the hazard probability to increase or decrease over the analysis period and the opportunity to model duration dependence. A recent study, Pryce and Gibb (2006), suggests that nonmonotonicity should also be modeled, allowing hazard rates to increase, remain constant, and decrease during different segments of the analysis period.

2.4.2 Time-on-Market as a Determinant of Selling Price

The straightforward hypothesis from search theory is that a longer time on the market, *ceteris paribus*, will produce a higher selling price. The longer a home is offered for sale, the greater the probability that a buyer with a high reservation price will arrive. Likewise, a seller with high search costs is willing to accept a lower selling price to achieve a speedier sale. Despite the intuitive appeal of this hypothesis, the empirical evidence of the positive relationship between time and selling price is not supported empirically. In a recent survey article on hedonic pricing variables, Sirmans et al. (2005) found a time-on-market variable appearing as a regressor in eighteen hedonic studies. The variable was positive and significant (as hypothesized by search theory) only once. It was negative and significant eight times and statistically insignificant nine times.

One possible explanation for the counterintuitive result is that most of the studies reported in the survey article used single equation models that failed to account for the endogeneity of selling price and time-on-market. Forgey et al. (1996) develop a two stage model in which a liquidity premium is measured in the first stage as the difference between expected selling time and actual selling time. The value of this premium is then included in the selling price equation of the second stage. They find that higher selling prices are indeed associated with longer expected selling periods, and houses that sell more quickly than expected command a price premium for liquidity.

However, Knight (2002) finds the more prevalent negative relationship when using a two-stage least squares model that controls for simultaneity and selectivity bias. One explanation for this that is not accommodated by one-period models is "negative herding", as described by Taylor (1999), wherein prospective buyers perceive a lower quality for homes that have been on the market longer.

While this "stigma effect" may contribute to lower selling prices for homes that take longer to sell, an even more plausible explanation is offered by Huang and Palmquist (2001). They address the endogeneity of selling price and selling time using a joint maximum likelihood technique and, consistent with Knight (2002), find a negative relationship. They propose that the result is observed because actual seller reservation prices are not observed in the data, only initial listing prices and ultimate selling prices. As marketing time for a home lengthens, sellers may find it necessary to adjust reservation prices downward in order to produce a sale. The result of this downward adjustment of unobserved reservation prices is lower observed selling prices for homes that have been on the market longer.

Huang and Palmquist (2001) stand out as the exception in the environmental hedonic literature. I am aware of no other study of environmental amenities or disamenities that includes time on market as a regressor in the selling price equation. If marketing time is correlated with the environmental variable of interest, this leads to omitted variable bias, and the higher the correlation, the more severe the bias. Consider a disamenity such as a contaminated waste site. It seems plausible that greater exposure to such a hazard might be correlated with a longer time on market as the pool of potential buyers, *ceteris paribus*, would be smaller. If the relationship of time on market with selling price is negative, as suggested by most studies, omitting time on market from the selling price regression would lead to a downward bias of the hazard's coefficient. In other words, the negative impact of the contaminated waste site would be overstated.[2]

2.4.3 Factors Influencing Selling Price and Selling Time

The factors that create imperfections in the market for houses likewise influence the selling prices and marketing periods for houses. Ignoring these imperfections leads to biased inferences from the results of hedonic regressions.

---

[2] Allen et al., forthcoming, is the only one paper addressing time on market in the residential rental market.

House Attributes

The standard hedonic model generates shadow prices for the physical characteristics of a house. However, some of a home's physical characteristics affect not only its composite price, but also its marketability. Two such attributes are a home's relative heterogeneity and its vacancy status. Haurin (1988) uses a duration model to explore the impact of house heterogeneity on marketing time. He reasons that the more atypical a house, the greater the uncertainty associated with its value, and therefore the greater the variance of potential offers. His hypothesis that the owner of an atypical house will wait longer to learn about the offer distribution is empirically supported with his data.

Zuehlke (1987) examines the impact of vacancy on time to sale. The seller of a vacant house has a more costly search than the owner of an occupied house, and thus becomes more likely with time to lower reservation price and to accept any given offer. He controls for censoring in his sample of sold and unsold homes (i.e. the complete duration of selling time for the unsold homes is unknown). Zuehlke finds that while vacant homes are less likely to sell initially, such homes exhibit positive duration dependence, while the hazard rate of occupied homes does not change significantly with time. Asking price also enters Zuehlke's model of time-on-market with higher asking prices corresponding with longer marketing period. Because most of the physical attribute variables that are significant in hedonic pricing models are insignificant in his time-on-market model, he suggests that list price and occupancy status are observable house attributes that may serve as good summary measures of seller characteristics.

Seller Characteristics

Rather than rely on proxies for seller characteristics, Glower et al. (1998) collect data directly related to seller motivation. They hypothesized that highly motivated sellers would set lower list prices and accept earlier, lower offers. They used a phone survey of home sellers to determine if the sale was motivated by a new job, and if so, how long before the new job commenced. They also collected information about the sellers' desired moving date, and whether they had made an offer or purchased another house. Using the survey information to gauge seller motivation, they find that "highly motivated sellers reduce time on market by up to 30% compared to sellers with a low motivation to sell." Their results, however, do not support their hypothesis of lower listing prices for motivated sellers.

Springer (1996) uses information available in multiple listing service (MLS) data to gauge the motivation of sellers. Remarks by the listing realtor to indicate the seller is relocating, offering a selling bonus, or is eager to sell are included as binary variables, as are property characteristics that would influence seller motivation, vacancy and foreclosure. In separate regressions of selling price and time on market on these variables, he finds that while all of the characteristics have a negative impact on selling price, only homes identified as foreclosures experience reduced marketing time. Thus, while the purpose of revealing seller motivation is usually to attract potential buyers and facilitate a quick sale, the unintended consequence is usually a weakening of the seller's bargaining position.

Genosove and Mayer (1994) examine the impact of another seller characteristic, homeowner equity in the house being sold. They hypothesize that equity constrained owners will set higher reservation prices and wait long to accept higher offers. Controlling for housing heterogeneity by using a fairly homogeneous set of condominiums in Boston, they find that sellers with higher loan-to-value ratios do in fact, signal higher reservation prices with higher asking prices, experience a longer marketing period, and ultimately sell at higher prices.

Seller Strategies

There are two main strategies available to the seller that can have an impact on marketing time and selling price. The most important of these is the choice of a listing price, as it determines the arrival rate of prospective buyers and sets a ceiling on the price for which the property can sell. The seller can also influence selling time by the decision to use a broker.

Empirical investigation of the listing price, selling price and time-on market nexus is extensive. Belkin et al. (1976) were among the first. They segmented housing data from Connecticut into submarkets based on price, and found a systematic negative relationship between time-on-market and a ratio of selling to listing price. In other words, the greater the discrepancy between listing and selling price, the longer homes took to sell. Kang and Gardner (1989) find the same relationship using [(Listing Price – Selling Price)/Selling Price] as the independent variable. Neither of these studies accounted for the endogenous relationship among listing and selling price and time-on-market, raising the potential for biased estimates. Yavas and Yang (1995) tested the relationship with a two-stage least squares model. They obtained predicted selling prices in the first stage, and in the second stage regressed days on market on the ratio of predicted selling price over listing price. Their results were ambiguous, with only two of four subsamples showing modest significance. When ordinary least squares was applied to the same data, the same negative and highly significant relationship as reported by Belkin (1976) and Kang and Gardner (1989) appeared. This suggests the simultaneity bias may be a legitimate cause for concern in evaluating the relationship.

Brokers have special knowledge of local housing markets such as identities of buyers and sellers, comparative values of properties, and recent price trends. As such, they can facilitate the matching of buyers and sellers and reduce the marketing time, as well as helping sellers select an appropriate listing price. The empirical evidence tends to support a reduced marketing time (Haurin 1988; Forgey et al.1996) although the support is not always strong (Knight 2002; Yavas and Yang 1995).

Bargaining Strength

Inasmuch as the observed transaction price is the result of negotiations, the price depends on the relative bargaining strength of seller and prospective buyer. The standard hedonic method does not allow for such effects, assuming that the shadow prices of house attributes are unaffected by bargaining strength. Harding et al. (2003) are able to estimate the effects of bargaining by including in the hedonic equation a vector of the sums of buyer and seller characteristics (to control for unobserved characteristics of the house), and a vector of the differences of buyer and seller characteristics (to measure the impact of buyer and seller attributes on bargaining power). For example, consider a binary variable for sex of the household head, one indicating male and zero female. The vector of sums would consist of zero where both buyer and seller are female, one if of different sex, and two if both male. The coefficient thus would capture the effect of unobserved characteristics of the house related to the sex of the buyers and sellers. The vector of differences would be plus one for a male seller and female buyer, zero for buyers and sellers of the same sex, and minus one for female seller and male buyer. Thus, a positive coefficient on this variable would suggest that males have greater bargaining strength in the transactions than do females. They find that women and first time buyers have less bargaining power than men and seasoned home buyers respectively, that wealth and income are negatively correlated with bargaining power[3], and that seasonal variations in prices may be driven by the presence of school-aged children in the families of buyers and sellers.

Another issue with respect to relative bargaining strength is whether the differences in negotiating power are reflected simply in the intercept of the hedonic equation, or also changes in the slopes of the attributes making up the hedonic equation. In other words, is it only the composite price of the house that is affected, or are the shadow prices of the individual house attributes affected as well? Harding et al. (2003) investigate this issue using house vacancy as a proxy for bargaining weakness on the part of the seller. They find strong evidence that bargaining power influences the negotiated price, and mixed evidence with respect to the individual attribute prices.

Spatial Competition

While each house is unique and has only one seller, similar houses compete with each other for a buyer. Turnbull and Dombrow (2006) investigate the spatial density of listings and observe that while a high density of listings in an area has a negative influence on price and time-on-market because of the competition effect, it simultaneously has a positive impact because of an externality effect (the arrival rate of buyers is higher in areas with many listings). They develop a means of separating these effects, and find that which effect dominates depends on whether the market as a whole is rising or falling.

---

[3] The authors suggest that this negative relation between the buyers' wealth and the bargaining power results from the diminishing marginal utility of wealth.

Temporal Factors

Time affects the selling price of homes in three ways. First, as discussed previously, the amount of time a home spends on the market influences the willingness of the seller to accept a lower price to expedite a speedier sale. Second, house values do not stay fixed during the selling period, but rather rise and fall with changes in supply and demand factors in the market as a whole. The longer a home remains on the market, the more likely such an influence will arise. Finally, the season of sale can influence the selling price as buyer behavior may be affected by weather conditions or family schooling concerns.

Time-of-sale may be controlled in two ways. If the time period of the data is relatively short or if the market during the period is relatively stable, a single time trend variable suffices, as in Turnbull and Dombrow (2006) or Forgey et al. (1996) for example. If, however, the data span a longer period, or the period is more turbulent, dummy variables for each month or quarter (e.g. Knight et al. 1994) are more desirable as a time trend variable would have the effect of smoothing the periodic market influence.

Season of sale is also a matter of concern. One would expect that spring and summer sales would be at higher prices, as weather is unlikely to have an adverse impact on property inspection by buyers, and spring and summer sales allow for the least disruption of schooling for children in the family. The empirical results for this control are quite mixed however (see, for example, Haurin 1988; Springer 1996; Forgey et al. 1996; Knight 2002; Harding et al. 2003).

Empirical Analysis of Interim Events

There have been a few efforts to adapt Lazear's (1986) theory to housing markets. Sass (1988), for example, tests the theory using higher priced houses, which have fewer prospective buyers, and newer and more recently sold homes, about which the information about value should be better. He does not have actual data regarding price reductions during the interim period, and instead uses the difference between initial listing price and ending selling price as the measure of price change. Read (1988) uses Lazear's theory as the basis for a price revision strategy for the profit maximizing seller. He uses numerical analysis to describe how sellers learn from the arrival rate of shoppers about the market value of their properties and then incorporate this information into reservation price changes.

Lack of data has severely hampered the empirical analysis of changes taking place between the initial listing and the ultimate sale. A few recent papers, however, have gathered data to investigate this interim strategy. Knight (2002), for example, has information about seller behavior during the selling period. Specifically, he has a record of all list price changes for homes selling in Stockton, California over a two-year period. About 38% of the homes changed list price at least once during the marketing period, confirming the commonplace nature of strategy revisions. The results of a probit model for the determinants of list price changes are consistent with costly search: the length of time on market and a home's vacant status increase the likelihood of a change. Heterogeneous homes and homes at either end of the price continuum are less likely to undergo list price changes, a result consistent with Lazear's theory: the more heterogeneous a product, the less is learned about its valuation by its failure to sell and the less the expected benefit of a price reduction. Further support for Lazear's price cutting theory is found in Herrin et al. (2004).

Merlo and Ortalo-Magne (2004) have not only data about list price changes, but also data reflecting the number of viewings by prospective buyers, and all offers made on a property between listing and sale. They consider listing price reductions fairly infrequent, although properties experiencing a change in listing price comprise a significant proportion (23%) of their sample of 780 properties in Yorkshire and London, England. They find that the size of the price reduction, if one occurs, is related to the length of time the home has been on the market. With respect to the offers received on a property, they find the offer is lower the longer a home has been on the market, a fact consistent both with Taylor's (1999) theory of negative herding, and with a perception by the buyer of a relatively weak bargaining position of the seller. Their data also provides evidence that the recorded transaction price is typically not the same as the first offer made, though properties are typically sold to the first potential buyer making an offer. This points out a weakness in existing complete information bargaining models that take price as fixed.

2.5 Directions for Further Research

Progress has been made, but the frequent conflicting results in studies of the home selling process suggest that much work remains to be done. There is considerable room in the literature, both theoretical and empirical, for study of the events between listing and sale. Extension of housing theory to incorporate search with learning models along the lines of Lazear (1986), would provide a framework for empirical testing of the data that is now becoming available regarding the interim between listing and sale. Changes in listing price during the process of selling a home provide information about the learning that takes place during the seller's search for a buyer. As an upper boundary for the unobservable reservation price of a seller, list price serves as an excellent proxy with which to study seller strategy.

The recent work of Pryce and Gibb (2006) modeling changing hazard rates opens another potentially fruitful avenue for learning more about the determinants of time-on-market, and there is a need to blend the superior information about time-on-market obtained from hazard models into the hedonic treatment of house price. Existing studies either ignore the simultaneity problem altogether, or address it with two stage least squares for which the time-on-market input is the result of ordinary least squares regression.

Especially relevant to this Volume's orientation, with the exception of Huang and Palmquist (2001) virtually nothing has been done to incorporate the home selling process into the hedonic study of environmental issues. Failure to consider time on market and its impact on selling price is a potentially serious omission. To the extent that time on market is correlated with the environmental variable of interest, biased estimation will result, and the higher the correlation, the greater the bias. The severity of the omitted variable problem is, of course, an empirical question. It can be answered by incorporating the time on market variable (frequently available in the data) as a regressor in the selling price equation and observing the change in the parameter estimate of the environmental amenity or disamenity. Beyond the mere inclusion of the time on market variable, consideration of the endogeneity of time and selling price could also yield important information. Replication of the Huang and Palmquist (2001) methodology using different sets of data would be a fruitful avenue of study.

Finally, very little has been done empirically with respect to the bargaining that takes place once a match between buyer and seller occurs. Yavas et al. (2001) explore the process in an experimental setting, and Arnold (1999) offers a sequential bidding process stemming from costly continued search on the part of buyer and seller, but virtually nothing has been done empirically to study the negotiation process. Collecting data about offers, counteroffers and rejections could provide a richer understanding of the end game of the selling process.

2.6 Conclusions

One may wonder about the importance of incorporating the home sellig process into hedonic pricing models. Virtually none of the environmental and segregation hedonic studies, and only a small percentage of hedonic pricing studies overall control for marketing time and its potential impact on parameter estimates. Most of those that include a time-on-market variable fail to recognize the endogeneity of time and selling price, and therefore merely substitue endogeneity bias for omitted variable bias. One would therefore be in good company in choosing to ignore the impact of selling process on selling price. This, of cours, is not a good reason to knowingly misspecify a model.

Some justification for ignoring marketing time is provided by the fact that there is theoretical justification for either a positive or a negative relationship with selling price. Empirically, however, the support for a negative relationship is fairly strong, especially among the studies correctly specifying the time-on-market variable.

In the end, the researcher must weigh the complexity of incorporating this concern against the potential result of ignoring it. If information regarding time-on-market is available, it should be used. It is possible, of course, that the endogeneity of time on market is not empirically important, as Jean Cavailhés et. al., this Volume, find using a Hausman test. Even if marketing time is not included in the final specification, a preliminary analysis such as this could reveal the importance of the home selling process on the study at hand.

References

Allen MT, Rutherford RC, Thomson TA (Forthcoming) Residential asking rents and time on the market. Journal of real estate finance and economics

Anglin P (1997) Determinants of buyer search in a housing market. Real estate economics 25: 567–589

Arnold MA (1999) Search, bargaining and optimal asking prices. Real estate economics 27: 453–481

Arnott R (1989) Housing vacancies, thin markets, and idiosyncratic tastes. Journal of real estate finance and economics 2: 5–30

Belkin J, Hempel DJ, Mcleavey DW (1976) An empirical study of time on market using multidimensional segmentation of housing markets. Journal of the American real estate and urban economics association 4: 57–79

Forgey FA, Rutherford RC, Springer TM (1996) Search and liquidity in single-family housing. Real estate economics 24: 273–292

Genesove D, Mayer CJ (1997) Equity and time to sale in the real estate market. American economic review 87: 255–269

Glower M, Haurin DR, Hendershott PH (1998) Selling time and selling price: the influence of seller motivation. Real estate economics 26: 719–740

Harding J, Knight JR, Sirmans CF (2003) Estimating bargaining effects in hedonic models: evidence from the housing market. Real estate economics 31: 601–622

Harding J, Rosenthal S, Sirmans CF (2003) Estimating bargaining power in the market for existing homes. Review of economics and statistics 85: 178–188

Haurin D (1988) The duration of marketing time of residential housing. AREUEA Journal 16: 396–410

Herrin W, Knight JR, Sirmans CF (2004) Price cutting behavior in residential markets. Journal of housing economics 13: 195–207

Horowitz JL (1986) Bidding models of housing markets. Journal of urban economics 20: 168–190

Horowitz JL (1992) The role of the list price in housing markets: theory and an econometric model. Journal of applied econometrics 7: 115–129

Huang JC, Palmquist RB (2001) Environmental conditions, reservation prices, and time on the market for housing. Journal of real estate finance and economics 22: 203–219

Kang H, Gardner M (1989) Selling price and marketing time in the residential real estate market. The journal of real estate research 4: 21–35

Kim S (1992) Search, hedonic prices and housing demand. The review of economics and statistics 74: 503–508

Knight JR (2002) Listing price, time on market, and ultimate selling price: causes and effects of listing price changes. Real estate economics 30: 215–237

Knight JR, Sirmans CF, Turnbull GK (1994) List price signaling and buyer behavior in the housing market. Journal of real estate finance and economics 9: 177–192

Knight JR, Sirmans CF, Turnbull GK (1998) List price information in residential appraisal and underwriting. Journal of real estate research 15: 55–70

Lazear EP (1986) Retail pricing and clearance sales. The american economic review 76: 14–32

Lippman SA, McCall JJ (1978) The economics of job search: a survey. Economic inquiry 14: 155–189

Merlo A, Ortalo-Magne F (2004) Bargaining over residential real estate: evidence from England. Journal of urban economics 56: 192–216

Pryce G, Gibb K (2006) Submarket dynamics of time-to-sale. Real estate economics 34: 377–415

Rosen S (1974) Hedonic prices and implicit markets: product differentiation in pure competition. Journal of political economy 82: 666–677
Read C (1988) Price strategies for idiosyncratic goods - The case of housing. AREUEA journal 16: 379–395
Sass TR (1988) A note on optimal price cutting behavior under demand uncertainty. The review of economics and statistics 70: 336–339
Sirmans CF, Turnbull GK, Benjamin JD (1991) The markets for housing and real estate broker services. Journal of housing economics 1: 207–217
Sirmans CF, Turnbull GK, Dombrow J (1995) Quick house sales: seller mistake or luck. Journal of housing economics 4: 230–243
Sirmans SG, Macpherson DA, Zietz EN (2005) The composition of hedonic pricing models. Journal of real estate literature 13: 3–43
Springer TM (1996) Single-family housing transactions: seller motivations, price, and marketing time. Journal of real estate finance and economics 13: 237–254
Taylor C (1999) Time-on-the-market as a sign of quality. Review of economic studies 66: 555–578
Turnbull GK, Dombrow J (2006) Spatial competition and shopping externalities: evidence from the housing market. Journal of real estate finance and economics 32: 391–408
Wheaton WC (1990) Vacancy, search, and prices in a housing market matching model. Journal of political economy 98: 1270–1292
Yavas A (1992) A simple search and bargaining model of real estate markets. Real estate economics 20: 533–548
Yavas A, Yang S (1995) The strategic role of listing price in marketing real estate: theory and evidence. Real estate economics 23: 347–368
Yavas A, Miceli T, Sirmans CF (2001) An experimental analysis of the impact of intermediaries on the outcome of bargaining games. Real estate economics 23: 251–276
Zuehlke TW (1987) Duration dependence in the housing market. Review of economics and statistics 69: 701–704

PART II
Applications to Urban Environment Issues

3 Hedonic Property Value Studies of Transportation Noise: Aircraft and Road Traffic

Jon P. Nelson

Pennsylvania State University, University Park, United States

3.1 Introduction

Noise from aircraft and road traffic is an example of an uncompensated external cost or externality. A negative externality is defined as a by-product of production or consumption activities that adversely affects third parties not directly involved in the associated market transactions. Environmental noises that exceed ambient levels can disturb valuable activities such as conversation, TV viewing, leisure, work or sleep, and in severe cases can have adverse effects on long-term health and thereby reduce productivity and quality of life.[1] The third parties can take defensive steps to avoid the physical effects of noise, such as screening their property using fencing or vegetation, installing air conditioning and insulation, or moving to a new residence. A role of economics is to help determine the socially optimal amount of noise and the appropriate mixture of source abatement, operational changes, and housing adjustments (relocation, zoning, soundproofing). Recent legislative changes, such as the European Commission's "Green Paper on Future Noise Policy" (EC 1996) and Directive 2002/49/EC on noise assessment (EC 2002), have focused attention on noise valuation as part of benefit-cost analyses of mitigation projects. The information from valuation studies also can be used for

---

[1] The unit of sound intensity is the decibel (dB), measured on a logarithmic scale. A tenfold increase in sound intensity is a 10 dB increase or roughly a doubling of perceived loudness. Sound-levels are weighted to account for human ability to hear sounds of different frequencies, e.g., the A-weighted sound level is used to describe sounds from transportation sources. Representative sound levels are a quiet suburban street (50 dBA); conversational speech at 3 feet (60 dBA); freight train at 100 feet (70 dBA); and busy city cross-streets (80 dBA). The statistical distribution of noise also is described by the levels in dBA exceed 10, 50, and 90% of the time: L_{10} (peak level), L_{50} (median), and L_{90} (background). Lastly, the day-night average sound level (DNL or L_{DN}) is the *equivalent* energy-averaged sound level (L_{EQ}) in dBA during a 24-hour period, with a 10 dB penalty for nighttime noise. "Equivalent" means the acoustical energy of the average steady-state sound equals the energy from the actual sounds.

A. Baranzini et al. (eds.), *Hedonic Methods in Housing Markets*, doi: 10.1007/978-0-387-76815-1_3,

cost-effective policy design, including the choice between regulations, noise pollution taxes, and tradeable permits.

Valuation of noise damages would be relatively straightforward if an explicit private market existed for tranquility, but in general this market is missing. In simple cases, a market can be created by assigning clearly-defined legal rights to either the polluter or the polluted. Aircraft operators and their customers value the surrounding airspace as an input to air travel and freight operations, and would be willing to pay for legal rights to ensure that the airspace is available for these purposes (Gillen 2003). For different reasons, airport neighbors also value the surrounding environment and would be willing to pay for their right to use the resource. Thus, in the absence of transaction costs, market exchange would solve the problem of noise abatement. However, the airspace is an example of a common property resource, where there is little or no delineation of use rights for private parties (Cheung 1987). Absent private ownership, the main alternative for allocation of common property is some system of government ownership and regulation. Regulation means that airports and their neighbors are given "rank" to enjoy different rights and privileges, which creates valuable implicit property rights. Under the Aviation Safety and Noise Act of 1979, the US Federal Aviation Administration declared 65 L_{DN} as the critical day-night average sound level for aircraft noise regulation, although evidence from complaints suggests that some fraction of the population is annoyed by lower noise levels. Due to increased transportation activity, income growth, and other economic changes, government ownership creates pressure for new abatement regulations and endogenous changes in rank. Economic analysis and valuation methods have the promise to provide objectivity in this essentially political process.

Economic valuation methods are divided into two categories: revealed preference methods such as the hedonic price (HP) method for housing values; and stated preference (SP) methods such as contingent valuation surveys. Revealed preference methods exploit the fact that there are private markets that are complementary to noise avoidance, including the market for residential housing. Suppose a house either has a quiet residential environment or it does not. The difference in market values of an identical house in these two environments yields an implicit discount for noise, which compensates the occupants of the noisy house. Informed market participants reveal this price as a result of purchase and sale decisions in the market for real estate. The sorting of buyers and sellers in a stable noise environment produces an outcome in which noisy houses tend to be occupied by individuals who have a low willingness to pay for quietude (imperturbables) and quiet houses tend to be occupied by those with a high willingness to pay. A change in the noise environment alters the relative supply of noisy and quiet houses, and creates a new equilibrium outcome. In practice, environmental conditions in residential neighborhoods are more complex. Noise is a localized public bad, so fixed proportions between houses and noises do not exist (Walters 1975). Potential buyers of houses can choose to live close to a busy highway or airport, far from these facilities, or somewhere in-between. They also can choose houses with physical attributes that partially offset the effects of noise.

The differences in housing values and noise levels yields a "noise discount" that falls as distance from an airport or highway increases. Regression analysis of real estate transactions is used to unbundle housing prices and calculate an implicit hedonic price for quiet. A difference in market value of $20,000 and a difference in noise exposure of 10 dB results in a hedonic price of $2,000 per dB, other things being equal. In order to avoid use of nominal values, this price is often expressed as a percentage of a base house (Walters 1975; Nelson 1980). If the market value of the house without noise is $200,000 and its value with noise is $180,000, the Noise Depreciation Index (NDI) is 1.0% per dB.

The main alternatives to hedonic valuation are survey methods that ask respondents to state their willingness to pay for environmental improvements, including the contingent valuation method, contingent ranking, conjoint analysis, and other SP models. These methods are still relatively new, but a number of survey-based studies of noise valuation are available. While the purpose of this chapter is to critically review recent studies using hedonic valuation methods, it is useful to include results from SP studies. An examination of survey-based results also serves to illustrate the strengths and weaknesses of the HP method. The next two sections of this chapter provide a brief history of hedonic valuation of noise and a topical outline. This is followed by a five-part discussion of issues that confront empirical researchers in this area.

3.2 Early HP Noise Studies and Prior Literature Reviews

Although the basic concepts date to 1928, Rosen's (1974) classic article on product differentiation and competition was an important theoretical contribution that formed the basis for much of the empirical work on housing markets using the HP model. Rosen's paper raised several theoretical issues that have not been entirely resolved, including the concept of two-stage estimation. Prior literature reviews that emphasize theoretical and welfare issues associated with the HP model include Freeman (1993), Haab and McConnell (2002), Palmquist (2005), and Taylor (2003, and in this Volume). There also have been several reviews of the empirical literature, including Boyle and Kiel (2001), Palmquist and Smith (2002), and Pearce et al. (2006).

The first major application of HP methods to aircraft noise was Emerson's (1972) study of housing sales for 1967 in the vicinity of the Minneapolis-St. Paul International Airport. Another early study by Paik (1972) examined housing values in US census data for 1960 for three areas: John F. Kennedy Airport, New York; Los Angeles International Airport; and Love Field Airport, Dallas. This early work was followed by HP studies of San Francisco International Airport (Dygert 1973), Toronto International Airport (Crowley 1973), National Airport, Washington, DC (Nelson 1975, 1978), and Heathrow Airport, London (Gautrin 1975). The latter study is notable for the analysis of the tradeoff between accessibility and noise disamenities. Reflecting possible access effects, a few studies have obtained a null effect of aircraft noise (Lipscomb 2003; Tomkins et al. 1998;

van Praag and Baarsma 2005).

Although several limited studies of highway noise and house prices appeared before Gamble et al. (1974), this was the first major study that applied HP methods to road traffic noise. They studied US interstate highways in four communities in New Jersey, Virginia, and Maryland. Other early work includes HP studies of traffic noise for Washington, DC (Nelson 1975, 1978), Chicago (Vaughan and Huckins 1975), and Toronto (Taylor et al. 1982), and a repeat-sales analysis for Spokane, Washington, by Palmquist (1982). The repeat-sales model is derived from the HP model by observing the sale of the same house at two or more points in time. Early European studies include a 1974 study for Stockholm by Hammar (cited in Navrud 2002) and a study of Copenhagen by Hjorth-Andersen (1978).

3.2.1 Meta-Analyses of Transportation Noise

By the year 2007, there were approximately 40 HP studies for airports in Canada and the US, and probably an equal number for non-North American airports. The aircraft noise literature was previously reviewed by Bateman et al. (2001), Nellthorp et al. (2007), Nelson (1978, 1980, 2004), Schipper (1999), and Schipper et al. (1998). Nelson (2004) conducted a meta-analysis of 33 estimates of the noise discount for 23 airports in Canada and the US. Using a variety of meta-analytical techniques, the NDI was between 0.50 and 0.70% per dB, with a weighted-effect size of about 0.67%.

The HP literature on road traffic noise has been reviewed by Bateman et al. (2001), Bertrand (1997), Navrud (2002), Nelson (1978, 1982), and Tinch (1995). Nelson (1982) reviewed nine empirical studies covering 14 different housing markets in Canada and the US. The mean NDI was 0.40% per dB. Using a formal meta-analysis, Bertrand (1997) compared 16 estimates from nine different HP studies. His work suggests an NDI for traffic noise as high as 0.64%. An empirical issue to be explored in the present survey is the extent to which more recent studies have altered the NDIs for aircraft and traffic noise. With this in mind, selected NDI values are reported for various studies and summarized at the end of the survey.

3.3 Research Outline

Following Rosen (1974), Freeman (1993), and Palmquist (2005), consumer preferences and the variety of available houses combine to produce an equilibrium hedonic price function. This function may be linear or non-linear. Individuals affect the price they pay for a house by choosing a different bundle of characteristics. However, as price-takers in a competitive market, they cannot affect equilibrium price schedules for characteristics. Thus, the heterogeneous nature of housing does not destroy the basic notion of a competitive price, and as a first approximation, estimation of the hedonic price function does not require socioeconomic data on the individuals residing in each house (see Knight, this Volume for an alternative perspective).

Empirically, there are two functions that are of interest. First, the hedonic price schedule can be estimated using data on prices of houses and their characteristics, including neighborhood attributes, accessibility, and environmental variables. From this schedule, marginal prices are calculated. Second, marginal prices can be combined with data on occupants' income and other socioeconomic variables to estimate an inverse demand or willingness to pay function. Ideally, inverse demands for all N characteristics are estimated jointly as a system of demand functions. Only a few HP studies for noise have estimated second-stage demand functions; see Day et al. (2007), McMillan (1979), Pommerehne (1988), and Wilhelmsson (2002). However, welfare measurements are possible using only marginal prices if the environmental change affects a small number of houses relative to the size of the market (Palmquist 1992a, 1992b). This is the case of a localized externality. Further, transaction and moving costs must be small enough so that the welfare gains are not offset by moving costs. If these costs are prohibitive, they place an upper-bound on the welfare change (Palmquist 2005).

In this chapter, I assume that noise is a localized externality, but transaction and moving costs are discussed below. Noise mitigation projects that affect large areas add complexity to the problem of welfare measurement using either HP or SP methods (Palmquist 2005; Taylor, this Volume). Given this stylized model, five empirical issues are identified for additional discussion: spatial heterogeneity and housing market segmentation; spatial autoregression and autocorrelation; housing market adjustment models and moving costs; alternative noise indices and community annoyance; and stated preference methods and hedonic prices.

3.4 Spatial Heterogeneity: Housing Market Segmentation

A housing market can be identified by a uniform hedonic price schedule, which is determined by the housing stock that makes up the market and characteristics of the occupants and neighborhood. An old issue in real estate economics is the existence and measurement of housing submarkets or market segmentation. A metropolitan housing market might be segmented according to structure type, structural characteristics, neighborhood amenities and disamenities, age of occupants, income, occupational or social class, and ethnic or racial identity (Goodman and Thibodeau 1998). Unlike many consumer products, houses are durable, infrequently traded, and short-run supplies are relatively fixed. Furthermore, alterations of physical features ("repackaging") is only possible within certain limits and many neighborhood attributes are either fixed or change slowly and infrequently over time. Spatial heterogeneity for hedonic prices is more likely to occur when households' demand for a particular characteristic is price inelastic and this preference is shared by a relatively large number of potential homeowners or renters (Day 2003). Early HP studies often used small samples that covered limited geographic areas, such as residential areas in close proximity to a major airport or busy highway. In these settings, segmentation is less likely to arise due to homogeneity of the sample of houses, neighborhood attributes, and occupants. However, the advent of GIS methods and computerized-data yield study samples that cover entire metropolitan areas, and which include thousands of housing sales and numerous locational variables. Empirical researchers are no longer faced with problems of a paucity of data and lack of variation, but instead must try to identify order amongst an abundance of sample observations.

The standard econometric test for homogeneity is the Chow F-test, but this test assumes that the model is correctly specified with regard to variables and functional form. Palmquist (2005) argues that an F-test will almost always reject homogeneity, given a large sample size. He suggests that investigators think about the types of transactions that are crucial to the environmental issue being addressed, and this might mean focusing on smaller areas or some subset of the sample. Similarly, a few noise studies have involved individuals from the real estate industry as a source of information about housing submarkets (Day et al. 2004; Feitelson et al. 1996; Frankel 1991). Also, rejection of the null for the overall regression need not imply a lack of uniformity for individual coefficients for submarkets. For individual coefficients, a Tiao-Goldberger F-test can be used (see Nelson 1979, 1981; Palmquist 1992a).

Baranzini and Ramirez (2005) examine the economic impact of noise in the Geneva market for apartments. A special feature of the Swiss housing market is the high proportion of renter-occupied housing (about 60–65%). They study the effects of road traffic noise on apartment rents using a sample of 13,034 apartments covering more than 7,000 buildings for the canton of Geneva. They also study the effects of airport noise for a restricted sample of 1,847 apartments. For the larger sample, there are 10,394 apartments in the private sector and 2,640 "public" apartments, which are subject to government regulation in the form of subsidized construction grants, rent controls, and occupant restrictions. The traffic noise data contains information on the day-night sound level (L_{DN}) at each building's facade, peak noise intrusiveness measured by ($L_{10} - L_{90}$), and an EU-version of the day-night metric, L_{DEN}, which includes a 5 dB penalty for evening noise and a 10 dB penalty for nighttime noise. The background noise level is 50 dB. Baranzini and Ramirez estimate semilog regressions for the two full samples and separate regressions for private and public submarkets. The regressions account for eight structural variables (number of rooms, floor level, age of building, etc.), four access variables, air pollution, and noise. For traffic noise, an increase in the mean noise level by one dB reduces private sector rents by 0.18% and public sector rents by 0.65%. A F-test rejects the equality of the NDIs. Further, the peak noise impact is 0.63% in the private sector and insignificant in the public sector. Hence, the evidence indicates separate markets for private and public apartments. The impact of airport noise is 0.66% and 0.79% per dB in the private and public submarkets. The airport NDIs agree substantially with prior studies.

A similar exercise for traffic noise is found in Rich and Nielsen (2004). Their initial sample covers 845 houses and 906 apartments in Copenhagen (40% of Danes live in apartments), but a 50 dB cutoff for background noise reduces the final samples to 238 houses and 472 apartments. The noise measure is the Danish equivalent of L_{DEN}. Rich and Nielsen argue that houses and apartments appeal to different consumer segments and statistical results show that the two markets are different. A non-linear Box-Cox function is used for the regressions, with two structural variables for each structure type, eight accessibility variables, seven neighborhood dummy variables, and traffic noise. Accounting for the non-linear relationship, the NDIs are 0.47% for apartments and 0.54% per dB for houses. A similar study by Grue et al. (1997) for Oslo obtains comparable results. The estimated NDIs are 0.24% for public apartments, 0.48% for private apartments, and 0.54% per dB for houses.

A more sophisticated approach to market segmentation is found in a series of papers by Day (2003) and Day et al. (2006) for Glasgow, Scotland, and Bateman et al. (2004) and Day et al. (2007) for Birmingham, England. The Glasgow sample covers 3,544 houses sold in 1986 and the Birmingham sample covers 10,889 residential dwelling sales in 1997. The environmental data include noise from aircraft, road traffic, and railroads. The background noise level is 55 dB. Due to the large number of socioeconomic and neighborhood variables, these studies use factor analysis to reduce the number of data dimensions. In order to identify submarkets, the studies also use cluster analysis. For Glasgow, there are four clusters: tenements occupied by ethnically Scottish residents; tenements occupied by ethnic minorities; larger urban properties occupied by upwardly-mobile young professionals; and larger properties in affluent suburban areas. For Birmingham, there are eight clusters defined by ethnic identity, age of occupants, wealth (affluent, poor), size of property (standard, large), and geographic location (north, south, west).

Using a semilog model, ordinary least squares (OLS) regressions are estimated for each submarket and the full sample. For Glasgow, a Chow test rejects the null and indicates the HP estimates are significantly different for each cluster. The traffic noise coefficients yield NDI values of –0.23, –0.46, –0.57, and a positive value of 0.38% per dB. A Tiao-Goldberger F-test rejects the null of uniform noise coefficients, even when the positive coefficient is excluded. A second set of estimates accounts for spatial autocorrelation and is obtained by using a generalized method of moments (GMM) estimator. Traffic noise coefficients are significantly negative for three of the four submarkets, with NDIs of –0.30, –0.47, –0.58, and 0.31% per dB. These values are quite close to the OLS estimates, except that significance levels increase. Aircraft noise is statistically significant for only one submarket, with a negative NDI of 0.40% per dB. For Birmingham, the regressions are based on a semiparametric model that accounts for spatial autocorrelation. Traffic and rail noise is significantly negative for five of eight submarkets and airport noise is significantly negative for only two submarkets. The traffic noise NDIs for Birmingham are in the range 0.18 to 0.55% per dB, which agrees generally with the estimates for Glasgow. The airport noise NDIs are 1.60% and 0.63% per dB, which suggest substantial differences among the submarkets. However, this result could simply reflect a non-linear hedonic price function.

Some of the results in these studies suggest that market segmentation is an important empirical issue for future researchers. However, the long list of locational and neighborhood variables are somewhat at a variance with the objectives of spatial modeling. Further, the non-linear nature of the hedonic price function will complicate tests for market segmentation. Advanced methods, such as those employed for Glasgow and Birmingham, are necessary to provide a convincing case for a segmented market.

3.5 Spatial Models: Autoregression and Autocorrelation

Econometric estimation of HP models by OLS requires, among other assumptions, the independence of residual errors. However, residuals in hedonic models are frequently spatially correlated or nonspherical, which means the OLS estimator is unbiased but inefficient and estimates of standard errors are biased. The most likely outcome is that residuals are positively correlated, which biases standard errors downward. Hence, confidence levels (t-statistics) for the coefficients are overstated, and confidence intervals and predicted values are understated. Spatially dependent errors can arise because (1) houses in close proximity to each other share common structural and neighborhood characteristics, so that disturbances are transmitted over space, and (2) the residuals contain systematic spatial information that is not captured by the regression model. For example, residences in the same geographic space share common environmental amenities and disamenities or houses may occupy similar locations in characteristics space, leading to a spatial-lag dependence (SLD) model. Furthermore, it is unlikely that all locational features and other relevant spatial variables are observed and quantified, which leads to an omitted variables problem. This results in a spatial-error dependence (SED) model. A similar argument applies if locational variables are measured with error. Finally, "adjacency effects" are spatial spillovers that are capitalized into housing prices, such as maintenance decisions by neighbors (Can 1992). In this case, spatial-lag dependence is endogenous and OLS coefficients are biased and inefficient.

Some of these problems can be overcome by increasing the number of locational variables, but this is not necessarily an efficient solution due to attendant collinearity problems. Some empirical applications omit all neighborhood-accessibility variables, and model the resulting autocorrelation in the error term (Dubin 1992). In general, it is expected that residual correlations decline as separation distance increases, reflecting a process of distance decay (Tobler's first law of geography). Hence, one simple econometric solution is to include a polynomial term for the latitude and longitude of each property. Alternatively, in the SLD model, neighboring observations are combined in the form of a spatially-weighted regressor, which is a distance-weighted average of the prices of other properties in the neighborhood. The definition of neighbors is typically based on the notion of distance decay as determined by empirical methods, such as the inverse of the square of distance with an arbitrary cutoff distance. Finally, in the SED model, residuals from neighboring properties are combined using a spatial-weights matrix.

The SED model is more appropriate when the researcher is interested in removing bias due to interdependence and the SLD model is used when the concern is with structural interaction. Use of these models has increased due in part to the ease of estimation using GMM procedures suggested by Kelejian and Prucha (1999).

Salvi (2003) applies spatial econometrics to measure the impact of aircraft noise on prices of single-family residences near the Zurich airport. He estimates a general spatial model using GMM techniques. The data set contains 675 housing sales during 1995 to 2002 and fourteen structural features for each house. Noise exposure is measured by the L_{EQ} metric over a 16-hour period and the background noise level is 50 dB. For the OLS model, the NDI is 0.74% per dB. Semi-variogram graphs of the sales prices and OLS residuals indicate that residual correlations decline rapidly with distance. The cutoff for the weighting matrix is set at distances of 300 or 600 meters (656 yards). Moran's I test and a nonparametric test rejects the absence of spatial autocorrelation for both cutoff distances. The spatial model includes the spatial error and a weighted lag of five continuous structural characteristics, but excludes the neighborhood variables. The GMM model is estimated with noise in a continuous form and, alternatively, with five dummy variables for noise increments of 3 to 5 dB. The continuous metric yields an NDI of 0.75% per dB. This result suggests that the spatial error component is small, both statistically and economically. For the semilog model with dummies for noise exposure, the effect of an additional dB in percentage terms can be approximated by $NDI = 100(\exp[B - 0.5 \cdot V(B)] - 1)$, where B is the noise coefficient and $V(B)$ is its variance (van Garderen and Shah 2002). With a background noise level of 50 dB, the five dummies yield NDIs of 0.48, 0.49, 0.63, 1.05, and 1.26% per dB. Hence, using dummy variables, damages rise sharply for the Zurich Airport at noise levels in excess of 65 dB. These estimates are within the range of values provided by previous studies, but demonstrate the importance of using dummy variables for each noise zone.

Theebe (2004) estimates the effects of traffic noise using a SED model, but some of the details are incompletely reported. His full data set contains more than 160,000 property sales in the western part of the Netherlands during 1997–1999, including abundant information on structural characteristics. The data set is split into five smaller samples by political jurisdictions, which are further divided into submarkets according to income, density, date of sale, and property type. Noise exposure is obtained for small areas using the L_{EQ} metric. The background noise level is 55 dB. In order to capture a non-linear relationship, noise exposure data are represented by nine dummy variables. Correcting for spatial autocorrelation, Theebe finds that traffic noise has little effect on house prices at sound levels below 65 dB. Above 65 dB, the NDI varies from 0.3 to 0.5% per dB. At the submarket level, the NDIs are somewhat larger, although less precisely estimated.

A third application of spatial econometrics is found in Cohen and Coughlin (2006). They study housing values in the vicinity of Atlanta's Hartsfield–Jackson International Airport, which is the world's busiest. The data set contains 508 housing sales during 2003, but only four structural variables (number of stories, bedrooms, bathrooms, fireplaces). Soundproofing of houses is an unobserved structural variable. Accessibility is measured by straight-line distance to the airport and neighborhood attributes are captured by dummies for each of six political jurisdictions. Noise exposure is represented by two dummy variables for L_{DN} values of 65 and 70 dB, with a background level of about 55–60 dB. Approximately 67% of observations are outside the 65 dB zone, 29% are in the 65–70 dB zone, and only 4% are in the 70–75 dB zone. This is less than satisfactory as only 19 houses in the sample are exposed to substantial noise levels. OLS estimates yield a negative, but insignificant, coefficient for the 65 dB zone and a significantly negative coefficient for the 70 dB zone. The NDI for the 70 dB zone is about 1.63 to 2.44% per dB, which is substantially larger than most prior estimates including other estimates for Atlanta. Next, Cohen and Coughlin incorporate spatial effects. They consider a general model with both a spatially-lagged dependent variable and spatial-error dependence. GMM estimates for the general model produce empirical results that are similar to the OLS model, but slightly smaller. Houses in the 70 dB zone sell for 20.8% less than houses in the buffer zone, so the NDI is about 1.39 to 2.08% per dB. Access to the airport also enhances housing prices after accounting for the effects of aircraft noise. The coefficient for the spatially-lagged dependent variable is significantly positive. The parameter estimate indicates that if all neighboring housing prices were to rise by 1%, the sale price of an individual house will rise on average by 0.54%.

Spatially-dependent errors present a major challenge to research on housing markets, but at present it is unclear if modeling of these errors leads to major changes in empirical results for the impact of noise. However, researchers should at least test for spatial correlation using Moran's I statistic and similar tests. Some additional evidence on this issue is presented below.

3.6 Housing Market Adjustment Models

Cross-sectional hedonic models are designed to capture long-run relationships, but policymakers and practitioners often express skepticism about this claim. Suppose, for example, that a new runway is being constructed at a major airport. This might be accompanied by an initial reduction of property values, followed by a slow recovery as new residents move into the area and capture the locational rents associated with access to the airport. If the increased noise adversely affects a large number of houses, the long-run price discount might increase as households move and bid for quieter houses (Walters 1975).

This adjustment process is complicated by moving costs, transaction costs, and asymmetric information associated with the purchase of a house. Future noise levels are not known with certainty, but sellers might have more accurate information about present and future environmental problems relative to potential buyers. This section examines several recent papers that account for housing market adjustment processes and associated events.[2]

Jud and Winkler (2006) study the expansion of the Greensboro-Winston Salem airport in North Carolina to accommodate a regional air-cargo hub for Federal Express. Announcement of the expansion took place in early 1998, and between 1998 and 2004 there were 508 news stories and 582 opinion and editorial pieces in the local newspaper related to the hub. For example, it was reported that the expansion would initially add 20 nighttime flights, which would be expanded to 126 flights per night by 2009. Local opposition groups and legal filings added to the publicity about the expansion. An environmental impact assessment was conducted by the Federal Aviation Administration and the final version was released to the public in late 2001. Among other things, it recorded the number of houses that were anticipated to be affected adversely by the expansion of the 65 dB and 70 dB zones. Hence, this is a setting with abundant public information about the event, and it seems likely the housing market would anticipate the expansion. Jud and Winkler measure the change in housing values for pre- and post-announcement time periods, but before the actual construction of the new airport facility. They estimate a HP model for a two-year period before the announcement and a five-year period after the announcement, where the important variables are two dummies for distance bands measuring proximity to the airport. A date-of-sale variable captures the effects of inflation and other housing market changes, including the 2001 recession and local plant closures. The pre-announcement sample covers 8,957 housing sales and the post-announcement sample covers 20,657 sales. Using a SLD model to correct for spatial dependence, they report that housing prices increased by 1.2% per year in the pre-announcement period, but declined by 0.84% per year in the post-announcement period. Properties closest to the airport (within 2.5 miles) sold at a discount of 0.2% before the announcement and a discount of 9.4% after the announcement. More distant properties (2.5 to 4.0 miles) sold at a discount of 2.7% before the event and a discount of 8.3% after the event. Both of the differences are statistically significant based on a Wald test. Using the mean property value and prior estimates of the NDI, the authors also calculate the housing market's anticipated change in aircraft noise levels due to the expansion. In the nearest distance band, the price change suggests an increase in the noise level of 11 to 18 dB. In the second band, the anticipated increase is 7 to 11 dB. Relative to the published noise contours, it appears that the housing market is anticipating a negative effect that exceeds the actual change in the L_{DN} metric. In part, this may indicate the shortcomings of the L_{DN} metric for measurement of community noise exposure and annoyance (Albee et al. 2006; Fidell 2003). It also indicates that individuals can overestimate noise levels.

A second event study is found in Pope (2007), except in this case the event occurs in the housing market. In March of 1997, the Raleigh-Durham International Airport (RDU) in North Carolina initiated a legally-binding noise disclosure re-

---

[2] Other HP studies of airport expansions are Cohen and Coughlin (2003), Konda (2002), and McMillen (2004a, 2004b). Poulos and Smith (2002) is a repeat-sales analysis of a new US interstate highway, while Julien and Lanoie (2002) and Wilhelmsson (2005) are repeat-sales analyses of traffic noise barriers and property values.

quirement to reduce liability for imposing noise damages on nearby housing. A North Carolina statute, passed in 1995, required that government agencies and owners of residential real estate provide prospective buyers with a property disclosure statement. RDU used its authority under this statute to develop a notification letter and noise exposure map that was mailed to all homeowners within the 55 to 70 dB noise zones. These materials were sent to real estate agents in the area and a "noise officer" from RDU was appointed to ensure compliance. A web site with "tips for homebuyers" also was developed. In order to model this event, Pope develops a strategic model of a housing market in which the fraction of informed buyers is a function of attentiveness and the benefits and costs of obtaining publicly-available information. A potential seller is assumed to have more accurate information about the house and neighborhood, so there is informational asymmetry about housing quality. When the fraction of informed buyers is below a threshold, the sales price of a house may not reflect its true quality. Hence, information asymmetry produces a setting in which the set of housing attributes that is considered relevant by a buyer is less than the full set, meaning that higher quality houses are underpriced. The testable hypothesis is that as the fraction of informed buyers increases, a high quality seller is able to charge a relatively higher price.

As a test of the model, Pope uses a sample of 16,856 single-family houses sold between 1992 and 2000. His data set contains a large number of structural variables, neighborhood variables at the census-block level, fixed-effects for time and location, airport accessibility, and dummy variables for aircraft noise and date of sale. The noise dummies indicate both the noise zone in which the house is located and the date of the disclosure letter. A semilog model is estimated for the full sample and for restricted subsamples according to year of sale. Using OLS, predisclosure houses in the 55–65 dB zone sell at a discount of about 2.3% and houses in the 65–70 dB zone sell for 5.1% less compared to houses at 50 dB. Both the SLD and SED models also are considered, with weight-matrices constructed using geographic coordinates. Using the author's preferred SLD model, predisclosure houses in the 55–65 dB zone sell at a discount of 1.9% and the 65–70 dB houses sell at a discount of 3.8%. The implied NDIs are about 0.19% and 0.25% per dB, respectively. The disclosure further reduces sales prices in the 65–70 dB zone by 2.1% and the total noise discount for these houses rises to 5.8%. The post-disclosure NDI is about 0.39% per dB, which is an increase of 55%. Pope concludes that conventional HP estimates may be substantially biased if real estate buyers are poorly informed about housing attributes.

An innovative study by Huang and Palmquist (2001) estimates the effects of road traffic noise on property values and selling time on the market. Using a search model borrowed from labor economics, they first present a stylized model of the seller's reservation price conditional on the distribution of potential offers, the probability of receiving an acceptable offer, and selling costs incurred by the owner. Hence, the reservation price will be lower, the lower is the probability of receiving an offer in a period. However, the effect of an environmental disamenity, such as noise, on duration is uncertain. The disamenity will lower the offer prices and the probability of receiving an acceptable offer, but this can lower the seller's reservation price. The lower reservation price results in lower expected time on the market, which makes the net duration uncertain. The empirical model of the seller's reservation price is based on a stochastic frontier production model. The market duration model takes the form of a hazard function for the probability of receiving an acceptable offer, which is modeled as a function of the reservation price and other variables that affect duration (noise level, square footage, season of the year). The model is estimated simultaneously using 499 single-family housing sales in a suburban area near Seattle, Washington. The road traffic noise metric is L_{10} in 2.5 dB increments and the background noise level is 55 dB. Highway noise significantly influences actual and reservation prices, but noise does not significantly affect duration. The NDI is about 0.56% per dB, which agrees closely with many prior estimates. The seller's expected reservation price is estimated to be about 95% of the actual sale price. Overall, duration has a negative effect on the reservation price, which implies that sellers lower their reservation prices as duration time increases (see also Knight in this Volume).

Wilhelmsson (2000) examines the effects of road traffic noise on housing prices and turnover rates in a suburb of Stockholm. His sample consists of 292 single-family houses sold between 1986 and 1995. Noise levels at each house are estimated using a traffic model and two variables are employed: the L_{EQ} metric and (L_{EQ} - 68 dB), which is interacted with a dummy variable that indicates the house has a view of the road. The second variable captures visual effects of the road at higher noise levels, but simultaneous use of two noise variables may create a collinearity problem in this study. A Chow test indicates that the model parameters are different for 1986–89 and 1990–95, but this is mostly due to the traffic noise coefficients. Wilhelmsson concludes that the average noise discount is 0.6% per dB. He also finds the turnover rate is somewhat higher for houses with a view of the road, but the difference is not statistically significant. Based on this finding, he argues that the existence of symmetric information in this market cannot be rejected. This finding parallels earlier results summarized in Nelson (1982) for other traffic noise studies.

Housing market adjustments present researchers with a number of interesting opportunities to extend the basic hedonic model and test newer propositions from economic theory, such as the effect of time on the market on housing prices and noise discounts (see Taylor, this Volume). Further, the next few decades are likely see a number of important changes in air transportation, such as new and expanded airports in developing countries (e.g. China) and restrictions on flight operations and procedures in developed countries. These emerging changes represent interesting opportunities for empirical research on housing market adjustments.

3.7 Alternative Noise Indices and Community Annoyance

In contrast to other environmental areas, scientific measures of noise exposure are designed to correlate with human perceptions of annoying sounds. In 1974, the US EPA adopted the L_{DN} metric as the single best noise index due to its reliable relationship between projected noise and surveyed reaction of people to noises (EPA

1974; FICON 1992). The index is widely used as a guide for acceptable land use in noise-impacted areas and as an indicator of ambient noise levels. The L_{DN} index takes account of the magnitude and frequency of all sound events that occur during an *average* 24-hour period, the number of events, and the increased sensitivity of people to nighttime noise. However, as an average, the index discards potentially important information about the distribution of noises that may be relevant for human annoyance and the economic relationship between noise and property values or rental prices. Albee et al. (2006) observe that noise sensitive individuals often report that an increased number of noise events is more annoying, even if the average noise level per event has fallen. Further, many noise exposure indices are calculated for an average day during a subject year and thus ignore variations due to peak traffic periods, weather-related changes in operations, wind direction, and seasonal differences in living conditions and lifestyle during the year. One alternative is to break L_{DN} into its component parts, with separate measurements for time-above given noise levels and number of events (Albee et al. 2006). A study that illustrates some aspects of this measurement approach is Levesque (1994). He represents noise conditions by three separate variables at each location: (1) number of events that exceed an Effective Perceived Noise Level (EPNL) of 75 dB; (2) mean EPNL; and (3) standard deviation of EPNL for all events exceeding 75 dB. Using a Box-Cox model, Levesque obtains significantly negative effects on property values for the number of events and mean noise level, with a stronger negative effect of the mean level. The noise variance is positive, which may be due to collinearity. Studies using this approach should compare results to L_{DN} and consider more than one peak noise level.

A second approach in the HP literature has been the use of a dummy variable for each noise zone or contour, rather than use of a continuous noise variable such as the L_{EQ} and L_{DN} indices. This approach has the advantage of allowing for nonlinear marginal effects due to increased sensitivity at higher noise levels. Cohen and Coughlin (2005) is an important study of the effects of aircraft noise and airport proximity on housing prices in the vicinity of Atlanta's Hartsfield–Jackson International Airport. They obtain a sample of 2,370 single-family property sales for the period 1995 to 2002. The data set contains a substantial number of structural variables, neighborhood variables at the census-block level, and public sector dummy variables. Noise contour data are obtained for 1995 and 2003, which permits an examination of changing prices over time. The properties are located in three noise zones: 65–70 L_{DN}; 70–75 L_{DN}; and a zone that is one-half mile outside of the 65 L_{DN} contour, which the authors characterize as a "buffer zone." Note that the properties in the buffer zone are likely to be subject to aircraft noise levels of 55–65 dB, which raises an issue of undercounting of the noise-impacted properties. The choice of a noise threshold depends in part on the importance of noise from non-aircraft sources, which the authors do not consider. Although 65 L_{DN} is the legislated ambient noise level for US airports, researchers should experiment with alternative ambient noise levels.

Cohen and Coughlin calculate the distance between each property and the airport as a measure of proximity or accessibility to air transportation services and airport employment. Due to the elongated shape of noise contours, there generally is a low correlation between aircraft noise and proximity. An important empirical issue is the shrinkage of the noise contours between 1995 and 2003, which can impart bias to the regression coefficients due to systematic measurement error. For example, the number of houses in the 70–75 dB zone declined from 249 in 1995 to 67 in 2003. Cohen and Coughlin address this issue by removing 727 houses from the sample that switched zones between 1995 and 2003. An alternative is to assign a dummy variable to houses that switch zones (see McMillen 2004a, 2004b). Using the reduced sample and a semilog OLS model, they find that houses in the 65 dB zone sell at a discount of 3.7% compared to houses in the buffer zone and houses in the 75 dB zone sell at a discount of 9.1%. The NDIs are about 0.74 and 0.91% per dB, respectively. They also consider the stability of the noise discount over time due, for example, to soundproofing and land purchases by the airport, increasing real incomes of residents, and displacement of noise-sensitive individuals. Adding a time trend for the 65 dB noise zone leads to mixed results, so it is unclear if the noise discount changed over time. In the reduced sample for the semilog model, the time trend is positive, but insignificant.

Another measurement approach is to make use of subjective annoyance relationships reported in the acoustics literature. One method is to use GIS and a noise model to determine the average noise exposure experienced at each house. Next, the exposure data are used to estimate the levels of human annoyance using some version of the nonlinear "Shultz curve," which captures the relationship between noise exposure and community annoyance (Fidell 2003; Fosgerau and Bjørner 2006; Miedema and Oudshoorn 2001; Ouis 2001). Thus, HP regression estimates can be compared for a cumulative metric and an index of annoyance, such as the percent of persons who are "highly annoyed". A second method is illustrated by innovative study by Baranzini et al. (2006). They use data from a Swiss noise perception survey to construct a subjective annoyance index for apartment buildings in Geneva. This index covers annoyance from all forms of noise, including traffic noise. Next, the annoyance index and the inverse of a Schultz curve are used to translate the subjective noise index to a "perceived dB" index. As a result, the researchers can experiment with three noise variables in HP regressions: (1) actual scientific daytime traffic noise; (2) actual scientific L_{DN} for traffic noise; and (3) perceived annoyance in dB for all sources of noise. A comparison of the actual and perceived noise metrics indicates that survey respondents tend to systematically overestimate noise exposure levels, especially at the lower end of the scale. This may reflect the fact that the Swiss noise survey covers all sources of noise or that survey respondents tend to overestimate low-probability events. The sample of apartment rents covers 2,794 observations. The scientific and perceived noise metrics produce similar values for the NDI. An increase in traffic noise reduces rents by 0.15 to 0.18% per dB. This result is comparable to that obtained in other Swiss studies, but slightly smaller than a NDI of 0.275% reported in Baranzini and Ramirez (2005). The authors conclude that scientific measurements of noise provide a satisfactory representation of individuals' perception of noise exposure, except possibly at the lowest intrusive noise levels.

Over the next decade, it seems likely that aviation regulators will encourage the use of additional noise metrics. This approval needs to be anticipated by economic researchers, so that econometric evidence can aid the selection of metrics and associated regulations. For example, additional attention should be devoted to the background noise level at which damages begin in the housing market and the impact (if any) of annoyance at lower decibel levels on housing values.

3.8 Stated Preference Methods and Hedonic Prices

The goal of a stated preference (SP) study is to construct a simulated market for an environmental commodity such that "consumers" will accurately and truthfully state their willingness to pay (WTP) for additional units of the commodity. In real markets for private commodities, consumers reveal their WTP by purchasing (or refusing to purchase) more or fewer units at different relative prices, other things being equal. According to Carson and Hanemann (2005), construction of a simulated market requires: (1) specifying the rules of the market in which the commodity is bought or sold through a bidding game, referendum, or preference ranking; (2) describing the environmental commodity being valued through use of photographs, quality ladders, or tape recordings; and (3) eliciting monetary values or indicators of value for the commodity, including the specification of a payment vehicle such as a tax increase or higher prices for gasoline and travel. Each step in this process can encounter difficulties that might bias the WTP responses, such as the implausibility of the hypothetical payment vehicle or the inability of respondents to understand the specific commodity they are being asked to value. For example, some survey studies have asked respondents to value a complete elimination of noise, which is not an advisable procedure. Because environmental commodities are public goods (locally or globally), there also can be strategic bias in the form of free-riding, which leads a respondent to state a WTP that is different from his or her true WTP. Further, economic theory provides no prediction how people faced with "purely hypothetical" choices will behave, and zero valuations and large WTP outliers are common outcomes in SP surveys. Relative to HP methods, the SP approach has the advantage of focusing more directly on the environmental commodity in question, avoiding imperfections in the housing market, and producing values that might apply in a wider variety of settings and circumstances. Further, in the HP model, it is not clear what aspects of annoyance due to noise and transportation activities are being capitalized in property values (TV interference, sleep disturbance, visual intrusion, air pollution, safety concerns, etc.). An appropriately designed survey could help determine those damages that are reflected in property values and the possibility of omitted damages such as health effects. Publication of the SP survey questions would aid this determination, although this practice is not often followed.[3] Early SP studies for noise are Plowden

[3] A false issue is the lack of comparability of values from HP and SP methods. A hedonic price is a capitalized value per dB. Treating the house as an annuity and using an appropriate discount rate, a hedonic price can be expressed as an annual or monthly value per dB; see Bjørner (2004a) and Saelensminde and Veisten (2006).

(1970) and Thorpe and Holmes (1976), while the recent literature is reviewed in Navrud (2002). A general problem in the SP literature for transportation noise is the wide variation of the WTP estimates.

Several noise studies have compared results from SP and HP models for comparable areas, but the results are mixed.[4] Pommerehne (1988) obtains a sample of 223 dwelling rents in Basel, Switzerland, including dwelling characteristics, accessibility, aircraft noise, traffic noise, and responses to an environmental-quality perception survey. In the CV survey, dwelling occupants were informed that they could reduce noise exposure by 50% by moving to another dwelling. Households were then asked about their current rent and the maximum acceptable rent increase for the quieter dwelling. The survey also obtained information about the respondent's income and family size. This information is used to estimate a survey-based WTP function. In the HP model for aircraft noise, the NDI is only 0.20% per dB. A HP linear model estimated by OLS yields a traffic noise NDI of 1.25% per dB. A non-linear model results in an NDI that increases in the noise level, rising from about 1.0% per dB for traffic noise at 40 dB to 1.50% at 75 dB. The nonlinear marginal prices also are used to estimate a second-stage WTP function for noise avoidance. Comparing the two sets of results, Pommerehne concludes that the WTP functions for traffic noise are similar, but the survey-based WTPs are somewhat lower than those derived from housing market data. However, for aircraft noise, the differences are more pronounced and the survey-based WTPs are higher at all noise levels. This may reflect survey response bias, since aircraft noise was not a serious problem in Basel (the airport is 10 miles from the city).

A second Swiss study was conducted by Soguel (1996) for the city of Neuchâtel. The CV survey asked 200 households to value a 50% reduction in traffic noise exposure. The payment vehicle was a hypothetical increase in the household's monthly rent. Respondents were divided into several categories based on the value of the WTP and other survey responses: indifferents (n = 59 respondents); free riders (30); insolvents (25); and receptive solvents (86). The WTP analysis is confined to 111 respondents who did not engage in strategic behavior and 86 of these individuals had a positive non-zero WTP for noise reduction. A Box-Cox regression model is used to estimate the WTP function, which reduces the influence of large bids. This model is estimated by OLS and by weighted least-squares in order to correct for a heteroscedasticity problem. The SP analysis yields an average monthly bid of about 70 SFr. The results from the survey-based WTP analysis are compared to a HP analysis for the same city. The HP analysis produced an NDI of 0.91% per dB, which results in a monthly WTP of 60 SFr for a 50% reduction in noise exposure. The author concludes that the SP

[4] Blomquist (1988) demonstrates that, due to sorting in the housing market, contingent values can be expected to differ systematically from the implicit hedonic values. If quiet houses tend to be occupied by noise-sensitive people, the contingent value will exceed the hedonic price. The opposite will be true for noisy houses occupied by imperturbables. This is a sample selection problem for SP studies; for other empirical evidence, see Carson et al. (1996). I am indebted to Jean Cavailhès for this point.

and HP estimates are similar.[5]

A third comparison study using both SP and HP methods was conducted by Bjørner (2004a, 2004b) for Copenhagen. Data for the CV analysis were collected using a mail survey, and the sample consists of 1,149 responses (53% response rate). The survey described a new noise-reducing road surface that would lower the noise level so that the respondent would no longer be annoyed (10–20 dB reduction). The WTP of each respondent was obtained using both open-ended bids and referendum-style valuation questions. The survey-based WTP values were analyzed by residence-type (apartments, houses) for five classes of respondents with positive bids: not annoyed (n = 45); slightly annoyed (85); moderately annoyed (198); very annoyed (257); and extremely annoyed (361). The WTP values rise from 45 EUR for the not-annoyed individuals to 361 EUR for the extremely annoyed. The overall mean value is 135 EUR for the road improvement project. A noise annoyance model (Schultz curve) is used to translate the WTP by class to an expected WTP per dB. The WTP per dB increases from 2 EUR at 55 dB to 11 EUR at 75 dB. The HP study uses a sample of sales prices for 2,505 apartments for the period 1996 to 2002. Noise exposure levels at each dwelling were calculated using a traffic model for the L_{EQ} metric, with a background level of 55 dB. Three different model specifications result in NDIs of 0.53, 0.54, and 0.58% per dB. The author concludes that the HP results correspond to values found in prior studies. A real discount rate of 2% is used to annualize the mean price in each of six noise zones. The annualized HP differentials are substantially higher than the WTP values calculated from the CV study. At 65 dB, the CV value is 6 EUR per dB per year and the HP value is 14 EUR per dB per year. These results conflict with Pommerehne (1988) and Soguel (1996).[6]

For aircraft noise, CV methods were applied in an innovative study conducted by Feitelson et al. (1996) for the Dallas-Ft. Worth Airport. The authors attempt to value the depreciation of real property due to noise and the loss of utility by residents who remain *in situ*. Using a telephone survey, homeowners near the airport were first asked to state their hypothetical willingness to pay for a standard single-family residence in an area with no aircraft noise and then they were asked to value the same residence with differing levels and types of noise exposure. Using a similar sequence of questions, apartment dwellers were asked how much monthly rent they would be willing to pay for a three-bedroom apartment. The full samples include 3,586 observations for homeowners and 2,662 for apartment dwellers. In the WTP regressions that omit zero valuations, most of the noise attributes are sta-

---

5 Navrud (2002) argues that CV questions used by Pommerehne and Soguel are not understandable by respondents. He suggests use of questions based on a reduction of annoyance or other qualitative comparisons, such as reducing daytime traffic noise to levels experienced on a Sunday morning (Barreiro et al. 2005).

6 Other SP traffic studies are Arsenio et al. (2006), Barreiro et al. (2005), Galilea and de Dios Ortúzar (2005), Garrod et al. (2002), Martin et al. (2006), Saelensminde (1999), and Wardman and Bristow (2004). Other SP aircraft studies are Bristow and Wardman (2006), Carlsson et al. (2004), Kriström (1997), van Praag and Baarsma (2005), and Wardman and Bristow (2007).

tistically significant, with larger negative coefficients for severe levels of noise. Noise insulation provides partial relief, but does not fully mitigate the adverse effects of noise. The NDIs are about 1.5% per dB for houses and 0.9% per dB for apartments. The authors note that the zero valuations provide information regarding respondents' unwillingness to tolerate severe aircraft noise, regardless of the noise discount in housing values or apartment rents. The proportion of zero responses rises as noise exposure increases, reaching 45% for homeowners and 35% for apartment dwellers if they were exposed to severe frequent noise from overflights (about 70–75 dB). Alternatively, the zero responses may reflect survey biases. The authors argue that WTP valuations are the outcome of a two-stage decision process. At severe noise levels, many individuals are unwilling to consider the residence, and thus their WTP drops to zero. They conclude that HP studies understate damages by failing to incorporate the losses to households who would like to relocate.

Stated preference studies represent an alternative method for valuation of noise damages. At present, the available estimates cover a wide range of WTP values and are simply not very robust. It is unclear if this reflects basic issues associated with the SP methodology (e.g., sample selection, various survey biases) or is an indication of underlying preferences for noise annoyance and mitigation.

3.9 Summary and Concluding Remarks

The preceding discussion demonstrates that there is a very active research program for hedonic studies of noise valuation. Interest in the area declined in the 1990s, but it now enjoys a healthy renewal. Researchers have taken advantage of advances in economic theory, newer econometric techniques, large disaggregated data sets, and GIS methods. Novel and innovative studies have appeared that estimate models not considered by earlier researchers. Survey-based studies now provide a useful supplement to the revealed values obtained from housing market data. However, policy applications of results from hedonic studies do not appear to have increased in frequency, especially in the United States. In this concluding section, I first offer summary comments on the use of hedonic models for valuation of transportation noise and then briefly discuss recent policy applications and final results.

The discussion in this chapter suggests five issues that researchers need to be aware of when estimating or using hedonic models.

- Market segmentation may be common in large samples of housing data. Researchers should guard against specification errors due to segmentation by appropriate use of Chow tests and other specification tests and by careful thinking about the research issue being addressed. Cluster analysis is another tool that has been used to address segmentation. However, these tools need to be applied carefully given a non-linear hedonic price function.

- Spatially-dependent errors present a major challenge to research on housing markets. This is due to the fact that econometric tools and software were designed for a spaceless world and the practical difficulty of observing all locational characteristics. Careful model specification can in some cases resolve the problem. However, simply adding more locational variables is not necessarily the best solution due to multicollinearity and the limitations of theory. Spatial statistics can be used to keep the hedonic model simple and augment the conventional HP model with models of spatial-error dependence.

- Housing market adjustments present researchers with opportunities to extend the basic hedonic model and test newer propositions from economic theory, such as the effects of asymmetric information, changes in noise valuation over time, and housing market imperfections. More studies in this area are needed to support applications of hedonic valuations.

- Noise measurement is a relatively old area of interest, but some studies have failed to heed past research. For example, quiet residential areas do not have a background sound level of zero decibels. Noise changes of 3 to 5 dB are generally noticeable, but some studies use dummy variables for differences of 10 dB or more, which is excessive. Attention needs to be paid to the appropriate nonlinear relationship between noise levels and housing prices or apartment rents. More attention also should be given to use of community annoyance metrics as an alternative to commonly employed noise indices.

- Stated preference surveys represent an alternative method for valuation of noise damages. These studies rely on hypothetical responses, whereas hedonic price studies use observed behavior and market responses. In order to estimate damages using a survey, SP researchers need to frame questions that simulate actual responses and tie these responses to realistic payment vehicles. This would appear easier for road traffic noise compared to aircraft noise, especially for the United States. Some existing studies suggest that SP and HP models yield comparable results, but interesting differences in noise valuations also have been uncovered.

There are three major policy applications for hedonic prices. First, cost-benefit analyses of specific noise mitigation and abatement projects, including airport expansions, curfews, quieter aircraft, traffic noise barriers, and improved roads and highways. Representative studies in this area include Bateman et al. (2005); De Vany et al. (1977); Morrison et al. (1999); Nellthorp et al. (2007); Nelson (1978); Nijland et al. (2003); Saelensminde and Veisten (2006); and Wilhelmsson (2005). Second, overall evaluations of the full social costs of transportation, which are studies of the "paid" and "unpaid" costs of motor vehicle and aircraft operations. Representative full-cost studies include Delucchi and Hsu (1998); Greene et al. (1997); Levinson and Gillen (1998); Levinson et al. (1998); Murphy and Delucchi (1998); Parry et al. (2007); Quinet (2004); and Schipper (2004). Third, studies have evaluated alternative policy instruments, such as the calculation of noise and congestion taxes and markets for tradeable permits. Representative studies of noise-congestion taxes are Brueckner and Girvin (2007); Hsu and Lin (2005); Newberry (2005); and Pearce and Pearce (2000). Tradeable permits are studied in

Bréchet and Picard (2007) and Hullah et al. (2007).

Continued refinement of HP and SP estimates of noise damage valuation will aid these policy applications. In particular, HP estimates of noise damages are more useful if marginal prices are stable over time and space, and therefore can be applied to welfare changes in similar environmental settings. Absent this stability, each HP estimate may only be useful for only its designed purposes. Thus, a general problem in environmental economics is the use of a WTP value or function from a given study area (or mode of transport) for a policy evaluation of another location or mode, which is referred to as the "benefit transfer" problem (Brookshire and Neill 1992; Rosenberger and Loomis 2003). Both unit value transfers and function transfers are possible. Several European countries have adopted standardized noise valuations for policy purposes, but many of these values are old or based on only a few studies (Saelensmine and Veisten 2006). These values could be improved through benefit transfer methods. Examples of recent benefit transfers of NDIs are Saelensminde and Veisten (2006) and Nellthorp et al. (2007).

Earlier reviews reported mean NDI values of 0.50 to 0.70% per dB for aircraft noise and 0.40 to 0.60% per dB for traffic noise (Bertrand 1997; Nelson 1980, 1982, 2004). For rough comparisons, the NDI values reported in this chapter can be combined to yield more recent estimates of noise valuations. For aircraft noise, the 24 estimates yield an unweighted mean value of 0.92% and a median value of 0.74% per dB. The interquartile mean for aircraft noise is 0.80% per dB. For traffic noise, the 25 estimates yield an unweighted mean value of 0.55% and a median value of 0.54% per dB. The interquartile mean for traffic noise is 0.51% per dB. The average values for aircraft noise are slightly higher than prior estimates, which may reflect rising real incomes as well as differences in econometric techniques. The average values for traffic noise also are slightly higher than prior estimates, although the differences are minor. Hence, a review of recent estimates of the NDI for aircraft and traffic noise suggests that the unit NDI values are reasonably stable over time, which is an encouraging finding for benefit transfers.

References

Albee W, Connor T, Bassarab R, Odegard R, Morrow C (2006) What's in your DNL? Wyle Labs, El Segundo, CA, US

Arsenio E, Bristow AL, Wardman M (2006) Stated choice valuations of traffic related noise. Transportation research D 11: 15–31

Baranzini A, Ramirez JV (2005) Paying for quietness: the impact of noise on Geneva rents. Urban studies 42: 633–646

Baranzini A, Schaerer C, Ramirez JV, Thalmann P (2006) Feel it or measure it: perceived vs. measured noise in hedonic models. Working paper, Geneva School of Business Administration, CH

Barreiro J, Sánchez M, Viladrich-Grau M (2005) How much are people willing to pay for silence? A contingent valuation study. Applied economics 37: 1233–1246

Bateman IJ, Day B, Lake IR (2004) The valuation of transport-related noise in Birmingham. Working paper, University of East Anglia, Norwich, UK

Bateman IJ, Day B, Lake IR, Lovett AA (2001) The effect of road traffic noise on residential property values: a literature review and hedonic pricing study. Scottish Executive Development Department, Edinburgh, UK
Bateman IJ, Turner RK, Bateman S (2005) Extending cost-benefit analysis of UK highway proposals: environmental evaluation and equity. Working paper, University of East Anglia, Norwich, UK
Bertrand NF (1997) Meta-analysis of studies of willingness to pay to reduce traffic noise. Msc dissertation, University College, London
Bjørner TB (2004a) Comparing the value of quiet from contingent valuation and hedonic pricing methods. Working paper, AFK, Copenhagen
Bjørner TB (2004b) Combining socio-acoustic and contingent valuation surveys to value noise reduction. Transportation research D 9: 341–356
Blomquist G (1988) Valuing urban lakeview amenities using implicit and contingent markets. Urban studies 25: 333–340
Boyle MA, Kiel KA (2001) A survey of house price hedonic studies of the impact of environmental externalities. Journal of real estate literature 9: 117–144
Bréchet T, Picard PM (2007) The price of silence: markets for noise licenses and airports. Working paper, Center for Operations Research and Econometrics, Catholic University of Louvain, BE
Bristow AL, Wardman M (2006) Valuation of aircraft noise by time of day: a comparison of two approaches. Transport reviews 26: 417–433
Brookshire DS, Neill HR (1992) Benefit transfers: conceptual and empirical issues. Water resources research 28: 651–655
Brueckner JK, Girvin R (2007) Airport noise regulation, airline service quality, and social welfare. Forthcoming in Transportation research B
Can A (1992) Specification and estimation of hedonic housing price models. Regional science and urban economics 22: 453–474
Carlsson F, Lampi E, Martinsson P (2004) The marginal values of noise disturbance from air traffic: does the time of day matter? Transportation research D 9: 373–385
Carson RT, Flores NE, Martin KM, Wright JL (1996) Contingent valuation and revealed preference methodologies: comparing estimates for quasi-public goods. Land economics 72: 80-99
Carson RT, Hanemann WM (2005) Contingent valuation. In: Mäler K-G, Vincent JR (eds) Handbook of environmental economics, vol II, Elsevier, Amsterdam, pp 821–936
Cheung SNS (1987) Common property rights. In: Eatwell J, Milgate M, Newman P (eds) The new Palgrave: a dictionary of economics, vol I. Macmillian London, pp 504–505
Cohen JP, Coughlin CC (2003) Congestion at airports: the economics of airport expansions. Federal Reserve Bank of St. Louis review 85: 9–25
Cohen JP, Coughlin CC (2005) Airport-related noise, proximity, and housing prices in Atlanta. Working paper, Federal Reserve Bank of St Louis, US
Cohen JP, Coughlin CC (2006) Spatial hedonic models of airport noise, proximity, and housing prices. Working paper, Federal Reserve Bank of St Louis, US
Crowley RW (1973) A case study of the effects of an airport on land values. Journal of transport economics and policy 7: 144–152
Day B (2003) Submarket identification in property markets: a hedonic housing price model for Glasgow. Working paper, University of East Anglia, Norwich, UK
Day B, Bateman IJ, Lake IR (2004) Omitted locational variates in hedonic analysis: a semiparametric approach using spatial statistics. Working paper, University of East Anglia, Norwich, UK
Day B, Bateman IJ, Lake IR (2006) Hedonic price analysis of road traffic noise nuisance. In: Pearce D (ed) Environmental valuation in developed countries. Elgar, Cheltenham, UK, pp 363-406
Day B, Bateman IJ, Lake IR (2007) Beyond implicit prices: recovering theoretically consis-

tent and transferable values for noise avoidance from a hedonic property value model. Environmental and resource economics 37: 211–232
Delucchi MA, Hsu S-L (1998) The external damage cost of noise emitted from motor vehicles. Journal of transportation and statistics 1: 1–24
De Vany A, Nelson JP, Walters AA (1977) Cost-benefit analysis: some illustrations. In: Noise abatement policy alternatives for transportation. National Academy of Sciences, Washington DC, pp 183–206
Dubin R (1992) Spatial autocorrelation and neighborhood quality. Regional science and urban economics 22: 433–452
Dygert PK (1973) Estimation of the cost of aircraft noise to residential activities. Ph.D. dissertation, University of Michigan, Ann Arbor, US
Emerson FC (1972) Valuation of residential amenities: an econometric approach. Appraisal journal 40: 268–278
European Commission (1996) European Commission green paper: future noise policy. EC, Brussels
European Commission (2002) Directive 2002/49/EC for the assessment and management of environmental noise. Official journal of the European Communities, L189/12. EC, Brussels
Feitelson EI, Hurd RE, Mudge RR (1996) The impact of airport noise on willingness to pay for residences. Transportation research D 1: 1–14
Fidell S (2003) The Schultz curve after 25 years: a research perspective. Journal of the acoustical society of America 114: 2007-2015
Fosgerau M, Bjørner TB (2006) Joint models for noise annoyance and willingness to pay for road noise reduction. Transportation research B 40: 164–178
Frankel M (1991) Aircraft noise and residential property values: results of a survey study. Appraisal journal 59: 96-110
Freeman AM (1993) The measurement of environmental and resource values: theory and methods. Resources for the Future, Washington DC
Galilea P, de Dios Ortúzar J (2005) Valuing noise level reductions in a residential location context. Transportation research D 10: 305–322
Gamble HB, Sauerlender OH, Langley CJ (1974) Adverse and beneficial effects of highways on property values. Transportation research record 508: 37–48
Garrod GD, Scarpa R, Willis KG (2002) Estimating the benefits of traffic calming on through routes. Journal of transport economics and policy 36: 211–231
Gautrin J-F (1975) An evaluation of the impact of aircraft noise on property values with a simple model of urban land rent. Land economics 51: 80–86
Gillen D (2003) The economics of noise. In: Hensher DA, Button KJ (eds) Handbook of transport and the environment. Elsevier, Amsterdam, pp 81–95
Goodman AC, Thibodeau TG (1998) Housing market segmentation. Journal of housing economics 7: 121–143
Greene D, Jones D, Delucchi MA (1997) The full costs and benefits of transportation. Springer-Verlag, Berlin
Grue B, Langeland JL, Larsen OI (1997) Housing prices: impacts of exposure to road traffic and location. Institute of Transport Economics, Oslo
Haab TC, McConnell KE (2002) Valuing environmental and natural resources: the econometrics of non-market valuation. Elgar, Cheltenham, UK
Hjorth-Andersen C (1978) Road noise and property values – some evidence from the Copenhagen area. Scandinavian journal of economics 80: 454–460
Hsu C-I, Lin P-H (2005) Performance assessment for airport noise charge policies and airline network adjustment response. Transportation research D 10: 281–304
Huang JC, Palmquist RB (2001) Environmental conditions, reservation prices, and time on the market for housing. Journal of real estate finance and economics 22: 203–219
Hullah PHC, Thompson T, de Lépinay I, Gjestland T (2007) MIME – Noise trading for air-

craft noise mitigation. Working paper, EUROCONTROL, Brétigny-sur-Orge, FR
Jud GD, Winkler DT (2006) The announcement effect of an airport expansion on housing prices. Journal of real estate finance and economics 33: 91–103
Julien B, Lanoie P (2002) The effect of noise barriers on the market value of adjacent residential properties. Working paper, CIRANO, Montreal, CA
Kelejian H, Prucha I (1999) A generalized moments estimator for the autoregressive parameter in a spatial model. International economic review 40: 509–533
Knight JR (2008) Hedonic modeling of the home selling process. In this Volume
Konda LS (2002) A comparison of methodologies to measure effects of airport siting decisions. Working paper, University of Texas, Austin, US
Kriström B (1997) Spike models in contingent valuation. American journal of agricultural economics 79: 1013-1023
Levesque TJ (1994) Modelling the effects of airport noise on residential housing markets: a case study of Winnipeg International Airport. Journal of transport economics and policy 28: 199–210
Levinson DM, Gillen D (1998) The full cost of intercity highway transportation. Transportation research D 3: 207–223
Levinson DM, Gillen D, Kanafani A (1998) The social costs of intercity transportation: a review and comparison of air and highway. Transport reviews 18: 215–240
Lipscomb C (2003) Small cities matter too: the impacts of an airport and local infrastructure on housing prices in a small urban city. Review of urban and regional development studies 15: 255–273
Martin MA, Tarrero A, González J, Machimbarrena M (2006) Exposure-effect relationship between road traffic noise annoyance and noise cost valuations in Valladolid, Spain. Applied acoustics 67: 945-958
McMillan ML (1979) Estimates of households' preferences for environmental quality and other housing characteristics from a system of demand equations. Scandinavian journal of economics 81: 174–187
McMillen DP (2004a) Airport expansions and property values: the case of Chicago O'Hare airport. Journal of urban economics 55: 627–640
McMillen DP (2004b) House prices and the proposed expansion of Chicago's O'Hare airport. Federal Reserve Bank of Chicago economic perspectives 28: 28–39
Miedema HME, Oudshoorn CGM (2001) Annoyance from transportation noise: relationships with exposure metrics DNL and DENL. Environmental health perspectives 109: 409–416
Morrison SA, Winston C, Watson T (1999) Fundamental flaws of social regulation: the case of airplane noise. Journal of law and economics 42: 723–743
Murphy JJ, Delucchi MA (1998) A review of the literature on the social cost of motor vehicle use in the United States. Journal of transportation and statistics 1: 15–42
Navrud S (2002) The state-of-the-art on economic valuation of noise: final report to the European Commission. Agricultural University of Norway, Oslo
Nellthorp J, Bristow AL, Day B (2007) Introducing willingness-to-pay for noise changes into transport appraisals: an application of benefit transfer. Transport reviews 27: 327–353
Nelson JP (1975) The effects of mobile-source air and noise pollution on residential property values. US Department of Transportation, Washington DC
Nelson JP (1978) Economic analysis of transportation noise abatement. Ballinger, Cambridge, MA, US
Nelson JP (1979) Airport noise, location rent, and the market for residential amenities. Journal of environmental economics and management 6: 320–331
Nelson JP (1980) Airports and property values: a survey of recent evidence. Journal of transport economics and policy 14: 37–52
Nelson JP (1981) Measuring benefits of environmental improvements: aircraft noise and

hedonic prices. In: Smith VK (ed) Advances in applied microeconomics, vol 1. JAI Press, Greenwich, CT, US, pp 51–75
Nelson JP (1982) Highway noise and property values: a survey of recent evidence. Journal of transport economics and policy 16: 117–138
Nelson JP (2004) Meta-analysis of airport noise and hedonic property values: problems and prospects. Journal of transport economics and policy 38: 1–27
Newberry DM (2005) Road user and congestion charges. In: Cnossen S (ed) Theory and practice of excise taxation. Oxford University Press, UK, pp 193–229
Nijland HA, Van Kempen EEMM, Van Wee GP, Jabben J (2003) Costs and benefits of noise abatement measures. Transport policy 10: 131–140
Ouis D (2001) Annoyance from road traffic noise: a review. Journal of environmental psychology 21: 101–120
Paik IK (1972) Measurement of environmental externality in particular reference to noise. Ph.D. dissertation, Georgetown University, Washington DC
Palmquist RB (1982) Measuring environmental effects on property values without hedonic regressions. Journal of urban economics 11: 333–347
Palmquist RB (1992a) Valuing localized externalities. Journal of urban economics 31: 59–68
Palmquist RB (1992b) A note on transactions costs, moving costs, and benefit measurement. Journal of urban economics 32: 40–44
Palmquist RB (2005) Property value models. In: Mäler K-G, Vincent J (eds) Handbook of environmental economics, vol II. Elsevier, Amsterdam, pp 763–819
Palmquist RB, Smith VK (2002) The use of hedonic property value techniques for policy and litigation. In: Tietenberg T, Folmer H (eds) The international yearbook of environmental and resource economics. Elgar, Cheltenham, UK, pp 115–164
Parry IWH, Walls M, Harrington W (2007) Automobile externalities and policies. Journal of economic literature 45: 373–399
Pearce B, Pearce D (2000) Setting environmental taxes for aircraft: a case study of the UK. Working paper, University of East Anglia, Norwich, UK
Pearce D, Atkinson G, Mourato S (2006) Cost-benefit analysis and the environment: recent developments. OECD, Paris
Plowden SPC (1970) The cost of noise. Metra Consulting Group, London
Pommerehne WW (1988) Measuring environmental benefits: a comparison of hedonic technique and contingent valuation. In: Bös D, Rose M, Seidl C (eds) Welfare and efficiency in public economics. Springer-Verlag, Berlin, pp 363–400
Pope JC (2007) Buyer information and the hedonic: the impact of a seller disclosure on the implicit price for airport noise. Forthcoming in Journal of urban economics
Poulos C, Smith VK (2002) Transparency and takings: applying an RD design to measure compensation. Working paper, North Carolina State University, Raleigh, US
Quinet E (2004) A meta-analysis of Western European external costs estimates. Transportation research D 9: 465–476
Rich JH, Nielsen OA (2004) Assessment of traffic noise impacts. International Journal of environmental studies 61: 19–29
Rosen S (1974) Hedonic prices and implicit markets: product differentiation in pure competition. Journal of political economy 82: 34–55
Rosenberger RS, Loomis JB (2003) Benefit transfer. In: Champ PA, Boyle KJ, Brown TC (eds) A primer on nonmarket valuation. Kluwer, Dordrecht, NL, pp 445–482
Saelensminde K (1999) Stated choice valuation of urban traffic air pollution and noise. Transportation research D 4: 13–27
Saelensminde K, Veisten K (2006). SILVIA project deliverable: cost-benefit analysis. Federation of European National Highway Research Laboratories, Brussels
Salvi M (2003) Spatial estimation of the impact of airport noise on residential housing prices. Working paper, Zurich Cantonal Bank, CH

Schipper Y (1999) Market structure and environmental costs in aviation: a welfare analysis of European air transport reform. Tinbergen Institute, Amsterdam

Schipper Y (2004) Environmental costs in European aviation. Transport policy 11: 141–154

Schipper Y, Nijkamp P, Rietveld P (1998) Why do aircraft noise estimates differ? a meta-analysis. Journal of air transport management 4: 117–124

Soguel N (1996) Contingent valuation of traffic noise reduction benefits. Swiss Journal of economics and statistics 132: 109–123

Taylor LO (2003) The hedonic method. In: Champ PA, Boyle KJ, Brown TC (eds) A primer on nonmarket valuation. Kluwer, Dordrecht, NL, pp 331–393

Taylor LO (2008) Theoretical foundations and empirical developments in hedonic modeling. In this Volume

Taylor SM, Breston BE, Hall FL (1982) The effect of road traffic noise on house prices. Journal of sound and vibration 80: 523–541

Theebe MAJ (2004) Planes, trains, and automobiles: the impact of traffic noise on house prices. Journal of real estate finance and economics 28: 209–234

Thorpe R, Holmes T (1976) Economic welfare impacts of urban noise. US Environmental Protection Agency, Washington DC

Tinch R (1995) The valuation of environmental externalities. Department of Transport, London

Tomkins J, Topham N, Twomey J, Ward R (1998) Noise versus access: the impact of an airport in an urban property market. Urban studies 35: 243–258

US Environmental Protection Agency (1974) Information on levels of environmental noise requisite to protect public health and welfare with an adequate margin of safety. EPA, Washington DC

US Federal Interagency Committee on Noise (1992) Federal agency review of selected airport noise analysis issues. FICON, Washington DC

van Garderen KJ, Shah C (2002) Exact interpretation of dummy variables in semi-logarithmic equations. Econometrics journal 5: 149–159

van Praag BMS, Baarsma BE (2005) Using happiness surveys to value intangibles: the case of airport noise. Economic journal 115: 224–246

Vaughan RJ, Huckins L (1975) The economics of expressway noise pollution abatement. Rand Corporation, Santa Monica, US

Walters AA (1975) Noise and prices. Oxford University Press, UK

Wardman M, Bristow AL (2004) Traffic related noise and air quality valuations: evidence from stated preference and residential choice models. Transportation research D 9: 1–27

Wardman M, Bristow AL (2007) Valuations of aircraft noise: experiments in stated preference. Forthcoming in Environmental and resource economics

Wilhelmsson M (2000) The impact of traffic noise on the values of single-family houses. Journal of environmental planning and management 43: 799–815

Wilhelmsson M (2002) Household expenditure patterns for housing attributes: a linear expenditure system with hedonic prices. Journal of housing economics 11: 75–93

Wilhelmsson M (2005) Valuation of traffic-noise abatement. Journal of housing and the built environment 20: 129–151

4 Pricing the Homebuyer's Countryside View

Jean Cavailhès[1], Thierry Brossard[2], Mohamed Hilal[1], Daniel Joly[2], François-Pierre Tourneux[2], Céline Tritz[2], Pierre Wavresky[1]

[1]INRA-CESAER, Dijon, France
[2]CNRS-ThéMA, Besançon, France

4.1 Introduction

In most developed nations big cities are expanding ever farther into the countryside. Rural populations are growing, whether with workers - commuters or the self-employed - retired people, or temporary residents. In France a "periurbanization" movement began in Ile-de-France in the 1960s and spread to the large provincial cities in the next decade before becoming a nationwide phenomenon (Le Jeannic 1997; Schmitt et al. 1998; Cavailhès and Schmitt 2002). So successful was this movement that by 1999 33% of the land area of France was periurban with 12.3 million people living there. Progression from 1990 to 1999 was remarkable, with the area concerned increasing by half (more than 6 million hectares) and an additional 3.5 million inhabitants being involved.

Most economists investigating this issue emphasize the role of "green" amenities and of "rural" life style in this movement. The choice between living in the city, in a periurban area, or in the remote countryside is the outcome of a trade-off between ease-of-access to employment centers and to public goods (like schools) associated with the urban fabric and to landscape and environmental amenities that are more specifically rural.

First we review the academic literature on valuing agricultural and wooded landscapes of rural residential areas. Then we present a case study of hedonic pricing of residential scenery around Besançon (France), before concluding.

A. Baranzini et al. (eds.), *Hedonic Methods in Housing Markets*, doi: 10.1007/978-0-387-76815-1_4,

4.2 Landscape and its Economic Valuation

"Landscape means an area, as perceived by people, whose character is the result of the action and interaction of natural and/or human factors" (European Landscape Convention). Beyond this definition the concept of landscape varies from one discipline to another. For ecologists landscape is an interacting system of exchanges of energy, matter, or information. For historians it is the heritage of the economic, cultural, or mythical exchanges that past societies maintained with the places where they lived. Psychologists take an interest in the mind's representation of landscape. For geographers what is paramount is the physical landscape and the imprint on it of the interplay of natural and/or anthropic systems. Economists look at landscape as non market goods providing residents or tourists with residential or recreational amenities. People are foremost here: it is a matter of analyzing their preferences for landscape, their resulting behavior, and the price they agree to pay to enjoy landscape, or to safeguard or enhance it.

Brossard and Wieber (1980, 1984) propose a system-based interpretation of landscape. Landscape breaks down into three interdependent sub-systems: a *productive system* where components of the mineral, plant and animal worlds interact, with the imprint of human action; a *visible system*, where the foregoing components are seen spatially depending on relief, perspective, their arrangement, and so on; and a *user system*, where landscape is a display for a specific individual, the subject matter of sensory perceptions and mental representations.

This conceptual framework is consistent with Lancaster's (1966) consumer economic theory: the view of landscape is the output of an individual production that uses an emitting system (physical features) as its input to produce utility through the tools of the senses and of the mind.

Economists have two sets of methods for evaluating the price of landscape (Garrod and Willis 1999). *Revealed preference methods* deduce price from the behavior of economic agents. The hedonic price method is the most common method (see Taylor, this Volume), but the transport cost method is used too: the cost laid out to go visit a site provides a mean from which to infer the site value for the visitor (Fleischer and Tsur 2000). *Stated preference methods* use surveys, with the responses obtained forming the study material. Of these methods, contingent valuation was long the most widely used (Willis and Garrod 1993) before being superseded by other techniques, such as choice experiment (Hanley et al. 1998).

Each of these methods has its advantages and drawbacks. Revealed preference methods study actual markets and the observed behavior of economic agents. They provide use values (residential with hedonic prices, recreational with transport costs). But it is not certain that the values obtained are those of the goods under study, for in the real world a great number of variables may interfere with the variables of interest, and thus the condition "all else being equal" never strictly holds. Stated preference methods analyze behavior in hypothetical scenarios. They may yield non-use values (legacies, use value for future generations). But it is not sure that stated behavior in a fictional scenario would be that adopted in the real world. Here we give precedence to the hedonic price method and it is this method that is used in the application presented in this chapter.

In the research presented below, we identify four types of variables that are used as landscape indicators: (i) ground cover (farmland, woodland, etc.), analyzed in two dimensions (from maps, aerial photos, satellite images), (ii) landscape ecology indices that add to the foregoing shape variables, (iii) distance between dwellings and specific objects (golf-courses, parks, green spaces, forests, etc.) insofar as the view of a landscape is dependent on such distance, and lastly (iv) the view of landscape that integrates the third dimension into the analysis thus corresponding to the actual view.

4.2.1 Ground Cover

Research based on ground cover generally concludes that the presence of farmland, woods or forests commands positive hedonic prices. Thus, among others, Des Rosiers et al. (2002) report that near Quebec (Canada) the presence of landscape attributes (forests, gardened landscapes, hedgerows) raises house prices by 7.7% on average. Other workers, though, such as Garrod and Willis (1994), Irwin (2002), Palmer (2003), and Smith et al. (2002), report opposing findings.

Results for farmland are ambivalent too, as they differ from one study to another. Roe et al. (2004) report a positive hedonic price, unlike Smith et al. (2002), whereas for Paterson and Boyle (2002) the effect is not significant either way.

Ground cover is sometimes analyzed in terms of the legal status of plots. Thus the presence of farmland, forests or woods that may later be built on (which is more often true for private than public property) devalues nearby housing while conversely a prohibition on any development on such land enhances property values (Irwin 2002). Cheshire and Sheppard (1995) report that around Reading and Darlington (UK) public green spaces where people can walk (parks, forests) command positive hedonic prices whereas farmland where people cannot go generally has a negative hedonic price.

We shall also touch on the use of stated preference methods using random utility theory (experimental choices, conjoint analysis). Roe et al. (2004) report, from a conjoint analysis, that the rich people value the proximity of farmland more highly than the poor. The rich are prepared to pay 6% more for residential property to benefit from an additional 10% farmland, the poor just 3% more. Those authors also conclude that farmland acts as an attractor in suburbanization and show substitutability between farmland (with an esthetic and non-use value) and public parks (with recreational value too). Dachary-Bernard (2005) uses the conjoint analysis method in a study of France's Armorica regional nature reserve and concludes that visitors are willing to pay to see wooded heathland.

It is worth remembering that findings for the land-use price of tree-covered land or farmland are not clear cut. In most cases, prices are positive but in a non-negligible number they are negative. This is paradoxical if one considers, as said in the introduction, that green living spaces are much desired. This paradox may result from the poor quality of land-use variables measured from maps or satellite pictures: these are not proper landscapes. So the analysis needs to be refined.

4.2.2 Landscape Composition and Landscape Ecology

To go beyond land use, geographers often use indices from landscape ecology such as the number of patches per hectare, their size, the boundary length between them, or synthetic indices such as entropy or the fractal dimension, or variables for analyzing shape, the complexity or uniformity that arises, and so on.

These studies are sometimes made from photographs. For example Palmer (2003) uses scores attributed by respondents to photos of the rural and touristic Cap Code area (Massachusetts, USA). He concludes they value water but not forest. He also shows that landscape ecology indices have insignificant impact, except for the length of hedgerows, which have a positive value.

Satellite pictures have been the most usual data source ever since landscape ecology first provided readily computable landscape composition variables that economists can use in hedonic models. Geoghegan et al. (1997) were the first to our knowledge to use such variables to estimate their hedonic prices. They report that in Maryland (USA), near Washington D.C., nearby forests or fields raise land values slightly (their effect is negative beyond a certain distance). Landscape fragmentation and diversity have a negative effect, except close to and far from Washington.

In France, Dumas et al. (2005) work through a hedonic price model in the Bouches-du-Rhône department with land-use and landscape-composition variables. An aggregation index has a positive hedonic price, while interspection, juxtaposition, and entropy indices have negative prices.

4.2.3 Distance from Farmland and Forest

The distance between a house and an object has long been included in hedonic price models. As early as 1973, Weicher and Zerbst showed that at Columbus (Ohio, USA) housing next to parks commanded higher values, except where there were too many users, which resulted in a fall in values.

Studies have proliferated since. For example, Bolitzer and Netusil (2000) report that in Portland (Oregon, USA) housing less than 500 m from a public garden is worth 1.5% more than more distant housing, and that the proximity of golf courses is valued even more highly. Like Weicher and Zerbst (1973) they report that being too close has negative effects because of congestion and noise. In a region near Helsinki (Finland) studied by Tyrväinen and Miettinen (2000), house prices fall by 5.9% per km with distance from the nearest forest park.

The proximity of wetland areas has positive hedonic prices in the Portland region (Oregon, USA), as reported by Mahan et al. (2000): an extra acre of the nearest wetland raises real-estate prices by $24.4 and moving 300 m closer raises prices by $440. The proximity of lakes is even more highly valued ($1,600 for being 100 m closer).

Other results are sometime surprising. Smith et al. (2002) conclude that, in the study region of North Carolina (USA), remoteness from a public park has a positive effect on real-estate prices: it seems people prefer to be farther away. However, as expected, prices fall with distance from golf courses and adjacent plots are much more expensive than average.

Several of the foregoing examples suggest that distance should be measured as a discrete rather than a continuous variable: it is a matter of being adjacent to the relevant landscape feature. This is what Thorsnes (2002) reports for housing projects in Michigan (USA). Properties adjoining forests are worth 19 to 35% more than other properties, but forests no longer affect prices when there is a road to cross to reach them. Hobden et al. (2004) obtain a similar result for a region close to Vancouver (Canada): plots adjoining green spaces are worth 2.8% more than average, and the additional value rises respectively to 6.9% and 11% for plots adjoining corridors and footpaths leading to large parks.

The role of distance seems to vary with the extent of urbanization, as shown by Anderson and West (2003) for St Paul – Minneapolis (USA) where, in the suburbs, distances to golf courses and to water (lake, rivers) only are significant whereas in the city the distance to parks also comes out positively.

The point to bear in mind is that the proximity of landscaped areas and of areas developed for recreational use (public gardens, golf courses, etc.) is valued more highly and that their adjacency generally means higher property values, unless they are so busy as to cause nuisances. And the effects of distance on property values tail off rapidly, vanishing beyond a few hundred meters.

4.2.4 The View of the Landscape

The view of a landscape is more difficult to quantify than the previous variables. One must shift from a view from above (map, aerial photo, satellite image) to an observer's view from the ground. Photography has long been used in this area. In recent years it has become possible to model the field of view from the ground through digital elevation models coupled to satellite images. Topography and/or visual barriers formed by features on the ground are thus taken into account.

Analysis of Landscape Preferences

The preferences of economic agents can be studied from scores attributed to landscape photographs by explaining those scores by the characteristics of the photos. The multiple regression method is therefore similar to a hedonic price equation, but the explained variable is a score. The conclusions of these often old studies are something of a rag-bag: Gobster and Chenoweth (1989), citing more than 80 references, list 1,194 terms used in 50 papers to describe esthetic preferences.

The often cited paper by Kaplan et al. (1989) accounts for a score given to landscape photos by four sets of variables: physical attributes (slope, relief, edge contrast, diversity, etc.), land use, sensation-associated variables, and finally perception variables (field of view, texture). In the rural area of Michigan (USA) under study, physical attributes do not adequately account for the score, surprisingly to the authors. Tree-planted lawns increase the score, farmland, brush and fallowland lower it, and other types (forests, meadowland) are neutral. The mysteriousness of a landscape has a positive impact on the score, which the authors claim is a classic result.

Recently Kaplan and Austin (2004) have reported that in a rural area near Detroit (USA), the view of nature from home is the highest scoring feature ahead of demand for space (plot, floor space). Other studies of this type have distinctive methods, such as those of Johnston et al. (2002) who analyze the layout of a project in Rhode Island (USA) by presenting plans and mock-ups to future inhabitants. They show that households prefer a development in a single, low-density, block with fragmented plots, and separated by hedgerows.

Estimating the Price of the Landscape Viewed

Bastian et al. (2002) use a quantitative-geography method to reconstruct the view of a landscape in the Rocky Mountains (Wyoming, USA) and apply the hedonic pricing method to the landscape so modeled. An observer's field of vision is analyzed for 360° from satellite pictures for ground cover and a digital elevation model for relief. Few landscape variables are significant except for landscape diversity, which is highly appreciated.

Paterson and Boyle (2002) also use a satellite picture and a digital elevation model to analyze the landscape seen in a rural area of Connecticut (USA). They obtain somewhat unstable results in that they differ with the type of variable (satellite view or ground view) and are sometimes counter-intuitive.

Cavailhès et al. (2007) study the hedonic price of landscapes seen in the periurban area around Dijon (France), using the same method for modeling the view from the ground as the one presented below for the Besançon area. They show that beyond a few tens or hundreds of meters, the fields of view and the features in them do not significantly influence house prices. However, nearby trees or fields seen from a house have positive hedonic prices and roads negative prices. The view itself matters: nearby trees that are hidden from view have a lower hedonic price than trees in view. Landscape ecology indices indicate positive prices for complex landscape shapes (mosaics, non connectivity, etc.).

The previous examples are for rural areas and are easier to analyze than examples for cities, where it is difficult to model the view partly because buildings vary in height and partly because the quality of a landscape depends on factors other than the presence of fields or woods. For Glasgow (UK), Lake et al. (1998; 2000) cannot determine the field of view from the digital elevation model alone: to allow for the height of buildings they have to go out and count the number of floors (limiting the count to a 500 m radius for reasons of time). They show that the view of a road lowers property values by 2.5%, regardless of traffic noise, which is accounted for elsewhere. Benson et al. (1998) also make systematic visits to houses in Bellinghan (Washington, USA) to determine the view of the ocean (and lakes). A full ocean view raises the price of houses within 0.1 miles of the coast by 68%, but by only 31% for houses more than two miles away.

Advances in geographic information systems (GIS) mean that multidimensional data analysis in complex urban environments can now be automated as shown by Baranzini and Schaerer (2007) for Geneva (Switzerland). They take account of the effect on rents of accessibility, noise, air pollution, and view. The view is modeled over a 1 km radius with a model combining a digital elevation model with a geographic information layer on building heights. Proximity, accessibility, and the view of certain landscape amenities (water, natural environment, mountains) have a positive influence on rental values, which is not true of other landscape attributes (negative effects of public gardens).

Let us retain from this brief survey of the literature first that the view itself must be introduced into landscape valuation models: land use as seen from the air is an overly coarse approximation, because the view of an observer on the ground is something very different. Secondly, if the quantity of view is important, what is seen also matters, so that the different types of view should be distinguished, and it matters what is seen. Finally, resolution or scale must be precise enough to make out small features or short distances, because it is not the same thing to be adjacent, a few tens of meters, or more than a hundred meters away from a feature whose size and height matter. It is understandable that such requirements entail sophisticated geographical methods. This relevant scale, which is always very large, may explain why studies using variables defined at the scale of several hundred meters or a kilometer yield volatile results that are sometimes counter-intuitive or different from one study to another.

4.3 Case Study: Periurban Landscape Prices in the Besançon Area

We now set out the results of a hedonic price evaluation of landscapes in a periurban belt around Besançon, a French city of some 150,000 inhabitants. This provides a detailed illustration of the methods and of the results they lead to.

4.3.1 Geographical and Economic Models, Study Region, and Data

In evaluating the hedonic prices of housing characteristics, the first stage of the approach *à la* Rosen (1974) is used. The method is discussed by Taylor in this Volume. We examine some of the econometric problems it raises and the solutions found after first presenting the study region and the geographical model used to define the landscape variables.

The Study Region

The study region is in the urban area of Besançon (France) which comprises an urban center and 223 periurban communes. Covering a surface area of 1,660 km² the urban area has 222,000 inhabitants, 53% of them living in the city of Besançon. The city itself is excluded from the study area as our landscape analysis model cannot be readily applied to the dense housing of cities, as discussed above. The 173 periurban communes used for the econometric estimates have fewer than 500 inhabitants, with an average density of 66 inhabitants/km².

In the 1990s the urban area gained 14,300 inhabitants. This increase was greater with distance from the city center: the population of Besançon grew by 0.4% per year, that of the suburbs by 0.9%, and that of the periurban belt by 1.2%.

Between 1990 and 1999, 13,300 people moved from the urban center to the periurban belt and 5,900 people moved in the opposite direction. Moreover, 72% of the 90,100 jobs in the study area were in Besançon. In the periurban belt 80% of the active population in employment worked outside of their residential commune. The high-level of residential mobility and of commuting between Besançon and its outskirts suggests that the study area meets the conditions of a single labor market and a single real-estate market that are required for applying the hedonic price model.

In 1999 the urban area had 103,050 homes, 16% more than in 1990. Over the period the number of homes increased faster than the population because of smaller families, more single parents, de-cohabitation, and more people living alone. Urban sprawl reinforced the number of detached houses, which alone are covered by our estimates: they accounted for 18% of housing built in Besançon itself, 81% in the suburbs, and 84% in the periurban belt.

Geographical Model

The geographical model is described by Joly et al. (2007); we summarize its main features here. The viewshed is analyzed using a digital elevation model and satellite images from which tall objects liable to block the view can be identified. For each cell in the study area (cells are squares with 7 m resolution), which we refer to as "base points", the 360° view outward is sampled by tracing a ray every 3°. A test is conducted for each cell encountered along each ray to determine by trigonometry whether the cell is seen or not (at eye level, 1.80 m from the ground), depending on the relief and the obstacles along the ray from the base point. The number of cells of each type, seen or not, is determined for each ray and the total for the 120 rays from the base point determines the viewshed and its contents. Moreover, each cell is geo-referenced in a system of Cartesian coordinates (the French "Lambert" system) so it can be connected in with the real-estate transaction data that is georeferenced using the same system.

Notice that the view from the ground concerns a small part of space only: for a house in the economic data base, a mean of 27% of cells within a radius of 280 m are visible, and the median is 5.5%.

To analyze the "views" of landscapes defined in this way, a land use layer localizing and identifying objects is combined with a digital elevation model of the topography and architecture of the space. Satellite images are processed by standard procedures in remote sensing science to correct their geometry, merge different satellite images and classify the pixels (see Joly et al. 2007). Twelve types of land use are identified: water, conifers, deciduous trees (aggregated into tree-covered land), crops, meadows, vineyards (aggregated into agriculture), bushes, roads, railroads (aggregated into networks), built areas, quarries, and trading estates. Some objects are ascribed a fixed height imposing a visual barrier: 15 m for deciduous trees, 20 m for conifers, 3 m for bushes, 1 m for vineyards and 7 m for houses. The other types (water, roads, railroads, fields) have zero height. The digital elevation model provides altitudes to the nearest 0.1 m for points 50 m apart on the ground.

To take into account the depth of the viewshed, six grounds are distinguished: less than 70 m from the observer, 70–140 m, 140–280 m, 280–1,200 m, 1.2–6 km, and 6–40 km.

Economic and Econometric Model

We start with a Rosen type model: $\ln P_i = X_i b + \varepsilon_i$, where $\ln P_i$ is the logarithm of the price of real-estate i, X_i the matrix of explanatory variables (including an intercept), b the vector of coefficients to be estimated, and ε_i an error term. The major concerns arising from this model are as follows. First there may be endogenous explanatory variables either because the market determines both the real-estate price and the quantity of certain attributes used to account for the price (Irwin, 2002; Knight, this Volume and Taylor, this Volume), or because the buyer chooses the price and the quantity of such attributes simultaneously (Epple 1987; Follain and Jimenez 1985). The instrumental variables method must therefore be used. Buyer characteristics are used as instruments (Epple 1987) and the main equation is calculated by the 2 SLS method.

Second there may be spatial autocorrelations. Most of these are allowed for by using a fixed-effect model. A dummy variable m_j characterizing the commune j is introduced into the equation, which becomes: $\ln P_{ij}=X_{ij}b+m_j+\varepsilon_{ij}$. The m_j values capture all the characteristics shared by the observations located in each commune, including badly measured or omitted variables. Thus, there are no inter-commune correlations between the residuals ε_{ij}. Nevertheless, correlations between residuals may exist at the intra-commune level. To check this possibility, a Moran's index between neighboring ε_{ij} values is computed, using a contiguity matrix where observations less than 200 m apart are neighbors, and the significance of this index is tested.

Third, multicollinearity between regressors often occurs in hedonic equations. Fortunately, the view from the ground reduces the links between landscape variables because the view is often blocked, mainly by houses situated more or less randomly on the ground, breaking the regular arrangement of objects, by blocking the view in a quasi-random way. This property is important for the econometric model: we chose the view from the ground because it is the actual view from detached houses, and this choice entails a pleasant statistical property by greatly reducing multicollinearity. To deal with remaining collinearity, we transform one of the correlated regressors to reduce or remove the statistical connection. Finally, we use the usual statistical tests: Hausman's method to test whether explanatory variables are endogenous or not; Sargan's method to test the validity of the instruments; significance of Moran's index between neighbor residuals; the homoscedasticity of residuals is submitted to White's test.

Data and Variables

The economic data come from lawyers, who register real-estate transactions in France. The database is made up of 997 sales of detached houses between 2001 and 2004, and records the price of the transaction and certain characteristics of the property and the economic agents involved. The variables used in the regressions are defined in Table 4.1. This database also includes variables used in the instrumental equation: the gender, occupation, age, marital status, and nationality of both buyer and seller.

Table 4.1 Variables

Abreviation	Definition
Structural variables:	
LSPACE	Living space [m²] (logarithm)
UNKNOWN LSPACE	Unknown living space (dummy)
LSPACE/LOT	Living space [m²] / lot size [m²]
2_BATHROOMS	Presence of a second bathroom
BASEMENT	Presence of a basement
POOL	Presence of a swimming pool
CAR PARK	Presence of car park
PERIOD OF CONSTRUCTION	Period of construction < 1850; 1850–1916; 1917–1949; 1950–1969 (reference); 1970–1980; 1981–1991; 1992–2004; unknown
LESS 5 YEARS	building constructed since less than 5 years, and resold
AN 2001 to AN2003	date of transaction: from 2001 to 2003 (2004 = reference)
SELLER OCC	Property occupied by the seller
BUYER OCC	Property already occupied by the buyer
PRIVATE	Transaction directly between private individuals
SALE OFFICE	Transaction by a real estate office
LAWYER OFFICE	Transaction by a real estate lawyer office (reference)
DIVISION	Previous transaction = division of estate
SUCC	Previous transaction = succession
NORMAL SALE	Previous transaction = normal sale (reference)
DIST TOWN HALL	Distance from the town hall
LOCAL BUYER	Buyer living in the urban area
Landscape variables:	According to grounds: <70 m, 70–140 m, 140–280 m, 280– 1200 m, 1.2–6 km, 6–40 km. Cells SEEN and UNSEEN are distinguished. Grounds may be merged
TREE	Number of cells of tree-covered area
TREE * LOT/LSPACE	Number of cells of tree-covered area * LOT/LSPACE
AGRI	Number of cells of agriculture
AGRI * LOT/LSPACE	Number of cells of agriculture * LOT/LSPACE
NETWORK	Number of cells of road/railroad
BUILT	Number of built cells
GREEN	Number of cells of agriculture + tree-covered area

Source: PERVAL

The landscape variables are made up of land-cover types in the six grounds (some of them in adjacent grounds are merged). Land-cover types are weighed up by the number of seen and unseen cells. Interaction variables are introduced between lot size and both trees and farmland (descriptive statistics show correlations between these land-cover types and lot size). Cells that are not introduced into the equation are the reference for the landscape variables. They are mainly made of cells located more than 1.2 km from the observer. Descriptive statistics show that the views of landscape are very sensitive to observations: the standard deviation is at least equal to the mean, and it is often twice or three times higher.

4.3.2 Results

The results are shown in Table 4.2. The coefficients give the effect on the logarithm of house price of the variation of one unit of explanatory variables (i.e. a 49 m^2 cell for landscape variables). The table does not show the parameters for the commune indicator variables.

Living space is endogenous (Student's t in the enhanced equation: – 4.0). Moreover, the living space, when unknown, is endogenous too (t: – 2.9). We therefore apply the instrumental variables method with the personal characteristics of buyer and seller when accepted as exogenous by Sargan's test. Other explanatory variables could be endogenous (see Knight, this Volume; Taylor, this Volume), in particular landscape attributes and the time-on-market (TOM), but they are here accepted as exogenous by the Hausman test. The calculation by 2 SLS yields an R^2 value of 0.58 (adjusted R^2: 0.48). Moran's index (observations less than 200 m apart, without weighting) shows there is no spatial correlation of residuals (significant at 11% level).

House Characteristics

The hedonic price of a square meter of floor space (the mean being 121 m^2) represents at the median point 0.9% of the price of a house. The dummy variable indicating the absence of floor space in the data base has a hedonic price that is higher than the mean price of houses where this variable is present. It is therefore on average large houses for which floor space is not indicated. Recent builds are valued more highly relative to the reference period (+ 17% for new builds); old buildings are not devalued. Real-estate prices surged 34% between 2001 and 2004. When the house is not vacant (it is occupied by the seller), the price is higher (+ 20%), and buyers from the Besançon urban area pay less than buyers from farther afield (– 8%), suggesting asymmetric information or market segmentation. The other results in Table 4.2 require no special comments insofar as it is landscape variables that are of interest here.

Table 4.2 Results

Stuctural Variables		Coefficient	T
INTERCEPT		11.9571	46.1
LSPACE		0.0086***	5.7
UNKNOWN LSPACE		0.9929***	4.6
LSPACE/LOT		-0.1515	-0.3
2_BATHROOMS		0.0879**	2.5
BASEMENT		0.0719***	2.7
POOL		0.1445**	2.5
CAR PARK		0.0531**	2.3
PERIOD OF CONST < 1850		-0.0127	-0.2
1850–1916		-0.1600**	-2.2
1917–1949		0.0471	0.8
1950–1969		Reference	
1970–1980		0.0995**	2.2
1981–1991		0.1108**	2.1
1992–2004		0.1559***	2.8
LESS 5 YEARS		-0.0894	-1.5
AN2001		-0.2929***	-4.6
AN2002		-0.1522***	-3.1
AN2003		-0.0954**	-2.1
AN2004		Reference	
SELLER OCC		0.1799***	6.6
BUYER OCC		-0.0897	-0.9
PRIVATE		0.0409	1.1
SALE OFFICE		0.0442	1.3
LAWYER OFFICE		Reference	
DIVISION		-0.0326	-0.6
SUCC		-0.0458	-1.3
NORMAL SALE		Reference	
DIST TOWN HALL (x 10)		0.0004	1.5
LOCAL BUYER		-0.0856***	-3.5
Landscape variables	GROUND	Coefficient	*T*
SEEN TREES	< 70 m	0.0192***	3.5
SEEN TREES *LOT SPACE	< 70 m	-0.1494***	-2.9
UNSEEN TREES	< 70 m	0.0093*	1.8
UNSEEN TREES*LOT SPACE	< 70 m	-0.0612	-1.4
SEEN TREES	70–280 m	0.0000	0.0
SEEN BUILT	< 70 m	0.0020	0.8

Table 4.2 (cont.)

SEEN BUILT	70–280 m	0.0003	0.3
SEEN NETWORKS	< 140 m	-0.0038*	-1.7
UNSEEN NETWORKS	< 140 m	-0.0024	-1.1
SEEN+UNSEEN AGRI	< 70 m	-0.0008	-0.3
SEEN+UNSEEN AGRI	70–280 m	0.0007**	2.4
SEEN+UNSEEN AGRI*LOT/SPACE	70–280 m	-0.0020	-1.2
GREEN	> 280 m	0.0001	1.1

Level of significance : *** < 1%; ** < 5%; * < 10%. Source: PERVAL

Landscape Attributes of Houses

Trees seen within 70 m of houses have a significantly positive hedonic price which, at the mean point of the residential area, is 2% for a cell or 11.6% for an additional standard deviation. The interaction variable between the number of tree-covered cells seen and the residential lot size is significantly negative: the larger the residential lot, the lower the price attached to the sight of trees or forests. Unseen trees in the same ground also have a positive hedonic price (significant at the 7% level) but half that of trees in view: the presence of nearby trees is a source of utility for inhabitants, but their mere presence counts less than the sight of them.

For farmland there is no need to distinguish between cells in view and out of view. The coefficient of fields closest to houses is insignificant, but farmland between 70 and 200 m has a positive hedonic price (at the 2% limit): €700, that is, 0.05% of the price of a house, for an additional standard deviation. Notice also a significant interaction between this variable and residential lot size, showing that both goods are substitutable in the consumption function. Distance is not involved in the same way for tree-covered land and for farmland. While proximity is much appreciated for forest, for farmland it seems that a certain distance is preferred: it is the presence of fields or meadows 200–300 m away that enhances real-estate values.

Road networks seen within the first 140 m around houses (and railroads, but these are scarce) have a significantly negative hedonic price of €5,100 (0.04%) for an additional standard deviation. When these networks are not in view in the same circle, their coefficient is insignificant. This yields the same conclusion as for the view of trees: although roads close to houses are a source of danger, noise, and pollution, it is the actual sight of networks, obviously combined with these nuisances, that leads to a lower real-estate value. The estimated depreciation is thus the result of this combination.

Notice lastly that fields of view beyond 280 m and the objects they contain have insignificant coefficients. This "short-sightedness" of households, to use the term of Cavailhès et al. (2007), may be due to the landscape characteristics of the region.

4.4 Summary and Conclusions

It is difficult to transpose the view of landscapes into quantitative variables that economists can plug into econometric models. Geographical methods range from photograph analysis to quantitative geography models using satellite pictures and digital elevation models. Explanatory variables range from psychology (mysteriousness, order, harmony, etc.) to landscape ecology. It is an area that is evolving rapidly, where results are still not stabilized because they derive from a small number of studies.

There are still not enough studies to untangle the economic tie-ins among variables and, until this can be sorted out, contradictory results may arise. Results differ from one study to another and even within the same study. For example, tree-covered land, which might be expected to have a positive hedonic price, may have a negative sign in some studies. Farmland is not highly valued everywhere either.

Let us retain from the case study of the Besançon area that first landscape price, whatever definition of it we adopt, is only a minor component of house price. In this area, tree-cover and farmland have positive hedonic prices, and networks negative prices, but only when these items are very close to houses and mostly when they are in view. Beyond a few tens of meters or 100–200 m at most, consumers appear indifferent to the presence of viewsheds and their contents.

This aspect related to the proximity between the source of the amenity and its beneficiaries must be set against public support for farming and forestry that is only loosely connected with the location of these activities relative to housing, or even not at all for most support packages. It is the presence of green areas close to housing that is positively valued by households. Local policies to enhance villages, to develop the appearance of public areas in villages, to bring greenery into the built-up areas, to encourage inhabitants to landscape their gardens, are justified by the "short-sightedness" of inhabitants.

Lastly, several of the studies examined conclude that the search for amenities and open spaces helps explain the periurbanization movement and the re-peopling of the countryside. The causes of cities extending toward their hinterlands have long been sought on the *push* side, the deterioration of city centers, the ghettoization and crime in US cities forcing the middle class toward the suburbs (Mieszkowski and Mills 1993). Nowadays, it is the *pull* side that holds the attention of those seeking to account for population movements toward periurban belts and rural areas.

References

Anderson ST, West SE (2003) The value of open space proximity and size: city versus suburbs. Working paper, Macalester College, St. Paul, United States

Baranzini A, Schaerer C (2007) A sight for sore eyes. Assessing the value of view and landscape use on the housing market. Working paper, Geneva School of Business Administration, Switzerland, available at SSRN: http://ssrn.com/abstract=981189

Bastian CT, McLeod DM, Germino MJ, Reiners WA, Blasko BJ (2002) Environmental amenities and agricultural land values: a hedonic model using geographic information systems data. Ecological economics 40: 337–349

Benson ED, Hansen JL, Schwartz AL, Smersch GT (1998) Pricing residential amenities: the value of a view. Journal of real estate finance and economics 16: 55–73

Bolitzer B, Netusil NR (2000) The impact of open spaces on property values in Portland, Oregon. Journal of environmental management 59: 185–193

Brossard T, Wieber JC (1980) Essai de formulation systémique d'un mode d'approche du paysage. Bulletin de l'association des géographes français 468–469: 103–111

Brossard T, Wieber JC (1984) Le paysage, trois définitions ; un mode d'analyse et de cartographie. L'espace géographique: 5–12

Cavailhès J, Brossard T, Foltête JC, Joly D, Hilal M, Tourneux FP, Tritz C, Wavresky P (2007) GIS-based hedonic pricing of landscape. Working paper, INRA, CNRS, Dijon, Besançon, France

Cavailhès J, Schmitt B (2002) Les mobilités résidentielles entre villes et campagnes. In: Perrier-Cornet P (ed) Repenser les campagnes. L'aube DATAR (edn), Gémenos, pp 35–65

Cheshire P, Sheppard S (1995) On the price of land and the value of amenities. Economica 62: 247–267

Dachary-Bernard J (2005) Une évaluation économique du paysage. Une application de la méthode des choix multi-attributs aux Monts d'Arrée. Economie et statistique, pp 57–80

Des Rosiers F, Thériault M, Kestens Y, Villeneuve P (2002) Landscaping and house values: an empirical investigation. Journal of real estate research 23: 139–161

Dumas E, Geniaux G, Napoléone C (2005) Les indices de l'écologie du paysage à l'épreuve du marché foncier. Revue d'économie régionale et urbaine 1: 83–106

Epple D (1987) Hedonic prices and implicit markets: estimating demand and supply functions for differentiated products. Journal of political economy 95: 59–80

Fleischer A, Tsur Y (2000) Measuring the recreational value of agricultural landscape. European review of agricultural economics 27: 385–398

Follain JR, Jimenez E (1985) Estimating the demand for housing characteristics. Regional science and urban economics 15: 77–107

Irwin EG (2002) The effects of open space on residential property values. Land economics 78: 465–480

Garrod GD, Willis KG, Saunders CM (1994) The benefits and costs of the Somerset Levels and Moors ESA. Journal of rural studies 10: 131–146

Garrod GD, Willis KG (1999) Economic valuation of the environment. Methods and case studies, Edward Elgar, Cheltenham

Geoghegan J, Wainger LA, Bockstael NE (1997) Spatial landscape indices in a hedonic framework: an ecological economics analysis using GIS. Ecological economics 23: 251–264

Gobster PH, Chenoweth RE (1989) The dimensions of aesthetics preference: a quantitative analysis. Journal of environment management 29: 47–72

Hanley N, Wright RE, Adamowicz V (1998) Using choice experiment to value the environment. Environmental and resource economics 11:413–428

Hobden DW, Laughton GE, Morgan KE (2004) Green space borders – a tangible benefit? Evidence from four neighbourhoods in Surrey, British Columbia, 1980–2001. Land use policy 21: 129–138
Irwin EG (2002) The effects of open space on residential property values. Land economics 78: 465–480
Johnston RJ, Swallow SK, Bauer DM (2002) Spatial factors and stated preference values for public goods: considerations for rural land use. Land economics: 481–500
Joly D, Brossard T, Tourneux FP, Tritz C, Cavailhès J, Hilal M, Wavresky P (2007) Using modeling to make a quantitative valuation of landscape. Working paper, CNRS-ThéMA, INRA-CESAER, Besançon, Dijon, pp 1–28
Kaplan R, Austin ME (2004) Out in the country: sprawl and the quest for nature nearby. Landscape and urban planning 69: 235–243
Kaplan R, Kaplan S, Bown T (1989) Environmental preferences. A comparison of four domains of predictors. Environment and behavior 21: 509–530
Lake IR, Lovett AA, Bateman IJ, Langford IH (1998) Modelling environmental influences on property prices in an urban environment. Computers, environments and urban systems 22: 121–136
Lake IR, Lovett AA, Bateman IJ, Day B (2000) Using GIS and large-scale digital data to implement hedonic pricing studies. International journal of geographical information science 14: 521–541
Lancaster KJ (1966) A new approach to consumer theory. Journal of political economy 74: 132–156
Le Jeannic T (1997) Trente ans de périurbanisation : extension et dilution des villes. Economie et statistique 307: 21–41
Mahan BL, Polasky S, Adams RM (2000) Valuing urban wetlands: a property price approach. Land economics 76: 100–113
Mieszkowski P, Mills ES (1993) The causes of metropolitan suburbanization. Journal of economic perspectives: 135–147
Palmer JF (2003) Using spatial metrics to predict scenic perception in a changing landscape: Dennis, Massachusetts. Landscape and urban planning 69: 201-218
Paterson RW, Boyle KJ (2002) Out of sight, out of mind? Using GIS to incorporate visibility in hedonic property value models. Land economics 78: 417–425
Roe B, Irwin EG, Morrow-Jones HA (2004) The effects of farmland, farmland preservation, and other neighborhood amenities on housing values and residential growth. Land economics: 55–75
Rosen S (1974) Hedonic prices and implicit markets: product differentiation in pure competition. Journal of political economy 82: 34–55
Schmitt B, Perrier-Cornet Ph, Blanc M, Hilal M (Eds) (1998) Les campagnes et leurs villes, Contours et caractères, INRA-INSEE
Sheppard S (1999) Hedonic analysis of housing markets. In: Mills ES, Cheshire P (eds) Handbook of regional and urban economics. Applied urban economics, pp 1595–1635
Smith VK, Poulos C, Kim H (2002) Treating open space as an urban amenity. Resource and energy economics 24: 107–129
Thorsnes P (2002) The value of a suburban forest preserve: estimates from sales of vacant residential building lots. Land economics 78: 626–441
Tyrväinen L, Miettinen A (2000) Property prices and urban forest amenities. Journal of environmental economics and management 39: 205–223
Weicher J, Zerbst R (1973) Externalities of neighbourhood parks: an empirical investigation. Land economics 49: 99–105
Willis KG, Garrod GD (1993) Valuing landscape: a contingent valuation approach. Journal of environmental management 37: 1–22

5 Semi-Parametric Tools for Spatial Hedonic Models: An Introduction to Mixed Geographically Weighted Regression and Geoadditive Models

Ghislain Geniaux, Claude Napoléone

INRA Ecodeveloppement, Avignon, France

5.1 Introduction

This chapter focuses on the contribution of semi-parametric tools such as Mixed Geographically Weighted Regression (MGWR) (Fotheringham et al. 1997) and Geoadditive Models (Hastie and Tibshirani 1993; Kammann and Wand 2003) that belong to the General Additive Models family (GAM), to explore the effects of distance regressors on price and/or spatial nonstationarity of implicit house price coefficient in hedonic functions. These tools have become essential with:

- Growing evidence in the economic literature of the multiplicity of amenity sources linked to space and location of houses. Amenity sources can be related to the distance to different public services, commercial facilities, noteworthy landmarks, tourist area, etc. Using monocentric models based on the single distance to Central Business District (CBD) is not sufficient to assess the effect of urban sprawl on land prices. Dominant models in economy fail to account for amenity values, congestion cost or social expenditure for public infrastructure (Brueckner 2001). The specification of hedonic OLS models may be quite difficult when numerous distance measures are candidate regressors, especially with respect to the colinearity issue. GAM is a powerful and flexible tool to explore distance effects with large samples.

- The upscale and downscale extension of available spatial descriptors provided by many public and private organizations has resulted in an explosion in the use of GIS in the last five years. This increased use of GIS by public administrations facilitates the introduction of finer descriptors of landscape, public services and social neighbourhoods in hedonic models. Working on large samples with a lot of finer descriptors of the environment and neighborhood involves

A. Baranzini et al. (eds.), *Hedonic Methods in Housing Markets*, doi: 10.1007/978-0-387-76815-1_5,

dealing with numerous local effects. In this case it is necessary to use multiple scales to analyze the structure of house prices (Quigley 1995). Locally weighted regressions such as Geographically Weighted Regressions (GWR) or MGWR, and GAM, enable estimation of spatially varying and invariant implicit prices in hedonic analysis.

The better the georeferencing of sales, the more numerous and precise the environmental, economic and social descriptors of the environment of a house. Moreover, the wider the geographical range of the sample, the more investigation of spatial heterogeneity and use of hedonic spatial models are required.

At the beginning of this chapter, we focus on methodological questions raised by using geolocalized house sales and distances to different "attractive areas" in hedonic models. In the two last sections, we describe spatially varying coefficient models. Attractive areas may be linked to urban services, but also to environmental quality, tourist awareness or public policies. Such a polycentric context with multiple distance regressors implies using suitable spatial econometrics tools, such as geoadditive models (Hastie and Tibshirani 1993; Kammann and Wand 2003). For example, geoadditive models enable estimation of the hedonic function with smoothing of every coordinate of a map which is able to capture the local effects of unobserved spatial variables. The geoadditive models are the most flexible and efficient alternative to Trend Surface Analysis models (see Des Rosiers and Thiérault 1996) and enable filtering out of large scale spatial trends with no computational burden in the case of large samples. In section 5.2, we give a summary of such semi-parametric tools in spatial hedonic models. In section 5.3, we provide an instructive illustrated example based on data from the Vaucluse District (a French district in Provence, south of France) in a rich data environment.

The effects of environmental descriptors, which are of primary interest in the context of non-market valuation, are generally assumed to be space invariant in hedonic analysis. This may be also the case for internal house characteristics (Fotheringham et al. 2002). However, there may be considerable spatial heterogeneity in hedonic models (Anselin 2001; Paez et al. 2001). The question of the spatial variability of coefficients calls not only for corrective methods, but may be of specific interest to evaluate the local effect of public policies. For example, links between farmland and the house market (or the market for developable land) reveals the ability of local public policies to preserve agricultural land and to control anticipation of land-use conversion (Plantinga et al. 2002; Geniaux and Napoléone 2005). Geographically Weighted Regressions (GWR) and Mixed Geographically Weighted Regressions (MGWR) provide flexible semi-parametric tools to obtain spatially variable coefficients. In section 5.3, we give a detailed description of GWR and MGWR techniques. Finally, in section 5.4, we compare estimations of spatially varying parameters obtained using MGWR and GAM.

5.2 Generalized Additive Models (GAM)

A Generalized Additive Model (Hastie and Tibshirani 1990) is an extension of the Generalized Linear Model (GLM) in which the linear predictor is specified as the sum of smooth functions of regressors. In such a semi-parametric model, the hedonic price function can be written as:

$$P_i = \beta X_i + f_1(x_{1i}) + f_2(x_{2i}) + f_3(x_{3i}) + \ldots + \varepsilon_i \qquad (5.1)$$

where P_i is the price of goods i, βX_i is the parametric part of the regression and f_j are smooth functions of the regressors x_j. Smooth function can be a function of several regressors. These models are estimated using penalized maximum likelihood estimation (P-IRLS for penalized iteratively re-weighted least square, with a smoothing parameter that balances fit and smoothness), for example by minimizing:

$$l(P) - \frac{1}{2}\sum_j \theta_j \int \left[f_j''(x) \right]^2 dx \qquad (5.2)$$

where l is the log-likelihood of the linear predictor, and θ_j are the smoothing parameters that control the tradeoff between goodness of fit and model smoothness. All the second terms act as a penalizing term where the smoothing parameters are multiplied by a given wiggliness measure of smooth functions. Optimization methods generally use Generalized Cross Validation (GCV, see next section) or minimization of the Unbiased Risk Estimator (UBRE, see Craven and Wahba 1979). UBRE is comparable to Akaike Information Criterion (AIC) in the GAM model (Wood 2004). To be solved, these models require us to work with a fixed and relatively low number of basis dimensions for the smooth function. Kim and Gu (2004) proposed a basis size of $n^{2/9}$, where n is the number of observations. This basis dimension acts as a bound on the flexibility of a term. The smoothing parameter controls the actual degree of freedom. In practice, only the basis dimension or the vector of knot[1] candidates sometimes needs to be fixed to control the final number of knots: if the basis dimension is not too low, the model fit is usually insensitive to the basis dimension (Wood 2006).

The latest developments of such models (Wood 2006) and their software implementation, like the *mgcv* and *semipar* packages for R software, provide essential tools for spatial hedonic analysis, allowing inference both on parametric and non-parametric terms. The main problem that remains with such spline tools is that not well-behaved distributions of regressors used in smooth functions may lead to knots that are specific to only a single data or to a small group of data. In such cases, it is probably better to choose the vector of knot candidates manually in order to exclude knots in intervals with missing data.

---

[1] Points where the different sections of a spline curve are joined.

5.2.1 GAM with Distance Regressors

First, a simple and interesting feature of the GAM model is that it allows investigation of the functional form of distance regressors using penalized spline smoothing (or "a penalized spline smooth"). Consider for example a polycentric area with L CBD. The regressor D_l describes the distance to CBD_l and the regressor X describes the house characteristics. A hedonic GAM model could be:

$$\log(P_i) = \beta X_i + \sum_{l=1}^{L} s_l(D_{li}) + \varepsilon_i \cdot \tag{5.3}$$

Working with a smooth of distance to a unique CBD in a non monocentric CBD context may lead to overestimation of the effect of distance. Let us consider the case of the Vaucluse district that is used as an example in the following subsection, in which more than five CBDs could influence the market for isolated houses. The optimized smooth term of the model:

$$log(P_i) = \beta X_i + s(Distance\ \ to\ \ Avignon_i) + \varepsilon_i \tag{5.4}$$

is a 9 basis dimension smooth with a highly significant level. As can be seen in Figure 5.1, the significant part of the smooth term, between 25 and 35 km, corresponds to one or another CBD located 30 km from Avignon (Avignon is the main town in the district). So it is not really the effect of distance to Avignon that this smooth term assesses. A first rule of thumb is to limit the maximum number of basis dimensions to five or six, in order not to capture effects of other CBD and to consider only continued significant effects of distance from 0 to $\overline{d}$ (where $\overline{d}$ corresponds to the radius of the area of influence of the CBD concerned), or from $\overline{d}$ to ∞.

After all, attractive areas are not always well known when the drivers of the housing market are not strictly correlated to employment, services and urban density. However, it may be useful to study the effect of distance to a given CBD, taking other CBDs and forces of attraction into account. A classical approach is to introduce spatial regressors that describe public goods, social neighborhoods, and environmental quality at different levels. Here again, analysis is limited to available data and it is not always certain that all important drivers are taken into account. A good way to deal with this problem is to use a GAM model with a smooth of distance to a given CBD and a smooth of longitude and latitude (Geoadditive Model). Supposing that location i is defined by (u_i, v_i) (longitude and latitude in the following example), we obtain:

$$log(P_i) = \beta X_i + s(Distance\ \ to\ \ Avignon_i) + s(u_i, v_i) + \varepsilon_i \cdot \tag{5.5}$$

Figure 5.2, where a more convenient control of basis dimension and a smooth of longitude and latitude are used, shows that distance to Avignon may have a significant decreasing effect (confidence level of 10 %).

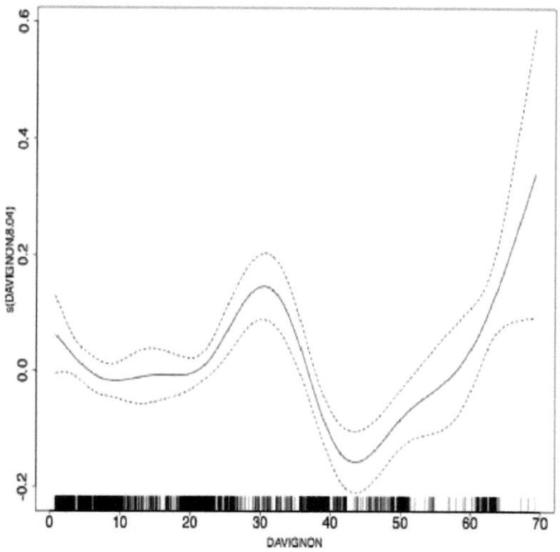

Fig. 5.1 Smoothed Term of Distance to Avignon in Equation (5.4). Data source: Public Notaries

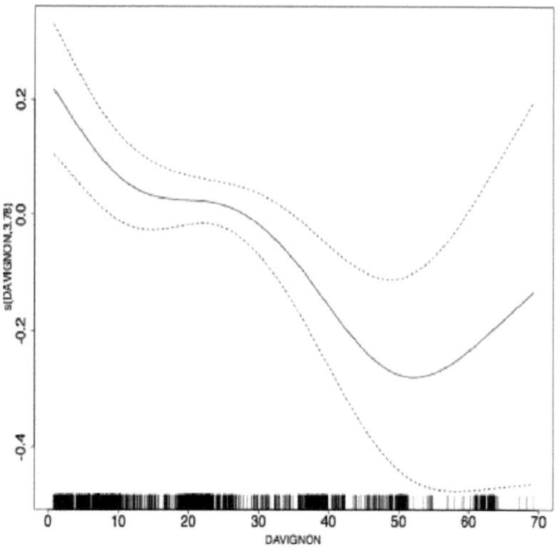

Fig. 5.2 Smoothed Term of Distance to Avignon in Equation (5.5) with $L = 1$ and a Smoothed Term of Longitude and Latitude. Data source: Public Notaries

5.2.2 GAM with Smooth Coordinates or Geoadditive Model

As already mentioned, the smoothing function may be a function of several terms. When the smoothing function includes the geographical location of the dependent variable (response term), Kammann and Wand (2003) called this type of model "Geoadditive Model". A geoadditive hedonic model could be:

$$log(P_i) = \beta X_i + s(u_i, v_i) + \varepsilon_i \, . \tag{5.6}$$

This model presents several interesting features. First, unlike most other spatial econometric models, e.g. Spatial Autoregressive (SAR) and Spatial Moving Average Processes (SMA) (see Anselin 1988), it does not require use of an $N x N$ weight matrix in computation, and allows estimation of large samples[2]. Second, it is better than a fixed effects model (with locational dummies, such as a municipalities dummy) to assess the specific effects of a single spatial regressor because the effects of other potential spatial regressors are captured by the smoothing function of the coordinates. This is right for spatial regressors that have a sufficiently large sphere of influence with respect to the smooth function chosen. It is this feature that allowed correct estimation of the effect of the distance to Avignon in Figure 5.2. Third, it could be used as a specification process tool in which spatial regressors are introduced step by step to reduce the explained sum of squares associated with the smoothed coordinates, in order to finally obtain a fully parametric model in which spatial heterogeneity is considerably reduced. Any spatial autocorrelation that may still be present could then be evaluated and corrected through classical spatial econometric tests (Moran's I, LMerr, LMlag, RLMerr, RLMlag, see Anselin and al. 1996) and models (conditional autoregressive model (CAR), spatial autoregressive model (SAR), spatial error model (SEM)). Figure 3 shows the plot of $s(u_i, v_i)$ for the Vaucluse house sales for the period 2000-2005, using 29 basis dimensions. Like other semi-parametric tools, it could be used to identify non-linear relationships and thresholds. These non-linear relationships and thresholds may lead to choosing a specific functional form of regressor or to stratifying the sample to work with more homogenous goods. It is a more efficient alternative to the trend surface analysis used in hedonic price analysis by Rosiers and Thériault (1996), and allows not only large scale spatial trends to be filtered out.

---

[2] We estimated such a model with a sample of 100,000 sales data with a 2 Mghz dual core / 2 Go RAM Mackbookpro in a reasonable time.

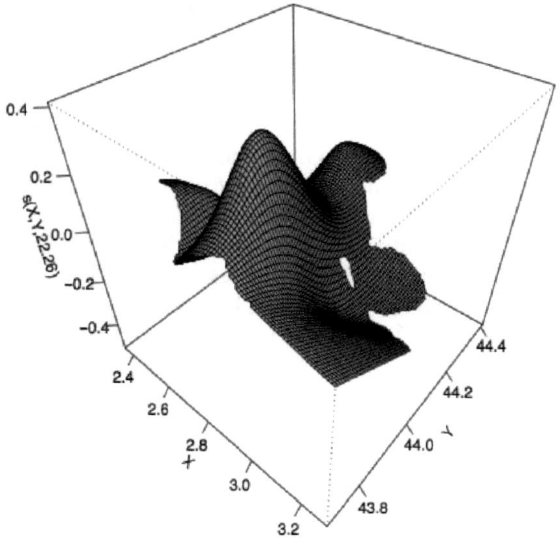

Fig. 5.3 Smoothed Terms of Longitude and Latitude in Equation (5.6). Data source: Public Notaries

5.2.3 Geoadditive Models with Spatially Varying Coefficients

The key features of geoadditive models is their capacity to provide estimations of spatially varying coefficients. To obtain such coefficients, we have to transform the coordinate's smooth terms by pre-multiplying them by a given regressor (Hastie and Tibshirani 1993). This enables evaluation of the spatial stationarity of a coefficient whose regressor is only slightly correlated to location. In order to separate the global location effect and the spatial variability of the regressor concerned, a coordinate smooth term is also introduced in the regression. The model takes the following form:

$$log(P_i) = \beta X_i + Z \cdot s(u_i, v_i) + s(u_i, v_i) + \varepsilon_i \,. \tag{5.7}$$

The correlation between location and the regressor Z can be evaluated before estimating the equation (5.7). Z can also be integrated in the X_i set with no computational difficulty. In this case, the p-value associated with the smooth term $Z \times s(u_i, v_i)$ can be considered as a stationarity test: when this term is non-significant then the stationary term of Z included in X_i is sufficient in the model.

5.3 An Example using GAM Models to Estimate Distances and Density Effects

In order to illustrate how to analyze the effects of different kinds of distances on house price, we estimate different GAM models using data on the 2000–2002–2004 period of house sales from the *Notary Public database* (isolated house with land) in the southern French District of Vaucluse. Vaucluse is an area that covers 3,567 km^2, and has a population of 529,000. Each sale is located by position determination technology with *(u, v)* coordinates. Among the 7,000 house sales that took place during this period, we selected a homogeneous sample of 2,553 isolated houses with garden (lot size lower than 1 hectare), sold privately, with no missing data concerning the main characteristics of the house, and with known longitude and latitude. A global GAM model that can be used as reference is:

$$log(P_i) = \beta X_i + s(u_i, v_i) + \sum_{k=1}^{K} s_k(D_{ki}) + s(d_i) + s(DI_i) + \varepsilon_i \quad (5.8)$$

where X are the house characteristics, D_k corresponds to the seven CBD distances, d_i corresponds to the distance to the nearest continuous high urban density area, DI_i is a density index, and (u_i, v_i) are longitude and latitude. In the Vaucluse district, there are seven potential CBD (Aix-Marseille Agglomeration, Avignon, Orange, Cavaillon, Apt, Pertuis and Manosque[3]) that may influence house prices, and 98 continuous high urban density areas that correspond to historic centers of the 151 municipalities of the Vaucluse district. To make the example easier to read, we introduce no other spatial descriptors than distance and density index in this section. For this example, we built three kinds of density indexes at the infra-municipality level, using a vector map of every building in the entire Vaucluse district (414,674 polygons) and a vector map of land-use zoning of each 151 municipalities (7,820 zones) classified in seven categories (Urban, Activities, Future Urban, Future Activities, Low urban density, Agriculture, Natural area)[4]. The first index is the ratio between the surface area of developed lots and the total surface area of each comprehensive land-use zone (denoted DIS). The second index is the number of built polygons per hectare of each comprehensive land use zone (denoted DINP). These two indexes were attached to each house sale of the sample, depending on the comprehensive land-use zone in which the sales was located. A third type of density index was computed directly for each house sale based on the distance to other existing houses. We then computed the sum and the variance of the distance to the k nearest neighbors, with $k \in \{1, 5, 15, 20, 50, 100, 200, 500, 1{,}000\}$ denoted DIV1, DIV5, ..., DIV1000.

---

[3] The Aix-Marseille Agglomeration, Pertuis and Manosque are located close to, but not in, the Vaucluse district.

[4] Generalization of local zoning used by French “ministère de l’équipement”.

5.3.1 Two Features of Geoadditives Models Illustrated with a "Wrong" Model

First, let us consider a "wrong" model that used a unique distance variable corresponding to the distance to the nearest of the six CBD resulting from a descriptive analysis of population and work data. The OLS model used here is:

$$log(P_i) = \beta X_i + \alpha(Distance\ to\ nearest\ CBD_i) + \varepsilon_i \tag{5.9}$$

Regression results gives a good adjustment ($R^2 = 0.6777$) in which distance to the nearest CBD coefficient $\hat{\alpha}$ is negative (-0.0030) and highly significant (p-value=0.0012), but with a maximum score corresponding to a 10% decrease in price (median score equal to 2%). A GAM estimation of the corresponding geoadditive model:

$$log(P_i) = \beta X_i + \alpha(Distance\ to\ nearest\ CBD_i) + s(u_i, v_i) + \varepsilon_i \tag{5.10}$$

indicates that distance effects, defined by the nearest CBD, are more significant with a coefficient $\hat{\alpha}$ equal to –0.0307. The implicit price is then 10 times higher than that given by the OLS estimation. Table 1 presents the results of this geoadditive model. Results of estimates of the implicit prices of characteristics are quite stable in the different models used in the following and will thus no longer be listed. Habitable area (SQRFOOT) in square meters and the mean habitable area per room (SQRFOOT/NBROOM) are the most significant characteristic in the model. Generally, purchasers choose a house based on their family needs and the choice of size and number of rooms is the most important: each additional square meter adds value to the house. However, a negative sign for the coefficient of the mean size of the rooms indicates that purchasers prefer a size near the mean and are averse to large rooms. The size of the lot (LOTSIZE) is the third most significant internal characteristic in our model. Not surprisingly, purchasers prefer large lots and each additional square meters adds value to the good. Other significant house characteristics are: a house with a swimming pool, a house classification (detached house, historic house, house in town, ruin, villa or not specified), the period the house was built (BEFORE 1850, 1850–1913, 1914–1947, 1948–1969, 1970–1980, 1981–1991, AFTER 1992), number of parking spaces, number of bathrooms (NBBATH), number of floors (NBFLOOR). The coefficient signs are as expected: the purchaser prefers a villa or a historic house, with a swimming pool and parking space. Number of bathrooms and floors are non-linear. The last internal characteristic accounts for the availability of the good (whether the house is available, occupied, or if the availability data is missing). In France, tenants have priority in sales, so the price of an occupied house is lower. Some sales context descriptors appear to have important effect on prices, like sales made by real estate agents (REALESTATEAGENT), previous change of ownership was a donation, a partition or a succession (PREVIOUS SALE TYPE) and the year of sale (YEAR). We showed that the intervention of a real estate agent increases prices.

Properties by donation lower the price, and are likely to accelerate the sale (in the case of succession, some taxes must be paid relatively quickly).

Table 5.1 Results of GAM Model (5.10)

Variables	Coefficient	Std. Error
Intercept	7.8031 ***	0.1375
Log(SQRFOOT)	0.7751 ***	0.0317
Log(SQRFOOT/NBROOM)	-0.3578 ***	0.0397
Log(LOTSIZE)	0.1421 ***	0.0089
SWIMMING POOL	0.1649 ***	0.0252
HISTORIC HOUSE	0.1147	0.0907
HOUSE IN TOWN	-0.2116 ***	0.0492
RUIN	-0.1358 *	0.0594
VILLA	0.1020 ***	0.0257
HOUSE TYPE NOT SPECIFIED	-0.0907 *	0.0422
BUILT BEFORE 1850	-0.0887	0.0609
BUILT 1850–1913	-0.1578 **	0.0557
BUILT 1914–1947	-0.1034 *	0.0521
BUILT 1948–1969	-0.1867 ***	0.0244
BUILT 1970–1980	-0.1443 ***	0.0217
BUILT 1981–1991	-0.1145 ***	0.0219
HOUSE IS OCCUPIED	-0.2088 ***	0.0440
HOUSE AVAILABILITY MISSING	0.0241	0.0931
NBBATH/NBROOM	0.4876 **	0.1791
NBFLOOR/NBROOM	0.1016	0.0719
$(\text{NBBATH/NBROOM})^2$	-0.2881	0.2086
$(\text{NBFLOOR/NBROOM})^2$	0.0397	0.0788
PARKING : 1 space	0.0801 ***	0.0165
PARKING : 2 spaces	0.0839 ***	0.0239
REALESTATEAGENT	0.0777 ***	0.0137
PREVIOUS SALE TYPE	-0.0506 **	0.0165
YEAR : 2002	0.2168 ***	0.0162
YEAR: 2004	0.4797 ***	0.0165
DISTANCE TO NEAREST CBD	0.0307 ***	0.0076
Approximate significance of smooth terms:	Edf	Est. Rank.
s(X,Y)	27.84 ***	29

R-sq.(adj) = 0.722, Explained deviance = 72.9%, GCV score = 0.0919, Scale est. = 0.089 n = 2,132, Signif. codes: *** 0.001 ** 0.01 * 0.05 . 0.1. The reference is an unoccupied detached house built after 1991 and sold in year 2000. Data source: Public Notaries.

Estimated OLS presents high spatial autocorrelation. Here and in the following example, we used a neighborhood weight matrix of 1, 5, 10 and 20 km to test spatial autocorrelation. Spatial autocorrelation of errors could not be rejected in the OLS model 5.9 for each weight matrix. Introducing such distance regressors does not lead to a significant reduction in spatial autocorrelation with LMlag, RLMlag, LMerr, and RLMerr tests (see Anselin et al. 1996). In contrast, the simplest geoadditive model 5.10 enables complete removal of spatial autocorrelation for 1, 5, 10 and 20 km neighborhood weight matrix.

5.3.2 In Search of a Better Model

The specification process used here consists of step-by-step evaluation of the effects of distance to identify their area of influence and their significance, while controlling the effects of other spatial regressors in the longitude/latitude smooth terms as in equation 5.5. Moreover the results of equation 5.6 shown in Figure 5.3 indicate that the most important effect of location is not related to a CBD but to awareness of a tourist area of special interest (centered on the villages of *Gordes* and *Roussillon*): for the sake of simplification, we called these distances "distance to tourist area" (DIST2TOURIST). We then also calculated these two specific distances and considered them as spatial regressor candidates among other 7 potential CBD distances. Distance to the nearest continuous high urban density area (DVILLAGE) was also introduced as a spatial regressor candidate at this stage.

For each of these 10 distances noted D_i^k, we estimated and plotted the results of the following model:

$$log(P_i) = \beta X_i + s(D_i^k) + s(u_i, v_i) + \varepsilon_i \quad \forall k = 1,2,...,10\,. \tag{5.11}$$

It appears that this segment of the housing market is hardly if at all influenced by CBD distances. After separate investigation of each distance smooth using GAM, only DAVIGNON (distance to Avignon), DAPT (distance to Apt) and DIST2TOURIST appeared to have significant effects on a $\left[0 - \overline{d}\right]$ segment, with at this stage, an unexpected repulsive effect of Apt. DVILLAGE, the distance to the nearest continuous high urban density became significant for houses located 3 km from the village limit. On the left side of Figure 5.4, it can be seen that the spatial variations of the coordinate smooth term in model 5.11 were considerably reduced when DIST2TOURIST was introduced.

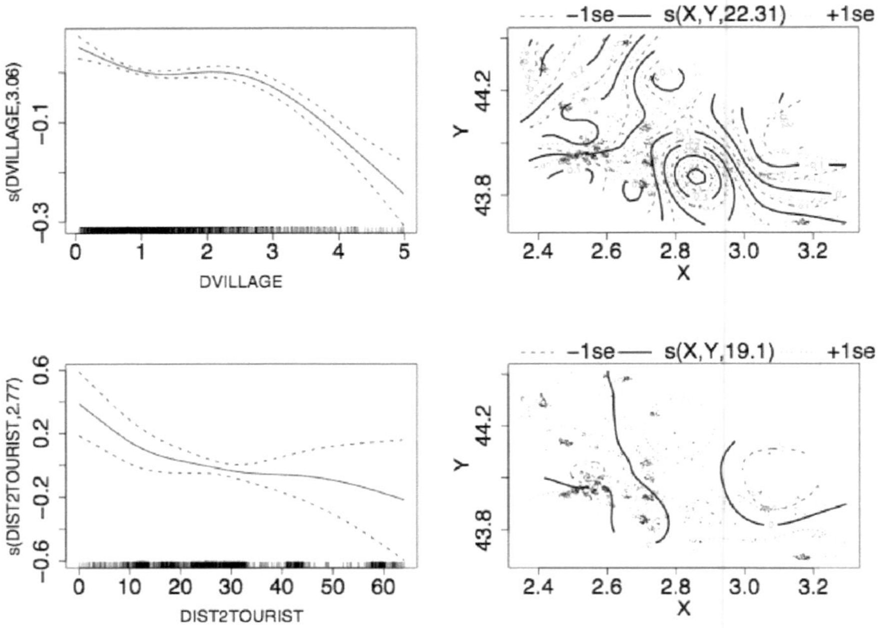

Fig. 5.4 Plot of each Smooth Term for DIST2TOURIST and DVILLAGE in the Corresponding Model (5.11). Data source: Public Notaries

The same specification process was used for the three different types of density index calculated, for which results are not detailed here. It appeared that the three kind of density indexes are rivals to explain house price and that sum and variance to the k nearest existing houses gives the most significant results. Moreover, the effects of variance of distances to the k nearest houses indicate that it could be interesting to introduce cross effect between indexes using small and large k. The intuition behind those cross effects is that high density at a large scale combined with low density in the immediate vicinity may be a desirable characteristic. Finally, the cross effects of the sum of distances to the 15 and 500 nearest houses, denoted DIV15 and DIV500, provided the most significant results.

At the final stage of the specification process, all the selected spatial regressor candidates were estimated in a global GAM model with all the smoothed terms. The results were quite similar to those obtained in model 5.11, which indicates that the coefficients are stable between a GAM model in which a spatial regressor is estimated alone and a GAM model in which other spatial regressors are included. Finally, we noted that Avignon has the largest area of influence as it spreads over a distance of 25 kilometers.

5.3.3 Choosing a Parametric Model

All the spatial regressors identified above are introduced in parametric form, as follows:

$$\begin{aligned} log(P_i) = \beta X_i &+ \alpha_1 I(DAVIGNON < 25km) \cdot DAVIGON \\ &+ \alpha_2 I(DAPT < 10km) \cdot DAPT + \alpha_3 I(DMARSEILLE < 60km) \\ &+ \alpha_4 I(DVILLAGE > 3km) \cdot DVILLAGE + \alpha_6 I(DIV15 > 1) \cdot DIV500 \\ &+ \alpha_7 I(DIST2TOURIST < 15km) \cdot DIST2TOURIST + \varepsilon_i \end{aligned} \tag{5.12}$$

where $I\ (X > x)$ is a dummy variable equal to 1 when $X > x$ and otherwise 0. Table 5.2 presents the results of the final OLS model. Note that due to the heteroskedastic form of the errors (Brush Pagan test = 80.48, df = 37, p-value = 0.000), Table 5.2 presents heteroskedastic robust estimations. As expected, distance effects within the area of influence of all selected distances were negative, with smaller effects beyond. Only distance to the "tourist area" remained significant and had a highly attractive effect on the whole area, and can be interpreted as the distance effect to the heart of the Luberon mountains. The cross effect of close low density with high density at a large scale was confirmed.

Table 5.2 Results of OLS Parametric Model (5.12) using heteroskedastic robust estimation

Variables	Coefficient		Std. Error
Constant	8.4715	***	0.1459
log(SQRFOOT)	0.7696	***	0.0364
log(SQRFOOT/NBROOM)	-0.3392	***	0.0457
log(LOTSIZE)	0.1482	***	0.0133
SWIMMING POOL	0.1583	***	0.0207
HISTORIC HOUSE	0.1713		0.1228
HOUSE IN TOWN	-0.2146	***	0.0615
RUIN	-0.1379	.	0.0790
VILLA	0.1158	***	0.0211
HOUSE TYPE NOT SPECIFIED	-0.0990	**	0.0373
BUILT BEFORE 1850	-0.0894		0.0793
BUILT 1850–1913	-0.1607	*	0.0748
BUILT 1914–1947	-0.0878		0.0619
BUILT 1948–1969	-0.1818	***	0.0229
BUILT 1970–1980	-0.1470	***	0.0189
BUILT 1981–1991	-0.1151	***	0.0186
HOUSE IS OCCUPIED	-0.1858	**	0.0564
HOUSE AVAILABILITY MISSING	0.0315		0.1354
NBBATH/NBROOM	0.6062	**	0.1976
NBFLOOR/NBROOM	0.1095		0.0812
$(NBBATH/NBROOM)^2$	-0.3981		0.2459
$(NBFLOOR/NBROOM)^2$	0.0439		0.0951

Table 5.2 (cont.)

PARKING : 1 space	0.0802	***	0.0165
PARKING : 2 spaces	0.0860	***	0.0249
REALESTATEAGENT	0.0747	***	0.0131
PREVIOUS SALE TYPE	-0.0528	**	0.0167
YEAR : 2002	0.2209	***	0.0165
YEAR : 2004	0.4789	***	0.0157
DAVIGNON < 25 km	-0.1762	***	0.0258
DAVIGNON = 25 km	0.0002		0.0012
DAPT < 10 km	-0.4706	***	0.0836
DAVIGNON = 10 km	0.0370	*	0.0148
DVILLAGE ≥ 3 km	-0.0375	**	0.0121
DVILLAGE < 3 km	0.0260	*	0.0114
DIST2TOURIST ≥ 15 km	-0.0116	***	0.0008
DIST2TOURIST<15 km	-0.0236	***	0.0024
(DIV15≤1)*DV500	0.0000		0.0001
(DIV15 >1)*DV500	-0.0002	*	0.0001

Residual standard error: 0.3009 out of 2,094 degrees of freedom Multiple R-Squared: 0.723, Adjusted R-squared: 0.7181, F-statistic: 147.7 on 37 and 2094 DF, Signif. codes: *** 0.001 ** 0.01 * 0.05 . 0.1. The reference is an unoccupied detached house built after 1991 and sold in year 2000. Data source: Public Notaries.

5.4 GWR and MGWR Tools

The GWR framework was introduced by Brundson, Fortheringham and Charlton in a series of articles (Brunsdon et al. 1996; Fotheringham et al. 1997; Brunsdon et al. 1998; Fotheringham et al. 1999). For a summary of this methodology see Fotheringham et al. (2002). The model used in GWR estimations can be expressed as:

$$y_i = \sum_{j=1}^{p} \beta_j(u_{i'}, v_{i'}) x_{ij} + \varepsilon_i \quad i = 1,2,..,n \,; i' = 1,2,..,n' \,; n' \leq n \tag{5.13}$$

where x_{ij} are the regressors that may include an intercept term. The main contribution of this framework is the use of specific properties of weighted regressions (WLS) to obtain a local estimation of parameters $\beta_j(u_i, v_i)$, with as many regressions as the number of focal points i'. When $i' = i$, n focal points are used to obtain a set of coefficients β for each observation. To determine the value of the p coefficients at location i defined by (u_i, v_i), we built a vector of spatial weights $W(u_i, v_i)$ based on the distances between the location i and other locations of the sample. This procedure was repeated for each focal point $i = 1, 2, \ldots, n$. We then obtained a spatial distribution of the p coefficients, denoted $\beta_j(u_i, v_i)$.

5.4.1 Weights Matrix

The most frequently used functions are based on a "Gaussian" transformation:[5]

$$W(u_i, v_i) = e^{-\left(\frac{di}{h}\right)^2}, \quad h > 0; i = 1, 2, \ldots, n.$$

This kernel's main argument is d_i, the vector of distances between location i and the other locations of the sample. Parameter h, called bandwidth, characterizes the decrease in weight with distance.

5.4.2 Estimation of GWR Coefficients

Using such an $n \times n$ weight matrix, $W(u_i, v_i)$, allows for spatial weighted regressions or GWR. Then for each location i, GWR consists in estimating a WLS model on a subsample defined by the matrix denoted W_i.[6] W_i has 0 $\forall i \neq j$, and $diag(W_i)$ is composed of elements of the ith column of $W(u_i, v_i)$. Then, for each i, local coefficients of GWR are given by:

$$\hat{\beta}(u_i, v_i) = [X'W_i X]^{-1} X'W_i Y. \tag{5.14}$$

It should be noted that focal points i are not necessarily observations and local estimations can be used for each possible location.

5.4.3 Estimation of MGWR Coefficients

The GWR model implies non-stationarity of each regression coefficient. This formulation may appear inadequate for many socio-economic variables that have global effects (taxes, interest rate, date, etc.) independent of individual localization. Moreover, GWR cannot be used with local polytomic variables (zone indexes: state, district, agricultural and environmental zones, etc.) since spatially varying coefficients associated with such polytomic variables may have no meaning. For adequate treatment of these problems, mixed models, or MGWR, were developed. This kind of model can be expressed as:

$$y_i = \sum_{j=1}^{q} \beta_j x_{ij} + \sum_{j=q+1}^{p} \beta_j (u_i, v_i) x_{ij} + \varepsilon_i \quad i = 1, 2, .., n \tag{5.15}$$

The intercept can be inserted between spatially varying coefficients $(j > q)$ or not $(j \leq q)$

---

[5] Other common structures are: bisquare where $W(u_i, v_i) = (1 - (d_i^2 / d^2))^2$ if $d_i \leq \bar{d}$ else $W(u_i, v_i) = 0$; and trisquare where $W(u_i, v_i) = (1 - d_i^3)^3$ if $d_i \leq \bar{d}$ else $W(u_i, v_i) = 0$

[6] In the case of a Gaussian kernel, all the observations are used but are weighted differently according to their localization. In the bisquare and trisquare cases (see note 5 above), only the observations near the focal point are used.

The MGWR was also introduced by the authors of the GWR, with a 7-step estimation, requiring *2 + p* GWR estimations, which is somewhat intensive in terms of computation. Mei et al. (2004, 2006) proposed a two-steps method, based on partial linear models developed in Speckman (1988) and Azzalini and Bowman (1997). This methodology appears to be suitable for empirical studies and large samples.

We denoted variables associated with stationary coefficients $\beta_c XC$ and variables associated with the non-stationary coefficients $\beta_v(u_i, v_i) XV$. To reduce excessive notation and for inference purposes, we can rewrite the estimation of the GWR hat matrix (Hoaglin and Welsch 1978) as:

$$S_v = \begin{pmatrix} XV_1 \left[XV'W_1XV'W_1\right] \\ XV_2 \left[XV'W_2XV'W_2\right] \\ \vdots \\ XV_n \left[XV'W_nXV'W_n\right] \end{pmatrix}$$

It is then possible to define a 2-step estimation of β_c and $\beta_v(u_i, v_i)$, where:

$$\text{Stage 1:} \quad \beta_c = [XC'(I-S_v)'(I-S_v)XC]^{-1} XC'(I-S_v)'(I-S_v)Y$$

$$\text{Stage 2:} \quad \beta_v(u_i, v_i) = [XV'W_iXV]^{-1} XV'W_i(Y - XC\beta_c) \qquad i = 1,2,..,n$$

Moreover, we can define the matrix XC as:

$$S = S_v + (I-S_v)XC[XC'(I-S_v)'(I-S_v)XC]^{-1} XC'(I-S_v)'(I-S_v)\,. \tag{5.16}$$

The fitted value of Y can be simply expressed in matrix formulation: $\hat{Y} = SY$. We note that, when every coefficient is non-stationary, then $X = XV$, and $\hat{Y} = SY$, so $S = S_v$ corresponds to GWR' fitted values. Finally, to make the Residual Sum of Square (RSS) formulation easier, we will denote $R = (I - S)$, where I is an $n \times n$ identity matrix.

5.4.4 Model Specification

Bandwidth Selection

Specification of GWR or MWGR models implies choosing a bandwidth h. Choosing h consists in identifying the relevant sub-samples for local regressions. After defining a threshold value linked to h level, observations have a very low weight ratio and a negligible impact on results. As Paez (2002) notes, choosing bandwidth h is, like the arbitrary choice of locations (u_i, v_i), one of the main problems of geographically weighted methods. As in all non-parametric estimation, the choice of bandwidth implies a trade-off between bias and variance. In order to solve this trade-off, Fotheringham et al. (2002) proposed using the General Cross Validation criteria introduced by Cleveland (1979) and Bowman (1984) for local regressions by kernel. Using such criteria, optimal bandwidth is the solution of:

$$\min_h n\sum_{i=1}^{n}\frac{\left[y_i-\hat{y}_{-i}(h)\right]^2}{(n-v_1)^2} \tag{5.17}$$

where $\hat{y}_{-i}$ is the fitted value $\hat{y}$ without observation i in order to avoid h converging to 0. $V_1 = Tr(S)$ is the effective number of parameters in the GWR and MGWR models. Fotheringham et al. (1999) also proposed a corrected AIC criterion for a given h:

$$AIC_c = 2n\log(\hat{\sigma})+n\log(2\pi)+n\left\{\frac{n+Tr(S)}{n-2-Tr(S)}\right\}. \tag{5.18}$$

For MGWR, Mei et al. (2004) proposed to adapt GCV, with the following program:

$$\min_h \sum_{i=1}^{n}\left(\frac{y_i-\hat{y}_{-i}(h)}{1-S_{ii}(h)}\right)^2 \tag{5.19}$$

where $S_{ii}(h)$ is the ith element of $diag(S)$ when the bandwidth value is h.

Non Stationary Tests on Parameters

As with all non-parametric procedures, the inference methodology is difficult to use as there no global distribution of estimated coefficients is specified. The difficulty here arises from the necessity of aggregating a large number of local regressions in a single test to answer a global question "Is the GWR model preferable to the OLS one?", which is equivalent to "Are coefficients spatially non-stationary?".

So first, we can test OLS against GWR. Three asymptotic tests allow such a hypothesis to be tested (Fotheringham et al. 1999; Leung et al. 2000a). Second, we can test the non-stationarity of each coefficient, one by one (Leung and al. 2000a). In this case, we consider that the GWR model may have some stationary parameters (in which case a MGWR model would be more appropriate).

Fotheringham et al. (1999) were the first to propose an asymptotic test for OLS against GWR alternatives. The test was based on results obtained by Kendall and Stuart (1977) to approximate the distribution for the statistic. They propose to test:

$$\begin{cases} H_0: \dfrac{\partial\beta_i}{\partial u} \equiv \dfrac{\partial\beta_k}{\partial v} \equiv 0 \quad \forall k \\ H_1: \dfrac{\partial\beta_i}{\partial u} \not\equiv \dfrac{\partial\beta_k}{\partial v} \not\equiv 0 \quad \forall k \end{cases}$$

The statistic proposed by Fotheringham and al. (1999) is constructed as:

$$F_{BFC99} = \frac{(RSS(H_0) - RSS(H_1))/\tau_1}{RSS(H_1)/\delta_1} \tag{5.20}$$

where $RSS = YRY$, $\delta_1 = Tr(R_1)$ and $\tau_1 = Tr(R_0 - R_1)$ has an approximate F-distribution equal to $F(\tau_1^2/\tau_2, \delta_1^2/\delta_2)$, where $\tau_2 = Tr[(R_0 - R_1)'(R_0 - R_1)]$ and $\delta_2 = Tr(R_1'R_1)$.

Leung and al. (2000a) proposed two alternative tests of the following hypothesis:

$$\begin{cases} H_0 : \beta_k(u_i, v_i) = \beta_k \quad \forall k, i \\ H_1 : \text{At least one of the } \beta_k(u_i, v_i) \text{ is varying with } i \end{cases}$$

They showed that if $E(\hat{y}_i) = E(y_i)\ \forall i$, then the RSS used in the two following statistical tests follow approximately a χ^2. The first test proposed supports the idea that under H_0 the ratio of the two RSS competing models is close to:

$$F_{LMZ1} = \frac{RSS(H_1)/\delta_1}{RSS(H_0)/(n - p - 1)}. \tag{5.21}$$

F_{LMZ1} has an approximate F-distribution equal to $F(\delta_1^2/\delta_2, n - p - 1)$, where $\delta_2 = [Tr(R_1'R_1)]^2$.

Their second test is constructed as follows:

$$F_{LMZ2} = \frac{(RSS(H_0) - RSS(H_1))/\tau_1}{RSS(H_0)/(n - p - 1)}. \tag{5.22}$$

F_{LMZ2} has an approximate F-distribution $F(\tau_1^2/\tau_2, n - p - 1)$.

Leung et al. (2000a) also proposed a test to check the variation of each set of parameters. As this test is computationally intensive and does not allow to test GWR vs. MGWR, we prefer to use the bootstrap approach proposed by Mei (2004) that allows stationary and/or significance of coefficients in MGWR models to be tested. This test is described in the following section.

Significance Tests

Using results of weighted regressions, we can easily dispose of local study statistics of every non-stationary coefficient for GWR or MGWR models. The spatial distribution of these statistical values may be a useful exploratory tool in the specification stage. We can easily distinguish coefficients that are significant from those that are not. Among the latter, we can identify variables that have a significant influence only in certain zones, and more generally, if the coefficient significance is spatially coherent.

Leung et al. (2000a) proposed a stepwise procedure to identify important variables to integrate in GWR models. It uses a statistic, analogue to F_{LMZ1}, that allows comparison of *RSS* in two GWR models, in which only one variable is added or omitted. For the forward selection, let M be a GWR model at a given step of the procedure, then the test to add variable k can be expressed as:

$$R_{LMZ}(+\beta_k x_k) = \frac{RSS(M+\beta_k x_k)/\delta_1(M+\beta_k x_k)}{RSS(M)/\delta_1(M)} \quad k \leq p \cdot \tag{5.23}$$

$R_{LMZ}(+\beta_k x_k)$ has an approximate F-distribution equal to $F(\delta_1^2(M+\beta_k x_k)/\delta_2(M+\beta_k x_k)), \delta_1^2(M)/\delta_2(M))$.

Mei (2004) proposed an inference framework of the MGWR model based on a bootstrap test. The proposed framework allows the significance and/or non-stationarity of each coefficient of MGWR to be tested, regardless of whether the coefficient is part of OLS, or GWR is part of the MGWR model. The only limitation is that the bootstrap requires repeated MGWR estimation, which is time consuming. The statistic proposed by Mei (2004) to test H_0 against H_1, in which H_0 corresponds to the stationary or the nullity of one of the p coefficient, is:

$$T = Y'(R_0 - R_1)Y/Y'R_1Y \,. \tag{5.24}$$

We computed $MGWR_0$, $MGWR_1$ and T in the first step. Using ε, the centered residuals of $MGWR_1$, we drew a bootstrap sample ε^* with replacement, computed $Y^* = S_0Y + \varepsilon^*$ and repeated it B times. Using (5.24), we then obtained T^* and computed the bootstrap p-value of the test:

$$p^* = \#\{T_i^*; T_i^* \geq T\}/B \,. \tag{5.25}$$

Spatial Autocorrelation Tests

Using MGWR (or GWR) does not preclude the presence of any remaining spatial autocorrelation, especially spatial autocorrelation based on another weighting structure than the one used in MGWR (or GWR). $\overline{W}$ denotes a specific weight matrix representing the underlying spatial structure of spatial autocorrelation. Let H_0 be the hypothesis that there is no spatial autocorrelation between the disturbances ε with $\varepsilon\,(\varepsilon \sim N(0, \sigma^2 I))$. Leung et al. (2000b) proposed the following expression of Moran's I_0 :

$$I_0 = \frac{\varepsilon' R' \overline{W} R \varepsilon}{\varepsilon R' R \varepsilon} \cdot \tag{5.26}$$

A three-moment χ^2 approximation of the p-value of I_0 can be used (see Leung et al. 2000b).

To our knowledge, there is no suitable spatial autocorrelation test for the MGWR model. To get around this problem, and due to the fact that the two final MGWR models have only one or two non-stationary coefficients out of more than 15 parameters, we used an empirical method to perform OLS spatial autocorrelation tests on the following models:

$$y_i = y_i - \sum_{j=q+1}^{p} \hat{\beta}_k(u_i, v_i) XV_i = \sum_{j=1}^{q} \beta_j x_{ij} + \varepsilon_i \quad i = 1, 2, .., n \cdot \tag{5.27}$$

For OLS regression (5.27), we then performed Moran's I test, unidirectional and bidirectional tests of the Spatial Autocorrelation and spatial lag models (LMerr, RLMerr, LMlag, RLMlag, see Anselin et al. 1996) with different spatial weight matrix.

5.5 Comparing the Estimation of Spatial Variable Coefficient Models by GAM and MGWR

To illustrate the similar features of MGWR[7] and geoadditive models, and particularly the relations between bandwidth in MGWR models and basis dimension in GAM, we compared estimations of the following models by MGWR and GAM:

$$\begin{cases} \text{GAM:} & log(P_i) = \beta X_i + s(u_i, v_i) + \varepsilon_i \\ \text{MGWR:} & log(P_i) = \beta_0(u_i, v_i) + \beta_1 X_i + \varepsilon_i \end{cases} \quad \text{M1}$$

$$\begin{cases} \text{GAM:} & log(P_i) = \beta X_i + SWIMMINGPOOL_i \times s(u_i, v_i) + s(u_i, v_i) + \varepsilon_i \\ \text{MGWR:} & log(P_i) = \beta_0(u_i, v_i) + \beta_1(u_i, v_i) \times SWIMMINGPOOL_i + \beta X_i + \varepsilon_i \end{cases} \quad \text{M2}$$

$$\begin{cases} \text{GAM:} & log(P_i) = \beta X_i + REALESTATEAGENT_i \times s(u_i, v_i) + s(u_i, v_i) + \varepsilon_i \\ \text{MGWR:} & log(P_i) = \beta_0(u_i, v_i) + \beta_1(u_i, v_i) \times REALESTATEAGENT_i + \beta X_i + \varepsilon_i \end{cases} \quad \text{M3}$$

For all MGWR estimations, we used the Gaussian weighting scheme. For M2 and M3, we estimated two bootstrap tests: one tests the nullity of the parameter under consideration, one tests the spatial stationarity of the same parameter. One notable difference between MWGR models and GAM for M2 and M3 is that the variable associated with the spatial varying parameter can also be included in the set of spatial stationary variables X_i in GAM. So in GAM, we can break down the

[7] All the preceding GWR and MGWR procedures were programmed in R language from an adaptation (email to geniaux@avignon.inra.fr for further information) of the SPGWR package (Bivand and Yu 2006).

variable between the stationary and non-stationary parts. This break-down is impossible in MGWR models because it leads to a non-full rank matrix.

In MGWR and GWR, the smaller the bandwidth h, the smaller the estimated degree of freedom *EDF*. So we propose to choose h following three different criteria to compare MGWR models and GAM: (i) GCV optimization (h^*); (ii) similarity of *EDF* between MGWR models and GAM estimations ($\bar{h}$); and (iii) minimization of difference between MGWR and GAM residuals (h).

In the example in section 5.2, we used a 30 basis dimension proposed by default in the *mgcv* library. Like for bandwidth in the MGWR estimation, in GAM, the results depend on the basis dimension: if we use more than 30 dimensions, both smoothed and non-smoothed parameters may change. Figure 5.5 illustrates changes in the estimated degree of freedom *vs* the residual sum of squares (RSS) when k is increased by increments of 10 between 0 and 300. We can see that above the level of 2,060 for RSS, the first derivative is no longer constant and starts to decrease: above this level, we pay too much for an increase in k. The curve breaks near the scale of $10\ n^{2/9}$ proposed by Kim and Gu (2004); in our case 50. As pointed out by Wood (2004), it is difficult to adopt a basis dimension of $10\ n^{2/9}$ for use in all circumstances; the modeler thus needs to choose a basis dimension that allows just the right flexibility. In the Geoadditive case, the issue is to choose a basis dimension that does not lead to spatial adjustment of the parameter for areas with few data[8]. Moreover, results have to be interpretable in terms of territorial analysis: it is possible to compare the evolution of the smoothed term on maps with a different basis dimension to obtain a trade-off between added spatial information and the basis dimension. In the following, we used a fixed basis dimension of 40 for the GAM estimation.

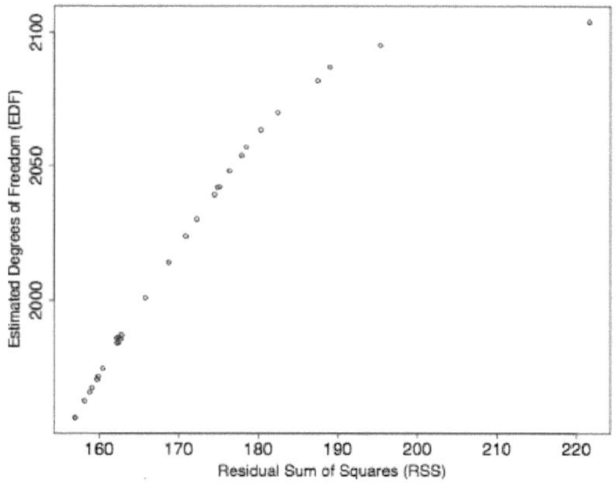

Fig. 5.5 Residual Sum of Squares (RSS) against Estimated Degrees of Freedom (EDF) with Basis Dimension $k \in [0, 300]$ Increased by Increments of 10. Data source: Public Notaries

[8] It also possible to choose the potential knots arbitrarily to avoid this problem, see Wood 2006 page 262.

5.5.1 Geoadditive Models vs. MGWR Spatial Varying Intercept

The estimations of M1 by GAM and MGWR for the non spatial varying coefficients are reported in Table 5.3:

Table 5.3 Comparison of MGWR and GAM Estimation of Stationary Coefficients in M1

	MGWR (OLS part) Coefficients			GAM Coefficient
	$h^* = 4.8$	$\bar{h} = 6.9$	$\tilde{h} = 7.5$	$k = 40$
log(SQRFOOT)	0.7600***	0.7712***	0.7734***	0.7670***
log(SQRFOOT/NBROOM)	-0.3411***	-0.3491***	-0.3498***	-0.3511***
log(LOTSIZE)	0.1431***	0.1421***	0.1423***	0.1424***
SWIMMING POOL	0.1724***	0.1682***	0.1678***	0.1700***
HISTORIC HOUSE	0.1161	0.0984	0.0923	0.1389
HOUSE IN TOWN	-0.2212***	-0.2274***	-0.2293***	-0.2101***
RUIN	-0.1480*	-0.1485*	-0.1498*	-0.1307*
VILLA	0.1023***	0.1104***	0.1130***	0.0972***
HOUSE TYPE NOT SPECIFIED	-0.0849*	-0.0888*	-0.0894*	-0.0895*
BUILT BEFORE 1850	-0.0829	-0.0772	-0.0741	-0.0937
BUILT 1850–1913	-0.1560**	-0.1589**	-0.1588**	-0.1636**
BUILT 1914–1947	-0.1032*	-0.1061*	-0.1062*	-0.1134*
BUILT 1948–1969	-0.1951***	-0.1972***	-0.1979***	-0.1896***
BUILT 1970–1980	-0.1468***	-0.1502***	-0.1511***	-0.1446***
BUITL 1981–1991	-0.1140***	-0.1207***	-0.1224***	-0.1126***
HOUSE IS OCCUPIED	-0.2133***	-0.2130***	-0.2134***	-0.2063***
HOUSE AVAILABILITY MISSING	0.0386	0.0325	0.0301	0.0324
NBBATH/NBROOM	0.3499.	0.4034*	0.4172*	0.4072*
NBFLOOR/NBROOM	0.1337.	0.1345.	0.1366.	0.1237.
$(\text{NBBATH/NBROOM})^2$	-0.1490	-0.1970	-0.2086	-0.1960
$(\text{NBFLOOR/NBROOM})^2$	-0.0090	0.0060	0.0081	0.0031
PARKING : 1 space	0.0788***	0.0746***	0.0733***	0.0796***
PARKING : 2 spaces	0.0940***	0.0897***	0.0878***	0.0845***
REAL ESTATE AGENT	0.0814***	0.0817***	0.0817***	0.0792***
PREVIOUS SALE TYPE	-0.0483**	-0.0479***	-0.0478**	-0.0507**
YEAR : 2002	0.2263***	0.2241***	0.2233***	0.2190***
YEAR : 2004	0.4805***	0.4815***	0.4815***	0.4767***
RSS	181.4868	187.4044	188.8177	187.4445
Estimated Degree of Freedom (EDF)	2,060.049	2,078.598	2,081.597	2,081.736
GCV	0.3060	0.3071	0.3076	not omparable

Signif. codes: *** 0.001 ** 0.01 * 0.05 . 0.1 Data source: Public Notaries.

For the $\tilde{h}$ criteria that gives 6.9 km, we can see that coefficients of the OLS part of both models are very similar. With a comparable EDF, i.e. with 7.5 km bandwidth ($\bar{h}$ criteria), the GAM model appears to be a little more efficient with a slightly lower RSS. With minimization of *GCV* (h^* criteria), we obtain a smaller bandwidth with $h^* = 4.8$ km that reduced the residuals relatively little compared with the loss of the degree of freedom.

The upper part of Figure 5.6 shows, using quartile classes, that for MGWR with $\tilde{h}$ bandwidth, spatial varying coefficients are also quite similar to the evaluation at the same location with the GAM spatial smooth. The performance of the four estimations is almost the same regarding the spatial auto-correlation issue. For weight matrix with 5, 10 and 20 km neighborhood weight matrix, and for the three bandwidths, MGWR does not result in spatial autocorrelation of residuals, as in the GAM estimation. For MGWR with weight matrix of a 1 km neighborhood weight matrix, spatial autocorrelation is clearly present for $\bar{h}$ and $\tilde{h}$ (p-value < 0.001) but the h^* bandwidth allows rejection of spatial autocorrelation of residuals at 5%. In the GAM estimation, absence of spatial autocorrelation of residuals is rejected at 5% but accepted at 1%. So for a comparable EDF with the same regressors, GAM seems to reduce the spatial auto-correlation of residuals in our sample more significantly than MGWR.

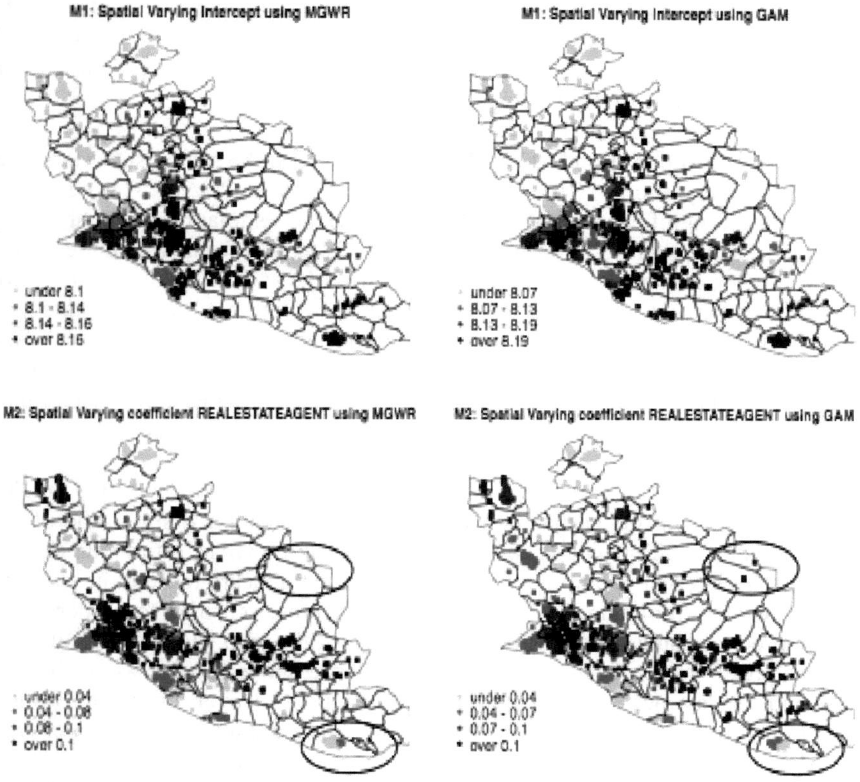

Fig. 5.6 Comparison of MGWR and GAM Estimations for M1 and M2 Models. Data source: Public Notaries

We note that in GAM M1 the house price can vary by ± 30% depending on the location of the house. Even if these variations are reduced to ± 13% by excluding the first and last deciles, our results highlight the importance of identifying the environmental, economic and social characteristics that explain these spatial variations in the implicit price.

5.5.2 Spatially Varying Coefficients: GAM vs. MGWR

To compare the M2 and M3 models, we considered two different spatial varying coefficients. The variables associated with these spatial varying coefficients were dummies, but estimations can be made in the same way with continuous variables. The most notable difference between GAM and MGWR is that the variables REALESTATEAGENT or SWIMMINGPOOL are included in the stationary set X_i in GAM but not in MGWR. Thus, the p-value associated to the spatial varying coefficient in M2 and M3 GAM models can be directly interpreted as a stationary test. In MGWR, we estimated two models – one in which the coefficient was included in the non-stationary set and one in which the coefficient was considered as stationary. Next we performed a bootstrap test as described in section 5.4.3. In the following, we estimated MGWR only with $\overline{h}$ in order to obtain estimations that are comparable with EDF.

In estimations of M1 and M2 by MGWR and GAM, the spatial stationary coefficients are very similar. The spatial varying coefficient REALESTATEAGENT appears to be significant in both models. In the GAM estimation, the spatial varying coefficient REALESTATEAGENT p-value is 0.0034 for a basis dimension of 15. The value of the spatial smooth is between -0.10 and 0.22, which can be considered as a percent (-10% to 22%) of the spatial evolution of the real estate agent implicit price. This evolution is around the constant implicit price of real estate agent estimated in GAM as 0.083. So the GAM estimation finds that the price of the house changes from -2% to + 30 % depending on whether a real estate intervenes and also depending on the location where the agent intervenes.

In MGWR, EDF is similar to the GAM models for a bandwidth of 6.9 km. The spatial varying coefficient lies between [-0.33, 0.36], with a first quartile of 0.04 and a mean of 0.084 which is comparable to that in the GAM estimation (mean = 0.083). The interval of implicit price variation first appears to be quite different, notably for the minimum. MGWR appears to be more sensitive to border effects and to produce some “outliers” near the borders of the map. However, only six locations give a value under -0.02 and almost 50 are above 0.30. If we exclude the first and the last percentile of this interval, we then recover similar intervals of variation from MGWR and GAM for the spatial varying coefficient REALESTATEAGENT. However, as can be seen in lower part of Figure 5.6, some coefficients, highlighted by circles, are quite different in GAM and MGWR.

For the spatial varying coefficient SWIMMINGPOOL, results in GAM and MGWR differed considerably. In GAM, the spatial varying coefficient SWIMMINGPOOL was not significant (p-value = 0.72) and led to an interval of [0.14, 0.18] if we still considered the value of the coefficient. In MGWR, we obtained an interval of [-0.05, 0.74], a first quartile equal to 0.11, and a third quartile equal to 0.23, while the means were similar in both estimations. Moreover more than 95% of the local estimate of this coefficient in MGWR gave student's t tests of more than 2.5. In MGWR, bootstrap tests confirmed the significance of the term against nullity (p-value = 0.0093, with 10,000 replications), but accepted spatial stationarity (p-value = 0.2389, with 10,000 replications). Thus we can conclude that SWIMMINGPOOL is stationary in both models.

Finally, results in GAM and MGWR converged regarding the spatial varying coefficients, but MGWR requires the systematic use of stationarity tests using bootstrap tests due to the absence of asymptotic tests for MGWR inference. This result highlights certain potential problems of GWR in which the significance of the coefficient measured by local student's t-tests in every sub-sample is not a guarantee that the coefficient really is non stationary even when the coefficients vary a lot. Moreover, available GWR asymptotic stationary tests (Fotheringham et al. 1999; Leung et al. 2000a) too often conclude that a coefficient is non stationary.

5.6 Conclusion

One of the main interests of MGWR and GWR tools in hedonic analysis, beyond the capacity to reduce spatial autocorrelation of residuals, is to offer a framework for dealing with the debatable hypothesis of perfect information on the house characteristics over large sample. For example, French census data indicates that more than 80% of people buy house no further than 20 km from their work location: most buyers probably mainly consider houses located in a target area. So for regional or national house sales databases, MGWR with an adapted bandwidth and weighting scheme can offer a convenient solution to avoid spatial segmentation and to keep in the model a set of stationary coefficients. MGWR generally enables a significant gain in model adjustment compared to OLS. However, Geoadditive models appear to be even better. GAM fits better than MGWR, is even more flexible in articulating stationary and non stationary coefficients, works well with a big sample and makes investigating non linearity easy. The question of colinearity needs to be better addressed in geoadditive models to avoid inappropriate conclusions about non stationarity.

References

Anselin L (1988) Spatial Econometrics: Methods and Models. Kluwer Academic Publishers, Dordrecht, The Netherlands.Kluwer Academic Publishers, Dordrecht, The Netherlands

Anselin L (2001) Spatial effects in econometric practice in environmental and resource economics. American Journal of Agricultural Economics 83: 705– 710

Anselin L, Bera AK, Florax R, Yoon MJ (1996) Simple diagnostic test for spatial dependance. Regional Science and Urban Economics 26: 77–104

Azzalini A, Bowman A (1997) Applied Smoothing Techniques for Data Analysis. Oxford University Press, NewYork

Bivand R, Yu D (2006) Geographically weighted regression. R package version 0.3-12, http://ncg.nuim.ie/ncg/GWR/index.htm

Bowman A (1984) An alternative method of cross-validation for the smoothing of density estimate. Biometrika 71: 353–360

Brueckner JK (2001) Urban sprawl: Lessons from urban economics. In: Gale WG, Rothenberg J (eds) Brookings-Wharton Papers on Urban Affairs. Brookings Institution Press, pp 65–89

Brunsdon C, Fotheringham AS, Charlton M (1996) Geographically weighted regression: A method for exploring spatial nonstationarity. Geographical Analysis 28: 281–298

Brunsdon C, Fotheringham AS, Charlton M (1998) Spatial nonstationarity and autoregressive models. Environment and Planning A 30: 957–993

Cleveland W (1979) Robust locally weighted regression and smoothing scatter-plots. Journal of the American Statistical Association 74: 829–836

Craven P, Wahba G (1979) Smoothing noisy data with spline functions. Numerische Mathematik 31: 377–403

Des Rosiers F, Thiérault M (1996) Houses prices, neighborhood factors and spatial dynamics: improving hedonic modeling using trend surface analysis. Working Paper, Faculté des sciences de l'Administration, Laval University, Québec, CA

Fotheringham AS, Charlton M, Brunsdon C (1997) Two techniques for exploring nonstationarity in geographical data. Geographical Systems 4: 59– 82

Fotheringham AS, Brunsdon C, Charlton M (1999) Some notes on parametric significance tests for geographically weigthed regression. Journal of Regional Science 39: 497–524

Fotheringham AS, Brunsdon C, Charlton M (2002) Geographically Weighted Regression: The Analysis of Spatially Varying Relationships. John Wiley & Sons, New York

Geniaux G, Napoléone C (2005) Rente foncière et anticipations dans le périurbain. *Economie et Prévision 68*: 77–92

Hastie TJ, Tibshirani R (1990) Generalized Additive Models. Chapman and Hall, London

Hastie TJ, Tibshirani R (1993) Varying-coefficient models. Journal of the Royal Statistical Society B55: 757–796

Hoaglin D, Welsch RE (1978) The hat matrix in regression and anova. The American Statistician 32: 17–22

Kammann EE, Wand MP (2003) Geoadditive models. Journal of the Royal Statistical Society C52: 1–18

Kendall M, Stuart A (1977) The advanced theory of statistics. Griffin, London

Kim YJ, Gu C (2004) Smoothing spline gaussian regression: more scalable computation via efficient approximation. Journal of the Royal Statistical Society B66: 337–356

Leung Y, Mei C, Zhang W (2000a) Statistical tests for spatial nonstationarity based on the geographically weighted regression model. Environment And Planning A32: 9–32

Leung Y, Mei C, Zhang W (2000b) Testing for spatial autocorrelation among the residuals of the geographically weighted regression. Environment And Planning A32: 871–890
Mei C (2006) Geographically weighted regression technique for spatial data analysis. Working Paper of School Science, Xi'an Jiaotong University
Mei C, He S, Fang K (2004) A note on the mixed geographically weighted regression model. Journal of Regional Science 44: 143–157
Paez A (2002) Spatial parametric non-stationarity: a variance heterogeneity approach. Working Paper, Centre for Spatial Analysis, School of Geography and Geology, McMaster University
Paez A, Uchida T, Miyamoto K (2001) Spatial association and heterogeneity issues in land price models. Urban Studies 38: 1493–1508
Plantinga A, Lubowski R, Stavins R (2002) The effects of potential land development on agricultural land prices. Journal of Urban Economics 52: 561–581
Quigley JM (1995) A simple hybrid model for estimating real estate price indexes. Journal of Housing Economics 4: 1–12
Speckman P (1988) Kernel smoothing in partial linear model. Journal of the Royal Statistical Society B50: 413–436
Wood S (2004) Stable and efficient multiple smoothing parameter estimation for generalized additive models. Journal of the American Statistical Association 99: 673–686
Wood S (2006) Generalized Additive Models: An Introduction with R. Chapman and Hall, CRC

6 Estimating Hedonic Models of Consumer Demand with an Application to Urban Sprawl

Patrick Bajari[1], Matthew E. Kahn[2]

[1]University of Minnesota and NBER, Minneapolis, United States

[2]University of California, Los Angeles and NBER, United States

6.1 Introduction

Hedonic regressions are one of the most commonly used techniques in applied microeconomics for the study differentiated product markets. Hedonic regressions date back at least 80 years (see Waugh 1928) and have been an active research area for several decades, with seminal contributions by Grillches (1971), Rosen (1974), Epple (1987) and Taylor (this Volume). In this chapter, we describe a flexible, but computationally simple approach for estimating structural models of consumer demand using hedonics. The framework is an application of Bajari and Benkard (2005) and Bajari and Kahn (2005), which builds on the classic Rosen hedonic two-step (Rosen 1974; Epple 1987). In a first stage estimation, a flexible home price regression is estimated using local linear regression. Second, using the results from the local linear regression, we recover the implicit price faced by each household in our data set and the marginal utility of each household for every product characteristic. This allows us to generate a nonparametric distribution of random coefficients for the various product characteristics in our data set. Third, we regress the random coefficients on consumer demographics in order to learn about the joint distribution of tastes and demographic characteristics.

As an application of our methods, we study the incentives for suburbanization by househods in a unique data set of housing purchases from Los Angeles during 2000–2003. In the year 2000, across all metropolitan areas, 54 % of employed heads of households lived in a single detached home and commuted to work by private vehicle. Flight from blight may explain some of the demand for suburbanization (Mieskowski and Mills 1993) but suburbanization is ubiquitous across the entire United States (Margo 1992; Glaeser and Kahn 2004). Suburban housing products offer several benefits. The housing stock is newer. The home's interior space and lot size are larger. Suburban communities tend to self select

A. Baranzini et al. (eds.), *Hedonic Methods in Housing Markets*, doi: 10.1007/978-0-387-76815-1_6,

richer, more highly educated households. Thus, on average, these communities offer greater local peer effects. In a monocentric city, a major cost of suburbanization is a longer commute. As employment has sprawled, this bundling of long commutes with new housing has been attenuated. Dispersed employment has shortened suburbanites' commute times (Gordon et al. 1989).

In this paper, we use Los Angeles county home transaction data from 2000 to 2003 to estimate how heterogeneous home buyers value the various attributes of urban versus suburban housing. In particular, we estimate the valuation for square footage, lot size, community characteristics and commute times to employment centers. Los Angeles is the right place to study the benefits and costs of suburban sprawl. For households with incomes above $53,000, 63% of employed Los Angeles heads of households live in single detached homes and commute to work by private vehicle[1]. This is a metropolitan area with dispersed employment centers (Giuliano and Small 1991). Only 6.5% of Los Angeles workers commute by public transit.

Our housing demand model yields estimates of the willingness to pay for the physical characteristics of the home such as its age, the structure's square feet and the lot size. In addition, we estimate willingness to pay for community attributes such as access to high human capital neighbors and the demographic composition of the neighborhood. We also provide new estimates of the willingness to pay to avoid commuting.

After measuring the private benefits of sprawl, we then use our estimates to investigate the welfare effects of two anti-sprawl policies. There is an ongoing concern that there is excess urban expansion in major U.S cities (for an overview see Nechyba and Walsh 2004). "Cities, it is claimed, take up too much space, encroaching excessively on agricultural land. [...] Excessive urban expansion also means overly long commutes, which generate traffic congestion while contributing to air pollution. Unfettered suburban growth is also thought to reduce the incentive for redevelopment of land closer to city centers, contributing to the decay of the downtown areas. Finally, by spreading people out, low-density suburban development may reduce social interaction, weakening the bonds that underpin a healthy society (Brueckner 2000)".

Using our housing demand model, we focus on the commute time consequences of low density living. In our first experiment, we shrink the lot size and square footage of all suburban homes. We then ask for each household, holding fixed each household's place of work, is the lower utility from smaller homes

---

[1] This fact is generated using the 1% Integrated Public Use Microdata Series (IPUMS) data from the 2000 Census of Population and Housing. The income cutoff of $53,000 represents the median household income for the set of Los Angeles households where the head of household works. For all Los Angeles heads of households who work, 47% live in detached housing and commute by private vehicle.

compensated for by the shorter commute? We also examine the incidence of this policy by demographic group to determine who are the winners and losers from such a policy. In our second policy experiment, we "monocentricize" Los Angeles by sending all employment back to the Central Business District. In this case suburban commutes become much longer. We estimate how much suburban home buyers would lose and how much urban home buyers would gain from such an employment sprawl reversal. Employment sprawl unbundles the commute time versus land consumption tradeoff. Our welfare analysis builds on recent work that has evaluated the intended and unintended consequences of different housing policies (see Arnott 1995; Glaeser and Luttmer 2003; Peng and Wheaton 1994; Phillips and Goodstein 2000; Thorsnes 2000).

6.2 The Data

The data source is First American Real Estate Solutions. First American's Metroscan houses a comprehensive database of residential, commercial, industrial and vacant property obtained from county assessors and other agencies. The data in Metroscan initially comes from the county assessor's office. We focus solely on single detached homes sold in Los Angeles county over the years 2000 to 2003. For each home, we observe its sales price, year built, unit square footage, and lot square footage. This specific information on the unit's physical size and its lot size are crucial inputs for measuring the demand for private space. Other data sources such as the Census of Population and Housing do not provide this information and the American Housing Survey surveys only a small number of homeowners in any metropolitan area.

Our data set provides each unit's street address. Thus, we know the unit's zip code, census tract and census bloc. Each census tract has an average of 4,000 people. We use these geographic identifiers to merge on data from the 2000 Census of Population and Housing. In particular, we merge on data regarding the socio-economic composition of the home owner's census tract and census block (namely the geographical area's educational attainment, racial and ethnic composition) and information on each census tract's population density and average one way commuting time in minutes. The 2000 Census data provides some tract level means by owner status. For example, we can construct the average household size and median household income for home owners in each census tract. We will use this information below when we discuss aggregation of consumer preferences.

The First American data provides us with the last name of each home purchaser. Based on this information, we assign each person a dummy variable that equals one if the last name is Hispanic and a second dummy variable that equals one if the last name is Asian[2]. In an immigrant city such as Los Angeles where Hispanics and Asians represent a large share of the population, it is important to recover housing preferences for such subgroups.

The data set includes over 173,000 transactions with a large enough number of transactions within zip codes to allow for within zip code hedonic estimation. We drop from the First American sample those observations that report a sales price of zero. We also trim the left and right tails of the pricing distribution dropping the bottom and top 1 percent of the pricing sample.

To appreciate the strengths of this data set it is useful to contrast it with more conventional micro data from the 2000 Census of Population and Housing. Home price data from the 2000 Census of Population and Housing is self reported and is top coded at $875,000. In addition, home prices are partitioned into only 23 mutually exclusive categories. The last six categories measured in $1,000s are 225, 275, 350, 450, 625, and 875. Clearly such crude categories could miss significant amounts of the "action" between communities. Census data only provides scanty information on the structure's quality such as the number of rooms and the unit's year built. Finally, the public use micro data are much more geographically aggregated. In the 5% sample of the 2000 Integrated Public Use Microdata Series (IPUMS), Public Use Microdata Areas (PUMAs) are identified. These are geographical units of roughly 100,000 people. In this paper, we seek to measure preferences for living in much smaller communities at the census block or census tract level.

While our data set has a number of advantages over traditional Census micro data for studying the demand for sprawled housing products, we must acknowledge the data set's limitations. As discussed above, we have very limited information on the demographics of each home buyer. In addition, unlike the Census, we do not have information on renters. Thus, the distributions of preferences we recover are for the select sample of households who chose to own and have purchased a home during the years 2000 to 2003 in Los Angeles county. In pooling repeat cross-sections over the year 2000 through 2003, we are assuming that the distribution of preferences is stable over this time period. A feature of the First American data base is that the data set only includes information on the most recent transaction. Thus, if a home sold in June 2000 and January 2002, we would not see the June 2000 transaction in our data set. To avoid attrition bias, we chose to include in our sample only homes that had transacted in the previous three years. We are confident for this short window that multiple sales are unlikely to be an important issue.

---

2 While we acknowledge that our assignment of people to ethnic categories based on last names may lead to some miscoding, this piece of household level information is useful for recovering preferences for specific subgroups of the population.

In Table 6.1, we report our sample's summary statistics. Home prices, structure quality and neighborhood attributes vary greatly across the county. Both average home prices and average commute times are much higher than the national average. The average sales price in our sample is $329,000. Relative to new Hispanic owners, the average new Asian buyer is living at much lower density and has a slightly lower average commute time to work. Hispanics are choosing communities where 54 percent of the community is Hispanic. Asians are more likely to choose communities with more college graduates.

Table 6.1 Summary Statistics for Los Angeles Homes Sold Between 2000 and 2003

Variables	Whole sample (N=173,507)		Asian Buyer (N=14,274)	Hispanic Buyer (N=50,766)
	Mean	Std. dev	Mean	Mean
Price [US$]	328,695	1,602,895	363,565	226,008
Structure [square feet]	1,568.579	648.046	1,793.183	1,332.150
Lot Size [square feet]	7,217.682	6,005.796	7,897.708	6,703.124
Age of Structure	48.105	20.940	43.171	51.420
Block Group % Black	0.084	0.145	0.039	0.095
Block Group % Hispanic	0.349	0.265	0.262	0.538
Block Group % College Graduates	0.265	0.188	0.333	0.152
Block Group Median Income [US$]	57,781.090	25,401.430	62,576.010	46,942.720
Population Density [1000 per square mile]	3.216	2.388	2.911	3.906
One Way Commute [Minutes]	4.970	4.970	31.392	31.903

Data source: First American and Census of Population and Housing

6.3 The Model

In this section, we build a model of housing demand for purchasers of single detached housing in Los Angeles county during the years 2000 to 2003. A home $j = 1, \ldots, J$ is modeled as a bundle of four types of characteristics. First are the structural characteristics of the home which will include attributes such as the structure's square footage, lot size and year built. The second set of characteristics are community attributes. In our application, this will include the average demographics of persons in census block, such as the fraction of college educated households and the racial composition of households. Third, is the commuting time from home to work. Finally, there will be some characteristics of the home that are observed by households, but not the economist[3]. Households solve the following static utility maximization problem:

$$u_{ij} = \max_j u_i(x_j, t_{ij}, \xi_j, c) \quad \textit{Subject to:} p_j + c \leq y_i \tag{6.1}$$

$$p_j = \mathbf{p}(x, \xi) \tag{6.2}$$

In equation (6.1), the term x_j represents the physical and the community attributes of home j, t_{ij} is the commute time for the head of household i for living in home j, keeping i 's place of work fixed. The variable ξ_j is a product attribute observed by the consumers but not the economist. Prices are determined in equilibrium by the interaction of buyers and sellers. The function **p** maps the characteristics (x, ξ) into their equilibrium prices. Note that households take prices as exogenous which is a plausible assumption if the housing market in Los Angeles is competitive. We are also assuming that recent home purchasers, who are migrants, believe that community attributes such as the percent of the community who are college graduates and the racial composition of the community are exogenous. We are only examining the demand for the migrant owners who recently bought into the community. Relative to the stock of owners and renters, this group is likely to be small and it reasonable to assume that they take the community attributes as exogenous. In equation (6.1), c is the nuemraire good with a price of 1 per unit.

Suppose that characteristic k is continuous and that j^* is household i's optimal housing unit. Then it must be the case that:

$$\frac{\partial u_i(x_{j^*}, t_{ij^*}, \xi_{j^*}, y_i - p_{j^*})}{\partial x_{j,k}} - \frac{\partial u_i(x_{j^*}, t_{ij^*}, \xi_{j^*}, y_i - p_{j^*})}{\partial c} \frac{\partial \mathbf{p}(x_{j^*}, \xi_{j^*})}{\partial x_{j,k}} = 0 \tag{6.3}$$

$$\frac{\dfrac{\partial u_i(x_{j^*}, t_{ij^*}, \xi_{j^*}, y_i - p_{j^*})}{\partial x_{j,k}}}{\dfrac{\partial u_i(x_{j^*}, t_{ij^*}, \xi_{j^*}, y_i - p_{j^*})}{\partial c}} = \frac{\partial \mathbf{p}(x_{j^*}, \xi_{j^*})}{\partial x_{j,k}} \tag{6.4}$$

At the optimal bundle of product characteristics, equation (6.4) must hold. This implies that the marginal rate of substitution between product characteristic k and the composite commodity must be equal to the implicit price.

In the model above, we have assumed that consumers are static utility maximizers. However, equation (6.4) is generated by dynamic models of housing demand, such as Dougherty and Van Order (1982). In these models, household's

---

[3] Omitting ξ_j from the demand system will generate biased estimates of the willingness to pay for product attributes (see Berry et al. 1995; Nevo 2001; Petrin 2002 and Bayer et al.2004).

period utility depends on consumption of housing services and a composite commodity. At any time period, households can invest in housing stock, buy bonds or purchase the composite commodity. This first order conditions for this model imply an equation similar to (6.4), except that u corresponds to the period utility and $\mathbf{p}$ corresponds to the user cost. We note that this first order condition only holds under stylized assumptions including no adjustment costs, time separable preferences and a competitive housing market. In our application, we will only apply the first order condition (6.4) to households that have recently moved. We recognize that this is a select sample of Los Angeles county residents. However, as we discussed above, we believe that this drawback is at least partially compensated for a superior data set on home prices than is available in the Census.

We will denote the characteristics used in application as follows:

- $SQFT_j$: The size of the home measured in square feet.
- $LOTSQFT_j$: The size of the lot that the home is located on measured in square feet.
- AGE_j: The age of home j.
- $PRICE_j$: The sale price of the home as recorded by First American.
- $RPRICE_j$: The owner's equivalent rent for the home defined as 0.075 times the sale price deflated to a 2000 base year.
- $MBLACK_j$: The percentage of people in the home's census block who are black.
- $MHISP_j$: The percentage of people in the home's census block who are Hispanic.
- MBA_j: The percentage of people over the age of 25 in the home's census block who are college graduates.
- $MINC_j$: The median income of households in the home's census block.
- ZIP_j: The zip code where the home is located.
- $COMMUTE_j$: The one way average commute time measured in minutes for workers who live in the home's census tract.

From a single cross section, it is obviously not be possible to recover a household's utility function globally. Following the literature on random coefficient discrete choice models, the utility specification we take to the data will be:

$$\begin{aligned} u_{ij} = {} & \beta_{i,1} \log(SQFT_j) + \beta_{i,2} \log(LOTSQFT_j) + \beta_{i,3} \log(AGE_j) + \beta_{i,4} \log(MBLACK_j) + \\ & \beta_{i,5} \log(MHISP_j) + \beta_{i,6} \log(MBA_j) + \beta_{i,7} \log(COMMUTE_{i,j}) + \beta_{i,8} \log(\xi_j) + c \end{aligned} \tag{6.5}$$

In equation (6.5), utility is a log-linear function of the product characteristics. The log specification allows product characteristics to have diminishing marginal utility. The terms $\beta_{i,k}$, $k = 1,...,8$ are referred to as random coefficients. These terms allow the marginal valuation of the (log) characteristics to be person specific, since the terms, $\beta_{i,k}$ are person specific. In commonly used models, such as the logit or multinomial probit, the economist assumes that $\beta_{i,k}=\beta_k$ for all i.

Therefore, our specification allows for a considerably richer specification of heterogeneity in tastes.

In most previous differentiated product studies, the $\beta_{i,k}$ are assumed to arise from a parametric distribution. Most commonly, they are assumed to be independently and normally distributed (see Berry et al. 1995; Petrin 2002 and Nevo 2001). In the context of our application, this is obviously a strong assumption. People with a higher valuation for big homes (i.e. high $\beta_{i,1}$) might be expected to value living in homes with larger lots (i.e. high $\beta_{i,2}$) and a higher proportion of college educated neighbors (i.e. higher $\beta_{i,6}$). This would not be consistent with the independence assumption. Furthermore, it is not clear, a priori why the random coefficients should have a normal distribution. Therefore, in our application, we will not impose any parametric distribution on $\beta_i = (\beta_{i,1},...,\beta_{i,8})$ and we will estimate the distribution of new home buyers' tastes nonparametrically.

It is worth noting that in (6.5), a random probit or logit error term is not included. As we shall discuss later, the model that we propose is just identified and therefore exhausts all of the degrees of freedom available in the data. Therefore, we can perfectly rationalize the observed data without using a random preference shock. We view this as a desirable feature of our model since when there are many choices available to consumers, random preference shocks may generate pathologies in the measurement of consumer welfare.

In our application, we will be interested in how the demographic characteristics of households in high sprawl areas differ from low sprawl areas. Therefore, we model the joint distribution of the random taste coefficients, β_i, and demographics. The demographic characteristics of the household we will consider are:

- $SIZE_i$: The number of people in the household.
- INC_i: The household's annual income.
- $ASIAN_i$: An indicator for whether the head of household is Asian.
- $HISP_i$: An indicator for whether the head of household is Hispanic.

For product $k = 1,...,8$ characteristics, we will append to the model (6.5) an additional equation of the form:

$$\beta_{i,k} = \alpha_{0,k} + \alpha_{1,k} SIZE_i + \alpha_{2,k} INC_i + \alpha_{3,k} ASIAN_i + \alpha_{4,k} HISP_i + \eta_{i,k}$$
$$E(\eta_{i,k} | SIZE_i, INC_i, ASIAN_i, HISP_i) = 0. \tag{6.6}$$

In equation (6.6), the random coefficient for product characteristic k is a function of household i's demographics and an idiosyncratic household level preference shock, $\eta_{i,k}$. Appending an equation such as (6.6) to a random coefficient model is common practice in the literature. This equation allows us to learn about the distribution of tastes conditional on demographics. Also, as we shall demonstrate in our identification section this will allow us to learn about preferences under a more appealing set of assumptions than by just imposing equation (6.5) alone.

In equation (6.6), the relationship between tastes and demographics is assumed to be linear. In general, with microdata on household level characteristics, this assumption will not be required. However, in our application, we cannot match household level demographics to the transactions. We only have access to demographic characteristics aggregated at the level of the Census tract. As a result, the estimation approach that we propose will require us to aggregate in order to estimate $\alpha_k = (\alpha_{0,k},...,\alpha_{4,k})$. Aggregation, in turn, requires an assumption of linearity.

It is worthwhile to contrast our estimation model with the classic hedonic two-step (see Cheshire 1998; Brown and Rosen 1982; Rosen 1974; Epple 1987; Eskelend et al. 2004). The framework that we apply is derived from Bajari and Benkard (2005) and has the following features. First, we allow for consumers to be heterogeneous in their willingness to pay for product attributes. In a linear hedonic regression, the implicit price for a product attribute is commonly interpreted as the marginal willingness to pay and does not differ across consumers. We consider a nonparametric framework that allows the marginal willingness to pay to freely differ across consumers. Second, we derive consumer preferences for omitted product characteristics that are observed by consumers but not by the economist. Finally, we discuss a framework that allows the economist to recover preferences in a hedonic model with discrete attributes. The standard analysis of the hedonic model exploits a first order condition to uncover structural willingness to pay. We apply here a nonparametric hedonic model that allows for all three of the properties discussed above.

6.4 Estimation

Our approach to estimation involves three steps. In the first step, we estimate the housing hedonic price function **p** using flexible, non-parametric methods based on the techniques described in Fan and Gijbels (1996) and applied in Bajari and Kahn (2005). Second, we recover a vector of random coefficients for each household by applying first order conditions for optimality. Finally, we recover the joint distribution of demographics and household demographics. We only have access to demographics aggregated at the level of Census tracts. Therefore we propose techniques to estimate household level preferences with this aggregated data. The first two steps of our estimator are similar to those used in Bajari and Benkard (2005) and Bajari and Kahn (2005). The last step is novel to this chapter.

6.4.1 First Step: Estimating the Hedonic Price Functional

In order to estimate the hedonic flexibly, we use methods from local linear methods discussed in Fan and Gijbels (1996). Fix a particular home j^*. In a local linear model, we assume that locally the hedonic price function **p** from equation (6.1) satisfies:

$$p_j = \alpha_{0,j^*} + \sum_k \alpha_{k,j^*}(x_{j,k} - x_{j^*,k}) + \xi_j \tag{6.7}$$

In equation (6.7), we assume that in a neighborhood of (x_{j*}, ξ_{j*}) the hedonic is approximately linear. However, unlike a linear regression, where the relationship between the dependent and independent variables is globally linear, here the relationship is only locally linear. Thus, the coefficients have a subscript $\alpha_{.,j^*}$ to emphasize that they will be specific to a particular bundle of characteristics (x_{j*}, ξ_{j*}).

Following Fan and Gijbels (1996), for any j^*, $1 \le j^* \le J$, we use weighted least squares to estimate $\alpha_{.,j*}$

$$\alpha_{j^*} = \underset{\alpha}{\arg\min}(\bar{\mathbf{p}} - \mathbf{X}\alpha)' \mathbf{W}(\bar{\mathbf{p}} - \mathbf{X}\alpha) \tag{6.8}$$

$$\mathbf{p} = [RPRICE_j], \mathbf{X} = [x_j], \mathbf{W} = diag\{K_h(x_j - x_{j*})\}. \tag{6.9}$$

In equations (6.8) and (6.9), $\bar{\mathbf{p}}$ is the vector of the owner's equivalent rent for all products $j = 1, \ldots, J$ in our cross section of homes, $\mathbf{X}$ is a vector of regressors, which correspond to the observed product characteristics and $\mathbf{W}$ is a matrix of kernel weights.

Note that the kernel weights $\mathbf{W}$ are a function of the distance between product j^* and product j. Thus, the local linear regression assigns greater importance to observations near j^*. Local linear methods have the same asymptotic variance and a lower asymptotic bias than the Nadaraya-Watson estimator, whereas the Gasser-Mueller estimator has the same asymptotic bias and a higher asymptotic variance than local linear methods. In our estimates, normal kernels with a bandwidth set equal to 1.5 times the sample standard deviation were used to construct the weights.

Our estimates of equations (6.8) and (6.9) allow us to recover an estimate of the unobserved product characteristic

$$\xi_{j^*} = p_{j^*} - x_{j^*}\alpha_{j^*}. \tag{6.10}$$

In equation (6.10), the unobserved product characteristic ξ_{j^*} is estimated as the residual to our hedonic regression. While there are certainly other interpretations of the residual in hedonics (e.g. measurement error in price), we believe that this interpretation is the most important in our data.

We use a reasonably large number of co-variates in many applications. Therefore we should not interpret these estimates as "nonparametric". However, compared to other flexible functional forms, in our experience and judging from our previous experience in Bajari and Kahn (2005), local linear methods appear to give much more plausible estimates of the implicit prices for housing product characteristics.

Equations (6.8) and (6.9) use the standard hedonic assumption that unobserved product characteristics are mean independent of observed product characteristics. This is a strong assumption that would be objectionable in practice. For instance, we do not have school quality data available by school district. To control for local school quality, we include zip code fixed effects. We believe that a community's racial composition and percent of adults who are college graduates will be highly correlated with school quality. Bayer et al. (2004) study of San Francisco's housing market in 1990 provides direct evidence that controlling for community socio-economics, objective data on school quality adds little information.

In a first step, we run a linear regression of owner equivalent rent on the single detached home's square footage, age and lot size and the census block's percent college graduate, percent black and percent hispanic and zip code fixed effects. Zip code fixed effects absorb a number of important attributes such as distance from major employment centers, the beach, climate, air pollution, local property taxes, crime and local high school quality. We then subtract the zip code fixed effects from the owner's equivalent rent. We then estimate the local linear regressions described in the previous section. This allows us to identify the implicit prices of the community characteristics using census block variation within a zip code. The average zip code has 14 census blocks within it. This emphasis of identifying willingness to pay for community attributes using within zip code community variation distinguishes our approach from previous hedonic studies such as DiPasquale and Kahn (1999). We use estimates from this linear hedonic regression to compute the implicit price of commuting[4]. This method relies heavily on a linearity assumption, which is less general than the nonparametric approach that we discussed above. Census data provides average commute times for each census tract. In using these data, we are implicitly assuming that the average place of work for new home buyers in a given census tract is the same as the average place of work for all tract residents (i.e renters and owners, long time stayers and recent migrants). Since almost everyone drives in Los Angeles, we do not have to worry about transit mode differences generating differences in commute times. If a census tract's average commute time is a noisy

4 When estimating this regression, we also include zip code fixed effects to control for unobserved community features at the level of the zip code.

measure of the average home buyer's true commute time, then this linear hedonic will under-estimate the marginal value of time.

6.4.2 Second Step: Recovering the Random Coefficients

Suppose that household i chooses home j^*. Let $\hat{\alpha}_{j*,k}$ be the coefficients of the local linear regression associated with x_{j^*}. These coefficients can be interpreted as the implicit prices faced by household i in the market. That is, we estimate the implicit price for characteristic k faced by household i, $\frac{\partial p(x_{j^*})}{\partial x_{j,k}}$, as $\hat{\alpha}_{j*,k}$.

Given an estimate of the implicit prices, we can generate an estimate of $\hat{\beta}_{i,k}$ of household i's random coefficient for characteristic k as follows by applying equations (6.4) and (6.5):

$$\hat{\beta}_{i,k} = \hat{\alpha}_{j^*,k} x_{j^*,k} . \tag{6.11}$$

By applying equation (6.11) for every household in our data set, we nonparametrically estimate the population distribution of random coefficients. The joint cumulative distribution function $F(\beta_i)$ can be estimated as using its empirical analogue:

$$\hat{F}(\overline{\beta}_i) = \frac{1}{I} 1\left\{\hat{\beta}_{i,k} < \overline{\beta}_{i,k} \ \text{for all } k\right\}. \tag{6.12}$$

In equation (6.11), function 1 {} denotes the indicator function.

In the cases where the characteristic k is discrete, we could follow Bajari and Benkard (2005) and Bajari and Kahn (2005) who propose a simple estimator for the preference parameters. In our application, all of the product characteristics are continuous and therefore this procedure is not required.

6.4.3 Third Step: Aggregation of Preferences

We would like to describe how new home buyers' willingness to pay for housing attributes varies as a function of buyer demographics. We have individual level data on buyers' willingness to pay for each product attribute but we only have aggregate owner demographics by census tract for the set of all owners who live in that tract. This section proposes an aggregation strategy for matching our "micro" data to readily available "macro" data.

The idea behind our approach to aggregation is straightforward. Naively, we would want to aggregate equation (6.6) within a single Census tract. From step two above, we have the value of the dependent variable for each household and we can calculate tract specific means, for home owners, for the demographic characteristics in equation (6.6). We are concerned that a OLS estimate of census tract average marginal willingness to pay for a housing attribute regressed on census tract demographics will not yield consistent estimates for how marginal willingness to pay for attributes varies by demographic groups.

To recover these preferences, a slightly modified approach is requied. We partition the $i = 1,....,I$ households into G groups each of size $n = G/I$.

We perform this partition at random. We could do this for instance by sampling from the households without replacement and assign the first n households to the first group, the second n to the second group and so forth. Then, for each $g \in G$, form an aggregated version of Eq. (6.6) as follows:

$$\frac{1}{n}\sum_{i\in g}\hat{\beta}_{i,k} = \frac{1}{n}\sum_{i\in g}\{\alpha_{0,k} + \alpha_{1,k}SIZE_i + \alpha_{2,k}INC_i + \alpha_{3,k}HISP_i + \alpha_{4,k}ASIAN_i + \eta_{i,k}\} \quad (6.13)$$

$$\overline{\beta}_{g,k} = \alpha_{0,k} + \alpha_{1,k}\overline{SIZE}_g + \alpha_{2,k}\overline{INC}_g + \alpha_{3,k}\overline{HISP}_g + \alpha_{4,k}\overline{ASIAN}_g + \overline{\eta}_{g,k}\,. \quad (6.14)$$

In equation (6.14), we define $\overline{\beta}_{g,k} = \sum_{i\in G}\hat{\beta}_{i,k}$, $\overline{SIZE}_g = \frac{1}{n}\sum_{i\in G} SIZE_i$ and so forth. Because of the nature of our data, we do not observe these values directly. However, we can estimate them as follows. In our census tract data, we observe $t(i)$ the tract in which every household i lives and the average values of the demographic variables for home owners in tract t. Let $SIZE_t$, INC_t, $HISP_t$ and $ASIAN_t$ denote these values. Then:

$$\overline{SIZE}_g = \lim_{t,n\to\infty}\frac{1}{n}\sum_{i\in g}\sum_{t} SIZE_t \cdot 1\{t(i) = t\}. \quad (6.15)$$

In equation (6.15), we estimate the average demographics of home buyers in group g by replacing it with the average of the tract that household i lives in. As the number of tracts and the size of the groups n become sufficiently large, we can consistently estimate $\overline{SIZE}_g$.

Let $\hat{SIZE}(g)$ be defined as $\hat{SIZE}(g) = \sum_{i\in g}\sum_t \hat{SIZE}_t \cdot 1\{t(i) = t\}$ and define $\hat{INC}(g)$, $\hat{HISP}(g)$ and $\hat{ASIAN}(g)$ similarly. The regression equation we will estimate is:

$$\overline{\beta}_{g,k} = \alpha_{0k} + \alpha_{1k}\hat{SIZE}(g) + \alpha_{2k}\hat{INC}(g) + \alpha_{3k}\hat{HISP}(g) + \alpha_{4,k}\hat{ASIAN}(g) + \overline{\eta}_{g,k} \quad (6.16)$$

Since we have constructed our groups at random, the expected value of $\overline{\eta}_{g,k}$ will be zero conditional on our covariates. We can therefore estimate (6.16) by regression. The coefficients α will be biased, but the bias will be small if the number of members n in each group g is sufficiently large[5].

6.5 Results

We begin by comparing average housing attributes in high sprawl and low sprawl areas. For all census tracts in our First American Data Set, we partition them into those whose population density is less than or equal to the 25th percentile (the high sprawl tracts) and those census tracts whose density place them in the 75th or higher percentile (the low sprawl tracts). For these two separate groups of tracts, we use our First American Data to calculate means of housing structure and community attributes. These are reported in Table 6.2. The average home in the sprawl tracts is newer having been built 38 years ago while the average home in the low sprawl tracts was built 65 years ago. Relative to low sprawl homes, homes in the sprawl areas have higher square footage and larger lots. In terms of community attributes, the sprawl homes have much lower rates of blacks and Hispanics and much higher rates of college graduates.

Table 6.2 Housing Attributes in High Sprawl and Low Sprawl Areas in Los Angeles

Housing Attributes	Sprawl	Low Sprawl	All
Price [US$]	388,597	231,466	328,695
Structure [square feet]	1,847.696	1,229.839	1,568.579
Lot Size [square feet]	8,715.238	5,359.013	7,217.682
Age of Structure	38.219	65.119	48.105
Tract % Black	0.065	0.149	0.084
Tract % Hispanic	0.220	0.603	0.349
Tract % College Graduates	0.345	0.130	0.265
Tract Median Income	71,821.770	34,474.620	57,781.090
Tract % Home Owners	0.775	0.363	0.648
Tract % in Poverty	0.079	0.252	0.118
Tract one way commute time in minutes	32.493	31.286	31.282
Tract one way commute time if all residents work in the Central Business District	39.983	22.813	32.706
Tract Population Density [1000 per square mile]	1.308	7.981	3.216
Count of Home Sales	68,199	19,387	173,507

We sort census tracts by their population density. We assign those tracts whose density is equal to or greater than the 75th percentile to the "Low Sprawl" category while tracts whose density is less than or equal to the 25th percentile are assigned to the "High Sprawl" category. Cell specific averages are reported. Data source: First American and Census of Population and Housing

[5] Due to collinearity issues we are not able to include a large number of explanatory variables in these second stage regressions. For example, we find that a census tract's percent Hispanic is highly negatively correlated with census tract average household income.

In the high sprawl areas, 35% of neighbors are college graduates while in the low sprawl areas 13% are college graduates. Ownership rates in high sprawl areas are much higher.

The one surprise that emerges in this comparison of high sprawl and low sprawl areas is the very small difference in average commuting times. Los Angeles is clearly not a monocentric city. Workers who live in the sprawl areas commute on average 32.5 minutes one way while workers in the low sprawl areas commute on average 31.3 minutes one way. In a monocentric city, this differential would be much larger. As pointed out by Gordon et al. (1989), and Glaeser and Kahn (2001), suburbanized employment allows suburban workers to reverse commute and drive at faster speeds at lower density[6].

6.5.1 Hedonic Pricing Estimates

The first step in implementing our three step estimation procedure is to estimate the hedonic pricing function. In Table 6.3, we display the distribution of implicit prices for the various product characteristics. Since we are using a nonparametric regression technique, each household faces a distribution of implicit prices. The average implicit prices all have the signs and magnitudes that are consistent with economic intuition. An extra square foot of interior space is priced at $9.08 per year whereas an extra foot of lot size is priced at $0.16 per year. Of the community characteristics, we note that the percentage of one's neighbors that are college graduates is heavily capitalized into the prices. Increasing the fraction of college educated neighbors by 10 percentage points will, on average, cost $1,619.9 per year. The racial characteristics of neighbors have smaller implicit prices. For instance, increasing the proportion of hispanics in block by 10 percentage points reduces real estate price by $19 per year. Increasing the percentage of blacks in one's census block by 10 percentage points reduces annual home prices by $1,466.

Table 6.3 Summary of Implicit Hedonic Prices Distribution

Variable	Mean	Std. Dev.	25%	50%	75%
Structure [square feet]	9.078	1.718	7.848	8.810	9.953
Lot Size [square feet]	0.159	0.083	0.126	0.167	0.207
Age of Structure	-9.463	33.946	-28.994	-19.556	2.386
Block % College Graduates	16,199.000	3,338.582	14,381.480	15,865.900	17,233.410
Block % Black	-14,656.590	3,694.453	-16,834.390	-14,127.700	-12,238.340
Block % Hispanic	-188.905	1,560.991	-737.908	-295.219	88.052

Data source: First American and Census of Population and Housing

[6] The third to last row of Table 6.2 reports a commuting counterfactual that we will discuss in detail below.

Table 6.4 reports two hedonic regressions where we include each census tract's average commute time as an explanatory variable. The standard errors are clustered by census tract. We find that the implicit price of an additional minute in the one way commute is -218.00. Suppose that the head of household in this sample works 5 days per year for 48 weeks per year. Every additional minute of a one way commute leads to an additional 8 hours in the car (480 minutes=5 days × 48 weeks × 2). This implies an opportunity cost of time of $27.30 per hour. The average household income for owners in the census tracts where the home sales we observe is $56,300.00 per year. This leads to an average (pre-tax wage) of $29.32 if the household works 48 weeks, 5 days per week and 8 hours per day[7]. At the margin, this is consistent with the intuitive argument that the value of commuting is (approximately) equated to the household's hourly wage[8].

Table 6.4. Linear Hedonic Price Regression to Recover Commuting Valuation

	With Zip Code fixed effects		Without Zip Code fixed effects	
	Coeff.	Std.err.	Coeff.	Std.err.
Age of Structure	-0.473	7.017	73.331	13.782
Structure [square feet]	10.965	0.644	10.957	0.613
Lot Size [square feet]	0.123	0.039	0.051	0.043
Tract % Black	-6,689.695	3,178.315	-2,237.928	1,553.685
Tract % College Graduates	20,574.020	2,498.553	47,787.220	3,026.263
Tract % Hispanic	326.082	1,444.595	4,475.481	1,393.349
One Way Commute [minutes]	-218.173	75.780	-488.231	93.102
Constant	8,399.406	3,237.439	4795.938	3,612.349
Observations	173,505		173,505	
R^2	0.14		0.13	

The dependent variable in the regression is the average owner's equivalent rent. Standard errors are adjusted for tract level clustering. Data source: First American and Census of Population and Housing

We have documented that the Los Angeles housing stock is highly heterogeneous (see Tables 6.1 and 6.2) and that the hedonic pricing function of housing attributes is highly non-linear (see Table 6.3). Tables 6.1 through 6.4 provide an explanation for the wasteful commuting puzzle (see Hamilton 1982; Cropper and Gordon 1991; and Small and Song 1992). While households dislike commuting (see Table 6.4), each household recognizes that they face a bundling problem. Their dream house may not be near their place of work. While all else equal, a commuter would want a shorter commute, all else is not equal. The full set of housing products is not available within each community. Facing this spanning

[7] This is the weighted average of census tract annual average household income for owners where the weights depend on what share of the home sales in our First American data base are from that census tract.

[8] The transportation economics literature has tended to find smaller opportunity cost estimates for the value of time averaging around 50 percent of one's hourly wage (see Small 1992).

constraint, rational households tradeoff extra commuting time in return for a preferred housing structure and a preferred community. There would only be a wasteful commuting puzzle if all homes are identical. In this case, utility maximizers become commute minimizers who should Tiebout sort by place of work.

6.5.2 Preferences Estimates

For each home buyer, we use our estimates of the implicit price he faces combined with our assumed functional form for the utility function, and his optimal consumption of this attribute, to recover his marginal valuation for various product characteristics. In order to present our estimates, it is most useful to change the units from the random coefficients in Eq. (6.5) to willingness to pay for a ten percent increase in consumption of the characteristic. This can be quickly computed for each household in our sample given our choice of the utility function. Suppose that household *i*'s current consumption of square footage is $SQFT_j$. Then willingness to pay for an extra square foot can be computed as:

$$\begin{aligned} WTPSQFT_i &= \beta_{i,1}\left(log(1.1 \times SQFT_j) - log(SQFT_j)\right) \\ &= \beta_{i,1}\, log(1.1) \end{aligned} \tag{6.17}$$

In Table 6.5, we present summary statistics for the empirical distribution of willingness to pay for housing attributes for all recent home buyers and for Hispanic recent home buyers. Recent home buyers care much more about structure size than lot size. The average recent home buyer is willing to pay \$1,430 for a 10 percent increase in structure size and only \$119 for a 10 percent increase in lot size. Hispanic owners have a lower demand for private space. Hispanics are willing to pay more for newer housing. In terms of community attributes, recent home buyers are willing to pay \$400 per year for a 10 percent increase in community residents who are college graduates. Hispanics reveal a positive but lesser demand for access to such peers. Community racial composition preferences appear small. All new home buyers are willing to pay \$88 per year to live in a community with 10 percent fewer black residents. Perhaps surprisingly, new Hispanic home buyers do not have a greater willingness to pay to live in a Hispanic community than the average home buyer.

Table 6.5 Differences in Consumer Willingness to Pay For Housing Attributes

	All New Home Buyers			
Variable	Mean TP	W25%	50%	75%
Square Feet	1,430.276	868.436	1,180.252	1,680.437
Lot Size	118.952	66.630	101.345	141.048
Age of Structure	-15.485	-120.937	-59.145	10.983
Tract % College Graduates	399.691	168.483	328.456	554.525
Tract % Black	-87.992	-115.014	-44.266	-9.116
Tract % Hispanic	-6.186	-17.178	-8.298	2.001

Table 6.5 (cont.)

		Hispanic New Home Buyers		
Variables	Mean WTP	25%	50%	75%
Square Feet	1,058.366	713.331	923.517	1,228.151
Lot Size	105.088	69.930	98.900	126.671
Age of Structure	-94.206	-148.276	-121.610	-61.611
Tract % College Graduates	231.611	92.974	173.721	307.285
Tract % Black	-94.741	-144.692	-48.272	-8.309
Tract % Hispanic	-9.678	-19.633	-11.100	-0.312

This table displays summary statistics for the population distribution of the willingness to pay for a 10 percent increase in each product characteristics. Data source: First American and Census of Population and Housing

In Table 6.6, we study the correlation between the willingness to pay for product characteristics. In most models with random coefficients, the correlation in tastes between different product characteristics is ignored. We find that the independence assumption commonly made in the literature appears to be strongly rejected by the data. Most of the signs are intuitively plausible with the exception of some of the race or age variables. We encourage the reader to note, however, that Table 6.5 suggest that the willingness to pay for many of these variables is not particularly large. As shown in Table 6.6, unit square footage and community percent college graduates are complements. We are surprised that new housing and larger interior space are not complements.

Table 6.6 Correlation Between Willingness to Pay for Characteristics

	Square Feet	Lot Size	Age of Structure	% College Graduate	% Black	% Hispanic
Square Feet	1.000					
Lot Size	0.189	1.000				
Age of Structure	0.538	0.369	1.000			
Block % College Graduate	0.822	0.135	0.560	1.000		
Block % lackB	0.156	0.245	0.115	0.213	1.000	
Block % ispaHic	0.464	0.056	0.004	0.341	0.315	1.000

Data source: First American and Census of Population and Housing

Using the aggregation approach presented above, we now test hypotheses concerning how willingness to pay for housing attributes varies as a function of home owner demographics. Table 6.7 reports six OLS regressions examining willingness to pay for housing attributes and the consumption of housing attributes. We do not use the full set of demographic characteristics in equation (6.16) because of collinearity. In columns (1), (3), and (5), we report willingness to pay for interior unit square footage, the home's lot size, and the age of the housing unit as a function of a household head's age, household size, and median income. Richer people greatly value indoor space. An extra $10,000 in income increases the willingness to pay for a 10 percent increase in indoor space by $240.

The income effect for lot size is much smaller. A $10,000 increase in household income increases the willingness to pay for a 10 percent increase in lot size by $9 per year. As shown in Table 6.7, controlling for household income, larger households are willing to pay less for more interior space and land. Our explanation for this counter-intuitive result is that household size proxies for per-capita income. For the same level of household income, larger families are poorer than smaller families and this income effect dominates any space demand effects. We are somewhat surprised by the negative income effect on the demand for new housing. At a point in time, a housing unit's age also bundles its "birth cohort". If homes built in the 1930s are very desirable, then it is possible that such a 70 year old home in the year 2003 could be in high demand *despite* its age. In columns (2), (4) and (6), we report how actual consumption of unit square footage, the home's lot size and the age of the housing unit differ by demographic group. Richer people are buying newer, larger homes.

Table 6.7 Willingness to Pay and Attribute Consumption as a Function of Household Demographics

	Unit Square Footage		Lot Size		Age of Unit	
	WTP (1)	Quantity (2)	WTP (3)	Quantity (4)	WTP (5)	Quantity (6)
Household Size	-80.147	-21.445	-8.062	-324.408	-16.820	-3.673
	(34.932)	(28.170)	(6.391)	(305.892)	(6.846)	(1.060)
Median Income [US$ 1,000]	23.971	14.997	0.916	14.661	3.213	-0.244
	(1.145)	(0.924)	(0.210)	(10.029)	(0.244)	(0.035)
Constant	110.079	650.055	84.667	1449.377	20.522	75.985
	(165.514)	(133.474)	(30.282)	(20.522)	(32.436)	(5.022)
Adjusted R^2	0.408	0.278	0.033	0.055	0.411	0.045

This table reports six separate OLS regressions. There are 1,000 "pseudo tracts used in each regression. Each dependent variable represents the willingness to pay for a ten percent increase in the attribute. Willingness to pay's units are dollars per year in owner's equivalent rent. The quantity regressions are average consumption of the characteristic within the tract regressed on demographic characteristics. Standard errors are reported in parentheses. Data source: First American and Census of Population and Housing

One of our methodological goals in this paper is to exploit both the "micro" information provided in the First American Data Base with the "macro" data from the Census. As discussed above, using information on each home buyer's last name we can identify home buyers who are Asian and Hispanic. In Table 6.8, we present another set of second stage preference regressions for housing structure attributes. For a household making an average of $56,300 per year, Asian households value large homes more. The differences in willingness to pay for lot size and age, while statistically different, do not appear to be very large in magnitude.

Table 6.8 Willingness to Pay for Structure Attributes as a Function of Household Demographics and Ethnicity

	Unit Square Footage		Lot Size		Age of Unit	
	Hispanic (1)	Asian (2)	Hispanic (3)	Asian (4)	Hispanic (5)	Asian (6)
Household Size	-102.344	48.955	9.193	-11.789	-38.307	-80.441
	(21.159)	(53.108)	(3.603)	(7.935)	(3.657)	(9.264)
Median Income [US$ 1,000]	19.041	28.238	1.589	1.219	3.074	3.777
	(1.094)	(1.348)	(0.186)	(0.201)	(0.189)	(0.235)
Constant	389.439	-397.220	-15.784	86.275	-122.31	-0.120
	(120.855)	(217.490)	(20.577)	(32.495)	(20.887)	(37.937)
Adjusted R^2	0.369	0.321	0.071	0.045	0.439	0.321

This table reports six separate OLS regressions. There are 1,000 "pseudo" tracts used in each regression. Each dependent variable represents the willingness to pay for a ten percent increase in the attribute. Willingness to pay's units are in dollars per year in owner's equivalent rent. The quantity regressions are average consumption of the characteristic within the tract regressed on demographic characteristics. Standard errors are reported in parentheses. Data source: First American and Census of Population and Housing

In Table 6.9, we report our estimates of how home buyers differ with respect to their willingness to pay for community composition. Increasing household income by $10,000 increases annual willingness to pay to live in a community with 10 percent more college graduates by $95. Unlike the demand for high human capital peers, our estimated income effects for community racial composition are quite small. Increasing a household's income by $10,000 increases annual willingness to pay to live in a community with 10 percent more black residents by $19 per year.

Table 6.9 The Willingness to Pay for Community Attributes as a Function of Household Demographics

	Census Block % College Graduates		Census Block % Black		Census Block % Hispanic	
	Coeff.	Std.err.	Coeff.	Std.err.	Coeff.	Std.err.
Household Size	-80.947	9.581	3.166	5.726	3.705	1.403
Median Income [US$ 1000]	9.670	0.314	1.881	0.188	0.384	0.046
Constant	23.781	45.397	-222.030	27.129	-43.396	6.648
Adjusted R^2	0.644		0.115		0.067	

This table reports 3 separate OLS regressions. There are 1,000 "pseudo tracts" used in each regression. Each dependent variable represents the willingness to pay for a ten percent increase in the attribute. Willingness to pay units are in dollars per year in owner's equivalent rent. Data source: First American and Census of Population and Housing

We next consider two policy experiments where we first raise suburban density and second make the employment patterns monocentric. We conduct these policy experiments using our estimated utility parameters using a partial equilibrium analysis. Ideally, we would allow for a general equilibrium analysis of these problems as in Bayer et al. (2004) and Epple and Sieg (1999). Our policy analysis only studies the partial equilibrium effects, household by household. Therefore, the results from our policy experiments should be viewed as tentative. However, we believe that at a minimum, this analysis is a first step to understanding the incentives faced by consumers from alternative policies that could be used to discourage urban sprawl.

6.5.3 Policy Exercise #1: Raising Suburban Density

By estimating the housing product demand model for new home buyers, we have recovered the marginal willingness to pay for lot size and for avoiding a longer commute. Even if we have misspecified the utility function, this is sufficient information for conducting our first policy exercise.

Sprawl may impose an externality. When a household purchases a large home on a large lot, this increases his neighbor's distance to work. There is no market that prices the effect of large lots and large homes on the commute of other persons. While sprawl entails costs, it is clear that it is also associated with benefits, since larger homes and larger lots are valued. We therefore engage in the following thought experiment. Commutes could be shorter if each home's lot were "squished". There may be a co-ordination failure that given that the vast majority of housing has already been built, households cannot contract to "squish" their housing structures closer together to explicitly tradeoff less lot size for a shorter commute.

Suppose that we scrunched the city by ten percent. This would have the following effects. First, everyone would live ten percent closer to work and the commuting distance would be decreased by ten percent. Second, lot sizes and home sizes would be ten percent small. Third, population density would increase by $1/_{0.9\times 0.9} = 1/_{0.81}$. Using data from the 1995 National Personal Transportation Survey on over 470 Los Angeles resident commuters, we estimate the following relationship between distance, population density and commuting time. The fitted equation that we use is:

$$log\,(commute) = 1.13 + 0.54 \times log\,(distance) + 0.074 \times log\,(density).$$

That is, the log commute time to work is linear function of the log distance to the place of work and the log population density.

In Table 6.10, we estimate the effect of this change on consumer welfare in partial equilibrium, that is, holding fixed their location, but scrunching the city. On average, this would lower utility by about $1,119 dollars per year. However, there is a wide dispersion around this number since there is heterogeneity in preferences for commuting time, home size and lot size.

Table 6.10 Welfare Effects of Compressing the City

Variable	Mean	Std. ev.D	25%	50%	75%
Loss from Small Unit Square Footage	3,160	1,988	1,918	2,607	3,713
Loss From Smaller Lot Size	263	28	147	224	312
Gain from Change in Commute	2,231	846	1,711	2,077	2,507
Net Gain/Loss	-1,192	2,220	-1,933	-715	98

Data source: First American and Census of Population and Housing

We note that almost all of the negative utility from scrunching the city is because this policy makes home buyers live in smaller homes. The loss in welfare from forcing them to have smaller lots is much smaller. In fact, if we shrink the lot size, but not the home size, the results suggest that on net people would be better off by about $2,000 per year.

For each household we use our aggregation approach to calculate how the "squished city" affects different demographic groups based on their willingness to pay. The results in Table 6.11 show that richer households, and larger households would be willing to pay more to avoid this compression.

Table 6.11 Distribution of Welfare Effects from Compressing the City

Variable	Coeff.	Std.err.
Household Size	459.581	84.632
Median Household Income [US$ 1000]	-54.603	2.775
Constant	922.972	401.002
Observations	1000	
Adjusted R^2	0.425	

Data source: First American and Census of Population and Housing

6.5.4 Policy Exercise #2: Monocentric Los Angeles

Our second policy exercise does not touch the existing residential housing stock. Instead, we propose to move all Los Angeles county employment back to the Central Business District. While nobody is proposing "monocentricizing" Los Angeles, it is of interest to calculate how home buyer well being has been affected by employment sprawl. As shown in Table 6.2, high sprawl residents have commute times that are only 1 minute longer than low sprawl residents. This indicates that most suburban residents must be working at suburban jobs. Employment sprawl has allowed them to avoid "monster" commutes by unbundling the commute versus land consumption tradeoff inherent in a monocentric city.

We now seek to measure this benefit of employment sprawl. To answer this question requires estimating what each household's commute time would be if they remained in their current home but worked downtown. For each zip code, we knew its distance to the Los Angeles Central Business District as defined by the Census in 1982 (see Glaeser and Kahn 2001 for details).

The 1995 National Personal Transportation Survey provides micro data on household commuting patterns, distances traveled and transport modes. We use the Los Angeles subsample of 471 commuters in this data set to estimate the relationship between household's commute time, and distance to work. We use this data to estimate an OLS regression that yields to: $commute = 9.2199 + 1.3538 \times distance$, with a R^2 of 0.417.

Employment sprawl has greatly benefited home buyers with a taste for larger newer housing structures. To demonstrate this, we use our First American data base's information on which zip code each household lives in to calculate its distance from the Central Business District (CBD). Plugging these values into the OLS regression equation, we predict what each home buyer's commute would be if he had to commute to the CBD each day. These counter-factual commute times are reported in the third to last row of Table 6.2. Home buyers in sprawl areas commute 7.5 minute less one way way than they would have if Los Angeles was monocentric (39.98–32.5). Home buyers in low sprawl areas would have much shorter commutes if Los Angeles was monocentric. This finding is quite intuitive. If all jobs were downtown, then people who live close to downtown in low sprawl areas would have shorter commutes. If willingness to pay to avoid commuting is \$29 per hour, then the average high sprawl home buyer would be willing to pay $\$(29/60) \cdot 7.5 \cdot 2 \cdot 240 = \$1{,}740$ per year for employment to stay sprawled.

In concluding this section, we must note that both of our policy experiments are partial equilibrium in nature. The Lucas Critique argues that substantive changes in government policy lead people to re-optimize. Yet in our experiments, we are assuming that home buyers choose the same housing product after the policy shock has taken place. For recent work that has attempted to build in such general equilibrium effects into residential sorting models see Sieg et al. (2002), and Bayer et al. (2004). In principal, it would be possible to compute such counterfactuals using our demand estimates. However, we were unable to merge data on individual specific place of work to our data. Thus, computing how households make their joint location/work decision was not possible and only a partial equilibrium analysis was possible.

Despite their limitations, we believe that these partial equilibrium policy experiments have useful lessons. Our first policy experiment suggests that there is a very large gap between the marginal valuation of land (as measured by the lot size) and the commuting externality it imposes. The current equilibrium is very far from efficient and could be improved, at least locally, by creating policies that encouraged homes to be built on smaller lots. The second policy experiment suggests that moving employment to a CBD would lead to large welfare losses. This suggests that the suburbanization of employment enhances the utility of many households.

6.6 Conclusion

Suburban home ownership embodies a tradeoff. Households face lower prices for newer, larger homes but are likely to spend more time commuting. Whether a household is willing to suburbanize hinges on its preferences over land consumption and avoiding commuting. Given that the educated tend to live in the suburbs, this will further encourage suburbanization for migrants who are willing to pay to live in high human capital communities.

Traditional census data cannot be used to measure this tradeoff. The housing data in the Census provides relatively little information on the types of housing households are purchasing. To provide new estimates of the private tradeoffs for new homeowners we have used recent transaction data in Los Angeles county. This investigation of housing demand for recent home buyers in Los Angeles county reveals that the demand for sprawled housing products is fueled by the demand for interior space and access to high human capital communities. We find little evidence that the racial composition of communities sharply affects willingness to pay for housing.

One puzzle that emerges from our structural estimates is the low willingness to pay for a home's lot size. As shown in table 6.2, in sprawl areas the lots are twice as big as in low sprawl areas. This finding is based on within zip code hedonic regressions. Within these zip codes, observationally identical homes on larger lots do not sell for a much greater price. One explanation for large suburban lots supported by minimum lot zoning is that these lots help create a "moat" to keep poorer people from moving into communities. While our hedonics recover zip code specific fixed effects, we cannot estimate the counter-factual of what would be the value of these zip code specific hedonic fixed effects if communities did not have minimum lot zoning. In the absence of such zoning, more poor people could enter these suburban communities and this would raise local crime levels and reduce local school quality and this would be capitalized into home prices.

In addition to reporting new estimates of how home buyers tradeoff housing attributes, we have used these estimates to investigate the welfare effects of two specific "anti-sprawl" policies. Given our large estimates of the willingness to pay to avoid commuting and our small estimates of the willingness to pay for lot size, we conclude that the average home buyer would support "compacting" Los

Angeles. We showed who would be the winners and losers from the radical anti-sprawl policy of moving all Los Angeles employment back to the Central Business District.

We have modeled Los Angeles county as a single housing market but in reality it is part of the greater Los Angeles region including other counties such as Orange, Ventura, San Bernardino and Riverside. The demand for sprawled suburban living continues to grow. Sixty miles east of Los Angeles county in Riverside county and San Bernardino county growth continues. Inland, in this warmer summer climate, average home prices are significantly lower. We expect that similar housing tradeoffs are taking place in such exurban fringe communities. This exurban growth should trigger employment to follow these suburbanites. This decentralization of employment will help to further reduce suburban residents' commute times.

References

Anas A, Arnott R, Small KA (1998) Urban spatial structure. Journal of economic literature 36: 1426–1464

Anderson S, DePalma A, Thisse J (1995) Discrete choice theory of product differentiation. MIT Press, Cambridge, United States

Arnott R (1995) Time for revisionism on rent control? Journal of economic perspectives 9: 99–120

Bajari P, Benkard CL (2005) Demand estimation with heterogeneous consumers and unobserved product characteristics: a hedonic approach. Journal of political economy 113: 1239–1276

Bajari P, Kahn ME (2005) Estimating housing demand with an application to explaining racial segregation in cities. Journal of business and economic statistics 23: 20–33

Bayer P, McMillan R, Ruben K (2004) The causes and consequences of residential segregation: an equilibrium analysis of neighborhood sorting. Working paper, Yale University

Benkard CL, Bajari P (2005) Hedonic price indexes with unobserved product characteristics. Journal of business and economic statistics 23: 61–75

Berry S, Levinsohn J, Pakes A (1995) Automobile prices in market equilibrium. Econometrica 63: 841–890

Brown JN, Rosen HS (1982) On the estimation of structural hedonic price models. Econometrica 50: 765–768

Brueckner JK (2000) Urban sprawl: diagnosis and remedies. International regional science review 23: 160–171

Brueckner JK (2001) Urban sprawl: lessons from urban economics. Brookings-Wharton papers on urban affairs 0: 65–97

Calfee J, Clifford W (1998) The value of automobile travel time: implications for congestion policy. Journal of public economics 69: 83–102

Cheshire P, Sheppard S (1998) Estimating the demand for housing, land and neighbourhood characteristics. Oxford bulletin of economics and statistics 60: 357–382

Cropper M, Gordon P (1991) Wasteful commuting: a re-examination. Journal of urban economics 29: 2–13
Cullen JB, Levitt SD (1999) Crime, urban flight, and the consequences for cities. Review of economics and statistics 81: 159–169
DiPasquale D, Kahn ME (1999) Measuring neighborhood investments: an examination of community choice. Real estate economics 27: 389–424
Dougherty A, Van Order R (1982) Inflation, housing costs, and the consumer price index. American economic review: 154–164
Epple D (1987) Hedonic prices and implicit markets: estimating demand and supply functions for differentiated products. Journal of political economy 95: 59–80
Epple D, Sieg H (1999) Estimating equilibrium models of local jurisdictions. Journal of political economy 107: 645–681
Eckland I, Heckman JJ, Nesheim L (2004) Identification and estimation of hedonic models. Journal of political economy 112: S60–S109
Fan J, Gijbels I (1996) Local polynomial modelling and its applications monographs on statistics and applied probability. (66) CRC Press, London
Giuliano G, Small KA (1991) Subcenters in the Los Angeles region. Regional science and urban economics 21: 163–182
Glaeser EL, Kahn ME (2001) Decentralized employment and the transformation of the american city. Brookings-Wharton papers on urban affairs 0: 1–47
Glaeser EL, Luttmer EFP (2003) The misallocation of housing under rent control. American economic review 93: 1027–1046
Glaeser EL, Kahn ME (2004) Sprawl and Urban Growth. Handbook of Urban Economics Volume IV, edited by Vernon Henderson and J. Thisse. North Holland Press, Amsterdam
Gordon P, Kumar A, Richardson HW (1989) The influence of metropolitan spatial structure on commuting time. Journal of urban economics 26: 138–151
Grilliches Z (1971) editor. Price Indices and Quality Change. Cambridge, Mass.; Harvard University Press
Hamilton BW (1982) Wasteful commuting. Journal of political economy 90: 1035–1051
Margo RA (1992) Explaining the postwar suburbanization of population in the United States: the role of income. Journal of urban economics 31: 301–310
McCulloch RE, Polson NG, Rossi PE (2000) A bayesian analysis of the multinomial probit model with fully identified parameters. Journal of econometrics 99: 173–193
Mieszkowski P, Mills ES (1993) The causes of metropolitan suburbanization. Journal of economic perspectives 7: 135–147
Nechyba T, Walsh RE (2004) Urban sprawl. Journal of economic perspectives 18(4), 177-200.
Nevo A (2001) Measuring market power in the ready-to-eat cereal industry. Econometrica 69: 307–342
Painter G, Gabriel S, Myers D (2001) Race, immigrant status and housing tenure choice. Journal of urban economics 49: 150–167
Palmquist RB (1984) Estimating the demand for the characteristics of housing. Review of economics and statistics 66: 394–404
Peng R, Wheaton WC (1994) Effects of restrictive land supply on housing in Hong Kong: an econometric analysis. Journal of housing research 5: 263–290
Petrin A (2002) Quantifying the benefits of new products: the case of the minivan. Journal of political economy 110: 705–729
Phillips J, Goodstein E (2000) Growth management and housing prices: the case of Portland, Oregon. Contemporary economic policy 18: 334–344

Rauch J (1993) Productivity gains from geographic concentration of human capital: evidence from the cities. Journal of urban economics 34: 380–400

Rosen S (1974) Hedonic prices and implicit markets: product differentiation in pure competition. Journal of political economy 82: 34–55

Sieg H, Smith VK, Banzhaf SH, Walsh RP (2002) Interjurisdictional housing prices in locational equilibrium. Journal of urban economics 52: 131–153

Small KA, Song S (1992) Wasteful commuting: a resolution. Journal of political economy 100: 888–898

Thorsnes P (2000) Internalizing neighborhood externalities. Journal of urban economics 48: 397–418

Waugh FV (1928) Quality factors influencing vegetable prices. Journal of farm economics 10: 185–196

Wheaton WC (1998) Land use and density in cities with congestion. Journal of urban economics 43: 258-272

PART III
Applications to Segregation and Discrimination Issues

7 Conceptual and Operational Issues in Incorporating Segregation Measurements in Hedonic Price Modeling

David W.S. Wong

George Mason University, Fairfax, United States

7.1 Introduction

The essence of hedonic price modeling is to establish the relationship between housing prices and housing attributes. Typically, housing attributes refer to structural characteristics of the unit. However, it is obvious that the price of a house is not just determined by its structural attributes, but also attributes of the neighborhood in which the unit is located. Neighborhood attributes can be physical properties of the neighborhood, such as street condition and proximity of employment centers, or environmental characteristics such as the types of vegetative cover. Another set of neighborhood attributes is associated with the demographic and socioeconomic characteristics of the residents. The intensity and nature of interaction between the population and the physical environment can also be regarded as neighborhood characteristics.

When modeling housing prices, both structural attributes of individual houses and neighborhood characteristics will be used. It is possible that multiple housing units are located within the same neighborhood. Therefore, neighborhood measures may be correlated among individual housing units or observations. Possible approaches to address this correlation at the neighborhood level include multilevel modeling and spatial regression framework. But for this chapter, the focus is not on the general methodological issues in hedonic price modeling, but to address both conceptually and in operation how population related characteristics at the neighborhood level can be derived and thus be incorporated in hedonic modeling. The specific population characteristic to be addressed is the racial-ethnic composition of the neighborhood. Racial-ethnic characteristics of a neighborhood are often addressed in the context of segregation, as segregated neighborhoods often carry a negative connotation and thus it adversely affects housing prices. In most econometric and hedonic models (e.g., Kiel and Zabel 1996; Myers 2004; Zabel, this

A. Baranzini et al. (eds.), *Hedonic Methods in Housing Markets*, doi: 10.1007/978-0-387-76815-1_7,

Volume; Bayer and Kahn, this Volume), housing price differentials are modeled as a function of housing structural and neighborhood characteristics, while the neighborhood characteristics include some simplistic descriptions of racial-ethnic mix.

The overall objective of this chapter is to evaluate how segregation is relevant in housing price determination and to suggest effective segregation measures that can be incorporated into housing price modeling. In other words, this chapter intends to provide insights on capturing neighborhood population characteristics as inputs to hedonic models. The objective is accomplished through the discussions of different facets of segregation at the conceptual level and various issues in using segregation measures at the operational level. I will first offer taxonomies of segregation based upon several defining dimensions. Then I will discuss the concepts of segregation in residential space in reference to housing price determination. Segregation is generally regarded as undesirable, but specific impacts (positive or negative) of segregation on a neighborhood and the processes have not been concretely addressed. There are also many types of segregation and only those that are relevant to housing price modeling will be discussed. Then I will address several segregation measurement issues that are relevant to housing price modeling in general. The issue of geographical scale and the nature of segregation will be the major emphases. Some measures appropriate for hedonic modeling will be reviewed.

7.2 Taxonomies of Segregation

There are many ways to define segregation. A retrospective approach is to review what has been studied, measured and analyzed in segregation studies. Massey and Denton (1988) examined information captured by the twenty selected measures that have been used in segregation studies. They concluded that there are *five dimensions* of segregation: evenness, exposure, concentration, centralization and clustering. These dimensions are useful in understanding the population distribution characteristics related to segregation, but they do not explain how segregation can negatively affect neighborhoods.

In the context of school segregation, Newby (1982) suggested that "opposition to segregation is an opposition to discrimination" (p. 19). This argument implies that when a population is segregated, besides encountering psychological isolation, it is also likely subject to discrimination, which is generally thought to be undesirable. While most people do not want to be subject to segregation, some populations volunteer to segregate themselves from the rest, such as the Amish population in Pennsylvania. A more common but subtle case of voluntary segregation is the gated community when the residents are separated from another group through memberships and/or physical access. It is unlikely that segregated community resulted from voluntary separation will bring along discrimination within the community, and this type should be treated differently from the undesirable segregation situations in modeling housing price. However, *voluntary* segregation of one group also implies *involuntary* segregation of the other groups.

Another implication of Newby's suggestion is that discrimination resulted from segregation has negative effects. The two general outcomes from discrimination are (1) receiving *disproportional burden* of certain negative effects and (2) the *denied access* to certain resources. The former one may be illustrated by the issue of environment justice where the disadvantaged populations are concentrated in neighborhoods bearing a disproportional level of environmental risk, such as pollution due to the proximity to hazardous sites (Perlin et al. 2001; Hite this Volume). In the later case, a neighborhood with high concentration of one population group may be given inferior recreational facility while accessing a better quality facility is difficult. In some cases, the two types of effects are not clearly distinguishable. For instance, when the water supplied to a neighborhood is of low-quality, people in that neighborhood are denied access to clean water. Similar arguments are applicable to school segregation.

While recognizing the nature that segregation may facilitate discrimination and in turn some population groups may be treated unfairly, it is also important to distinguish different types of segregation. Segregation can happen in various *social-geographical spaces*: residential, work, school, cultural-religious, and entertainment. Segregation is sometime acceptable in cultural-religious space as different cultural and religious groups organize activities focusing on their own groups, but it is generally not acceptable in residential, work and school spaces in most western countries. Therefore, many studies focus on segregation in these social-geographical spaces.

But within each of these social-geographical spaces, population may be divided into subgroups according to different *population variables*. For instance, in residential space, *race or ethnicity* of the population is often used to subdivide the population into groups in order to evaluate the level of segregation among these groups. Another common variable used in dividing the population into subgroups is *income or poverty status* (Jargowsky 1996). In the work space, *gender* is often used as a variable to create population groups, but other population-demographic variables, such as race-ethnicity and age can also be used

Based upon the discussion above, taxonomies of segregation include voluntary and involuntary, involve different geographical-social spaces where segregation occurs, the population characteristics which can be used to divide the population into subgroups for comparison, and different positive or negative impacts resulting from discrimination facilitated by the segregated situations.

7.3 Segregation and Hedonic Pricing Modeling

One of the bases of hedonic models is that the price of a housing unit is determined by both structural and neighborhood characteristics. The level of segregation in the neighborhood can be regarded as a neighborhood characteristic and thus a determinant of housing price. Many hedonic models include some measures reflecting the neighborhood racial-ethnic mix. However, one conceptual issue in current segregation studies is in defining segregation. When the study area exhibits possibly uneven distribution of population, investigators often employ popular segregation measures, and then relate the segregation values to the phenomenon being studied. This process is often performed without considering how segregation may be conceptually relevant to the phenomenon. It rarely evaluates what aspect or type of segregation the measure may reflect effectively. The link between segregation and its impacts or effects on the phenomenon being studied is often not established. Generic measures of segregation can easily be employed to evaluate a population, but whether those measures are appropriate to evaluate the specific concerns of segregation in the study context and to reflect the impacts of segregation were not examined in the past. As a result, the measures employed may not capture what the study may need.

Therefore, it is important to first identify the type of segregation that one is concerned about and then the conceptual relationships between that type of segregation and housing price. In the context of hedonic price modeling, segregation in the residential and school spaces are the most relevant. Within these two spaces, one has to identify the population characteristics most relevant to the modeling context. Numerous population variables can be used to divide the population into subgroups in the housing price modeling framework. The most common variable is probably the race-ethnicity based variables. In the North American context, African American or black is usually regarded as the minority group and black percentage or concentration is often the focus. However, recent immigration patterns have changed the landscape such that other minority groups are increasing their roles in shaping the North American metropolitan system (e.g., Johnston et al. 2003). But besides race-ethnicity, other variables can also be used: income level or poverty status, type of occupation or employment, education level, and home ownership status, etc. It is true that these variables are often not independent of each other (Hughes and Madden 1991). In general, these are socioeconomic variables that can be used to divide the population into groups in order to evaluate the level of segregation.

In addition, we need to identify the relationships between segregation and housing price. These relationships are often in the form of negative impacts with the exception of voluntary segregation. As mentioned before, the type of impacts from segregation (over-burdened by some undesirable attributes or denied access to resources) should be explicitly postulated in the housing price modeling, as it may affect how the level of segregation should be evaluated in operation. The overburdening of environmental risk to one residential group in the environmental justice context is a typical example of how housing prices may be affected (Segerson 2001; Brasington and Hite 2005; Hite this Volume). Neighborhoods of disadvantaged groups or with high poverty level likely suffer from inadequate or substandard infrastructure, such as recreational and medical facilities (e.g., Massey 1990; Yankauer 1950). It is preferable to identify and adopt the segregation measure which can best capture the potential impacts of the segregated situation but most popular measures of segregation are not effective in capturing these negative impacts resulting from segregation.

7.4 The Use of Segregation Measures in Hedonic Modeling

Part of the procedure in hedonic modeling is to identify or derive variables describing the neighborhood characteristics. The level of segregation of a neighborhood can be a legitimate neighborhood attribute. Unfortunately, few segregation indices have been used in hedonic modeling partly because of several operational and methodological issues.

7.4.1 Concepts of Segregation vs. General Description of Racial-Ethnic Mix

Previously, I described some of the impacts from discrimination originating from or facilitated by segregation. However, the literature also recognizes the presence of racial prejudice against the population of a neighborhood (Yinger 1978, 1979). In this context, prejudice is defined as "a feeling or an attitude toward a group or individual" (Kiel and Zabel 1996, p.144). It is likely that in this context, the feeling or attitude is negative. In a neighborhood, if a population group is highly concentrated or segregated, the group will be more identifiable and thus is more likely subject to prejudice in the housing market.

While it is quite challenging to reflect the level of prejudice a group and its neighborhood may receive, it is common to use some racial-ethnic mix variables to capture the potentials that the neighborhood is subject to a certain level of prejudice. These variables can be as simple as percentage of a specific racial-ethnic group found in the enumeration unit or percentage of population in specific population categories as defined by other socioeconomic variables such as occupation types and education levels. Many attempts in modeling housing price have used these simple percentage variables as neighborhood characteristics (e.g., Myers 2004; Kiel and Zabel 1996). However, most of these simple percentages are not regarded as segregation measures conceptually in the literature as they merely reflect population shares by a group or multiple groups in an area.

Numerous ways have been proposed to define segregation. Newby (1982) suggested that segregation implies spatial separation among different population groups. While following Newby's suggestion, many researchers, especially geographers called for an explicit spatial treatment of segregation. The five dimensions of segregation suggested by Massey and Denton (1988) seem to be spatial in nature, but most of them are in fact aspatial when they are implemented by corresponding measures. Some researchers have argued that there are fewer than five dimensions (Brown and Chung 2006; Reardon and O'Sullivan 2004). The aspatial nature of most existing segregation measures will be discussed later. The important point is that simple percentages for a specific population group are not adequate to reflect the natures of segregation. To a certain extent, percentages can be regarded as a simple form of the evenness measure, similar to the entropy-based diversity measure, which is a function of the racial-ethnic mix of a region (White 1986; Reardon and Firebaugh 2002). Percentages are usually limited to two-group comparison, but the diversity measure can accommodate multiple groups.

7.4.2 Global vs. Local Measures

A simple fact is that most segregation measures developed so far are global measures. They are labeled as "global" not that they describe the situation of the entire world, but rather they describe the study region as a whole, in contrast to describing the situations of various sub-regions or neighborhoods within the study region. This usage of the terms is consistent with spatial statistics parlance where global measures are summary measures for the entire study region and local measures are used to depict the spatial variability at the local scale within the study area (Anselin 1995; Getis and Ord 1992). It has been a trend in both geographical research and spatial statistics to shift from global scale analysis to local scale study using local spatial statistics, including regression techniques (Fotheringham 1997).

In the review provided by Massey and Denton (1988), twenty measures of segregation were evaluated and all of them can be regarded as global measures. Such measures can be used for hedonic modeling if housing observations are distributed across multiple regions or cities and a segregation value can be computed for each region or city as a regional variable. In this case, the segregation value may be used to explain inter-city differences in housing price attributable to city-level segregation. This approach in modeling housing price is not very common and is not without problems. The more likely situation is that housing observations are distributed within a city or a region and summary global measures will be of little value to explain the intra-city or intra-region housing price variation.

Therefore, to include segregation information in hedonic modeling, it is necessary to derive segregation values for neighborhoods where the housing units are located. In other words, we need a segregation value for each neighborhood or local areal unit, and this value can be obtained from employing local segregation measures as neighborhood attributes. Although most segregation measures are global measures, some local measures do exist and have been adopted. The local version of the diversity index is very easy to compute and has existed for quite sometimes. Formally, the diversity level of a unit *i* is

$$H_i = \sum_{k}^{n} p_k * ln\, p_k \qquad (7.1)$$

where p_k is the proportion of the *k-th* population group in the areal unit, and there are *n* population groups in the unit. This measure can be computed for each unit and a map can be compiled to show the varying diversity level in the study region. Then the diversity value for each unit can be treated as a neighborhood characteristic in the hedonic model. The higher the value of H_i, the higher is the level of diversity or lower is segregation. The upper bound of the index is ln(*n*). Therefore, the index can be scaled to (0, 1). It is important to note that the index is not group-specific in the sense that the index will be zero, indicating no diversity as long as an area is exclusively dominated by one group regardless of which group dominates the area. Also, the formulation in Equation 7.1 does not reference the regional diversity level. However, regional level diversity can be used to standardize the local measure.

Local diversity can be regarded as an evenness measure. Another highly recommended evenness measure for segregation is the *D* index of dissimilarity. The global version has been used probably most frequently in segregation studies. A local version has been suggested by spatially disaggregating the index (Wong 1996). Briefly, for each unit *i*, the local dissimilarity index can be defined as

$$D_i = \frac{a_i}{A} - \frac{b_i}{B} \qquad (7.2)$$

where a_i and b_i are the population of the two groups in unit *i*, and *A* and *B* are the total populations of the two groups in the entire study region. Note that this index can be positive, indicating that group *a* is more concentrated than *b*, and negative, indicating that group *b* is more concentrated than *a* in the unit. It should be bounded between 1 and –1. As each unit will have a value showing the evenness of the two groups, the value can then be used as a neighborhood characteristic to serve as an input to hedonic models. Figure 7.1 shows the D_i values of Washington, DC at the census block group level by comparing whites and blacks with whites corresponding to group *A* and blacks corresponding to group *B* in Equation 7.2. Therefore, a positive D_i reflects that whites are disproportionally more than blacks in unit *i*, and vice versa. In Figure 7.1, it is apparent that whites were distributed in higher proportions than blacks on the western or northwestern side of the city while blacks had higher proportions in the east.

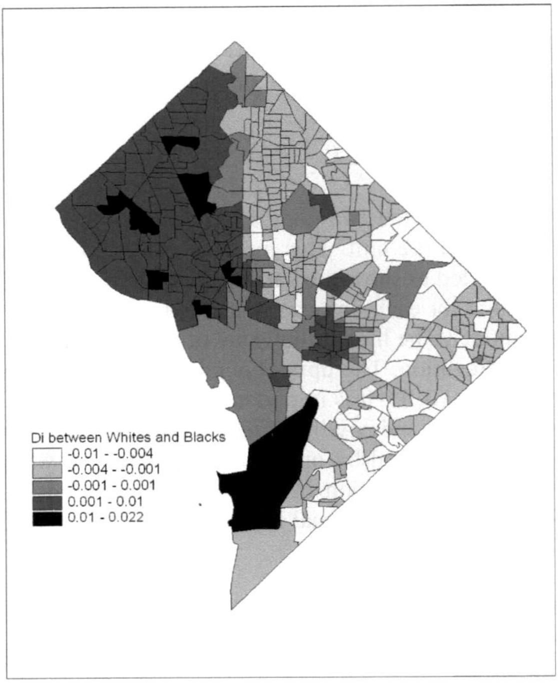

Fig. 7.1 D_i between Whites and Blacks at the Census Block Group Level, Washington, DC, 2000 Census. Data source: U.S. Bureau of the Census Summary File 1

Another dimension of segregation is exposure or isolation. The popular exposure measure is also a global measure (Lieberson 1981). The global measure can be disaggregated to derive a local form using a methodology developed by Wong (1996). However, modified or spatial local versions of the index by incorporating spatial or neighborhood information have been suggested, partly based upon the spatial interaction modeling literature (Wong 2002). The general idea is that in the original formulation of the exposure indices, only the population within the same areal unit will be evaluated and the results from individual units are all aggregated to provide a summary for the entire region. In the proposed spatial local indices, exposure between groups across areal units is accounted for by the simple formulation

$$a_i \sum_j c_{ij} b_j \tag{7.3}$$

where a_i and b_j are the two groups in units i and j, and i can be equal to j. The exposure of group a to b is moderated by c_{ij}, which in its simplest form is a binary variable indicating if i and j are neighbors. Obviously more sophisticated specifications of spatial relationship, such as a distance-based specification can be used instead of the binary neighborhood specification.

More detailed information about this set of indices can be found in Wong (2002). Each areal unit will then have a measure reflecting how one group is exposed to another group. Note that exposure is not a symmetrical concept. The exposure of group *a* to *b* at a given location will unlikely be the same as the exposure of group *b* to *a*. Therefore, the indices are group and location-specific. This local version has been used to assess neighborhood effects on health performance (Grady 2006).

The centralization dimension of segregation is highly dependent upon the structure of cities or regions and therefore, it will not be discussed in this section. For the concentration dimension, many measures have been proposed in the geographical literature (Massey and Denton, 1988). One might easily perceive this dimension as simply population density. High concentration implies high density such that a relatively large population occupies a relatively small amount of space. Another interpretation is that the population is restricted or confined to a small territory and thus it limits their interaction or opportunities mixing with other population groups.

This dimension is a function of density, and in turn may be a function of area. Different from the dimensions of evenness and exposure which involve the comparison of two or more population group, concentration dimension may involve only one population group, and population density of that group is the focus. Hoover index (Hoover 1941) is probably one of the earliest indices for measuring concentration. Another concentration measure commonly used in geography while density is not explicitly taken into account is the location quotient. The location quotient of an areal unit *i* is defined as

$$Q_i = \frac{S_i / P_i}{S / P} \tag{7.4}$$

where S and P are the subgroup population and the total population, respectively, in the entire study area. The S_i and P_i are the subgroup and total populations in the individual areal unit *i*. The quotient will be one if the share of the subgroup in the unit is the same as the subgroup in the entire region. Quotient values smaller than one indicate that the group is less concentrated than the regional situation, and vice versa. Note that comparing the location quotients of two population groups is similar to the local evenness measure of D_i in Equation 7.2.

Location quotients are often mapped to show spatial patterns of concentration. Therefore, the quotient can be used as a neighborhood characteristic. Figure 7.2 shows two maps using whites and blacks as the two subgroups in deriving the quotient for Washington DC. Note that the maximum of Q_i for whites was close to 3 while the maximum of Q_i for blacks was only 1.5. In other words, whites were highly concentrated in some areas while the concentration level of blacks was much less.

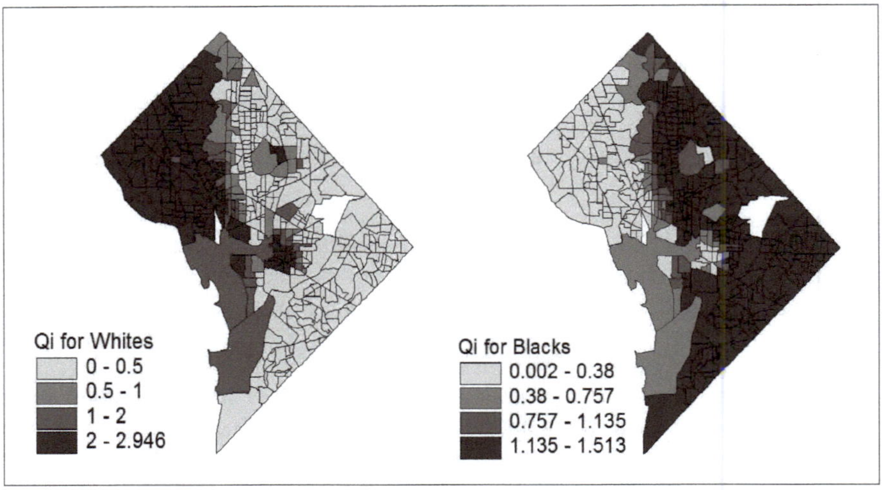

Fig. 7.2 Location Quotients for Whites and Blacks in Washington, DC. Data source: U.S. Bureau of the Census Summary File 1

Two characteristics of using location quotient deserve attention. First, the current approach deals with one population group at a time, but segregation involves more than one group. By using the quotient on individual groups, it does not deal with segregation directly and effectively. Second, the calculation of location quotients does not involve area to derive density but uses the total population as the base. Therefore, the density in the quotient is not per areal unit but per person in the total population. By mapping the location quotients, spatial patterns, if any, can be reviewed. These patterns are formed not just due to where each of the high or low values is located (absolute locations), but are also dependent upon the values of surrounding areas (relative locations). By examining the spatial patterns of the high and low concentration areas, one may develop an impression of how the population is clustered, the last dimension of segregation.

The clustering dimension is probably the most spatial among all dimensions of segregation. In Massey and Denton's review, all clustering measures incorporate certain spatial information, such as unit adjacency information and distance measures. A subset of clustering measures is essentially spatial autocorrelation measures in the spatial statistics literature. These measures include Moran's I and Geary's Ratio (Wong and Lee 2005). They are intended to measure the direction and degree of correlation or similarity across areal unit for a single variable. But like most segregation measures, they are global measures – one value for the entire region.

Local versions of these spatial autocorrelation measures have been proposed (Anselin 1995) and they were labeled as local indicators of spatial autocorrelation (LISA). A common misconception about these local measures is that they can identify "hot spots" and "cold spots." One needs to recognize that these measures evaluate the level of similarity or correlation among areal units, and therefore they cannot distinguish clusters of high values from clusters of low values. The local version of *G-statistic*, or G_i is more appropriate for hot-spot analysis (Getis and Ord 1992). Another limitation of using local spatial autocorrelation statistics in evaluating neighborhood segregation is that most measures consider only one variable or population group, though bivariate spatial autocorrelation statistics have been proposed (Lee 2001).

7.4.3 Aspatial vs. Spatial Segregation Measures

A major limitation with existing segregation measures, regardless of global or local, is the assumption that population in an areal unit will not cross over unit boundaries to interact with population of another group in other (neighboring) units. This assumption is definitely problematic, and is an artifact of using ecological or aggregated data such that population data are tabulated and reported according to enumeration units. Because of such nature of the data, there is a tendency to overestimate the level of segregation, as population is prohibited to cross over to other units to interact with other population groups. Spatial separation among groups is artificially imposed. To remove or at least reduce the impacts of this artificially inflated segregation, evaluation of segregation should implicitly allow people to interact over space, or at least in the surrounding neighborhood.

This framework has been adopted in creating several spatial segregation measures. In measuring multi-ethnic segregation, Wong (1998) proposed using the concept of composite population count. The composite population count, for instance, of population group a in areal unit i is defined as

$$ca_i = \sum_r d(a_r) \tag{7.5}$$

where a_r is the population count of a group a in areal unit r, $d(.)$ is a function defining the neighborhood of i, r refers to an areal unit within the study region, and r can be i. In other words, the composition population count of group a in unit i includes all populations of group a in the neighborhood of i, assuming that people can move and interact freely within the neighborhood. Then measures of segregation based upon this composite population counts will implicitly account for interaction among ethnic groups across areal units within the neighborhood. The composite population count framework is the simplest form of more sophisticated and general spatial smoothing methods that were suggested more recently, especially in the light of addressing the scale dependence of the modifiable areal unit problem (MAUP) (Wong 1997; Reardon and O'Sullivan 2004; Wu and Sui 2001).

Based upon this framework, a multi-group spatial version of D was suggested as a global segregation measure (Wong 1998). Using a similar approach, Wong (2002) proposed a spatial version of the diversity index computed for each areal unit. Specifically,

$$H_i = -\sum_k^n \left[\left(\frac{CP_{ik}}{CP_i} \right) ln \left(\frac{CP_{ik}}{CP_i} \right) \right] \tag{7.6}$$

where CP_{ik} is the composite population count for population group k in areal unit i, and CP_i is the total composite population count for areal unit i. In other words, values inside () in Equation 7.6 are the composite population proportions. Note that the composite population count framework can also be applied to location quotient (Eq. 7.4), though the conceptual meaning is not too clear.

In this chapter, I modify this framework slightly to introduce another local version of D measure, LD_i, which is the D measure evaluated at the local neighborhood around a reference unit i. I will argue that even though D is originally used to depict evenness, when space is introduced, its local form can reflect a different segregation dimension – exposure. Formally, this local version $LD_i(d)$ is

$$LD_i(d) = \sum_{j=0}^n I_d \left(\left| \frac{a_j}{A} - \frac{b_j}{B} \right| \right) \tag{7.7}$$

where all terms are defined as in Equation 7.2, and the $I_d(.)$ is a indicator function (0, 1), such that if unit j is within distance d from i, the function will be 1, otherwise 0. The general idea is to compute the traditional dissimilarity index but at a local scale, and the local neighborhood is defined by the distance threshold. Areal units within the threshold will be included in the evaluation to provide an indication of the level of evenness within the neighborhood i, not the entire study area like the traditional D index.

Therefore, we can alter the size of neighborhood definition to explore the spatial extent of segregation. As shown in Figure 7.3, two renderings of the LD_i based upon different distance thresholds (or buffers) for Washington, DC are shown together with a map showing the proportions of white in the region. As for any true spatial measures, LD_i will suffer from boundary or edge effect. That is the units located close to or along the regional boundary will not be evaluated correctly because its neighborhood relationship has been truncated by the artificial delineation of the region. Several methods have been suggested to "correct" boundary effects and none is perfect (Griffith 1985; Griffith and Amrhein 1983). I chose to include a ring or buffer of units surrounding Washington, DC as shown in the first map in Figure 7.3.

In Figure 7.3, two maps using two neighborhood definitions (i.e., d) of 1,000-meter and 5,000-meter buffers were rendered. The size of the buffer or neighborhood definition implies the spatial extent of resident's interaction space. Clearly, it varies by individuals. Elderly and children will have smaller interaction spaces, but young adults and adults should have bigger. The two buffer sizes chosen here are for illustrative purposes. According to Equation 7.7, LD_i reflects the unevenness of the two groups within the neighborhood surrounding areal unit i. The higher the value, the more uneven is between the two groups within the neighborhood. Based upon the first map in Figure 7.3, it is obvious that Washington, DC has a general east-west division such that west (or northwest) is predominantly whites and east is predominantly blacks. As a result, units in the middle section have relatively uneven population mix and thus they have relatively high LD_i values. On the contrary, units located at the eastern and western ends are highly homogeneous and therefore, their LD_i values are relatively low.

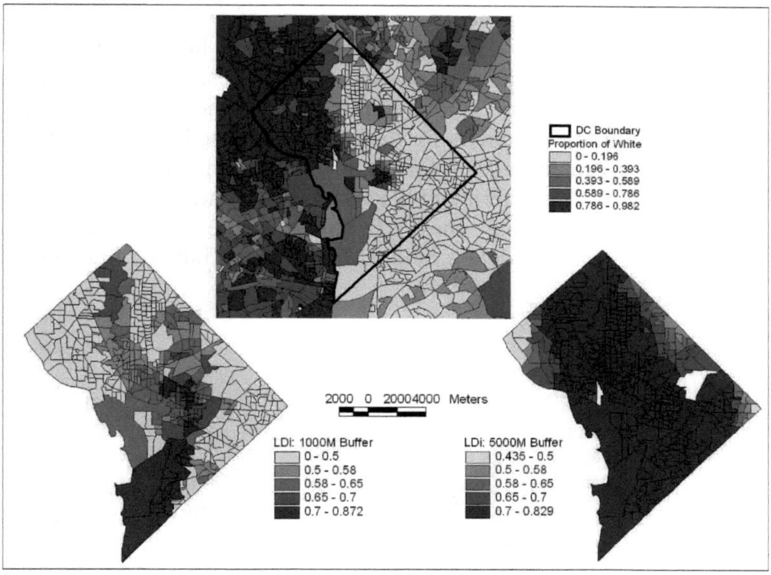

Fig. 7.3 Local D_i with 1000M and 5000M Buffers, Washington, DC.
Data source: U.S. Bureau of the Census Summary File 1

According to the traditional interpretation of the index of dissimilarity D, higher D value is less desirable and more segregated as the population is distributed unevenly. Two major problems are associated with this conceptualization. First, the traditional D is aspatial because it does not include any geographical information explicitly and thus it cannot capture the spatial distribution and relationship of population effectively. It essentially concerns only the population mix of individual unit, but not across units. As a result, if units are exclusively occupied by one group, it will be perfectly segregated even if the two groups are in neighboring units. This issue, sometimes known as the checker-board problem, has been illustrated thoroughly by White (1983), Morrill (1991), and Wong (1993). Closely related to the first problem, the second problem of the formulation of D is that the boundaries are treated as real barriers inhibiting interaction, while in many cases, those boundaries were drawn for statistical gathering and reporting purposes. Thus, two neighboring units with different population mixes can possibly have a high degree of inter-group interaction, and therefore, lower the level of segregation.

With this understanding, LD_i in essence reflects the level of heterogeneity within the defined neighborhood. A low LD_i value indicates that the neighborhood is highly homogeneous, which also implies that the population in the neighborhood do not have much interaction with the other group. On the other hand, units with high LD_i values have relatively heterogeneous neighborhoods and therefore provide the opportunities for inter-group interaction if unit boundaries are not real barriers to interaction. Note that the dissimilarity index D is originally a measure of evenness, the interpretation of its local version, LD_i, has incorporated the exposure dimension and switched the original meaning of D completely. Highly uneven neighborhoods should have low segregation, and homogeneous neighborhoods are segregated. Traditionally, darker colors represent the more segregated neighborhoods and vice versa. Therefore, in Figure 7.4, the coloring schemes were switched around with darker colors for the more segregated areas, and lighter colors for the less segregated units. As a result, the eastern and western ends were highlighted. While on the eastern end blacks were separated from whites, and the western end is just the opposite. These LD_i values can be regarded as a neighborhood variable for hedonic modeling. It is spatial in nature but no group-specific.

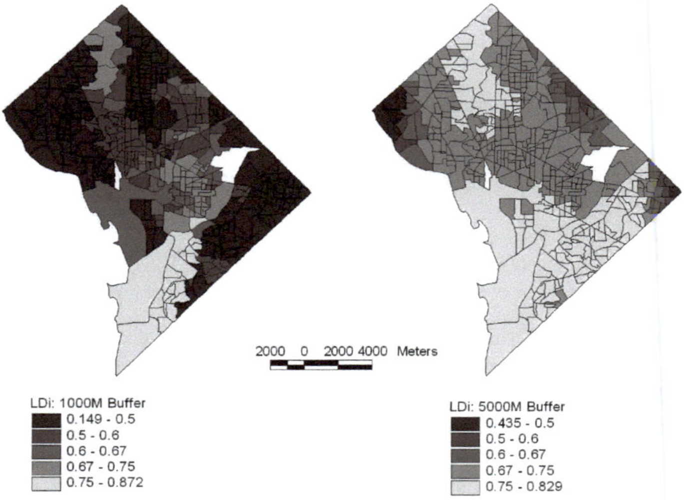

Fig. 7.4 Local *Di* with 1,000M and 5,000M Buffers with Darker Colors for more Segregated Areas. Data source: U.S. Bureau of the Census Summary File 1

7.4.4 The Nature and Impacts of Segregation

The last operational issue regarding the use of segregation measures in hedonic modeling is about the effectiveness of adopted segregation measures in reflecting the nature of segregation. Besides facilitating the formation of prejudice toward a population group, segregation may lead to discrimination as reviewed before. The two types of discrimination are overburdened by undesirable conditions and the denied access to resources or services; both conditions can affect housing price of a neighborhood. The issue is whether current measures of segregation can reflect these types of undesirable conditions effectively. All measures we have discussed so far, including all those measures classified into the five segregation dimensions by Massey and Denton (1988), are not designed to measure the levels of mistreatment received by the residents or ill conditions in the neighborhood. Essentially they measure population distribution disregarding the sources of undesirable conditions or the nature of access restriction to resources.

In order to take into account the undesirable situations due to segregation, one has to first identify the source of the undesirable condition and/or the process or nature through which the population is denied of access to certain resources. Then these sources and processes have to be incorporated into the measures adopted. For instance, a typical example in environmental justice is the presence of a noxious facility in the neighborhood. If the neighborhood is highly segregated, then this particular population group will be subject to disproportional burden of the undesirable effects from the facility. The measure should be able to reflect the burdens shared by different groups. If the segregated population is denied access to a particular facility, the measure should be able to show that the population group in the neighborhood has to pay more, both in monetary and non-monetary terms, to access a similar facility elsewhere.

It is quite clear that current segregation measures were not designed to be effective in this type of evaluation. Some measures in geography and spatial analysis could possibly serve as the bases for this type of measures, but most of them were not intended to take different population groups into account. Therefore, there is a significant deficiency in this direction of segregation research.

7.5 Summary and Conclusion

Including segregation measures in modeling housing price is logical in the sense that segregation can be treated as a neighborhood characteristic which may have impacts on housing price. Conceptually, how segregation is related to housing price has not been thoroughly theorized, and their relationship has been very much investigated with the data-driven empirical approach. In fact, the concept of segregation has not been clearly defined. One of the objectives of this paper is to briefly elucidate the segregation concept by identifying the potential impacts of segregation. Segregation has been regarded as undesirable in most situations (with some exceptions) and is expected to negatively affect housing price. Therefore, it is important to assess the impacts of segregation on housing price.

Operationally, several issues serve as the obstacles in incorporating segregation measures in modeling housing price. Some issues are purely methodological such as the need to develop local or neighborhood scale versus the traditional city or regional scale measures to serve as inputs to model housing price. Other issues are related to what aspects of segregation should be measured or quantified to explain housing price variation over space. Some methodological advances were made in the past two decades in developing spatial and local measures, but some basic conceptual issues are still in need for further investigation.

References

Anselin L (1995) Local indicators of spatial association - LISA. Geographical analysis 27: 93–115

Brasington DM, Hite D (2005) Demand for environmental quality: a spatial hedonic analysis. Regional science and urban economics 35: 57–82

Brown LA, Chung SY (2006) Spatial segregation, segregation indices and the geographical perspective. Population, space and place 12: 125–143

Fotheringham AS (1997) Trends in quantitative methods I: stressing the local. Progress in human geography 21: 58–96

Getis A, Ord JK (1992) The analysis of spatial association by use of distance statistics. geographical analysis 24: 189–206

Grady SC (2006) Racial disparities in low birthweight and the contribution of residential segregation: A multilevel analysis. Social science and medicine 63: 3013–3029

Griffith DA (1985) An evaluation of correction techniques for boundary effects in spatial statistical analysis: contemporary methods. Geographical analysis 17: 81–88

Griffith DA, Amrhein CG (1983) An evaluation of correction techniques for boundary effects in spatial statistical analysis: traditional methods. Geographical analysis 15: 352–360

Hoover EM (1941) Interstate redistribution of population, 1850–1940. Journal of economic history 1: 199–205

Hughes MA, Madden JF (1991) Residential segregation and the economic status of black workers: new evidence for an old debate. Journal of urban economics 29: 28–49

Jargowsky PA (1996) Take the money and run: economic segregation in U.S. metropolitan areas. American sociological review 61: 984–998

Johnston RJ, Poulsen MF, Forrest J (2003) Ethnic residential concentration and a "new spatial order?":exploratory analyses of four United States metropolitan areas, 1980-2000. International Journal of Population Geography 9: 39-56

Kiel KA, Zabel JE (1996) Housing price differentials in U.S. cities: household and neighborhood racial effects. Journal of housing economics 5: 143–165

Lee SI (2001) Developing a bivariate spatial association measure: an integration of Pearson's r and Moran's I. Journal of geographical systems 3: 369–385

Lieberson S (1981) An asymmetrical approach to segregation. In: Peach C, Robinson V, Smith S (eds) Ethnic segregation in cities. University of Georgia press, Athens, United States, pp 61–82
Massey DS (1990) American apartheid: segregation and the making of the underclass. American journal of sociology 96: 329–357
Massey DS, Denton NA (1988) The dimensions of residential segregation. Social forces 67: 281–315
Morrill RL (1991) On the measure of geographical segregation. Geography research forum 11: 25–36
Myers CK (2004) Discrimination and neighborhood effects: understanding racial differentials in US housing prices. Journal of urban economics 56: 279–302
Newby RG (1982) Segregation, desegregation, and racial balance: status implications of these concepts. The urban review 14: 17–24
O'Sullivan D, Wong DWS (2007) A surface-based approach to measuring spatial segregation. Geographical analysis 39: 147–168
Perlin SA, Wong DWS, Sexton K (2001) Residential proximity to industrial source of air pollution: interrelationships among race, poverty, and age. Journal of air and waste management 51: 406–421
Reardon SF, Firebaugh G (2002) Measures of multi-group segregation. Sociological methodology 32: 33–67
Reardon SF, O'Sullivan D (2004) Measures of spatial segregation. Sociological methodology 34: 121–162
Rosen S (1974) Hedonic price and implicit markets: product differentiation in pure equilibrium. Journal of political economy 82: 34–55
Segerson K (2001) Real estate and the environment. Journal of real estate and economics 22: 135–139
White MJ (1983) The measurement of spatial segregation. American journal of sociology 88: 1008–1018
White MJ (1986) Segregation and diversity measures in population distribution. Population index 52: 198–221
Wong DWS (1993) Spatial indices of segregation. Urban studies 30: 559–572
Wong DWS (1996) Enhancing segregation studies using GIS. Computers, environment and urban systems 20: 99–109
Wong DWS (1997) Spatial dependency of segregation indices. The canadian geographer 41: 128–136
Wong DWS (1998) Measuring multiethnic spatial segregation. Urban geography 19: 77–87
Wong DWS (2002) Modeling local segregation: a spatial interaction approach. Geographical and environmental modelling 6: 81–97
Wong DWS, Lee J (2005) Statistical analysis and modeling of geographic information. Wiley and Sons, New York
Wu X, Sui DZ (2001) An initial exploration of a lacunarity-based segregation measure. Environment and planning B: planning and design 28: 433–446
Yankauer A (1950) The relationship of fetal and infant mortality to residential segregation: an inquiry into social epidemiology. American sociological review 15: 644–648
Yinger J (1978) The black-white price differential in housing: some further evidence. Land economic 54: 187–206
Yinger J (1979) Prejudice and discrimination in the urban housing market. In: Peter Mieszkowski P, Straszheim M (eds) Current issues in urban economics. Johns Hopkins University press, Baltimore, Maryland, pp 430–468

8 Using Hedonic Models to Measure Racial Discrimination and Prejudice in the U.S. Housing Market

Jeffrey E. Zabel[1]

Tufts University, Newton, United States

8.1 Introduction

Given the longstanding goal of racial equality in the USA (and elsewhere), there have been many attempts to measure the presence of racial discrimination in the housing market. In this context, racial discrimination is an action whereby nonwhites are treated differently than whites in some aspect of the housing market.[2] Given the complexity of the housing market, racial discrimination can manifest itself in a number of ways. First, suppliers of housing can price discriminate and charge nonwhites more than whites. Second, whites can by force, threat, or collusion prevent nonwhites from living in certain areas. This can include some forms of zoning or racial covenants that can restrict the types of individuals that can purchase houses in certain areas or towns. Third, real estate agents can steer nonwhites away from white neighborhoods and hence deny nonwhites access to these areas. Fourth, nonwhites can be denied mortgages at a higher rate than whites, all else equal. Fifth, lenders can refuse to write loans in certain high minority areas; this is known as redlining. Sixth, lenders can charge higher prices to nonwhites for mortgages by offering higher interest rates or by forcing them to apply for private mortgage insurance.

---

[1] The author would like thank Steve Ross for useful comments and particularly the Editors of this Volume for their very careful reading of and insightful comments on earlier drafts of this chapter.

[2] While racial discrimination has been the focus in the Unites States, discrimination against foreigners is more pertinent elsewhere such as in Europe. The framework established here for analyzing racial discrimination can also be applied to discrimination against other groups.

A. Baranzini et al. (eds.), *Hedonic Methods in Housing Markets*, doi: 10.1007/978-0-387-76815-1_8,

There are numerous ways of detecting discrimination in the housing market. First, one can observe the actual process of discrimination. For example, discrimination by real estate agents can be observed through the use of paired testing experiments, also known as audit studies. A number of such studies have been conducted in the USA (the most recent in 2000) and they show that while discrimination against blacks has declined over time, it is still present in a variety of forms (Yinger 1998; Ross 2005). Second, one can directly observe and measure residential segregation, which is a particular outcome of discrimination. This can be accomplished using one of the numerous segregation measures such as indices of exposure and dissimilarity (see Wong in this Volume). Third, one can analyze differential treatment of nonwhites in the mortgage market. Direct evidence points to lower approval rates (Munnell et al. 1996) and redlining (Tootell 1996). Indirect evidence is found by analyzing racial differentials in homeownership rates (e.g. Deng et al. 2003). Fourth, one can analyze whether price differentials by race exist in the housing market. This can be accomplished by estimating house price hedonic equations that include measures of race. A fifth method is based on a general equilibrium model of the housing market. This allows one to identify racial preference parameters that derive from an underlying utility function (e.g. Bayer et al. 2004 and Bayer, this Volume). A related method borrows from the industrial organization literature to model the housing market as being made up of multiple products with different characteristics. One can then show whether or not an individual's willingness to pay for one of these characteristics such as the racial makeup of the neighborhood, depends on the individual's race (Bajari and Kahn 2005 and Bajari and Kahn, this Volume).

The focus of this chapter is on the fourth of these methods for detecting discrimination in the housing market. Initially, a general framework for detecting discrimination based on the hedonic model of house prices will be established. Then, this framework will be used to evaluate the literature. This paper is limited to an analysis of the U.S. housing market since this is the basis of most of the research on discrimination in the housing market (but see Harrison et. al. (2005) for an analysis of housing discrimination in the European Union). The burst of energy in the 1970s devoted to estimating discrimination and prejudice in the housing market using hedonic house price models has been followed by a relative dearth of such studies in the past twenty-five years. This might be due to a change of focus to other forms of discrimination in the housing market (i.e. forms three through six above). Also, with the advent of estimable forms of the general equilibrium urban model, it is now possible to analyze the impact of racial preferences on residential patterns in urban areas in a general equilibrium framework rather than the inherently partial equilibrium framework that underlies the studies based on hedonic models.[3] Another reason is that the data requirements for accurately estimating discrimination using hedonic models are particularly onerous. Given these difficulties, along with other econometric issues that arise in specifying and estimating

---

[3] Two versions of the computable general equilibrium model have been developed by Epple and Seig (1999) and Bayer et al. (2004).

the hedonic model, it is recommended that the focus should be on trends in racial discrimination in the housing market rather than on point estimates from cross-section data. Of course, this only adds to the data requirements for estimating these trends.

When discussing housing discrimination, it is important to distinguish between three concepts: discrimination, prejudice, and segregation. In this context, prejudice is a preference for neighbors of the same race. Discrimination is an action whereby nonwhites are treated differently than whites in any aspect of the housing market. Segregation is an outcome; the physical separation of groups. In this context, this refers to residential segregation. One way to relate these three concepts is by the following schematic:

(S.1)	prejudice ⇒	discrimination	⇒ segregation
(S.2)		prejudice	⇒ segregation

Of course, the arrows can go the other way too. As Yinger (1995) points out, discrimination and prejudice are mutually reinforcing. Furthermore, segregation can cause prejudice since a lack of interaction among races can serve to reinforce racial stereotypes that can lead to prejudice. Yinger states that "residential segregation is one outcome of a complex system in which prejudice, segregation, discrimination, and racial or ethnic disparities are simultaneously determined. [....] Most scholars now recognize that racial and ethnic prejudice and discrimination are both the causes and consequences of residential segregation" (p. 122).

Cutler et al. (1999) distinguish between centralized racism where whites get together to restrict nonwhite choices and hence nonwhites pay more for housing, and decentralized racism where individually whites choose to pay more to live in white communities (thereby constraining white choices) and hence pay more for housing. Centralized racism is a special case of (S.1) and decentralized racism a special case of (S.2).

The hedonic house price model is based on actual housing market outcomes that are affected by both the supply of and the demand for housing. One can thus distinguish between (S.1) and (S.2) in terms of their impacts on these two components of the housing market. The supply of housing is affected when nonwhites are excluded from purchasing units in certain areas and when the seller charges a higher price to nonwhites (S.1).[4] The demand side of the market is affected when the buyer's reservation price depends on the racial makeup of the neighborhood (S.2). In this sense, we see that discrimination directly affects the supply of housing and prejudice directly affects the demand for housing. All forms of discrimination discussed in the initial paragraph affect the supply of housing to nonwhites. It is important to point out that observing the market outcome that the price of a

[4] King and Mieszkowski (1973) refer to Becker (1957) in noting that prejudiced landlords will only rent to blacks at a premium.

house is affected by race in some way does not necessarily allow one to distinguish between these two causes, discrimination and prejudice, since one affects the supply of housing and the other affects the demand for housing. In order to clearly distinguish between supply-side and demand-side impacts, one would need to estimate supply and/or demand equations for housing.

Typically, market outcomes are observed in the form of sales prices for houses since in the USA information on rents is more difficult to obtain. Given utility maximization by consumers and profit maximization by producers (in the case of new units) or overlapping reservation prices by buyers and sellers in the case of resales, sales prices can be related to the characteristics of the units in a functional form known as the hedonic house price model:

$$P_{klt} = \mathrm{f}\left(sc_{kt}, a_{lt}; \beta_t\right) \tag{8.1}$$

where P_{klt} is the sales price of unit k in location l at time t, sc_{kt} is a vector of structure characteristics for unit k at time t, a_{lt} is a vector of locational amenities for location l at time t, and β_t is a vector of parameters that are the weights that relate the structure characteristics and locational amenities to the sales price P_{klt}. Rosen (1974) shows that under certain conditions, these weights can be interpreted as the willingness to pay (WTP) for the associated characteristic (see Taylor, this Volume).

Without discrimination, buyer characteristics do not appear in this hedonic model. Furthermore, without widespread discrimination against a specific race, individuals of that race should be able to buy the desired unit for a lower price from a seller who is not charging a higher price based on race. Hence the race of the buyer should not affect the price. Only when there is widespread discrimination can the race of the buyer affect the price of the unit.

Locational amenities can include the characteristics of neighbors if there are widespread preferences for such characteristics. Thus individuals might have preferences for neighbors who are of a certain race, religion, ethnicity, and/or income level. In which case, these characteristics will appear in the hedonic function (eq. 8.1). To allow for discrimination and racial preferences (prejudice) to affect prices, the hedonic model in equation (8.1) can be modified as follows:

$$P_{iklt} = \mathrm{f}\left(sc_{kt}, a_{lt}, nw_i, pctnw_{lt}; \beta_t\right) \tag{8.2}$$

where nw_i is an indicator of the race of the buyer of unit k and $pctnw_{lt}$ is the percent of neighbors who are nonwhite.[5]

[5] Other measures of racial composition are possible (see Wong, this volume). The percent of neighbors who are nonwhite is used here since this has traditionally been used in the literature that is pertinent for this analysis.

The hedonic equation models housing market outcomes and hence reflects interactions between supply and demand. Again, one has to be careful about interpreting the coefficients as representing individual preferences. One assumption needed to interpret the coefficients as WTP is that the market is in equilibrium. Second, it is assumed that there is no bundling of goods; the market is "thick" in that it includes a continuum of choices. But this may not hold in practice. For example, one reason that one might see a high level of racial segregation is that the integrated areas may not have the other characteristics that nonwhites desire when looking for a place to live.

While racial prejudice is typically viewed as whites preferring to live near other whites, nonwhites can also have a preference to live near other nonwhites. This can result in nonwhites paying more to live in neighborhoods with a high percentage of nonwhites. Still, one must not view de facto segregation as evidence of either overt discrimination by whites or of preferences of nonwhites to live with nonwhites. It is clear that residential choice is a complex process that involves many factors on both the supply and demand side. For example, whites typically have higher incomes than nonwhites and there is a lot of residential sorting by income. The end result can be sorting by race. Further, one must recognize that preferences are endogenous and potentially self-reinforcing. Current preferences for whites and nonwhites to live with those of the same race are likely driven by past discrimination and the ensuing segregation. Cutler et al. (1999) find a large persistence in relative segregation across cities in the twentieth century. Aaronson (2001) finds that neighborhood racial and income composition are very persistent. He also finds that house prices are highly persistent and have positive feedback effects on high-income families and negative effects on the percent of nonwhites in the neighborhood. Aaronson also finds that spatial dependence may matter; that is, spillover effects from nearby neighborhoods are important. This can explain the long lives of highly segregated areas that encompass multiple neighborhoods. Further, as Schelling (1971) shows, high levels of segregation are possible even if most nonwhites and whites have a desire for integration. Hence the resulting high level of segregation may not represent the true preferences of nonwhites (and whites) who prefer integrated neighborhoods.

In fact, other than discrimination and prejudice/preferences, there are at least five reasons for racial segregation; 1) income differences, 2) demographic differences, 3) occupational differences, 4) different preferences for other factors, and 5) a lack of integrated neighborhoods with other desired characteristics such as good schools, little crime, and good access to jobs. One needs to control for these other factors before determining if discrimination and prejudice/preferences can explain racial residential patterns. Ioannides and Zabel (2007) estimate a residential location model that includes the percent nonwhite in the census tract interacted with the race of the head of household along with a host of other factors such as household income. They also interact the race of the head of household with a binary variable that indicates if the percent of nonwhites in the census tract is greater than 50%. They find that the impact of an increase in percent nonwhite is to lower the likelihood of whites residing in the neighborhood while it increases the likelihood of nonwhites residing in the neighborhood. Further, for nonwhites, the likelihood of residing in the neighborhood is even greater if the dominant race in the neighborhood is nonwhite. Bayer et al. (2004) show that in the San Francisco Bay area, raising black incomes to the same level as white incomes can create enough middle class black households to form middle class black neighborhoods such that segregation can actually increase. But see Ihlanfeldt and Scafidi (2002) who find that preferences play a small role in the residential location of nonwhites.

In Section 8.2, four versions of the hedonic house price model are developed that allow for racial discrimination and prejudice. These include Bailey's (1959) Border model and Yinger's (1976) Amenity model. In Section 8.3, four issues complicating the analysis of racial discrimination using the hedonic house price model are addressed: 1) Schelling outcomes, 2) omitted variable bias due to a lack of significant neighborhood characteristics, 3) endogeneity, and 4) appropriate data and levels of aggregation. In Section 8.4, the existing literature is reviewed in the context of the models developed in Section 8.2 and the problems highlighted in Section 8.3. In Section 8.5, future directions of research are discussed.

8.2 Modeling Framework

In this section, the framework for measuring discrimination and prejudice in the housing market must be established. Initially, the general hedonic model is developed. Then four models that allow for discrimination and prejudice are presented and the parameters associated with the racial variables are interpreted. The next section includes a discussion of four issues that need to be addressed when estimating one of these four models.

8.2.1 The General Hedonic Model

Let P_{knmt} be the price of house k, in neighborhood n, in Metropolitan Statistical Area (MSA) m, at time t. Assume that the natural log of P_{knmt} is a function of house characteristics (sc_{kt}) and neighborhood characteristics (N_{nmt}):

$$\ln P_{knmt} = \mathrm{f}\left(sc_{kt}, N_{nmt}; \beta_{0mt}, \beta_{1mt}, \beta_{2mt}, v_k, v_n, \varepsilon_{knmt}\right). \tag{8.3}$$

Note that in this general model, coefficients β_{0mt}, β_{1mt}, and β_{2mt} vary across time and MSAs. This is a recognition that housing markets are no larger than MSAs and hence coefficients can vary across these markets. The terms v_k and v_n are unit and neighborhood effects that capture unobserved structure and neighborhood factors that affect the price, and ε_{kmnt} is a random error term.

Typically, individual characteristics do not enter the hedonic equation but in the case of racial discrimination, the race of the owner can enter the model. Further, if individuals care about the characteristics of their neighbors, these will be included in the vector of neighborhood amenities in equation (8.3). In particular, one can care about the race of one's neighbors or, in a summary way, the racial makeup of the neighborhood such as the percent nonwhite. For now, a general function of these racial variables is added to equation (8.3) but it is assumed that the remaining terms enter linearly:

$$\ln P_{iknmt} = \beta_{0\mathrm{mt}} + \beta_{1\mathrm{mt}} sc_{kt} + \beta_{2\mathrm{mt}} N_{nmt} + \mathrm{f}_{nw}\left(nw_i, pctnw_{nmt}; \beta_{mt}^{nw}\right) + v_k + v_n + \varepsilon_{knmt} \quad (8.4)$$

where nw_i is an indicator that the owner is nonwhite and $pctnw_{nmt}$ is the percent nonwhite in neighborhood n. The coefficients that relate to discrimination and racial preference are allowed to vary across time and MSAs. This is because it is likely that discrimination will vary across MSAs and change over time (Kiel and Zabel 1996).

8.2.2 Four Models of Discrimination and Prejudice in the Housing Market

The general function $\mathrm{f}_{nw}(\cdot)$ in equation (8.4) allows for many possible functional forms of the impact of the racial variables on house prices. Initially, a simple functional form is presented and then increasingly complex specifications are considered. To simplify matters, the analysis will be confined to one MSA and one time period so that the "*mt*" can be dropped from the subscripts for the model variables and coefficients.

Linear specifications for nw_i and $pctnw_{nt}$ are included in Model 1:

$$\ln P_{ikn} = \beta_0 + \beta_1 sc_k + \beta_2 N_n + \beta_3 nw_i + \beta_4 pctnw_n + v_k + v_n + \varepsilon_{ikn}\,. \quad (8.5)$$

For Model 1, $\Delta nw = 100 \cdot \left[exp(\beta_3) - 1\right]$ is the average percent difference in price for a buyer who is nonwhite relative to a buyer who is white. Racial discrimination will lead to nonwhites paying more for a comparable unit than whites; that is $\Delta nw > 0$. This could either occur because prejudiced sellers require nonwhites to actually pay more for a unit or because the supply of housing available to nonwhites is restricted and this drives up the price for a comparable unit relative to what whites pay. Next, $\Delta pctnw = 100 \cdot \left[exp(\beta_4) - 1\right]$ is the average percent difference in price for a one percentage point increase in the percent nonwhite in the neighborhood. Preferences for neighbors who are white will result in lower prices in neighborhoods with a higher percentage of nonwhites; that is $\Delta pctnw < 0$. If $\Delta pctnw > 0$ then this is an indication that, on average, the higher the percentage of nonwhites in the neighborhood, the higher the price of the unit. This can be the result of preferences for neighbors who are nonwhite or because the supply of housing available to nonwhites is restricted and hence this drives up the price for a comparable unit relative to what whites pay (the neighborhoods where nonwhites live will tend to be concentrated with nonwhites). In this case, one cannot determine specifically if prejudice or discrimination is present in the housing market but only that at least one of these two causes exists.

An influential model in the literature on housing discrimination is the "border" model developed by Bailey (1959). The standard general equilibrium urban model has been generalized to allow for racial preferences along the lines of Bailey's border model by, among others, Rose-Ackerman (1975). The general assumption is that nonwhites prefer to live near whites while whites prefer *not* to live near nonwhites. The result is a perfectly segregated city with nonwhites living in the center and whites in the suburb. Preferences are specified to be a function of the distance from the border between these two areas. At the border, the price that nonwhites and whites will pay is the same. After this point, the white bid-rent function is always above the nonwhite bid-rent function and the white bid-rent function can initially rise with distance from the border. In this model, whites pay more and nonwhites less for housing when whites are prejudiced than when they are not. Bailey's Border Model is presented in Figure 8.1.

A version of the Border model was estimated by King and Mieszkowski (1973). Model 1 can be modified to produce a variation of the Border model and is referred to as Model 2.[6]

$$\begin{aligned} lnP_{ikn} = \beta_0 + \beta_1 sc_k + \beta_2 N_n + \beta^{nw}_{NONW} nw_i \cdot NONW_n + \beta^{nw}_{BORD} nw_i \cdot BORDER_n + \\ + \beta^{w}_{NONW} w_i \cdot NONW_n + \beta^{w}_{BORD} w_i \cdot BORDER_n + \beta^{w}_{WHITE} w_i \cdot WHITE_n \\ + v_k + v_n + \varepsilon_{knt} \end{aligned} \qquad (8.6)$$

where w_i is the binary indicator that the owner is white and $NONW_n$ and $BORDER_n$ are binary variables that define the nonwhite and border areas (based on the percent nonwhite in the neighborhood; for example King and Mieszkowski use 60% and 3% cutoffs to define these areas).

6 There are no nonwhites residing in WHITE in King and Mieszkowski's dataset so they do not include the term $w_i \cdot WHITE_n$ in their model.

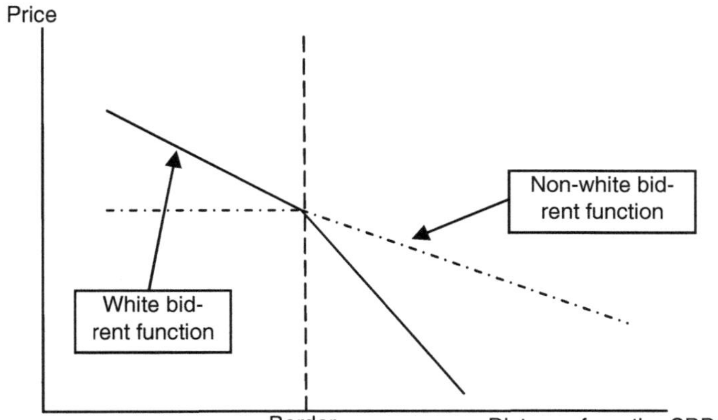

Fig. 8.1 Bailey's Border Model. Source: generated by the author

The coefficients $\beta^{nw}_{NONW}, \beta^{nw}_{BORD}, \beta^{w}_{NONW}$, and β^{w}_{BORD} are measures of price differentials for units owned by nonwhites and whites in *NONW* and *BORDER* compared to the left-out area; *WHITE* (note that the superscript indicates the race of the owner and the subscript the area of residence). See Figure 8.2 for a visual representation of this version of Bailey's Border model. In Model 2, price discrimination implies that nonwhites pay more for equivalent housing than whites; $\beta^{nw}_{NONW} > \beta^{w}_{NONW}$, $\beta^{nw}_{BORD} > \beta^{w}_{BORD}$ and $\beta^{w}_{WHITE} < 0$. Exclusion of non-whites from white areas implies that $\beta^{nw}_{NONW} > 0$; nonwhites pay more for equivalent housing in *NONW* compared to what they would pay in WHITE.[7] White prejudice implies that $\beta^{w}_{NONW} < \beta^{w}_{BORD} < \beta^{w}_{WHITE}$ and preferences for integration by nonwhites implies $\beta^{nw}_{BORD} > 0$. Note that the signs of these coefficients do not necessarily reveal the full set of preferences and discriminatory practices since they can combine supply-side and demand-side effects. For example if $\beta^{w}_{NONW} > 0$ this could indicate exclusion (a supply-side effect) since prices are higher in *NONW* but it could mask white prejudice since this would be consistent with $\beta^{w}_{NONW} < 0$ (a demand-side effect).

[7] Note that exclusion of non-whites from white areas can also result in $\beta^{w}_{NONW} > 0$ since whites will also have to pay more in NONWITE given that demand for housing is greater for nonwhites.

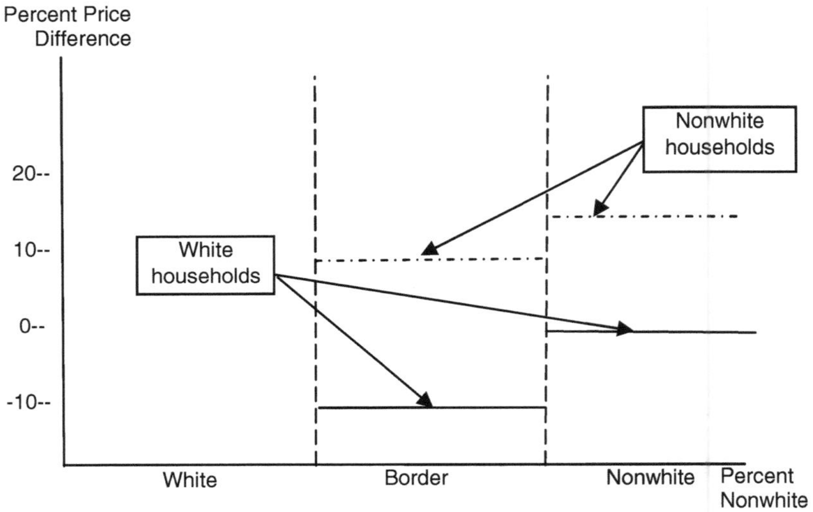

Fig. 8.2 Border Model (Model 2). Source: generated by the author

For the city to be perfectly segregated, as entailed by the border model, the incomes for all whites must be higher than those for all nonwhites. Yinger and Courant (1977) relax this unrealistic assumption and allow for there to be overlap in the distributions of incomes for nonwhites and whites. In this case, the bid-rent functions of nonwhites and whites can intersect at some point beyond the border. Past this point, wealthier nonwhites will out-bid whites and the result is two nonwhite areas surrounding one white area; hence the border model is not an equilibrium outcome. Further, both poor and rich whites are worse off than under the border outcome. It is then in the best interest of whites to try to prevent wealthier nonwhites from moving to the periphery. Thus, the border model is not consistent with nonwhite and white preferences when incomes overlap and the housing market is competitive. One way to reconcile this model is to assume positive search costs for housing and preferences by some whites to not sell to nonwhites. Then nonwhites may find it too costly to search for housing in whites areas (Courant 1978). The other way to reconcile the model is to assume non-competitive behavior in the form of discrimination by whites against nonwhites by exclusion.

An alternative to the Border model was developed by Yinger (1976). This model is referred to as the "Amenity" model since the percent nonwhite in the neighborhood is treated as a local amenity that is capitalized into house prices. The only difference between this model and the Border model is the way racial preferences are specified; in the latter, preferences are a function of distance to the border while in the former they are a function of the proportion of nonwhites in the surrounding area /neighborhood.

One further characteristic of the Amenity model is that the coefficient of the amenity variable percent nonwhite is allowed to vary across neighborhoods. A negative coefficient is expected in largely nonwhite areas since both whites and nonwhites prefer areas with fewer nonwhites. In integrated areas, a negative coefficient is an equilibrium outcome for both nonwhites and whites if nonwhites prefer integrated areas with the highest percentage of whites. The problem with the Amenity model is that it is an equilibrium model for whites but not necessarily for nonwhites if nonwhites prefer integrated neighborhoods. If the coefficient on percent nonwhite is negative in largely white areas, nonwhites cannot be in equilibrium. This outcome can only arise if discrimination prevents nonwhites from moving into their preferred location. Model 3 is a generalized specification of the Amenity model as presented in Yinger (1978):

$$\begin{aligned} ln\,P_{ikn} = {} & \beta_0 + \beta_1 sc_k + \beta_2 N_n + \beta_{NONW}^{nw} \cdot nw_i \cdot NONW_n + \beta_{BORD}^{nw} \cdot nw_i \cdot BORDER_n \\ & + \beta_{NONW}^{w} \cdot w_i \cdot NONW_n + \beta_{BORD}^{w} \cdot w_i \cdot BORDER_n + \beta_{WHITE}^{w} \cdot w_i \cdot WHITE_n \\ & + \beta_{NONW}^{pctnw,nw} \cdot nw_i \cdot pctnw_n \cdot NONW_n + \beta_{BORD}^{pctnw,nw} \cdot nw_i \cdot pctnw_n \cdot BORDER_n \\ & + \beta_{WHITE}^{pctnw,nw} \cdot nw_i \cdot pctnw_n \cdot WHITE_n + \beta_{NONW}^{pctnw,w} \cdot w_i \cdot pctnw_n \cdot NONW_n \\ & + \beta_{BORD}^{pctnw,w} \cdot w_i \cdot pctnw_n \cdot BORDER_n + \beta_{WHITE}^{pctnw,w} \cdot w_i \cdot pctnw_n \cdot WHITE_n \\ & + v_k + v_n + \varepsilon_{ikn} \end{aligned} \tag{8.7}$$

The amenity model is displayed in Figure 8.3. Note that the coefficients $\beta_b^{pct,a}$ for a = *nw, w* and b = *NONW, BORD, WHITE* measure the impact of *pctnw* on house prices for nonwhites and whites in the three neighborhoods (hence the corresponding variables are triple interactions between *pctnw*, race, and neighborhood. Yinger does not allow for the impact of *pctnw* to differ for whites and nonwhites. Hence, the model that he estimates is a special case of Model 3 where the impact of *pctnw* across neighborhoods is measured by the common (across the races) coefficients $\beta_{NONW}^{pctnw}, \beta_{BORD}^{pctnw}$, and β_{WHITE}^{pctnw}. This implies that the impact curves for white and nonwhite households are parallel in Figure 1 in Yinger (1978) whereas they are allowed to have different slopes in Figure 8.3.[8]

One problem with this approach is that the values of *pctnw* that are used to divide up the areas can be arbitrary. For example, King and Mieszkowski (1973) use 3% and 60% nonwhite as breakpoints and Myers (2004) uses 15% and 30%. Yinger (1978) chooses the divisions based on minimizing the sum of squared errors; 40% and 80%.

[8] Also, there are no nonwhites living in *WHITE* in Yinger's dataset. This further restricts the model that Yinger actually estimates. This is also why there is no curve for nonwhites in *WHITE* in Figure 1 in Yinger (1978)

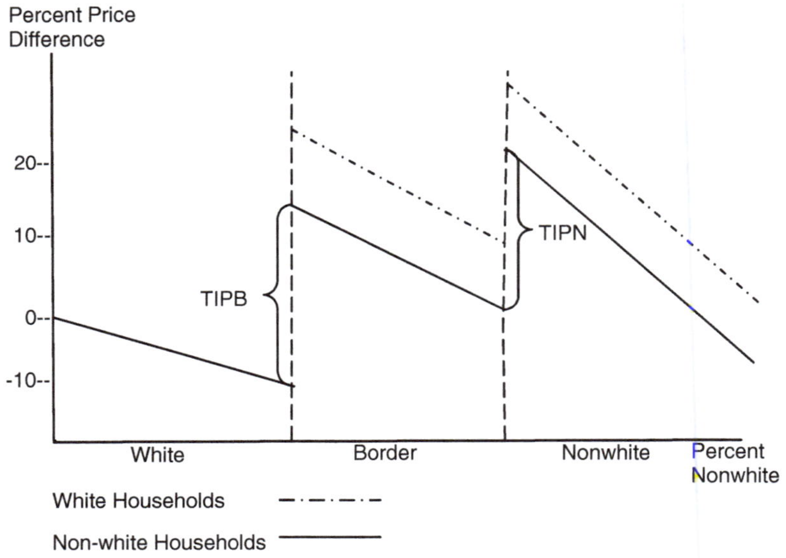

Fig. 8.3 Amenity Model (Model 3). Source: generated by the author

One can view this as a model with segmented markets where *NONW*, *BORDER*, and *WHITE* represent three separate markets (though the coefficients for *sc* and *N* are assumed to be the same). This now allows for the model to capture more complex preferences such as whites preferring to live with whites and nonwhites preferring integrated neighborhoods. White preferences to live with whites will imply that $\beta_{NONW}^{pctnw,w}$, $\beta_{BORD}^{pctnw,w}$, and $\beta_{WHITE}^{pctnw,w}$ are all less than zero. On the other hand, if nonwhites prefer to live with other nonwhites; $\beta_{NONW}^{pctnw,nw}$, $\beta_{BORD}^{pctnw,nw}$, and $\beta_{WHITE}^{pctnw,nw}$ will all be greater than zero. Note that in Yinger's specification, where the impact of *pctnw* is the same for whites and nonwhites, the above preferences lead to conflicting signs for these now common coefficients. The result can be a mixture of signs since *NONW* neighborhoods will be dominated by nonwhites and hence their preferences may dictate the sign of β_{NONW}^{pctnw} while *WHITE* neighborhoods will be dominated by whites and hence their preferences may dictate the sign of β_{WHITE}^{pctnw}.

One can use the above model to measure the difference in house prices between a unit in an all-white neighborhood and one in neighborhoods with different percentages of nonwhites. These differences will depend on which neighborhood type the specific value of *pctnw* falls into. So consider three values, $PCTNW_W$, $PCTNW_B$, and $PCTNW_{NW}$ (all greater than zero) to indicate three values of *pctnw* that result in the unit being in a *WHITE*, *BORDER*, or *NONW* neighborhood. Then, for white households, the price differential between the unit in the all-white neighborhood and the other three neighborhoods would be (similar differences can be constructed for nonwhite households):

$$DIFF(PCTNW_W) = \beta_{WHITE}^{pctnw,w} PCTNW_W$$
$$DIFF(PCTNW_B) = \beta_{BORD}^{w} + \beta_{BORD}^{pctnw,w} PCTNW_B$$
$$DIFF(PCTNW_{NW}) = \beta_{NONW}^{w} + \beta_{NONW}^{pctnw,w} PCTNW_{NW}$$

If whites prefer to live with other whites, these three values will be negative. One could also construct similar differentials for units in all-nonwhite and integrated neighborhoods to measure the preferences for nonwhites to live with nonwhites.

Finally, one can measure the differences in prices of units that are located on either side of the frontier between *NONW* and *BORDER* and between *BORDER* and *WHITE*. Yinger (1978) claims that these can be interpreted as measures of discrimination through the exclusion of nonwhites from specific neighborhoods. Let $PCTNW^B$ and $PCTNW^{NW}$ be the values of *pctnw* at the frontiers between *WHITE* and *BORDER* and *BORDER* and *NONW*, respectively. The price differential between houses on the *BORDER* and *WHITE* sides of the frontier between these two neighborhoods is:

$$TIPB = \beta_{BORD}^{w} + \left(\beta_{BORD}^{pctnw,w} - \beta_{WHITE}^{pctnw,w}\right) \times PCTNW^{B}.$$

The price differential between houses on the *NONW* versus the *BORDER* sides of the border between these two neighborhoods is:

$$TIPN = \beta_{NONW}^{w} - \beta_{BORD}^{w} + \left(\beta_{NONW}^{pctnw,w} - \beta_{BORD}^{pctnw,w}\right) \times PCTNW^{NW}.$$

Racial discrimination through the exclusion of nonwhites from white (border) neighborhoods will lead to a positive value of TIPB (TIPN). Both TIPB and TIPN are displayed in Figure 8.3. Note that TIPB and TIPN can also be calculated using the coefficients for nonwhites (versus whites as above).

One other issue to address is the appropriate level of aggregation at which the "neighborhood" is measured. Kiel and Zabel (1996) use the census tract while Myers (2004) uses the ten nearest neighbors as surveyed in three special waves of the American Housing Survey. Kiel and Zabel (2008) use variables at both levels of aggregation. This recognizes that individuals can care about the race of the neighbors on their street, S_{sw}, and in the census tract where the latter could proxy for the racial make-up of the public schools (e.g. Downes and Zabel 2002) that would depend on the percent nonwhite in the school district or town, T_w (if the two are similar) where s and *w* index street and town, respectively. Thus Model 4 is a generalization of Model 1 that allows for two levels of neighborhood:

$$\begin{aligned} ln\, P_{iksw} = \beta_0 + \beta_1 sc_k + \beta_{21} S_{sw} + \beta_{22} T_w + \beta_3 nw_i + \beta_{41} pctnw_{sw} + \beta_{42} pctnw_w \\ + v_k + v_s + v_w + \varepsilon_{iksw} \end{aligned} \quad (8.8)$$

Further generalizations along the lines of Models 2 and 3 are possible.

8.3 Complications Arising in Estimating Racial Impacts on House Prices

There are a number of issues to address when estimating the models developed in Section 8.2 that bring into question the appropriate interpretation of the estimated coefficients for the racial variables in Models 1 to 4. In this section, we discuss, in turn, the following four issues; 1) Schelling outcomes/tipping, 2) omitted variables bias, 3) endogeneity, and 4) the appropriate data for estimating these models.

8.3.1 Schelling Outcomes/Tipping

Schelling (1971) developed a model of neighborhood choice where individuals care about the racial composition of their neighbors. Whites are assumed to be indifferent to the racial make-up of their neighborhood up to a critical level of nonwhite concentration. This critical level is referred to as a "tipping point." Schelling's model is based on a sequential decision-making process where individuals who wish to do so can move. The result is a segregated neighborhood even though the initial distribution may have been integrated. Schelling's model reveals the unintended consequences of individual interactions. The dynamics of the so called "spatial proximity model" or "social interactions model" are driven by externalities; an individual's residential location decision affects the neighbors' utilities and this is not priced in the housing market; how much one person will pay for a house is not affected by how that person's decision to live in a neighborhood affects the neighbors' utilities. Pancs and Vriend (2007) show that Schelling's model of segregation is robust – individual preferences for integration can be made more extreme and the result is still segregation. Pancs and Vriend point out that the consequence of this finding is that policies that attempt to alter individual preferences towards integration will be ineffective in producing integrated outcomes.

Schellings' work has made the concept of tipping an important part of the discussion of racial residential composition, yet actual empirical evidence of tipping is rare. This is partially due to the fact that residential choice is a very complicated process and isolating the impact of a particular factor is difficult. Recently, Card, Ma, and Rothstein (2007, henceforth CMR) use census tract data from 1970 to 2000 to test for discontinuities in the dynamics of neighborhood racial composition. That is, there is expected to be very different, discontinuous changes in white population on either side of the tipping point. CMR estimate the location of the unknown tipping points for more than 100 metropolitan areas in the U.S; the mean tipping point in the 1970 – 1980, 1980 – 1990, and 1990 – 2000 periods was 11.83, 13.53, and 14.46 percent minority, respectively. Thus tipping points have increased over time. CMR show that this trend can be explained by demographic changes. They point out that it is crucial to allow the tipping point to differ across cities. Otherwise, no tipping point is found (as in Easterly 2005). CMR find that the tipping point is higher in cities with more tolerant whites. It is also related to racial composition, racial income differences, density, crime rates and measures of past racial tension.

CMR develop a model of tipping that is based on the bid-rent (inverse demand) functions for whites and nonwhites. This model predicts that rents will not exhibit discontinuities around tipping points though no such prediction is possible for house prices. Using the census data, CMR find modest evidence of discontinuities in rents and house values around tipping points. This result has an impact on how to specify the percent of nonwhites in the hedonic model; there should not be discontinuous changes in prices at the border (e.g. β^{w}_{NONW} and β^{nw}_{NONW} in Model 3 should be zero, though the CMR model does not incorporate potential discrimination through exclusion). The CMR approach could also be used as a rigorous approach to determining the boundaries between the different neighborhoods as specified in Model 2 and Model 3.

8.3.2 Omitted Variable Bias Due to Lack of Significant Neighborhood Characteristics

One confounding factor in measuring the impact of discrimination and prejudice on house values is the likelihood that omitted variables will bias the results. Kiel and Zabel (1996) show that the impact of leaving out the neighborhood indicators on the coefficient for the race of the homeowner is substantial. Typically, obtaining information on the appropriate set of neighborhood characteristics that affect house prices is difficult for multiple cities. These would include school quality, crime levels, environmental quality, job accessibility and block-level characteristics such as density, noise, aesthetics, and general upkeep. For example, Li and Brown (1980) are able to include a large number of neighborhood characteristics but only for 781 sales of single-family houses in 1971–1972 in 15 suburban towns in the southeast sector of the Boston MSA. One alternative is to use census data to proxy for neighborhood characteristics. Of course, one must be careful about using variables such as median household income since it is likely to be endogenous.

A second solution to the omitted variables bias problem is to use repeat sales; i.e. take first-differences. The impacts of the race of the homeowner and the percent nonwhite in the neighborhood would be identified by changes in these variables across sales periods. The use of repeat sales requires multiple sales for the same unit and can suffer from sample selection bias since houses with multiple sales are not necessarily a random sample of all housing units. One can imagine a scenario where a number of contiguous neighborhoods have tipped and there are a large number of sales that can potentially influence the estimates particularly since identification depends on units where there is a change in the race of the owner and the percent nonwhite in the neighborhood.

A third solution would be to use town fixed effects. These will capture any unobserved town characteristics that are correlated with the percent nonwhite and hence will alleviate any associated bias.[9] Given that the neighborhood is disaggregated below the town level (e.g. census tract or block), the impact of *pctnw* will be identified by within-town differences in this variable. The problem with this approach is that it is not possible to measure the impact of individual town-level variables with a cross-section of data. This is a problem when estimating the impact of school quality when the district coincides with the town. This could be a problem with measuring racial impacts if multiple levels of neighborhood are used where one level is the town-level.

8.3.3 Endogeneity

Another complication with the hedonic model is, because of neighborhood sorting, the racial composition of the neighborhood is endogenously determined and hence variables that measure the racial make-up of the neighborhood are not likely to be exogenous. Typically, the percent nonwhite in the neighborhood has been treated as exogenous and this can lead to bias when estimating the house price hedonic. Two approaches to obtaining instruments are to use boundary fixed effects (Bayer et al. 2004) or the average of the percent nonwhite in the neighborhoods inhabited by observationally identical homeowners (Bayer and Ross 2007).

8.3.4 Appropriate Data

An important issue concerns the appropriate data with which to estimate racial impacts on house prices. This is a simpler problem when only estimating a cross-section model but omitted variable bias problems can then be harder to solve and it is not possible to estimate trends in the racial impacts. Ideally, one would want data on all relevant factors that affect house prices; particularly neighborhood characteristics. This includes the race of the homeowner which is often not available; particularly with sales data.[10] One example is the American Housing Survey (AHS). Another source of data is the Integrated Public Use Microdata Series (IPUMS). The problem with this dataset is that it generally identifies no geographic areas with fewer than 100,000 inhabitants. A final recourse is to gain access to confidential census data at the household level. The one problem with these datasets is that they include owners' house valuations and not sales data. While this might seem problematic, Kiel and Zabel (1999) show that the bias is,

---

[9] See (Clapp et. al. 2007) for an example of town fixed effects in the context of measuring school quality.

[10] One possible solution would be to merge sales data with Home Mortgage Disclosure Act (HMDA) data that will provide information on the race of the homeowner. I thank Pat Bayer for this making this point.

on average, 5% and, other than length of tenure, this bias is unrelated to observable characteristics of the owner, house, and census tract.

One thing to take away from this analysis is that the results of changes over time in coefficients for racial variables in hedonic regressions are likely to be more reliable than individual coefficient estimates at one point in time. This requires data across time (either a panel or independent cross-sections). In this case, the main issue is obtaining measures of the percent nonwhite in the neighborhood at different points in time. Until recently this has been difficult to obtain since the main source of this type of information has been the decennial censuses. Now the American Community Survey fills in the gap by collecting census information every year. The drawback is that this is based on a random sample of the population and it is not collected at the same level of geographic detail as the decennial census. A few states provide information at the elementary school district level but nothing as small as a census tract is given.

Another issue is the appropriate level at which to measure the neighborhood. Typically percent nonwhite is measured at the census tract level. Kiel and Zabel (1996) analyze discrimination and prejudice in the housing market at the census tract level. They note that carrying out the analysis at the census tract level may mask heterogeneity in racial composition within the tract. Myers (2004) uses the special waves of the AHS data for 1985, 1989, and 1993 to construct measures of racial composition at the cluster level which consists of about 10 nearest neighbors. She points out that the cluster-level may be too narrow a measure to capture racial effects at the neighborhood level. Kiel and Zabel (2008) further investigate this issue of the appropriate geographic level at which to measure racial composition by including variables at both the cluster and tract levels. They find evidence that both levels are important and their importance varies across regions. This highlights the need for a more disaggregated analysis at the MSA level that includes measures of racial composition at both the street and town level.

Goodman (1977) estimates hedonic models using sales data from 1967–1969 in New Haven, Connecticut (U.S.). He includes neighborhood variables aggregated to the tract and block group levels in separate regressions. The R^2 for the latter model is slightly higher (0.8388 vs 0.8353). Generally, the coefficient estimates are comparable across regressions. One important difference is the impact of the racial variables which are significant with the expected signs when aggregated at the block group level but not at the tract level.

Typically, it is assumed that housing markets are no larger than metropolitan areas in the U.S.. Hence it is advisable to estimate the impact of discrimination and prejudice on house values separately for each MSA. Kiel and Zabel (1996) show that these impacts vary across the four cities in their analysis. Further, as already mentioned, Card et al. (2007) find that tipping points vary across cities. Estimating a single house price hedonic for the whole country (i.e. U.S.) can easily miss evidence in specific MSAs (e.g. Myers 2004; Cutler et al. 1999). This means that it is necessary to obtain enough observations per MSA to be able to estimate separate hedonic regressions for each MSA.

8.4 Literature Review – Current Evidence on Racial Discrimination and Prejudice in the U.S. Housing Market

In this section, the literature on racial discrimination and prejudice in the housing market is discussed and results are evaluated in reference to the models developed in Section 8.2 and the complications discussed in Section 8.3. We focus on recent contributions to the literature that allow for a synthesis of the latest findings using hedonic house price models to determine the existence and scope of discrimination and segregation in the U.S. housing market.

To set the stage, information on the extent of prejudice and segregation in the U.S. is provided. First, the most recent surveys show that white attitudes have changed; whites are more willing to live with nonwhites than in the past (Yinger 1995). Further, Card et al. (2007) show that tipping points across U.S. metropolitan areas have increased over time. Still, there is evidence of persistent negative racial stereotypes and more subtle forms of racial discrimination (Bobo 2001). Second, segregation has declined over time yet the rate of change is slow and past attitudes still influence today's pattern of racial segregation in the U.S. Cutler et al. (1999) provide a thorough analysis of the birth and development of ghettos in twentieth-century U.S. They find three divisions: 1) 1890–1940: birth of the ghetto, 2) 1940–1970: ghettos expanded and consolidated and, 3) 1970–1990: segregation fell throughout the country and most in the South and West. The decrease in segregation was due to the drop in neighborhoods that were exclusively white and not the neighborhoods that were exclusively black; between 1960 and 1990, the percentage of suburban census tracts that were less than one percent black fell from 70 percent to 40 percent while the share of census tracts that were at least 90 percent black doubled in both suburban and urban areas. Cutler et al. (1999) note that the relative segregation of different cities has been much more persistent and appears to be strongly correlated with city size. Glaeser and Vigdor (2001) find that segregation continued to decline in the 1990's with an average decrease of 5.5%.

It is recognized that there are many reasons for the current level of racial segregation other than discrimination and prejudice such as differences in income, demographic characteristics, occupations, and preferences for factors other than the racial composition of the neighborhood. Based on the recent evidence, particularly that in Cutler et al. (1999), Ross (2005) concludes that discrimination in the housing market has declined "substantially" and it "does not significantly constrain the residential outcomes of minorities." That said, there are still large disparities in homeownership rates between whites and nonwhites. Evidence in the mortgage market points to lower approval rates (Munnell et al. 1996) and redlining (Tootell 1996) and the evidence from paired testing studies of housing discrimination (the most recent in 2000) shows that while discrimination against blacks has declined over time, it is still present in a variety of forms (Ross 2005).

Given this background, we look at the evidence on how racial discrimination and prejudice have been capitalized into the price of housing. The burst of energy in the 1970s devoted to estimating discrimination and prejudice in the housing market using hedonic house price models has been followed by a relative dearth of such studies in the past twenty-five years. Recent studies have tended to focus on discrimination in the mortgage market and by real estate agents. The results of the studies discussed below are summarized in Table 8.1.

Cutler et al. (1999) is an example of a recent study that estimates Model 1. They use IPUMS data to estimate house price regressions across MSAs for 1940, 1970, and 1990. Due to data restrictions, they can only include the percent black in the census tract in 1970 (along with a binary variable to indicate whether the owner is black). They also include the median tract income and the percent of the population that lives in housing built within the previous 30 years as controls for neighborhood quality. The estimated coefficient on the percent black is 0.088 and it is significant at the 1% level. Cutler et al. (1999) interpret this as evidence of exclusion or black preferences to live with blacks. They note that if median income is omitted from the model, the coefficient estimate for the percent black is negative. The estimated coefficient on the indicator of black ownership is -0.117 and significant at the 5% level. This appears to be contrary to the finding of exclusion. One problem with the Cutler et al. (1999) analysis is that they estimate one regression for the whole U.S. (even MSA dummies are not included). Thus they cannot pick up the variation in the impact of race on house prices across MSA's.

As discussed in Section 8.2, King and Mieszkowski (1973) estimate the Border model as specified by Model 2. They use data from 1968 and 1969 on 220 rental units in New Haven, Connecticut (U.S.). They find evidence of discrimination in the border area where blacks pay 7% more than whites but no such evidence in the black area where prices are similar for whites and blacks. Given that these latter coefficients are positive (around 9%), this is viewed as evidence of exclusion. The only neighborhood characteristics included are the mean test score for the local elementary school and the distance to downtown. Only the latter variable is significant. Hence these results are likely to be biased due to a lack of neighborhood quality indicators. Further, the sample size is quite small.

Table 8.1 Summary of Existing Studies

Study	Data	Unit of Observation/Neighborhood level	Model	Results
Glaeser, Cutler, Vigdor (1999)	IPUMS data for 1940, 1970, and 1990	City in 1940 and 1990, Census tract in 1970	1	Evidence of decreasing discrimination over time. In 1970, evidence of discrimination in the form of exclusion or preferences for blacks to live with blacks.
King and Mieszkowski (1973)	220 Rental units in New Haven, Connecticut in 1968–1969	School district	2	Discrimination in Border areas; blacks pay more than whites. Evidence of exclusion based in black area; both blacks and whites pay more.
Cicerone (1994)	AHS data for Boston in 1985	Zone – at least 10,000 residents	2	Blacks paid less than whites; evidence is inconsistent with discrimination.
Chambers (1992)	AHS data for Chicago in 1975 and 1979	Zone – at least 10,000 residents	2	Blacks pay less in black border and white areas; inconsistent with discrimination.
Yinger (1978)	Transaction data for St Louis in 1966	Census tract	3	Blacks paid more than whites; evidence of discrimination. Blacks paid more to live in the Boundary versus the white area; evidence of exclusion. Houses with a higher percent back sold for less in the white, border, and black areas; evidence of white prejudice.
Kiel and Zabel (1996)	Philadelphia, Denver, and Chicago for 1978–1991	Census tract	3	Evidence of decreasing discrimination in all three cities; increasing prejudice in Denver and Philadelphia and decreasing prejudice in Chicago.
Myers (2004)	National version of AHS for 1985, 1989 and 1993	Neighborhood cluster	3	Blacks paid more than whites; evidence of both discrimination and prejudice.
Kiel and Zabel (2008)	National version of AHS for 1985, 1989 and 1993	Neighborhood cluster and census tract	4	Evidence of discrimination in the South, prejudice in the Northeast, Midwest; former focused at the tract level, latter focused at the cluster level.

Source: generated by the author

Yinger (1978) estimates the amenity model (Model 3) using transactions data for St. Louis in 1967. The results show that blacks pay 15% more for housing than whites; evidence indicative of discrimination. Further, blacks pay 50% more to live in the Boundary versus the white area; evidence of exclusion. Finally, the coefficient estimates for percent black are -0.6, -0.8, and -1.9 for the white, border and black areas; respectively; evidence of white prejudice. One drawback of this analysis is the small number of observations in some of the areas; for example there are no blacks in the white area and only seven in the Border area.

Chambers (1992) uses a special version of the American Housing Survey (AHS) for Chicago in 1975 and 1979 where the lowest level of geography that is identified is the "zone" (an area that contains at least 100,000 residents). Chambers estimates a version of the Border model that includes separate impacts of the race of the owner in four areas; black, black border, white, and Spanish border and binary indicators for the black and black border areas. He finds significant discounts for black owners in the black border and white areas in both 1975 and 1979. The negative coefficients for the black border are contrary to what one would find if whites were undertaking discriminatory actions against blacks. The binary indicators for the black and black border areas are not significant and hence do not provide evidence of exclusionary actions against blacks.

Cicerone (1994) uses the 1985 AHS data for Boston that also includes the zone variable used by Chambers. He includes binary indicators for the race of the owner and whether or not the zone was at least 25% black. Cicerone finds that blacks paid from 19 to 41% less for houses than did whites. This is a similar result to what Chambers found. Given that the zone is such a large area and given the lack of objective measures of neighborhood quality in the AHS, these results could be picking up the fact that blacks tended to live in lower quality neighborhoods than did whites rather than any indication of racial factors, per se, affecting house values.

Kiel and Zabel (1996) analyze discrimination and prejudice in the housing market in Philadelphia, Denver, and Chicago for the 1978 – 1991 period using the metro-level AHS. They were able to merge in tract-level data from the 1980 and 1990 censuses since they had access to proprietary census tract information for the AHS. They estimate a version of Model 3 where *NONW*, *BORDER*, and *WHITE* are defined to be tracts with percent nonwhite greater than 60, between 10 and 60, and less than 10, respectively. They include median household income, median age, percent blue collar workers, percent of residents over 25 years old with a high school degree, percent vacant units, and percent of units with less than one occupant per room in the census tract to capture neighborhood quality. Kiel and Zabel (1996) find evidence of increasing prejudice in Denver and Philadelphia and decreasing prejudice in Chicago over time. Further, they find evidence of decreasing price discrimination in all three cities over time. An important result of their analysis is that the existence of discrimination and prejudice varies across the three cities. Further, this is one of the few studies that estimates impacts over time so that trends in discrimination and prejudice can be determined.

Myers (2004) uses the special waves of the National version of the AHS for 1985, 1989, and 1993 to construct measures of racial composition at the cluster level. She does not include information on the racial composition at the tract level since she does not have access to the proprietary data that indicates the tract the unit is located in. Myers estimates a single house price model for the U.S. that includes regional dummies. She finds evidence of discrimination; blacks paid an additional 10% compared to whites. She also finds evidence of prejudice; house values declined as the percentage of blacks in the cluster increased. Myers' results are open to the same criticism as those of Cutler et al. (1999); estimating the model at the national level does not allow for the variation in racial impacts across MSAs in the U.S.

Kiel and Zabel (2008) further investigate this issue of the appropriate geographic level at which to measure racial composition by including variables at both the cluster and tract levels. That is, they estimate a version of Model 4. They do this using the same dataset as Myers along with access to proprietary information about the census tract in which each house is located. Given the small number of observations per MSA, a thorough analysis can only be carried out for the four census regions; Northeast, Midwest, South, and West. Thus their results are only suggestive of possible discrimination and prejudice in the housing markets in these regions. Kiel and Zabel (2008) find that the coefficients for the indicator of the homeowner's race do not appear to be greatly affected by which level of geography is included in the model. The evidence indicates that there is discrimination in the South but not in any of the other three regions. The results suggest that including the measure of racial composition at either the tract or cluster level picks up the total impact on house prices due to preferences about racial composition at both the cluster and tract level. This may not be too surprising given the high correlation between the proportion of nonwhites at the cluster and tract levels in this data. Still, this total effect can obscure preferences for racial composition manifesting themselves in different ways at the cluster and tract level if both geographic measures are not included. There is evidence of prejudice in the Northeast and in the Midwest; the former is focused at the tract level while the latter is focused at the neighborhood cluster level. Not surprisingly, the results on discrimination and prejudice vary across the regions. This highlights the need for a more disaggregated analysis at the MSA level that includes measures of racial composition at both the street and tract (or town) level.

8.5 Conclusion

This chapter has investigated the impact of racial discrimination and prejudice on the housing market as evidenced in hedonic house price models. First, four hedonic models that allowed for the impact of racial discrimination and prejudice were developed. Then four complicating issues that arise in estimating these models were discussed. With this framework established, the literature on the impact of discrimination and prejudice (and the related concept of segregation) on house prices in the U.S. was reviewed. One important result is that there are very few relevant studies from the past twenty-five years. One reason for this lack of analysis is that recent efforts have been focused on other sources of evidence on discrimination in the housing market by mortgage brokers and real estate agents. A second reason is that the data requirements for obtaining accurate estimates of racial impacts in hedonic house price models are quite severe. Given the differences in racial concentrations and attitudes across cities, racial discrimination and segregation are best analyzed at the city-level rather than at the national level. This means that datasets such as the national version of the AHS are not useful since there are not enough observations to estimate models at the MSA level. Further, given the many complications involved in being able to obtain accurate estimates of the impact of race on house prices, one should not place too much emphasis on individual coefficient estimates at one point in time. More believable inferences are likely to come from changes over time in coefficients for racial variables in hedonic regressions. This adds to the difficulty in obtaining the necessary data to come up with believable estimates. Thus one recommendation is the need for complete datasets at the MSA level to be able to accurately estimate trends in racial effects over time.

Another recommendation is to use the results/method of Card et al. (2007) to estimate tipping points as a means for determining the border between the nonwhite and border area. This can supplant the fairly ad hoc procedure used in the literature for choosing the borders between areas in the Border and Amenity models.

One assumption of the model underlying the Border and Amenity models is that the racial preferences of whites and nonwhites are homogeneous. This has led to equilibrium conditions only in special cases. But, in reality, racial preferences of all whites, even within a single market, are not the same. Thus, an extension of the general equilibrium urban model with racial preferences would be to allow these preferences to be heterogeneous for whites and nonwhites. This might allow for a more general equilibrium outcome and might also add new facets to the resulting hedonic models.

References

Aaronson D (2001) Neighborhood dynamics. Journal of urban economics 49: 1–31

Bailey MJ (1959) A note on the economics of residential zoning and urban renewal. Land economics 35: 288–292

Bajari P, Kahn ME (2005) Estimating housing demand with an application to explaining racial segregation in cities. Journal of business and economic statistics 23: 20–33

Bayer P, McMillan R, Ruben K (2004) An equilibrium model of sorting in an urban housing market. Working paper no 10865, NBER, Cambridge, United States

Bayer P, Ross SL (2007) Identifying individual and group effects in the presence of sorting: a neighborhood effects application. Discussion paper 07–03, Center for economic studies, U.S. Census Bureau, Washington D.C.

Becker GS (1957) The economics of discrimination. University of Chicago press, Chicago

Bobo L (2001) Racial attitudes and relations at the close of the twentieth century. In: Wilson WJ, Mitchell F (eds) In American becoming: racial trends and their consequences. Academy press, Washington DC

Bond EW, Coulson NE (1989) Externalities, filtering, and neighborhood change. Journal of urban economics 26: 231–249

Card D, Ma A, Rothstein J (2007) Tipping and the dynamics of segregation. Working paper no 13052, NBER, Cambridge, United States

Chambers D (1992) The racial housing price differential and racially transitional neighborhoods. Journal of urban economics 32: 214–232

Cicerone A (1994) An Analysis of Racial Price Differentials in the Boston Area Housing Market. Unpublished Ph.D. dissertation, Northeastern University, Boston Massachusetts

Clapp JM, Nanda A, Ross SL (2007) Which school attributes matter? The influence of school district performance and demographic composition on property values. Forthcoming in Journal of urban economics

Courant PN (1978) Racial prejudice in a search of the urban housing market. Journal of urban economics 5: 329–345

Courant PN, Yinger J (1977) On models of racial prejudice and urban residential segregation. Journal of urban economics 32: 272–291

Cutler DM, Glaeser EL, Vigdor JL (1999) The rise and decline of the american ghetto, Journal of political economy 107: 455–506

Deng Y, Ross SR, Wachter S (2003) Racial differences in homeownership: the effect of residential location. Regional science and urban economics 33: 517–556

Downes TA, Zabel JE (2002) The impact of school characteristics on house prices: Chicago 1987–1991. Journal of urban economics 22: 1–25

Easterly W (2005) Empirics of strategic interdependence: the case of the racial tipping point. Working paper no 5, New York University DRI

Epple D, Seig H (1999) Estimating equilibrium models of local jurisdictions. Journal of political economy 107: 645–681

Frankel DM, Pauzner A (2002) Expectations and the timing of neighborhood change. Journal of urban economics 51: 295–314

Glaeser EL, Vigdor JL (2001) Racial segregation in the 2000 census: promising news. Center on urban and metropolitan policy, The Brookings Institution, Washington D.C.

Goodman AC (1977) A comparison of block group and census tract data in a hedonic housing price model. Land economics 53: 483–487

Harrison M, Law I, Phillips D (2005) Migrants, Minorities and Housing: Exclusion, Discrimination and Anti-Discrimination in 15 Member States of the European Union, European Monitoring Centre on Racism and Xenophobia, Vienna, Austria

Ihlanfeldt KR, Scafidi B (2002) Black self-segregation as a cause of housing segregation: evidence from the multi-city study of urban inequality. Journal of urban economics 51: 366–390

Ioannides Y, Zabel JE (2007) Interactions, neighborhood selection, and housing demand. Forthcoming in the journal of urban economics

Kiel KA, Zabel JE (1996) House price differentials in U.S. cities: Household and neighborhood racial effects. Journal of housing economics 5: 143–165

Kiel KA, Zabel JE (1999) The accuracy of owner provided house values: the 1978–1991 american housing survey. Real estate economics 27: 263–298

Kiel KA, Zabel JE (2008) Location, location, location: The 3L approach to house price determination. Forthcoming in the Journal of Housing Economics
King AT, Mieszkowski P (1973) Racial discrimination, segregation, and the price of housing. Journal of political economy 81: 590–606
Li MM, Brown J (1980) Micro-neighborhood externalities and hedonic housing prices. Land economics 56: 125–141
Munnell AH, Browne LE, Tootell GMB, McEneaney J (1996) Mortgage lending in Boston: interpreting HMDA data. American economic review 86: 25–53
Myers CK (2004) Discrimination and neighborhood effects: understanding racial differentials in US housing prices. Journal of urban economics 56: 279–302
Pancs R, Vriend NJ (2007) Schelling's spatial proximity model of segregation revisited. Journal of public economics 91: 1–24
Rose-Ackerman S (1975) Racism and urban structure. Journal of urban economics 2: 85–103
Rosen S (1974) Hedonic prices and implicit markets: product differentiation in pure competition. Journal of political economy 82: 34–55
Ross SL (2005) The continuing practice and impact of discrimination. Working paper: 2005–19, Department of economics, University of Connecticut
Schelling TC (1971) Models of segregation. RM–6014–RC, The Rand Corporation, Santa Monica
Tootell GMB (1996) Redlining in Boston: do mortgage lenders discriminate against neighborhoods? Quarterly journal of economics 111: 1049–1079
Yinger J (1976) Racial prejudice and racial residential segregation in an urban model. Journal of urban economics 3: 383–396
Yinger J (1978) The black-white price differential in housing: some further evidence. Land economcs 54: 187–206
Yinger J (1979) Prejudice and discrimination in the urban housing market. In: Mieszkowski P, Straszheim M (eds) Current issues in urban economics. Johns Hopkins University press, Baltimore, Maryland
Yinger J (1995) Closed door, opportunities lost. Russell Sage Foundation, New York
Yinger J (1998) Housing discrimination is still worth worrying about. Housing policy debate 9: 893–927

9 The Problem with Environmental Justice Studies (And How Hedonics Can Help)

Diane Hite

Auburn University, Auburn, United States

Focus on environmental justice has intensified since President Clinton issued an executive order in February, 1994 requiring that all government agencies investigate the potential impact of any proposed policy on the environment of disadvantaged classes. Bullard (1996) broadly defines environmental justice as providing equal environmental and health protection under governmental laws and regulations. Specifically, environmental inequity is associated with unequal application of environmental and other social regulations, unequal exposure to environmental hazards, improper risk assessment, exclusionary zoning, and exclusionary practices that prevent minorities from participating in environmental decision making. It has been clearly demonstrated that better community organization and decision-making is a powerful factor in preventing sitings of noxious facilities (Berry 2003), and access to information is critical in this effort (Kellogg and Mathur 2003; Shapiro 2005).

Although environmental disamenities are aesthetically unpleasant, the more important public policy issue concerns human health and productivity impacts, since exposure to toxic substances may result in health problems for a portion of the population that is less likely to have private health insurance. Environmental quality may also contribute significantly to lost labor productivity; for example, Ho (2007) finds significantly reduced work hours for individuals exposed to higher levels of toxic releases. Further, the environmental justice concept can be extended to the built environment, where lack of access to grocery stores has a negative impact on health via improper diet as well as from poor sanitary conditions (Frumkin 2005), and sociologists such as Wilson and Kelling (1982) Sampson and Groves (1989) and Cohen et al. (2000) find links between neighborhood decay, antisocial behavior and other public health problems like increased occurrences of sexually transmitted diseases.

A. Baranzini et al. (eds.), *Hedonic Methods in Housing Markets*, doi: 10.1007/978-0-387-76815-1_9,

However, perhaps the most salient point is that those consuming the most – the wealthy – are visiting the negative byproduct of their consumption on the less fortunate. For example, Mitchell and Dorling (2003) find that the poor in England are disproportionately exposed to auto emissions, even though they are the class with the lowest rates of car ownership; Loh and Sugerman-Brozan (2002) similarly point to the effects of diesel emissions in minority neighborhoods of Boston[1].

The nature of environmental justice has made it a topic of interest for researchers in a number of disciplines, primarily law, sociology, urban planning, geography, and to a more limited extent, economics. Because enforcement of and protection under environmental laws and regulations require proof of wrong-doing, it appears straightforward to turn to statistical methods to make the case. And once damages are established, it is necessary to use generally accepted statistical methods to account for the costs of the wrong-doing, if restitution is to be made. However, the underlying causes of inequitable environmental outcomes are so complex that the straightforward application of standard statistical methods is generally unsatisfactory. For example, some may argue that disadvantaged households are simply willing to give up better environmental quality in order to gain access to other local public goods (e.g. Yandle and Burton 1996). Because hedonic house price analysis can help capture potential tradeoffs in willingness to pay among various property characteristics, its use to analyze environmental price discrimination and to apply a test of envy-free distributions may be fruitful, as will be presented in this paper. An economic, value-based approach also has the advantage of providing estimates of monetary harm that cannot be captured in the standard environmental justice literature.

It should be noted that the costs to lower socioeconomic groups may be understated in standard analysis because of the external nature of environmental damages. For example, individuals in lower classes are less likely to have health insurance, and are more likely to develop more costly medical conditions as a result of preventative measures. In addition, even if the disadvantaged have information about potential environmental dangers in their neighborhoods, they are likely unable to afford to move away from the hazard. Because any econometric analysis of market data cannot fully address these problems, it is possible that a cost-benefit criterion, that uses marginal utility of income weights, would be a useful framework within which consider environmental justice problems.

This paper is organized as follows: first, I present an exhaustive review of the seminal and current literature on environmental justice, predominantly from a sociological and economic point of view; next I present the foundations for applying hedonic techniques to housing data to measure the distribution of environmental quality in neighborhoods; then I discuss further shortcomings of the proposed he-

[1] Although there is a literature concerned with international aspects of environmental justice – for example the pollution haven hypothesis (Strohm 2002) and global warming (Norgaard 2006) – this paper deals only with domestic environmental justice concerns.

donic methods and suggest some additional ways to refine the aforementioned models using recent contributions in econometrics, as well as provide concluding comments.

9.1 Literature Review

Much of the earliest contribution to the environmental justice (EJ) literature has come from the sociology discipline. Among others, sociologists have much contributed to shaping the conceptual basis for EJ analysis. Bullard (1996) defines and clarifies the conceptual issues surrounding EJ. Jacobson et al. (2005) further define EJ into process equity – the process that leads to unequal distribution of environmental quality – and outcome equity – the end result of the process, which is largely what is observed by the empirical researcher. For example, Morello-Frosch (2002) examines how industrial and demographic processes across the landscape have contributed to unequal outcomes, and Platt (2005) examines historical factors leading to environmental inequities in Chicago and Manchester, UK. Helfand and Peyton (1999) provide a coherent conceptual model of EJ and Boerner and Lambert (1997) survey popular and media accounts of environmental discrimination. An important factor in the process of environmental discrimination in housing markets can likely be traced to the well-documented practices of redlining and steering of minorities by real estate agents (Nothaft and Perry 2002; Zenou and Boccard 2000; Ondrich et al. 2000; Page 1995; Yinger 1986). Yinger (1997) extends this literature by developing a search model to estimate discrimination costs associated with search by minority homeowners. Similarly, time-on-market before a house sells has been found to be significantly related to racial composition of a neighborhood (Hite 2006c).

As previously mentioned, much of the empirical EJ literature has been concerned with siting issues, examining the correlation of environmental quality with underlying demographics. Studies that take a more sophisticated approach to the siting issue are Hamilton (1993, 1995), and Kriesel et al. (1996). Hamilton is primarily interested in firms' decisions to increase output of a disamenity in the face of collective action, while Kriesel et al. examine exposure of disadvantaged groups to a number of toxic substances using the Environmental Protection Agency's Toxic Release Inventory. The evidence from these studies appears to suggest that disproportionate exposure to environmental disamenities appears to exist in both urban and rural areas. In contrast to these studies, Been (1993, 1994) notes that most siting studies correlate *current* demographics, not necessarily the demographics at the time of the siting; Been's studies find that when taking dynamics into account, there is no evidence of discrimination in siting. Similarly, Anderton et al. (1997) do not find that disamenities are disproportionately sited in minority neighborhoods, but do find that assigning superfund status is generally slower in minority neighborhoods, meaning that minorities are exposed to disamenities for a longer time than in other neighborhoods. Baden and Coursey (2002) find some evidence for discrimination against Hispanics only.

The results of these studies have been somewhat mixed, quite possibly because of problems associated with aggregation level – most commonly census tract, census block or ZIP code – or problems of identifying or controlling for multiple disamenities. In addition, there are a number of measures of disamenities to examine. Partly in response to environmental justice concerns, a wide range of data have become available in the U.S. for empirical researchers; the United States Environmental Protection Agency (USEPA) has collected the data making it available electronically, notably at the Right to Know website (www.rtk.net). Among the data available are the Toxic Release Inventory (TRI) that contains annual data on releases into air, water and land. Another database that has been used with some frequency is the Comprehensive Environmental Response, Compensation and Liability Information System (CERCLIS), which contains data on superfund sites nationally. A third database used less frequently is the Accidental Release Information Program (ARIP), which documents chemical accidents. One weakness of most of these data is that they do not measure differences in toxicity levels.[2] One of the very few papers that addresses this issue is Bouwes et al. (2001), which develops a measure of relative risk by accounting for toxicity levels, transport and fate in the TRI data.

Derezinski et al. (2003) use 1990 census block group (CBG) data combined with ARIP to examine the distribution of health risk associated with chemical accidents. Their study finds strong correlation between risk and low income households, but finds a smaller effect with respect to race. Goetz and Kemlage (1996) control for cost and demand factors that would drive firm location decisions, and find that high-minority counties are more likely to be associated with hazardous waste treatment facilities location. Hockman and Morris (1998) examine health outcomes associated with environmental justice – cancer rates, and low birth weight – along with the association between race and income on environmental cleanup and location of noxious facilities. Ho and Hite (2006) also find higher cancer rates and releases in counties with more predominate minority populations. In a somewhat different twist, Sadd et al. (1999) and Morello-Frosch et al. (2002) find implications for environmental outcomes in terms of school siting.

Geographic information systems are being used increasingly in the EJ literature. For example, Glickman (1994) employs geographic information system (GIS) data in order to create risk-based measures that differentiate between acute and chronic environmental hazards. Pearce et al. (2006) demonstrate how combining emissions and GIS can be used to create a detailed model of particulate matter pollution dispersion in New Zealand. Using a highly geographically specific model, they find that suppliers of pollution do not consume it.

However, simple correlations of cross-sectional data entirely miss the dynamics

[2] It is also well-established that the geocoding variables in these databases are highly inaccurate.

of urban change (Lambert and Boerner 1997); that is, the sitings may have taken place before the area was inhabited by the under class. Researchers thus consider that perhaps disadvantaged groups move to the area where disamenities are located, and thus are not being discriminated against. Cameron and Crawford (2003) examine changes in the demographic composition of census tracts near seven Superfund sites located in urban areas and find some evidence of minorities moving to risky areas, many of whom are single parent households with children. I argue later that moving to a hazard is likely a result of price discrimination; that is, it is more costly for minorities to buy good environmental quality as part of their house than it is for other socioeconomic groups. An additional possibility is that price discrimination is exacerbated (or caused by) redlining and/or steering.

There is a dearth of studies based on individual or household data, which should seem to an important foundation for examining EJ. Among the exceptions is Hokby and Soderqvist (2003), who use contingent valuation survey data to develop demand curves for a variety of environmental disamenities, and use the demand curves to develop a set of willingness to pay (WTP) elasticities. The conclusion from their analysis is that environmental quality is also regressively distributed in Europe. Another important paper, which not only uses hedonics, but also instruments for risk associated with Superfund sites is Gayer (2000). Gayer considers welfare changes in the form of marginal risk reduction from environmental improvements, examining how benefits vary according to neighborhood demographics. Gayer's findings suggest the disadvantaged gain more from environmental cleanup than do advantaged populations. Based on other hedonic models, racial price differentials have been found in housing markets (see Kiel and Zabel 1996 for a review); such differences may also be correlated with environmental quality. Papers taking a social choice perspective include Millimet and Slottje (1999) who use a Gini coefficient approach to develop an environmental welfare function.

9.2 Conceptual Framework

I propose two utility-based, household-level hedonic approaches to measuring environmental price discrimination, which would ideally use household or individual-level demographic data. Publicly available demographic data in the U.S. are generally unavailable in such a way as to merge individuals' characteristics with detailed data on environmental quality; by observing choice of house in a given neighborhood, the method proposed here can at least partially control for unobservable sorting. In addition, hedonics are important because they can capture tradeoffs between environmental quality and other property characteristics, e.g. number of rooms in a house, better public schools or freeway access. I suggest that under ideal conditions, marginal price differentials for environmental quality estimated from hedonic models can be used to examine environmental price discrimination.

9.2.1 Hedonic Models of Environmental Discrimination

I outline two approaches to test for environmental inequality. The first uses the hedonic model to estimate property characteristic marginal implicit prices, which can be used in a counterfactual decomposition to test for price discrimination. The second is based on a random utility model, which can be used to create tests based on concepts of equity first proposed by Foley (1967) and then expanded upon by Varian (1974), Baumol (1986), Pazner and Schmeidler (1978) and others. The two models differ in that the first does not explicitly model utility levels, but isolates the marginal implicit price of environmental quality, while the second approach considers utility levels associated with different levels of environmental quality.

9.2.2 Environmental Price Discrimination

The traditional hedonic price model used in the first approach is useful to analyze discrimination, since it can separate the total price of a home into expenditures on individual property characteristics, such as environmental quality. Similar models have been used by Baumol (1986) to analyze energy policy, urban economists, such as Hughes and Madden (1991) and Gabriel and Rosenthal (1991), to test the hypothesis that discrimination can lead to inefficient location choice with respect to the work place, and by labor economists such as Oaxaca (1973) to test for wage discrimination in labor markets.

Extending the hedonic concept to location choice is straightforward, and particularly useful to examine whether households are really trading environmental goods for others.

The hedonic price model (HPM) as formalized by Rosen (1974) forms the basis for the first empirical test for environmental discrimination. The model in question takes on the standard assumptions that a composite good, such as a house, is comprised of a number of characteristics, each with its own implicit price, which contribute to the total house value (for more details, see Taylor, this Volume).

The annual price of housing services is called the hedonic rent function (HRF), which at the household level, represents expenditure on annual housing services, i.e.

$$HRF = R(H, N, L, E; \delta) \tag{9.1}$$

where H is a vector of structural characteristics, N is a vector of neighborhood characteristics and local public goods, L is a vector of locational attributes, E is a vector representing environmental attributes and δ represents demographic characteristics of home purchasers.

To simplify, let H, N, L, and all but one element of the E vector, e, be subsumed in Z[3]. Holding all elements of Z constant and suppressing δ, let e be an element of the set of environmental characteristics of interest and write it as $R(H,N,L,E) \equiv R(Z,e)$.

One approach is to take an arbitrary first order Taylor series expansion such that $R(Z,e) = \sum_{i \in N} \frac{\partial R}{\partial z_i} z_i + \frac{\partial R}{\partial e} e + \xi$ where ξ is the remainder term of the expansion. For sufficiently small ξ, we can write the *HRF* as

$$R(Z,e) \cong \sum_{i \in N} \frac{\partial R}{\partial z_i} z_i + \frac{\partial R}{\partial e} e. \tag{9.2}$$

The rent for housing services of a property then consists of the sum of marginal implicit prices for characteristics, $\frac{\partial R}{\partial z_i}$ and $\frac{\partial R}{\partial e}$, times the quantities of characteristics and environmental goods purchased. From Eq. (9.2), let $r_{z_i} = \frac{\partial R}{\partial z_i}$, and $r_e = \frac{\partial R}{\partial e}$, then write the nonlinear budget constraint as

$$y = \sum_{i \in N} r_{z_i} z_i + r_e e + p_x x, \tag{9.3}$$

where x is the numeraire good and p_x=1[4]. To investigate the effect of consuming different levels of e and x while holding all other expenditures on characteristics constant, the budget constraint can be rewritten as

$$y' = r_e e + x, \tag{9.4}$$

where $y' = y - \sum_{i \in N} r_{z_i} z_i$, with all z_i held constant, representing the disposable income available to purchase environmental quality.

Figure 9.1 illustrates two households, one from class A, and one from class B both of which face the same implicit prices for all housing services *except* the environmental characteristic, e. In the situation illustrated, if the numeraire good were held equal, then the class A household, consuming fixed level of environmental quality, $\bar{e}$, faces a marginal implicit price of r_e^A for $\bar{e}$ that is higher than the marginal implicit price paid by class B (r_e^B).

Consuming the same level of numeraire good x, class A households could consume more of the Hicksian good if they were to face class B 's implicit price for environmental quality, r_e^B. The implicit price differential for $r_e^A - r_e^B$ the quantity of environmental quality at $\bar{e}$ suggests the existence of discrimination against class A, in that on the margin, they must pay a higher price for environmental quality. Nonetheless, it is still possible that in a statistical setting, it may

[3] The method discussed here is generalizable to multiple indicators of environmental quality, but this example is limited to one for ease of exposition.

[4] The numeraire good in this discussion is assumed to be annaul income less house rental value.

be difficult to identify whether the difference is due to tastes or discrimination; however, it is difficult to imagine that so long as environmental quality is a normal good that when facing the same levels of numeraire good that one would choose worse environmental quality when its price is higher.

This result leads to a potential test for environmental equity using a hedonic pricing model. That is, if households in class A pay a higher marginal implicit price for environmental quality than do individuals in class B, *ceteris paribus*, then the price differential represents price discrimination against class A.

From a slightly different perspective, it is apparent that a type A household consuming environmental quality $\bar{e}$ at price r_e^A could achieve a higher utility level if they were faced with the price of type B households.

The *HRF*, which represents an estimated expenditure function for housing services, can be used to empirically examine the situation depicted here. It is notable the difference in marginal prices changes with environmental quality levels; thus, examining the differential at only one point along the environmental quality continuum may result in under – or possibly – over-estimation of the full welfare impact. Empirically, this problem is addressed by solving the differential for each individual household and summing over households, but this could still result in distortions in traditional welfare measures.

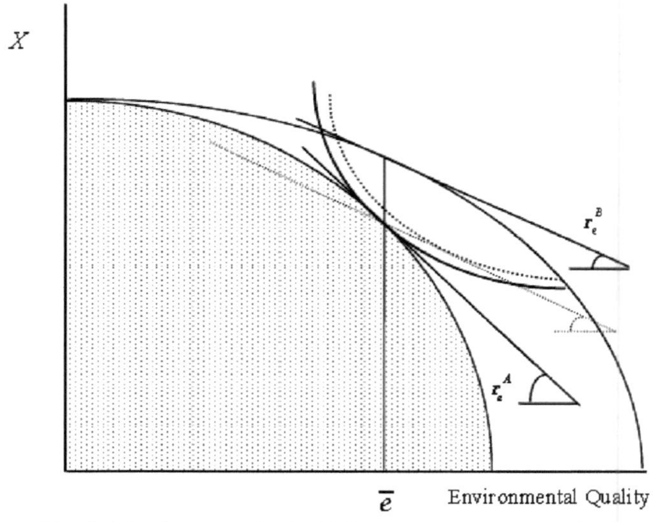

Fig. 9.1 Environmental Discrimination. Source: Hite (2006a)

9.2.3 Envy and Equity

Although a number of measures of justice have been proposed by Rawls (1971) and others, Foley's (1967) no-envy criterion is the easiest to implement in empirical models. No-envy requires that for each individual A with utility $U^A(C^A)$ there is no other individual B such that

$$U^A(C^B) > U^A(C^A). \tag{9.5}$$

That is, if individual A is free to choose her optimal bundle of consumption goods, C^A, there will be no bundle C^B consumed by another individual, B, that would yield a higher level of utility.

Figure 9.2 illustrates a case in which person A could increase her utility by consuming the bundle of housing services C^B. The fact that we observe person A consuming C^A rather than C^B suggests that A is barred from consuming her utility maximizing bundle.

To extend the equity criterion to the present context, we can simply assume that instead of individuals A and B, we are dealing with classes, or types, of individuals, A and B, where types are assumed to have different preferences (Varian 1974; Baumol 1986).

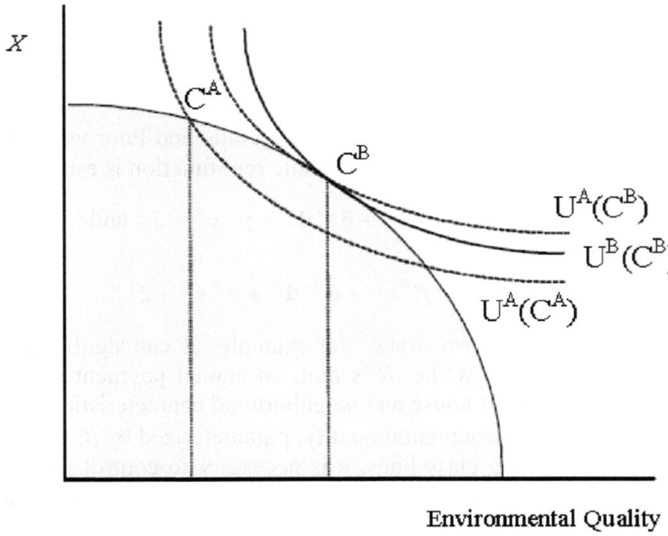

Fig. 9.2 No Envy Criterion. Source: Hite (2000)

If the situation represented by inequality (Eq. 9.5) is observed, then it may be safe to assume that some external barrier exists, e.g. discrimination, such that individuals in class A are barred from consuming C^B, otherwise C^B would be consumed by any rational class A individual.

It is fairly straightforward to incorporate the no-envy criterion into a simple endogenous choice model of housing service bundles that include different levels of environmental quality and it is what I illustrate in Section 9.3.2 below.

9.3 Empirical Framework

9.3.1 Price Discrimination

The first proposed analysis can be carried out by stratifying a sample of house transactions according to the groups of interest, i.e. advantaged vs. disadvantaged. This example follows Hite (2000), in which a sample of housing transactions is stratified twice, once into predominantly black and predominantly white census block groups, and again into predominantly poor and nonpoor census block groups. The data used in the original analysis combines a full year's (1990) auditors' records on individual house sales in four study areas in Franklin County, Ohio, U.S.A., with block group (about 455 households in each) census data on demographics, combined with measurements of distances to four landfills. The study areas include all houses within 3.5 miles of the four landfills, and the landfills distances were used as a measure of environmental quality.

To examine price discrimination, Black vs. White, and Poor vs. Rich strata are compared. For each of the two strata, a hedonic rent function is estimated, i.e.

$$ln\ R^A = \boldsymbol{\alpha}^{A\prime}\mathbf{Z}^A + \beta^A e^A + \boldsymbol{\delta}^{A\prime}\mathbf{d}^A + \gamma^A x^A + \xi \text{, and} \tag{9.6}$$

$$ln\ R^B = \boldsymbol{\alpha}^{B\prime}\mathbf{Z}^B + \beta^B e^B + \boldsymbol{\delta}^{B\prime}\mathbf{d}^B + \gamma^B x^B + \xi \tag{9.7}$$

where A and B denote the two strata – for example, A can signify Black or Poor and B can signify Rich or White. R is rent, an annual payment calculated from house price, $\mathbf{Z}$ is a vector of house and neighborhood characteristics parameterized by $\boldsymbol{\alpha}$ and e represents environmental quality, parameterized by β. Even though the models are stratified along class lines, it is necessary to control for demographic differences within strata, thus $\mathbf{d}$ represents a vector of demographic characteristics parameterized by $\boldsymbol{\delta}$. Finally, x represents the numeraire good, calculated as the census block group income level less house price. Tests performed using Chi-square statistics determine that market segmentation exists in terms of class and landfill proximity.

Once the models have been estimated, a counterfactual decomposition can be used to predict house prices and marginal implicit prices of Class A types given the environmental quality characteristic and numeraire good level of the Class B types; these predictions are then compared to Class A types' own predicted prices. In other words, for household i the comparison is between the two models 9.6 and 9.7, with resulting estimated values

$$\hat{R}_i^A = e^{\left(\hat{\boldsymbol{\alpha}}^{A\prime}\mathbf{Z}_i^A + \hat{\beta}^A e^A + \hat{\boldsymbol{\delta}}^{A\prime}\mathbf{d}^A + \hat{\gamma}^A x^A\right)}, \text{ and} \tag{9.8}$$

$$\hat{R}_i^{A|B} = e^{\left(\hat{\boldsymbol{\alpha}}^{A\prime}\mathbf{Z}_i^A + \hat{\beta}^B e_i^{*B} + \hat{\boldsymbol{\delta}}^{B\prime}\mathbf{d}^B + \hat{\gamma}^B x^B\right)}. \tag{9.9}$$

In equations 9.8 and 9.9, class A's environmental price and numeraire good are switched. The reason that other house characteristics are not switched is to maintain the household at its initially chosen housing bundle. If all characteristics were included, it is most likely that subtle variations in environmental marginal prices would be swamped by the effects of other characteristics, resulting in an inability to isolate any source of discrimination.

The converse predictions are also generated, i.e. $\hat{R}^B$ and $\hat{R}^{B|A}$. It is important to note that person i, coming from group A obviously cannot have B' s same level of e, and in nonlinear specifications, implicit price of environmental quality is a function of e.

Thus an adjustment must be made, such that $e_i^{*B} = e_i^A \frac{\bar{e}^B}{\bar{e}^A}$, and the numeraire good is adjusted similarly. In this case, $\bar{e}^A$ and $\bar{e}^B$ are class mean levels of environmental value. For example, empirically it was discovered that households in predominantly black neighborhoods are located systematically closer to a landfill than households in predominantly white neighborhoods; this means that to assign houses in black neighborhoods a similar implicit price as the houses in white neighborhoods, it is necessary to systematically adjust distances. The adjustment essentially moves the group that is closer to the landfill to a location further away.[5] Because the predictions are generated for each household in a similar way, it is possible to perform paired t-tests of $\Delta^A = \hat{R}^A - \hat{R}^{A|B}$ and $\Delta^B = \hat{R}^B - \hat{R}^{B|A}$. That is, for each A class household in the sample, the rent based on B's environmental quality and numeraire good (Equation 9.9) is subtracted from A's actual predicted rent (Equation 9.8). The null hypothesis is that the two rent values are not statistically different than zero; values of the test statistic that exceed critical levels of the t-value for paired tests suggest that the null cannot be accepted. The test assumes that the error distribution of the underlying model is lognormal.

---

[5] This is an ad hoc adjustment, and future research should develop better methods to assign prices among groups based on sorting behavior.

As an example of the test setup, suppose Δ^A represents the difference in predicted rent for Poor households and the predicted rent the Poor would experience with the implicit price of environmental quality that is experienced by the Rich. In this scenario, we would want to know if the poor pay a higher price for environmental quality than they would if they were rich, and the proper null would $\Delta^A = 0$ if no price differential were to exist, and its expected value would be positive under the alternative. Conversely, if the hypothesis is that the Rich group is getting a better deal on environmental quality, we would examine Δ^B ,expecting its value to be significantly negative if the Rich are indeed better off.

9.3.2 No-Envy Criterion

The no-envy criterion is empirically adaptable to endogenous location choice models. In the most basic application, once again imagine two classes of house buyers, Poor/Rich, or Black/White. Under common assumptions of the hedonic model, individuals purchasing homes chose a bundle of structural, neighborhood and environmental services in such a way as to maximize utility, where utility is defined similarly to the rent function, that is, $U = U(Z, e; \delta)$. However, as in all random utility models, only average utility functions of individuals in classes A and B are observed, based on their choices of location. Thus, empirically the researcher observes location choice as an average utility function plus a random error for each class:

$$U_0^A = \overline{V}_0^A + \varepsilon_0^A \tag{9.10}$$

$$U_1^A = \overline{V}_1^A + \varepsilon_1^A \tag{9.11}$$

and

$$U_0^B = \overline{V}_0^B + \varepsilon_0^B \tag{9.12}$$

$$U_1^B = \overline{V}_1^B + \varepsilon_1^B . \tag{9.13}$$

Equations (9.10) and (9.12) with subscript 0, represent the utility levels for individuals of classes A and B whose houses are in areas with relatively bad environmental quality, while equations (9.11) and (9.13), with subscript 1 relate to individuals in each class whose houses are located in areas with better environmental quality. An individual of a given class should choose to locate in an area with poor environmental quality only if $U_0^i > U_1^i$, $i = A, B$. Thus utility maximizing households would choose housing bundles that include tradeoffs among various housing characteristics, with the choice of poor environmental quality being compensated for by increases in other characteristics. An individual of a given class should therefore choose to locate in an area with bad environmental quality only if $\overline{V}_0^i + \varepsilon_0^i > \overline{V}_1^i + \varepsilon_1^i$ or $\varepsilon_0^i - \varepsilon_1^i > \overline{V}_1^i - \overline{V}_0^i$. Identification of the probit model requires that only the difference in utilities be included in the econometric model.

Assuming that utility is derived directly from consumption of the characteristics of a property at a given location, j, utility can be denoted as a linear combination of a vector of characteristics, that is $V_j = Z'_j\alpha + \varepsilon_j$. Taking derivatives of V_j with respect to the different Z_j 's, the estimated parameters represent the marginal contributions that characteristics make to individual utility. Furthermore, the first order conditions suggest that utility is maximized when the ratio of parameters, or the marginal rate of substitution is equal to the ratio of prices, that is $\partial V/\partial Z_1 \,/\, \partial V/\partial Z_2 = \beta_1/\beta_2 = \hat{p}_1/\hat{p}_2$ where $\hat{p}_1$ and $\hat{p}_2$ represent marginal implicit prices. Thus a utility maximizing household observed consuming low levels of environmental quality is presumed to choose a housing bundle that maximizes their utility level, and the probability of locating in an area with bad environmental quality should be higher as a result.

To implement the model, the data within each stratum (Race and Income) are split into two additional groups with respect to environmental quality, one group for households living in areas with good environmental quality, and the second for households in areas with poor environmental quality. Then, location becomes an endogenous choice variable, and a binary random utility model is estimated with location as the dependent variable and quantities of characteristics, taxes, and the numeraire good as explanatory variables, that is

$$\Pr(y^i = 1) = F(\boldsymbol{\alpha}^{i'}\mathbf{Z}^i;\boldsymbol{\delta}) \tag{9.14}$$

if class $i = A, B$ is located in an area with bad environmental quality; and

$$\Pr(y^i = 0) = [1 - F(\boldsymbol{\alpha}^{i'}\mathbf{Z}^i;\boldsymbol{\delta})] \tag{9.15}$$

otherwise. Thus, utility is a function of property characteristics, including rent, Z, environmental quality, e, and consumer characteristics, $\boldsymbol{\delta}$. The procedure used is similar to the regression analysis, except that the regressand is now an endogenous choice variable representing level of environmental quality.

Gabriel and Rosenthal (1989) suggest tests for discrimination in location choice of housing with respect to the workplace that can be used here. The model given by equations 9.14 and 9.15 is run for each of the race and income strata, and simulations are performed in which probability shares for class A are calculated with the parameters of class B and vice versa. That is for class A

$$H_0 : Pr(A|B) - Pr(A) = z^* \text{ vs. } H_A : Pr(A|B) - Pr(A) < z^*, \tag{9.16}$$

and for class B

$$H_0 : Pr(B|A) - Pr(B) = z^* \text{ vs. } H_A : Pr(B|A) - Pr(B) > z^* \tag{9.17}$$

where z^* represents a critical value of the normal distribution. In words, if the probability of a class A (Black or Poor) household locating in an area with poor environmental quality would be lower if they could consume class B 's bundle rather than their own, then a rational household should do so. If not, the implication would be that there is some barrier to consuming the utility maximizing bundle. Conversely, discrimination would also be indicated if individuals in the advantaged classes were more likely to be located in areas where there is poor environmental quality by consuming the disadvantaged classes' bundles.

9.3.3 Previous Findings

Previous studies based on the methods presented here (Hite 2000, 2006b) have found evidence that environmental discrimination is disproportionately experienced by individuals living in predominantly black census block groups[6] (CBGs), as compared to those living in poor CBGs.[7] In these papers, the environmental disamenity of focus is landfills, and strata are based on the mean sample values of percentage of black households and percentage of households below the poverty level in a CBG. Further, in the endogenous choice framework, houses located less than 1.5 miles from a landfill are considered to have poor environmental quality.

Predicted rents based on the framework presented in equations 9.8 and 9.9 show that households in predominantly black CBGs could gain significantly if they faced the same implicit price as those in whiter CBGs faced. That is, the expected yearly housing expenditure for households in black neighborhoods – if they had the same marginal implicit price for environmental quality as those in white neighborhoods – would be $3,554, about $450 less per year than the $3,918 predicted for this stratum. Conversely, if households in predominantly white neighborhoods paid the same implicit price for environmental quality as do those in black neighborhoods, their predicted yearly expenditures for housing services would be about 129% of actual ($10,467 vs. $8,130).

On the other hand, when examining the price of environmental quality across poverty strata, CBGs with a high percentage of households below the poverty line fare better with respect to environmental quality ($3,600 vs. $6,620) than neighborhoods with a lower percentage of households below the poverty line ($8,261 vs. $5,073). This suggests that environmental discrimination is concentrated in black neighborhoods, contrary to the popular notion that discrimination is correlated with income.

---

6 A Census Block Group is the smallest geographic unit for which 10% data from the decennial census is tabulated.

7 The studies were performed in the Columbus (Ohio, U.S.), OH metropolitan area, using 1990 housing transactions. Based on racial dissimilarity indices for major metro areas in Ohio, and nationally, Columbus ranked 78th nationally in segregation, compared to Cleveland and Cincinnati (ranked 8th and 14th respectively). In addition, the sample used was taken within 3.5 miles of landfills, thus the results could change if the sample had been based on a wider geographic area, or had been drawn from a more segregated metro area.

The results from the test of hedonic implicit prices are substantiated by tests based on the random utility framework outlined in equations (9.16) and (9.17). In this case, the mean predicted probability that households in predominantly black CBGs will be located close to a landfill is 0.24; however, if households in black CBGs were to face the same bundle as those in white CBGs, the mean probability of being located near landfills is cut by more than half (0.10). Similarly to the implicit price analysis, those in white CBGs would be more likely to live less than 1.5 miles from a landfill under the black households' relative prices for housing services (0.20 vs. 0.16 actual). These results suggest that an envy-free distribution of environmental goods does not exist between those in black and white neighborhoods.

Consistent with the implicit price analysis, CBGs with a high percentage of households below the poverty line are far more likely to locate *further* from a landfill than those with a low percentage of households below the poverty line. That is, the mean predicted level of environmental quality chosen by a poor household would be *worse* if the poor household faced a rich household's bundle of consumption goods. At the same time, wealthy households would significantly increase their probability of living near a landfill by consuming the poor stratum's bundle.

It should be noted that these models suffer from a variety of frailties. First, the results may be sensitive to the geographic unit of observation; in this case, two distances from a landfill were analyzed. It may be more appropriate to perform the analysis with a multinomial logit, using census geography, as in Ionnides and Zabel (2007). Second, the models presented here are partial equilibrium; however the simulations presented here may be subject to general equilibrium effects as demonstrated by Banzhaf and Walsh (2006). Finally, as with many models of discrimination, it is difficult to identify whether the results stem from discrimination or preferences.

9.4 Potential for Methodological Advances

The methods outlined in the previous section provide some promise to advance the environmental justice literature; however, previous applications (Hite 2000, 2006a) have not fully accounted for a number of potential problems. For example, these studies were conducted prior to widespread access to geographic information systems software, which enables accurate matching of spatially referenced data. Thus, they do not control for various environmental disamenities such as toxic releases. This exacerbates the unobserved heterogeneity that still exist in the data; although the proposed approach attempts to control for sorting and trade-offs among property characteristics, it is impossible to control for unmeasured charac teristics. Another issue related to sorting is the possibility of endogenous stratification when creating the subsamples in the analyses.

As previously noted, the level of data aggregation is a serious problem facing the hedonic researcher. For example, demographic data generally available to the public in the USA is at the CBG level, while it would be desirable to have such information at household level. However, in the USA there are some public data sources that provide household demographic data, but in this case, location is not released, so that examining impacts of environmental quality and other local public goods is impossible. One method that has been used to obtain demographic data is household surveys (e.g. Brasington and Hite 2006, Ho 2007, and DeParisot 2007) but nonresponse has the potential to seriously bias the results. Nonetheless, future research into environmental discrimination would be improved by primary data collection of individual household characteristics.

Possibly the most serious issue when estimating hedonic models where environmental disamenities exist is the potential truncation in the observation of transactions. In particular, reservation willingness to accept in areas where environmental quality is poor may exceed the WTP of potential buyers. In addition, in such areas the market is also likely to be quite thin. Thus, individuals who want to sell their houses may simply not be able to afford to do so. The standard hedonic model simply cannot capture this market distortion. A related problem is the fact that, according to US Census, homeownership rates for black households in 2005 were significantly lower for African Americans (48.2%) than for white households (75.8%), suggesting that home-ownership opportunities for black households may be limited to areas with worse environmental quality. Because renter data for a group that rents more often than buys is not used in the U.S., the results from hedonic methods may be even more misleading.

Urban sprawl is another factor contributing to increased segregation as blacks become more concentrated in inner cities, where environmental quality is worse; suburbanization of job opportunities has followed, resulting in spatial mismatch in the labor market (for an analysis of urban sprawl, see Bajari and Kahn, this Volume). Nonetheless, recent advances in econometrics and data availability discussed below may be used to improve the type of study proposed here. As previously noted, the data used to estimate any kind of EJ model, even hedonics, is fraught with unobserved heterogeneity, due to sorting and migration by residents and siting decisions by industry; in addition problems associated with general equilibrium changes should be accounted for. Instrumental variables approaches will thus be vital to moving the EJ literature forward. Good instruments are difficult to find in hedonic data, but some recent studies have made progress to address this problem. To control for sorting, Epple and Seig (1999) develop a general equilibrium model that uses ranks of variables as instruments, while Bayer et al. (2006) create instruments based on surrounding neighborhoods. Hite (2006b) uses cluster analysis to create expected values of neighborhood characteristics for "similar" census block groups to be used in instrument creation. Bayer et al. (2006) use a unique instrumenting method, reception of pollutants originating at more distant sources to help break the endogeneity of firm location and pollution levels.

Another strategy that has become popular in the recent environmental hedonic literature is spatial econometrics (e.g. Boxall et al. 2005; Cohen and Coughlin 2006); in theory, spatial models would help to control for unobservable spatial correlation in the regression error (Brasington and Hite 2005). However, it is not clear that these models are as effective as instrumental variables models in controlling for unobserved heterogeneity. For example, Kim et al. (2003) compare willingness to pay elasticities for SO_2 reduction from OLS and spatial models and find very little difference between the two. Spatial models may also be improved by inclusion of dissimilarity indices, which have the potential to better capture spatial heterogeneity in the degree of segregation (see Wong, this Volume, for a discussion of segregation measures). Such indices have been used both at the metropolitan area as in Cutler et al. (1999) and at the census block group level as in Jauregui (2006). Incorporating dissimilarity and spatial models into the analytical framework presented here may hold promise for isolating the effects of environmental discrimination.

It is obvious that the environmental justice issue is quite dynamic. That is, the timing of siting of an environmental disamenity in conjunction with changing demographic composition of neighborhoods near disamenities, make it particularly difficult to identify environmental inequities. Thus use of difference-in-difference models with multi-year data is another method that holds potential for disentangling the complex relationships between household characteristics and environmental quality. Banzhaf and Walsh (2006) represent an application of both difference-in-difference and general equilibrium modeling of environmental justice.

A final econometric method holding promise for EJ models such as those developed in this chapter is quantile regression. Since the tests here are based on Oaxaca's decomposition, it is useful to examine innovations for decomposition from the labor literature. Recently, Machado (2005) demonstrated a methodology for quantile decompositions, which illuminate the effects of different characteristics upon the wage distribution. In addition, Machado made the contribution of using bootstrapping to create equal-sized samples for the decomposition. It would be a fairly straightforward exercise to examine the effects of housing and demographic characteristics on the distribution of house prices in a similar way. Doing so would help to determine degrees of impact; for example, are houses of all values impacted uniformly by environmental disamenities (as assumed by regression models), or are less expensive houses less impacted than high value houses? Another possibility is to examine the degree to which disadvantaged households are exposed to disamenities – are the exposures more concentrated above a given percentage of minority inhabitants? In a somewhat similar vein, Maasoumi and Millimet (2001) propose using stochastic dominance models to examine the full distributional effects of toxic releases.

With the advent of geographically referenced data and powerful geographic information systems (GIS) software, better measures of environmental quality can be developed. In many cases researchers have been limited to distance to disamenity measures as a proxy for environmental quality, but such measures cannot capture intensity or toxicity of many forms of emissions. Using GIS, Mennis (2002), Buzzelli and Jerrett (2004), Anselin and Lozano (2006), De Parisot (2007) and Ho and Hite (2006) among others use kriging[8] of observed point observations to create environmental quality surfaces rather than distance to capture variations in environmental quality that are obscured in distance measures. Also, many previous studies have uniformly applied an environmental value to some geographic unit such as a census tract or ZIP code. This practice allows a significant amount of measurement error to enter the data. For example, some studies apply a uniform value from a toxic release to an entire census block group or tract, when in reality, the source may be located near the border of the area. GIS can help cure this problem by allowing identification of fairly precise location of disamenities, enabling the researcher to create variables that reflect relatively small buffers around affected properties as compared to the more general practice of using linear distance from disamenities; buffers can also be created to account for factors such as prevailing winds.

9.5 Conclusion

Environmental justice has been largely ignored by economists, perhaps because of the fragility of data and methods that have been available in the past. However, as discussed in this chapter, many of the ingredients for successful analysis are now available to researchers, offering an opportunity to move the literature forward. Such advances would be useful for those who are charged with measuring potential impacts of new policies on the disadvantaged.

In addition to measuring potential policy impacts, the methods suggested here should be useful in calculating losses in environmental law suits. Standard hedonics have typically been used in the legal arena, but by simply comparing differences of predicted values of houses in areas with environmental disamenities to those without cannot capture the full extent of the losses from the methods proposed in this paper. The better econometric methods, including new types of instruments and spatial statistics, coupled with increased data accessibility outlined here can only improve the outlook for economists working in the area of environmental discrimination.

Despite the efforts to refine the data and econometric methods in the hedonic,

[8] Kriging is a geostatistical smoothing method, which create values of unobserved data based on observable data.

future research may be greatly improved combining home-owner surveys with other data sources. Surveys could inform the analysis and help illuminate causes of sorting by obtaining individual risk perceptions, knowledge of disamenities, and rankings of the factors that influence household location decisions. In addition, such surveys could potentially be used to uncover systematic differences in lending rates and steering by real estate agents.

References

Anderton DL, Oakes JM, Eagan KL (1997) Environmental equity in superfund - Demographics of the discovery and prioritization of abandoned toxic sites. Evaluation review 21: 3–26

Banzhaf SH, Walsh RP (2006) Do people vote with their feet? - An empirical test of environmental gentrification. Discussion Paper 06–10, Resources for the future, Washingto DC, available at http://www.rff.org/rff/Documents/RFF-DP-06–10.pdf_

Anselin L, Lozano N (2006) Spatial econometric aspects of the consideration of submarkets in hedonic house price models. Selected paper, North american regional science council annual meeting, Toronto, CA

Baden BM, Coursey DL (2002) The locality of waste sites within the city of Chicago: a demographic, social, and economic analysis. Resource and energy economics 24: 53–93

Baumol WJ (1986) Superfairness: applications and theory. The MIT Press, Cambridge

Bayer P, Keohane N, Timmins C (2006). Migration and hedonic valuation: the case of air quality, social science research network, Working paper W12106, NBER, Cambridge, United States, available at http://ssrn.com/abstract=892131

Bayer P, McMillan R, Rueben KS (2004) An equilibrium model of sorting in an urban housing market. Social science research network, Working paper W10865, NBER, Cambridge, United States, available at http://ssrn.com/abstract=612067

Been V (1994) Locally undesirable land uses in minority neighborhoods – disproportionate siting or market dynamics. Yale Law Journal 103: 1383–1422

Been V (1993) What's fairness got to do with it – environmental justice and the siting of locally undesirable land uses. Cornell Law Review 78: 1001–1085

Berry GR (2003) Organizing against multinational corporate power in cancer alley: the activist community as primary stakeholder. Organization and environment 16: 3–33

Boerner C, Lambert T (1995) Environmental injustice. Public interest 118: 61–82

Bouwes NW, Hassur SM, Shapiro MD (2001) Empowerment through risk-related information: EPA's risk screening environmental indicators project. Working papers, Political economy research institute, University of Massachusetts, Amherst, MA

Boxall PC, Chan WH, McMillan ML (2005) The impact of oil and natural gas facilities on rural residential property values: a spatial hedonic analysis. Resource and energy economics 27: 248–269

Brasington DM, Hite D (2006) A mixed index approach to identifying hedonic price models. Louisiana State University, Department of economics and Auburn University, Department of agricultural economics and rural sociology, Social science research network, available at http://papers.ssrn.com/sol3/papers.cfm?abstract_id=928252

Brasington DM, Hite D (2005) Demand for environmental quality: a spatial hedonic analysis. Regional science and urban economics 35: 57–82

Bullard RD (1996) Environmental justice: it's more than waste facility siting. Social science quarterly 77: 493–499
Buzzelli M, Jerrett M (2004) Racial gradients of ambient air pollution exposure in Hamilton, Canada. Environment and planning A 36: 1855–1876
Cameron TA, Crawford GD (2003) Superfund taint and neighborhood change: ethnicity, age distributions, and household structure. University of Oregon Economics Department Working Papers 2003-38, University of Oregon Economics Department
Cohen DA, Spear S, Scribner R, Mason K, Kissinger P, Wildgen J (2000) Broken windows and the risk of gonorrhea. American Journal of public health 90: 230–236
Cohen JP, Coughlin CC (2006) Spatial hedonic models of airport noise, proximity, and housing prices. Working papers, Federal reserve bank of St. Louis, pp 2006–2026
Cutler DM, Glaeser EL, Vigdor JL (1999) The rise and decline of the American ghetto. Journal of political economy 107: 455–506.
De Parisot C (2007) Property value impacts and risk perceptions: a hedonic analysis of Anniston, Alabama. Masters thesis, Auburn University, Auburn, US
De Parisot C, Ho SC, Hite D (2006) Determinants of risk perception and property value impacts associated with the solutia PCB plant and the Anniston chemical warhead incinerator: results of a direct mail survey. Selected paper, Auburn, AL, SERA 30 Annual Meeting, May
Derezinski DD, Lacy MG, Stretesky PB (2003) Chemical accidents in the United States, 1990–1996. Social science quarterly 84: 122–143
Epple D, Sieg H (1999) Estimating equilibrium models of local jurisdictions. Journal of political economy 107: 645–681
Foley D (1967) Resource allocation and the public sector. Yale economic essays 7: 45–98
Frumkin H (2005) Health, equity, and the built environment. Environmental health perspectives 113: A290–A291
Gabriel S, Rosenthal S (1989) Household location and race. Review of economics and statistics 71: 240–249
Gabriel S, Rosenthal S (1991) Credit rationing, race and the mortgage market. Journal of urban economics 29: 371–379
Gayer T (2000) Neighborhood demographics and the distribution of hazardous waste risks: an instrumental variables estimation. Journal of regulatory economics 17: 131–155
Glickman TS (1994) Measuring environmental equity with geographical information systems. Renewable resources journal 116: 17–21
Goetz SJ, Kemlage DJ (1996) TSD facilities location and environmental justice. Review of regional studies 26: 285–300
Hamilton JT (1993) Politics and social costs: estimating the impact of collective action on hazardous waste facilities. Rand journal of economics 24: 101–125
Hamilton JT (1995) Testing for environmental racism: prejudice, profits, political power? Journal of policy analysis and management 14: 107–132
Helfand GE, Peyton LJ (1999) A conceptual model of environmental justice. Social science quarterly 80: 68–83
Hite D (2000) A random utility model of environmental equity. Growth and change 31: 40–58
Hite D (2006a) A hedonic model of environmental justice. Working paper, available at http://ssrn.com/abstract=884233
Hite D (2006b) Out of market transactions as neighborhood quality indicators in hedonic house price models. Working paper, Auburn University, Department of agricultural economics and rural sociology, Auburn, US
Hite D (2006c) Welfare impacts of an environmental disamenity: a survival model approach. Working paper, available at http://ssrn.com/abstract=883343

Ho SC (2007) Three essays on toxic chemical releases, house values, health and labor productivity. Ph.D. dissertation, Auburn University, Auburn, US
Ho SC, Hite D (2006) Economic impact of environmental health risks on house values in southeast region: a county-level analysis. Working paper, available at http://ssrn.com/abstract=839211
Hockman EM, Morris CM (1998) Progress towards environmental justice: a five-year perspective of toxicity, race and poverty in Michigan, 1990–1995. Journal of environmental planning and management 41: 157–176
Hokby S, Soderqvist T (2003) Elasticities of demand and willingness to pay for environmental services in sweden. Environmental and resource economics 26: 361–383
Hughes MA, Madden JF (1991) Residential segregation and the economic status of black workers. Journal of urban economics 29: 28–49
Ioannides Y, Zabel JE (2007) Interactions, neighborhood selection, and housing demand. Forthcoming in Journal of urban economics
Jacobsen JO, Hengartner NW, Louis TA (2005) Inequity measures for evaluations of environmental justice: a case study of close proximity to highways in New York city. Environment and planning A 37: 21–43
Jauregui A (2006) Three essays on real estate, environmental, and urban economics using the hedonic price model technique. Ph.D. dissertation, Auburn University, Auburn, US
Kellogg WA, Mathur A (2003) Environmental justice and information technologies: overcoming the information-access paradox in urban communities. Public administration review 63: 573–585
Kiel KA, Zabel JE (1996) House price differentials in U.S. cities: household and neighborhood racial effects, Journal of housing economics 5: 143–165
Kim CW Philipps TT, Anselin L (2003) Measuring the benefits of air quality improvement: a spatial hedonic approach. Journal of environmental economics and management 45: 24–39
Kriesel W, Centner TJ, Keeler AG (1996) Neighborhood exposure to toxic releases: are there racial inequities? Growth and change 27: 479–499
Lambert T, Boerner C (1997) Environmental inequity: economic causes, economic solutions. Yale Journal on regulation 14: 195–234
Loh P, Sugerman-Brozan J (2002) environmental justice organizing for environmental health: case study on asthma and diesel exhaust in Roxbury, Massachusetts. Annals of the american academy of political and social science 584: 110–124
Maasoumi E, Millimet DL (2001) Socio-economic composition and uniform partial ranking of us county-level environmental quality. Departmental working papers 0510, Department of economics, Southern Methodist University, pp 1–26
Machado J (2005) Counterfactual decomposition of changes in wage distributions using quantile regression. Journal of applied econometrics 20: 445–465
Mennis J (2002) Using geographic information systems to create and analyze statistical surfaces of population and risk for environmental justice analysis. Social science quarterly 83: 281–297
Millimet DL, Slottje D (1999) The distribution of pollution in the United States: an environmental Gini approach. Departmental working papers 9902, Department of economics, Southern Methodist University, pp 1–31
Mitchell G, Dorling D (2003) An environmental justice analysis of british air quality. Environment and planning A 35: 909–929
Mohai P (1996) Environmental justice or analytic justice? reexamining historical hazardous waste landfill siting patterns in metropolitan Texas. Social science quarterly 77: 500–507

Morello-Frosch R (2002) Discrimination and the political economy of environmental inequality. Environment and planning C: Government and policy 20: 477–496
Morello-Frosch R, Pastor M, Sadd J (2002) Integrating environmental justice and the precautionary principle in research and policy making: the case of ambient air toxics exposures and health risks among schoolchildren in Los Angeles. Annals of the american academy of political and social science 584: 47–68
Norgaard KM (2006) We don't really want to know: environmental justice and socially organized denial of global warming in Norway. Organization and environment 19: 347–370
Nothaft FE, Perry VG (2002) Do mortgage rates vary by neighborhoods? Implications for Loan pricing and redlining. Journal of housing economics 11: 244–265
Oaxaca R (1973) Male-female wage differentials in urban labor markets. International economic review: 693–709
Ondrich J, Ross SL, Yinger J (2000) How common is housing discrimination? Improving on traditional measures. Journal of urban economics 47: 470–500
Page M (1995) Racial and ethnic discrimination in urban housing markets: evidence from a recent audit study. Journal of urban economics 38: 183–206
Pazner EA, Schmeidler D (1978) Egalitarian equivalent allocations: a new concept of economic equity. Quarterly journal of economics 92: 671–687
Pearce J, Kingham S, Zewar-Reza P (2006) Every breath you take? Environmental justice and air pollution in Christchurch, New Zealand. Environment and planning A 38: 919–938
Platt HL (2005) Shock cities: the environmental transformation and reform of Manchester and Chicago, Chicago and London. University of Chicago Press
Rawls J (1971) A theory of justice. Harvard University press, Cambridge
Rosen S (1974) Hedonic prices and implicit markets: product differentiation in pure equilibrium. Journal of political economy 82: 34–55
Sadd J, Pastor M, Boer JT, Snyder LD (1999) Every breath you take...: the demographics of toxic air releases in southern California. Economic development quarterly 13: 107–123
Sampson RJ, Groves WB (1989) Community structure and crime: testing social-disorganization theory. American journal of sociology 94: 774–802
Shapiro MD (2005) Equity and information: information regulation, environmental justice, and risks from toxic chemicals. Journal of policy analysis and management 24: 373–398
Stretesky PB, Lynch MJ (1999) Environmental justice and the predictions of distance to accidental chemical releases in Hillsborough County, Florida. Social science quarterly 80: 830–846
Strohm LA (2002) Pollution havens and the transfer of environmental risk. Global environmental politics 2: 29–36
Varian HR (1974) Equity, envy and efficiency. Journal of economic theory 9: 63–91
Wilson JQ, Kelling GL (1982) Broken windows: the police and neighborhood safety. Atlantic monthly (March): 29–38
Yandle T, Burton D (1996) Reexamining environmental justice: a statistical analysis of historical hazardous waste landfill siting patterns in metropolitan Texas. Social science quarterly 77: 477–492
Yinger J (1986) Measuring racial discrimination with fair housing audits: caught in the act. American economic review 76: 881–893
Yinger J (1997) Cash in your face: the cost of racial and ethnic discrimination in housing. Journal of urban economics 42: 339–365
Zenou Y, Boccard N (2000) Racial discrimination and redlining in cities. Journal of urban economics 48: 260–285

10 Distinguishing Racial Preferences in the Housing Market: Theory and Evidence

Patrick Bayer[1], **Robert McMillan**[2*]

[1] Duke University, Durham, United States
[2] University of Toronto, Toronto, Canada

10.1 Introduction

Given the extent of residential segregation on the basis of race and ethnicity in U.S. cities, it is unsurprising that a long line of research in social science has attempted to better-understand the causes and consequences of segregation. One prominent branch of that literature has used housing market data on the observed patterns of residential sorting and corresponding housing prices to make inferences about (i) the nature of household preferences for the racial composition of their neighborhoods and (ii) the extent to which segregation is driven by centralized discriminatory forces versus the decentralized location decisions of households, given their preferences (Zabel, this Volume, and Hite, this Volume).[1]

Building on that literature, the current chapter summarizes a series of theoretical and empirical issues related to the role of race in housing markets. It starts with a discussion of the challenges involved in identifying racial preferences using housing market data. To that end, Section 10.2 of the chapter sets out a simple model of racial sorting to illustrate the relationship between racial preferences and the equilibrium (hedonic) price of a neighborhood's racial composition.

---

* We are grateful to Pat Bajari, Steve Berry, Sandra Black, Hanming Fang, Fernando Ferreira, Edward Glaeser, Kim Rueben, Chris Timmins and Jacob Vigdor for valuable discussions about the ideas contained in this paper. A portion of the research in this paper was conducted while the authors were Special Sworn Status researchers of the U.S. Census Bureau, working at the Berkeley and Triangle Census Research Data Centers. Research results and conclusions expressed are our own and do not necessarily reflect the views of the Census Bureau. This paper has been screened to ensure that no confidential data are revealed.

[1] See Bayer and McMillan (2006) and Cutler et al. (1999) for an extensive discussion.

A. Baranzini et al. (eds.), *Hedonic Methods in Housing Markets*, doi: 10.1007/978-0-387-76815-1_10,

This discussion highlights a number of key insights. First, we show that in a segregated equilibrium, the preferences of those households with the strongest tastes for segregation tend to be infra-marginal and, as a result, are not fully reflected in the hedonic price of race. Instead, the hedonic price function reflects the preferences of those households on the margin of choosing neighborhoods with varying racial compositions – i.e., households that reside in more integrated neighborhoods. Thus, even in the presence of strong self-segregating preferences, neighborhood race is likely to be only slightly (if at all) capitalized into house prices. A second insight that our simple theoretical model delivers is that, without additional assumptions, the sign of the coefficient on neighborhood race in a hedonic price regression does not distinguish the existence of centralized discriminatory forces.

Having laid out this theoretical framework for discussing the relationships among racial preferences, discrimination and hedonic prices, we take up a first empirical issue – the systematic correlation between neighborhood race and unobserved neighborhood quality – in Section 10.3. The fact that black households typically have less income and wealth than white households suggests that blacks will typically live in lower-quality houses and neighborhoods. To the extent that many aspects of quality are likely to be unobserved in even the best datasets, one naturally expects a negative correlation between the fraction of blacks in a neighborhood and the error term in a hedonic price regression.

Because of the inherent difficulty of isolating variation in neighborhood sociodemographics uncorrelated with unobserved aspects of neighborhood and housing quality, empirical researchers have generally elected to recognize the endogeneity of neighborhood sociodemographics as a limitation of their analysis – see Cutler et al. (1999) and Bajari and Kahn (2005 and this Volume), for example. In other cases, researchers have isolated variation in neighborhood sociodemographics within Census tracts or other broader regions. But in such cases, the underlying factors causing the variation in neighborhood sociodemographics below the Census tract level remain unobserved and thus the endogeneity problem associated with the correlation of neighborhood race and unobserved neighborhood quality remains.

Given these fundamental difficulties, Section 10.3 describes the results of one of our recent papers. Specifically, in Bayer et al. (2007), we provide a new strategy for addressing the endogeneity of neighborhood sociodemographics by extending an influential approach developed in the context of hedonic price regressions by Black (1999). Black's boundary discontinuity design (BDD) includes school boundary fixed effects in hedonic price regressions to control for the correlation of school quality and unobserved neighborhood quality. Intuitively, differences in house prices at school attendance zone boundaries reflect only the discontinuity in the right to attend a given school, providing an estimate of the value that households place on the difference in school quality across the boundary.

Our key insight is that the sorting of households across boundaries generates variation in neighborhood sociodemographics that is primarily related to an *observable* aspect of neighborhood quality – in this case, schools. Thus, to the extent that one can control for differences in school quality on opposite sides of the boundary, a BDD provides a plausible way to estimate the value that households place on the characteristics of their immediate neighbors. In a hedonic price regression setting, we show that the inclusion of boundary fixed effects reduces the magnitudes of the coefficients on the income and education of one's neighbors by 25 and 60 percent, respectively. This is consistent with the intuitive notion that higher-income and better-educated households select into neighborhoods with better amenities. Even more noteworthy, the magnitude of the coefficient on the fraction of black neighbors declines to zero. This implies that the negative correlation of housing prices and fraction of black neighbors observed in the Census data we use, and reported systematically in the previous literature, is driven mostly by the correlation of race and the unobserved neighborhood quality captured by the boundary fixed effect.

In Section 10.4, we take up a second empirical issue that arises because there are very few predominantly black, high-amenity neighborhoods in any U.S. cities. While over 11,000 Census tracts in U.S. metropolitan areas are at least 40 percent college-educated, for example, a mere 44 of these tracts are also at least 60 percent black.[2] Thus, in general, in order to choose high-amenity neighborhoods, households must live with a higher fraction of white neighbors. This *bundling* of neighborhood race and amenities violates a core assumption of hedonic demand models, which implicitly assume that households are able to select the level of consumption of each element of the bundle of neighborhood attributes to satisfy the associated first-order condition. In contrast, discrete choice models provide a natural approach to account for the fact that households are constrained to choose among the set of existing choices (bundles).

10.2 A Simple Model of Racial Sorting

This section sets out a simple model of racial sorting to illustrate the relationship between racial preferences and the equilibrium (hedonic) price of a neighborhood's racial composition. We begin with a graphical characterization of preferences and hedonic prices in two simple settings.

Figure 10.1 illustrates the equilibrium in a setting in which households value a single amenity that is in fixed supply. In the figure, the downward-sloping line represents the marginal willingness-to-pay (MWTP) curve for the households in the market. If only a few houses in the market have this amenity, as represented by

---

[2] Moreover, 33 of these 44 tracts are located in just four metropolitan areas: Baltimore-Washington, Detroit, Los Angeles, and Atlanta.

H_1, the hedonic price of the amenity would reflect the MWTP of a household with a relatively strong taste, as indicated by p_1* in the figure. If, on the other hand, the amenity were widely available, its hedonic price would generally reflect the MWTP of someone much lower in the taste distribution, as indicated by p_2*. In this way, the equilibrium price of the amenity is set by the household on the margin of purchasing a house with the amenity, and will be a function of both its supply and the distribution of preferences.

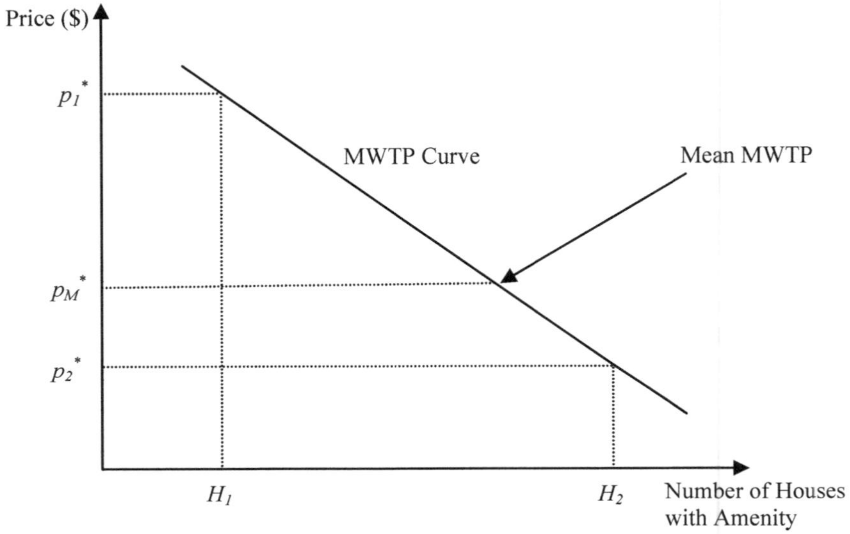

Fig. 10.1. Demand for an Amenity in Fixed Supply. Source: Bayer et al. (2007)

Of course, many housing and neighborhood characteristics are supplied on a more continuous basis throughout a metropolitan area. To gain some intuition about the relationship of the hedonic price to preferences in this case, it is helpful to consider a simple characterization of the equilibrium when households value only a single location attribute – e.g., school quality – that varies across the neighborhoods of the metropolitan area. Figure 10.2 provides a graphical depiction of this case. Because a metropolitan area contains many schools, the equilibrium difference in housing prices between each pair of schools ranked according to quality is the MWTP of the household on the corresponding boundary between schools. These equilibrium prices are represent by the p_j^* terms on the vertical axis. If there are roughly an equal number of students in each school, averaging the equilibrium price over all of the houses in the sample corresponds roughly to the mean MWTP of all households. Consequently, for attributes that vary more continuously throughout the region, there is likely to be only a slight difference between the mean preferences estimated in the heterogeneous sorting model and the coefficients of the hedonic price regression.

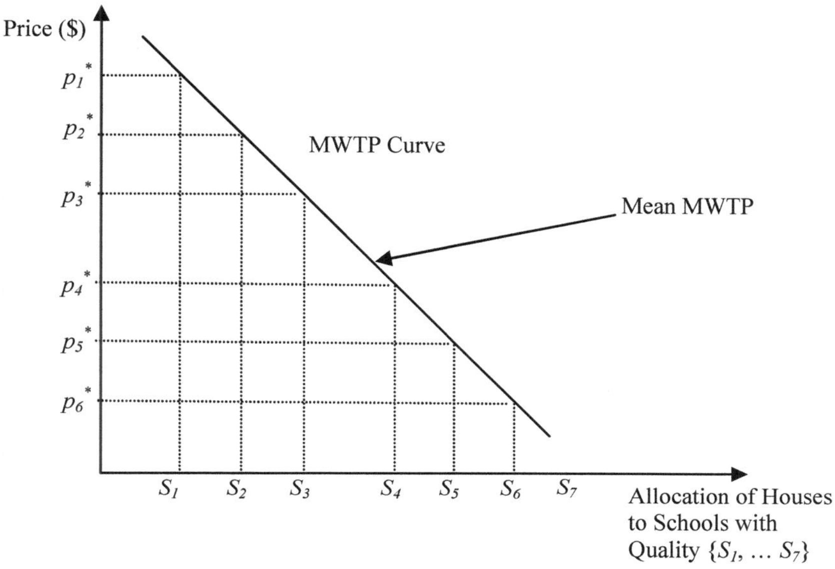

Fig. 10.2. Demand for School Quality. Source: Bayer et al. (2007)

10.2.1 Racial Preferences and Hedonic Prices

The above examples provide an intuitive way of thinking about the relationship of preferences and hedonic prices. In the case of an amenity in fixed supply, we would generally expect the hedonic price to reflect the preferences of the marginal person just indifferent between buying a house with and without the amenity. In this case, there is a single 'boundary' between houses that possess or do not possess the amenity. For amenities that vary more continuously throughout a region, there are many "boundaries" and, as a result, a simple hedonic price regression is likely to capture something much closer to mean preferences.

For racial preferences, the equilibrium in most US metropolitan areas likely combines the characteristics of these two simple examples. Given the relatively small fraction of black households (11 percent on average) and the substantial degree of racial segregation, most US metropolitan areas have a large number of neighborhoods and communities that are nearly perfectly segregated. In this sort of equilibrium, the preferences of those households with the strongest tastes for segregation tend to be infra-marginal and, as a result, are not fully reflected in the hedonic price of race. Instead, we would generally expect the hedonic price of neighborhood race to more directly reflect the preferences of those households on the margin of choosing neighborhoods with varying racial compositions – i.e., households that reside in more integrated neighborhoods. In this way, it is entirely possible for the hedonic price of race to be small in magnitude even in the face of strong segregating preferences.

To illustrate this insight more formally, we develop a simple model of racial sorting. The goal of this exercise is to illustrate the differential role of marginal versus infra-marginal households on the hedonic price function. A serious empirical analysis needs to go well beyond the simple model developed here; we discuss a couple of additional important empirical issues in Sections 10.3 and 10.4 below.

The model that we develop is a simple special case of the vertical sorting model developed in Epple et al. (1984, 1993) and in Epple and Sieg (1999). Households are either black or white and choose neighborhoods according to the following utility function:

$$U_{ij} = \beta_i \times Pblack_j - p_j \tag{10.1}$$

where i indexes households and j neighborhoods, $Pblack_j$ is the fraction of black household in neighborhood j and p_j is the price of housing in neighborhood j. β_i characterizes the preferences of household i for black neighbors; preferences can be either positive or negative and are distributed in the black and white populations according to f_b and f_w, respectively. Given their preferences and equilibrium prices, households choose to reside in one of J neighborhoods of fixed (but not necessarily equal) size. Housing prices adjust to clear the market.

To approximate the equilibrium in US cities we make one further assumption – that f_b stochastically dominates f_w. This amounts to assuming that the black population as a whole has weakly stronger preferences for living with black neighbors than the white population in the sense of distributions. This does not preclude a large region of overlapping preferences – i.e., values of β_i that are shared by some white and some black households. An equilibrium in this model is characterized by the stratification of households across neighborhoods on the basis of their preferences for black neighbors. The equilibrium price of race is set by households with values of β_i that make them marginal for living in mixed race communities.

10.2.2 Characterizing the Sorting Equilibrium: An Example

The insights that we develop from this model or racial sorting can be readily seen through a couple of simple examples. Consider first an example in which black households make up 20 percent of the population and have β's uniformly distributed between +200 and –200 and white households make up 80 percent of the population and have β's uniformly distributed between +100 and –1,500. Finally, assume there are 20 neighborhoods of equal size. Equilibrium in this setting takes the following form:

Table 10.1 Equilibrium Distribution of Neighborhood: Example 1

N'hood	% of Population	% Black	Range of β Dist	Equilibrium Price
1	5%	100%	(+200,+100)	50
2–7	30%	50%	(+100,-200)	0
8–20	65%	0%	(-200,-1,500)	100

Source: Authors' own calculations

To solve for the equilibrium distribution of neighborhoods in this simple model, we first order households by their preferences for neighborhood race. We then assign the five percent of households with the strongest positive taste for black neighbors to Neighborhood 1, the 5 percent with the next strongest taste to Neighborhood 2, and so on. Equilibrium prices (which are determined up to an additive constant) are then calculated so as to leave individuals on the boundary of neighborhoods with varying racial composition indifferent between those neighborhoods. When there are multiple neighborhoods with the same racial composition, the model does not actually determine how the households with varying racial preferences assigned to these neighborhoods sort themselves among these neighborhoods.

In equilibrium, mixed race neighborhoods develop for the portion of the preference distribution that overlaps for whites and blacks and households with stronger preferences for black or white neighbors live in completely segregated neighborhoods. Given the smaller size of the black population, one segregated black neighborhood arises compared to thirteen segregated white neighborhoods.

Of most direct interest to our earlier discussion is the price associated with each neighborhood. In equilibrium, relative prices must make the household with marginal preferences indifferent. In this example, an individual with β=100 must be indifferent between the 100 percent and 50 percent black neighborhoods. Likewise, an individual with β=200 must be indifferent between the 0 percent and 50 percent black neighborhoods.

This requires that, relative to the mixed race community, the price be \$50 higher in the segregated black community and \$100 higher in the segregated white community, respectively. Note that given the linear utility function assumed above, equilibrium prices are only determined up to an additive constant, i.e., if a constant *K* were added to prices in all communities, each household's choice would be unaffected.

Given this equilibrium it is useful to compare what an estimated hedonic price regression would return relative to the distribution of preferences. In this example, a hedonic price regression estimated on the generated data would return a coefficient on *Pblack* of \$–127. Notice that mean preferences are \$0 for blacks, \$–750 for whites, and \$–600 for the full population. Thus, the equilibrium price of neighborhood race does not reflect mean preferences directly. This is because the households with the strongest segregating preferences are infra-marginal with respect to the determination of equilibrium prices. The hedonic price regression reflects the preferences of those that are marginal to living in mixed race neighborhoods.

These insights have important ramifications not only for the estimation of the hedonic price function but for the use of hedonic demand estimation.[3] In particular, because the preferences of the households with the strongest segregating preferences are not reflected in the equilibrium price function, there is no way that derivatives of the price function can reveal those preferences. Thus, when the equilibrium is characterized by many nearly perfectly segregated neighborhoods alternative estimation strategies, such as discrete choice models, may yield better preference estimates. We return to a discussion of the relative merits of hedonic demand versus discrete choice models in Section 10.4 below.

10.2.3 A Second Example

A slight change to the above example makes it clear that whether the hedonic price regression returns positive or negative coefficients does not depend on the strength of racial preferences in general, but on the region of overlapping preferences. In particular, consider a second example identical to the first in every way except that black households have slightly stronger preferences for living with black neighbors: in this case, β's uniformly distributed between +400 and 0. Equilibrium in this setting takes the following form:

Table 10.2 Equilibrium Distribution of Neighborhood: Example 2

N'hood	% of Population	% Black	Range of β Dist	Equilibrium Price
1–3	15%	100%	(+400,+100)	50
4–5	10%	50%	(+100,0)	0
6–20	75%	0%	(0,-1,500)	0

Source: Authors' own calculations

In this case, the region of overlapping preferences falls on the positive side of the origin and a hedonic price regression would return a coefficient on *Pblack* of $45. Thus, whether the hedonic price regression yields a positive or negative coefficient in this model is determined by where exactly the distributions of white and black preferences overlap.

More generally, in a heavily segregated world, hedonic prices tend to inform us about the nature of preferences of households that are close to indifferent between living in segregated neighborhoods of either kind. Thus, even in the presence of strong self-segregating preferences, we might expect neighborhood race to be only

[3] See Bajari and Benkard (2005), Bajari and Kahn (2005), Ekeland et al. (2002), Epple (1987), Heckman et al. (2003), Nesheim (2001), and Rosen (1974) for extensive discussion of hedonic demand estimation.

slightly (if at all) capitalized into house prices. This suggests that much of the negative correlation between housing prices and the fraction of blacks households in a neighborhood typically reported in U.S. data is likely to reflect the correlation of neighborhood race with unobserved neighborhood quality (an issue that we take up in Section 10.3).

10.2.4 Decentralized Versus Centralized Racism

This simple model of racial sorting also helps to illustrate the difficulty of distinguishing racial preferences from certain forms of centralized discrimination in the housing market. Centralized discrimination can take many forms including actions by realtors, mortgage companies, or sellers that make it more difficult or costly for black households to purchase homes in predominantly white neighborhoods or hostile actions towards new black residents in predominantly white neighborhoods.

Perhaps the easiest (but certainly not the only) way to incorporate centralized discrimination into our simple model is to assume that white households face an implicit additional price that varies with the percentage of black households in a neighborhood equal to $200 \times Pwhite$. Incorporating this change into the utility function of black households corresponds to shifting the distribution of β up by 200 for black households:

$$\begin{aligned} U_{ij} &= \beta_i \times Pblack_j - p_j - 200 \times (1 - Pblack_j) \\ &= (\beta_i + 200) \times Pblack_j - p_j - 200 \end{aligned} \tag{10.2}$$

But this is observationally equivalent to the change in black preferences that we considered in moving from the first to the second example above. Thus, the equilibrium in this case is identical to that presented for the second example above.

The key insight that the equivalence of the second and third examples delivers is that it is generally impossible to distinguish decentralized preferences from centralized discrimination using data from a single cross-section without imposing stronger *a priori* assumptions about the functional form that discrimination takes or the nature of preferences. Centralized discrimination will in fact tend to increase the estimated coefficient on percent black in the hedonic price regression but whether the coefficient is greater than or less than zero in equilibrium will be a function of both the location of the region of overlap between black and white preferences and the strength of centralized discriminatory forces.

10.3 The Correlation of Neighborhood Race and Amenities

Having laid out this theoretical framework for discussing the relationship among racial preferences, discrimination, and hedonic prices, we now take up two empirical issues in turn. In this section, we examine the implications of the systematic correlation between neighborhood race and unobserved neighborhood quality, drawing on the empirical analysis in Bayer et al. (2007).

The primary data set used in that analysis is drawn from the restricted-access version of the 1990 US Decennial Census. This dataset provides information for the full sample of households that filled out the long form questionnaire, approximately 15 percent of the population. For each household, these data provide a wide range of economic and demographic variables, including the race/ethnicity, age, educational attainment, and income of each household member. In addition, the data also characterize each household's residence: whether the unit is owned or rented, the corresponding rent or owner-reported value, property tax payment, number of rooms, number of bedrooms, type of structure, and the age of the building.

For our purposes, the most important feature of this restricted-access Census dataset is that it characterizes the location of each individual's residence and workplace very precisely; these locations are specified at the level of the Census block (a region with approximately 100 individuals) rather than the publicly available Census Public Use Microdata Area (PUMA) (a region with an average of 100,000 individuals). This precise geographic information allows us to examine the way that households and houses change on a block-by-block basis anywhere within our study area.

The study area for our analysis includes data drawn from six contiguous counties in the San Francisco Bay Area: Alameda, Contra Costa, Marin, San Mateo, San Francisco, and Santa Clara. We focus on this area for two main reasons. First, it is reasonably self-contained: a very small proportion of commutes originating within these six counties in 1990 ended up at work locations outside the area, and vice versa. Second, the area is sizeable along a number of dimensions: it includes over 1,100 Census tracts, 4,000 Census block groups, and almost 39,500 Census blocks, the smallest unit of aggregation in the data. Our full sample consists of around 650,000 people in 242,100 households.

10.3.1 Sorting at Boundaries

We gathered school attendance zone maps for as many elementary schools as possible in the Bay Area, for the period around the 1990 Census. Our final attendance zone sample consists of 195 elementary schools – just under a third of the total number in the Bay Area. From this sample, we excluded boundaries that coincide with school district boundaries, city boundaries, or large roads, since they could potentially confound our identification strategy.

For Census blocks falling within these attendance zones, we follow a simple procedure to assign a boundary. For each block, we calculate the perpendicular distance from the block population centroid to the nearest school attendance zone boundary. We then locate the closest 'twin' Census block on the other side of that boundary. If a given block has a lower score than its twin, it is designated as being on the 'low' side of the boundary; otherwise it is designated as being on the 'high' side of the boundary. We restrict attention to boundaries for which we have Census data on both high and low sides.

To motivate our approach, we start with a descriptive analysis of sorting at school attendance zone boundaries using these data. Given a discontinuity in local school quality at school boundaries, one might expect that residential sorting would lead to discontinuities in the characteristics of households residing on opposite sides of the same boundary; so even if a school boundary was initially drawn such that the houses immediately on either side were identical, one would expect households with higher incomes and education levels to sort onto the side of the boundary with the better school.

We present descriptive evidence that sheds light on household sorting in the region of school attendance zone boundaries, taking advantage of the block-level information provided in the restricted version of the Census to measure the characteristics of housing units and households in a precise way on each side of a given boundary.

Throughout, we focus on boundaries for which the test score gap comparing low and high sides is in excess of the median gap (38.4 points). Significant differences in prices across these boundaries are expected if households have strong preferences for school quality.

We begin with a series of figures that summarize the movement of variables in the boundaries' region. The figures are constructed with the following procedure: (i) regress the variable in question on boundary fixed effects and on distance-to-the-boundary dummy variables; (ii) plot the coefficients on these distance dummies.

Thus a given point in each figure represents this conditional average (in 0.02 mile bands) at a given distance to the boundary, where negative distances indicate the "low" test score side. All averages are normalized to zero at the closest point on the low side of the boundary.

By construction, as shown in top left panel of Figure 10.3, there is a clear discontinuity in average test score at the boundary. For the Census sample considered, the magnitude of the discontinuity is around 75 points (which is approximately a standard deviation).

The top right panel of Figure 10.3 shows a similar pattern for the test scores assigned to a dataset that includes all housing transactions in the Bay Area between 1992–1996. The bottom left panel of Figure 10.3 shows the difference in house prices using the Census data, which corresponds to approximately $18,000 at the threshold.

Using the more precisely measured house values drawn from the transactions dataset in the bottom right panel shows a similar seam: $20,000 difference right at the boundary.

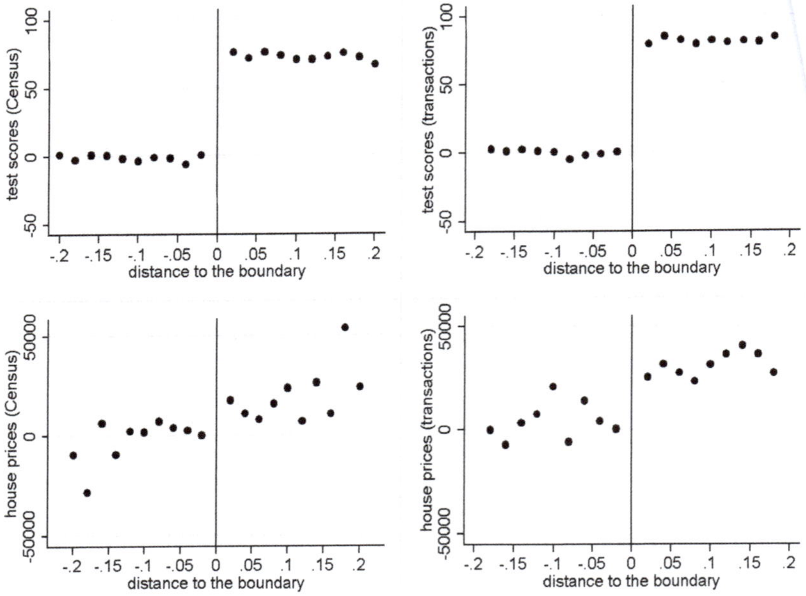

Fig. 10.3 Test Scores and House Prices around the Boundary. Notes: Each panel in this figure is constructed with the following procedure: (i) regress the variable in question on boundary fixed effects and on 0.02 mile band distance-to-the-boundary dummy variables; (ii) plot the coefficients on these distance dummies. Thus a given point in each figure represents this conditional average at a given distance to the boundary, where negative distances indicate the "low" test score side. Data sources: US Census of Population, California Dept of Education, and Dataquick

As Black (1999) pointed out, if all housing and neighborhood amenities are continuous at the boundary, then those differences in price would solely correspond to the observed gap in school quality. Given the proximity of houses across the boundary, it is probably reasonable to expect a somewhat similar housing stock at the threshold.[4] We test this assumption by first comparing housing characteristics. The panels of Figure 10.4 show that the housing variables drawn from the Census, average number of rooms, ownership, and year built are in fact continuous through the boundary. The same is true of the housing variables associated with the recent transactions in our alternative data set.

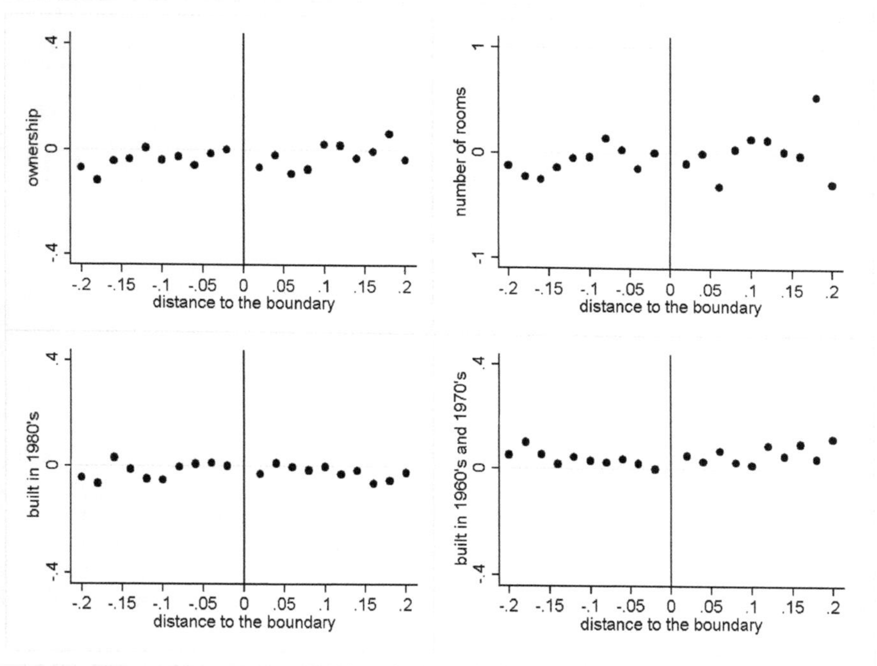

Fig. 10.4 Census Housing Characteristics around the Boundary. Notes: Each panel in this figure is constructed with the following procedure: (i) regress the variable in question on boundary fixed effects and on 0.02 mile band distance-to-the-boundary dummy variables; (ii) plot the coefficients on these distance dummies. Thus a given point in each figure represents this conditional average at a given distance to the boundary, where negative distances indicate the `low' test score side. Data sources: US Census of Population, California Dept of Education, and Dataquick

In contrast, Figure 10.5 presents a different story with respect to the people inhabiting those houses. On average, the households on the high test score side of the boundary have more income and education, and are less likely to be black.

[4] It is important to keep in mind that these school attendance zone boundaries are not school district boundaries, not city boundaries, and not aligned with rivers or major roads.

This observed sorting at attendance zone boundaries naturally suggests that household preferences for schools are heterogeneous.

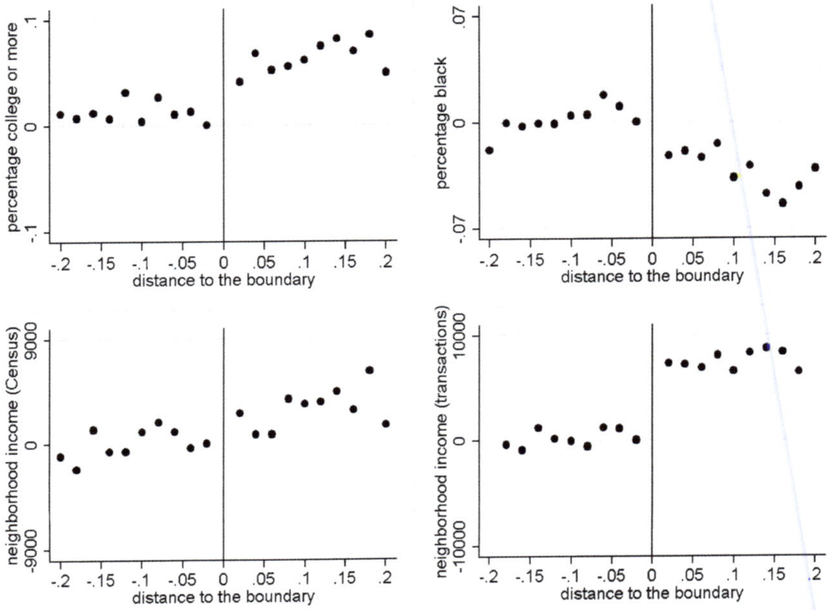

Fig. 10.5 Neighborhood Sociodemographics around the Boundary. Notes: Each panel in this figure is constructed with the following procedure: (i) regress the variable in question on boundary fixed effects and on 0.02 mile band distance-to-the-boundary dummy variables; (ii) plot the coefficients on these distance dummies. Thus a given point in each figure represents this conditional average at a given distance to the boundary, where negative distances indicate the `low' test score side. Data sources: US Census of Population, California Dept of Education, and Dataquick

10.3.2 Hedonic Price Regressions

We now explore the implications of observed sorting at school attendance zone boundaries in the context of hedonic price regressions. Our main estimating equation relates the price of house h to a vector of housing and neighborhood characteristics X_h and a set of boundary fixed effects, θ_{bh}, which equal one if house h is within a specified distance of boundary b and zero otherwise:

$$p_h = \beta X_h + \theta_{bh} + \xi_h . \tag{10.3}$$

To maximize the sample size in our baseline analysis, we include both owner- and renter-occupied units in the same sample. To put these units on a comparable basis, we convert house values to a measure of monthly user costs using a hedonic regression that returns the average ratio of house values to rents for housing units with comparable observable characteristics; we do so for each of 40 sub-regions of the Bay Area.[5]

Table 10.3 reports estimates for the key parameters for a total of eight specifications of this hedonic price regression, using the monthly user cost of housing as the dependent variable. The reported specifications differ along three dimensions: (i) whether neighborhood sociodemographics are included in the specification, (ii) whether boundary fixed effects are included, and (iii) whether the sample consists of houses within 0.20 miles versus 0.10 miles of a boundary. All of the specifications include a full set of controls for housing and neighborhood characteristics, which are listed in the table notes.

Table 10.3 Key Coefficients from Baseline Hedonic Price Regressions

Sample	Within 0.20 Miles of Boundary		Within 0.10 Miles of Boundary	
Observations	27,548		15,122	
Boundary Fixed effect	No	Yes	No	Yes
Panel A: Exluding Neighbourhood Sociodemographic Characteristics				
	(1)	(2)	(5)	(6)
Average test score (in standard deviations)	123.7	33.1	126.5	26.1
	(13.2)	(7.6)	(12.4)	(6.6)
R^2	0.54	0.62	0.54	0.62
Panel B: Including Neighbourhood Sociodemographic Characteristics				
	(3)	(4)	(7)	(8)
Average test score (in standard deviations)	34.8	17.3	44.1	14.6
	(8.1)	(5.9)	(8.5)	(6.3)
% census block group black	-99.8	1.5	-123.1	4.3
	(33.4)	(38.9)	(32.5)	(39.1)
% block group college degree of more	220.1	89.9	204.4	80.8
	(39.9)	(32.3)	(40.8)	(39.7)
Average block group income (/10,000)	60.0	45.0	55.6	42.9
	(4.0)	(4.6)	(4.3)	(6.1)
R^2	0.59	0.64	0.59	0.63

All regressions shown in the table also include controls for whether the house is owner-occupied, the number of rooms, year built (1980s, 1960-1979, pre-1960), elevation, population density, crime, land use (% industrial, % residential, % commercial, % open space, % other) in 1, 2, and 3 mile rings around each location. The dependent variable is the monthly user cost of housing, which equals monthly rent for renter-occupied units and a monthly user cost for owner-occupied housing, calculated as described in the text. Standard errors corrected for clustering at the school level are reported in parentheses. Data sources: US Census of Population, California Dept of Education, and Dataquick

[5] Separate estimation for each sub-region (a Census PUMA) allows the relationship between house values and current rents to vary with expectations about the growth rate of future rents in the market. The average estimate of the ratio of house values to monthly rents is 264.1

Comparing the coefficients on neighborhood sociodemographic characteristics in the specifications shown in columns (3) and (4) of Table 10.3 provide an estimate of the bias associated with the sorting of higher-income and better-educated households into neighborhoods with different levels of unobserved quality. In particular, the inclusion of boundary fixed effects leads to a 25 percent decline in the coefficient on the average income of one's neighbors, from $60 to $45 per month (for a $10,000 increase), and a 60 percent decline in the coefficient on the fraction of neighbors that are college educated, from $220 to $90 per month. These results suggest that analyses which fail to control for the correlation of neighborhood sociodemographics with unobserved neighborhood quality are likely to overstate the extent to which neighborhood socioeconomic characteristics are capitalized into property values in a significant way.

The effects for neighborhood race are perhaps even more interesting. With the inclusion of boundary fixed effects, the coefficient on the percent of one's neighbors who are black changes from $100 to $2. This implies that the racial composition of a neighborhood is not capitalized directly into housing prices; instead, the large negative correlation of housing prices and the fraction of black households in a neighborhood reflects in its entirety the correlation of unobserved aspects of neighborhood quality with neighborhood race. This empirical finding is, to the best of our knowledge, new to the literature. While many prior studies have documented the correlation of race and housing prices, ours is the first to use a boundary discontinuity design to address the correlation of neighborhood race and unobserved neighborhood quality.

As the discussion of Section 10.2 suggests, the statistically and economically insignificant coefficients on neighborhood race in specification (4) by no means imply that households do not have strong racial preferences – on the contrary, the heterogeneous preferences we estimate in a broader model of residential sorting developed in Bayer et al. (2007) indicate that households have strong self-segregating preferences. Rather, the fact that race is not capitalized into housing values suggests that households are able to sort themselves across neighborhoods on the basis of race without the need for price differences to clear the market.

10.4 The Bundling of Neighborhood Race and Amenities

In this section, we describe a second empirical issue – the bundling of neighborhood race and neighborhood amenities. Here, we draw on some motivating facts concerning the availability of neighborhoods across all U.S. cities developed in Bayer and McMillan (2006). In that paper, we show that (i) there are few neighborhoods combining high-fractions of both college-educated and black individuals in almost every metropolitan area in the United States and (ii) that faced with the resulting trade-off between black versus other college-educated neighbors, college-educated blacks choose a very diverse set of neighborhoods in each metropolitan area.

More specifically, using publicly-available Census Tract Summary Files (SF3) from the 2000 Census, we characterize the distribution of race and neighborhood quality for all neighborhoods in U.S. metropolitan areas. A 'neighborhood' in this section corresponds to a Census tract, which typically contains 3,000 to 5,000 individuals, and we summarize neighborhood quality in a single dimension – the fraction of residents who are college-educated. In terms of racial composition, we focus on non-Hispanic black and non-Hispanic white individuals 25 years and older. Non-Hispanic blacks and whites respectively constitute 11.1 and 69.5 percent of the U.S. population 25 years and older residing in metropolitan areas. Among blacks, 15.4 percent have a four-year college degree, while the comparable number for whites is 32.5 percent.

Looking at all the Census tracts in the United States, we show that while neighborhoods combining high fractions of both college-educated and white individuals are abundant in all metropolitan areas, very few neighborhoods combine high fractions of both college-educated and black individuals. For example, while 22.6 percent of all US tracts are at least 40 percent college-educated, only 2.5 percent of tracts that are at least 40 percent black and only 1.1 percent of tracts that are at least 60 percent black meet this education threshold. In fact, there are only 44 neighborhoods in the whole country that are both 60 percent black and 40 percent college educated. Moreover, in addition to being scarce in general, these neighborhoods are concentrated in only a handful of metropolitan areas, most notably Baltimore-Washington DC, indicating that the availability of such neighborhoods in most metropolitan areas is even more limited.[6]

The scarcity of neighborhoods combining high fractions of both black and college-educated households means that neighborhood race and many other neighborhood characteristics are explicitly linked in the set of residential options available to most households: in order to choose neighborhoods with more college-educated neighbors, households must typically live with a greater fraction of whites.

---

[6] Of the 44 tracts that are at least 60 percent black and 40 percent college-educated, for example 14 are in Baltimore-Washington DC, 8 in Detroit, 6 in Los Angeles, and 5 in Atlanta. Of the 142 tracts that are at least 40 percent black and 40 percent college-educated, almost two-thirds are in the Metropolitan Statistical Areas (MSAs) listed above along with Chicago and New York.

10.4.1 Hedonic Demand Estimation

This bundling of neighborhood race and other neighborhood attributes has serious consequences for the use of hedonic methods to infer preferences. The central assumption of hedonic demand estimation is that households face a continuous hedonic price function and choose the level of consumption of each amenity or attribute in order to maximize utility. This assumption fails to hold whenever households consume a level of a neighborhood attribute that puts them on a boundary constraint. This is why hedonic demand estimation of racial preferences breaks down when a sizeable part of the population lives in perfectly segregated neighborhoods – as discussed in Section 10.2. The strong bundling of neighborhood attributes and race suggests that such boundary constraints are likely to bind in many more instances. In particular, bundling implies that at many points in multi-dimensional space of neighborhood attributes it is simply not possible to increase consumption of one attribute (fraction of black neighbors) without increasing consumption of another (fraction of college-educated neighbors).

In light of the failure of the central assumption of hedonic demand estimation, one alternative is to use a different approach to estimate preferences – more on this below. If researchers do use hedonic methods, however, estimation would likely be improved by specifying a flexible hedonic price function with the bundling of neighborhood race and neighborhood attributes in mind. One way to do this is to allow for interactions between neighborhood attributes. Including these interaction terms would permit the possibility that the hedonic price of additional college-educated neighbors may rise steeply near the implicit constraint that arises due the bundling of neighborhood race and education. An even more flexible approach to the estimation of the hedonic price function is the local linear approach developed in Bajari and Kahn (2005) and Bajari and Benkard (2005). In this case, the hedonic price function is estimated separately for each house/neighborhood using weights based on the proximity of other houses/neighborhoods in both geographic and attribute space. The key advantage of this approach is that it naturally allows the hedonic price function to vary flexibly near any constraints in the attribute space.

10.4.2 An Alternative Approach to Estimating Preferences – Discrete Choice

Discrete choice estimation provides an alternative framework for inferring preferences.[7] This approach is used widely in economics and does not require that household consumption of a particular attribute satisfies a first order condition. This is especially desirable when estimating racial preferences given the extent to

[7] See McFadden (1973, 1978) for some of the key initial developments of discrete choice models. Cropper et al. (1993) compares hedonic demand and discrete choice estimation directly.

which households are likely to lie on a boundary constraint with respect to neighborhood race.

Discrete choice estimation trades heavily on the notion of revealed preference: a household's chosen house/neighborhood must have provided greater indirect utility than those not chosen. We develop and estimate an equilibrium model or residential sorting based on an underlying discrete choice framework in Bayer et al. (2005). While a full characterization of that model is beyond the scope of this chapter, it is important to point out that the discrete choice framework also requires assumptions for identification, most notably an assumption about the distribution of idiosyncratic preferences for houses and neighborhoods.

The discrete choice approach also has a second key advantage. Because it is incredibly difficult to solve the system of partial differential equations that characterize the hedonic equilibrium when the attribute space is multi-dimensional, researchers cannot generally conduct general equilibrium counterfactual simulations with an estimated hedonic demand system. The equilibrium model of sorting that we develop in Bayer et al. (2005), however, lends itself quite easily to general equilibrium counterfactual simulations.

10.5 Conclusion

This chapter highlights a number of key theoretical and empirical issues that arise in attempting to infer preferences for neighborhood racial composition in observational data. We focus on three key areas. First, in the context of a simple model of racial sorting, we draw attention to the difficulty of identifying the operation of centralized racial discrimination using observational data and illustrate the relationship between racial preferences and the equilibrium (hedonic) price of neighborhood racial composition. Second, we discuss the likely correlation of neighborhood race and unobserved neighborhood quality in most data sets, then present evidence that this correlation is indeed substantial, before describing an attractive solution to the associated endogeneity problem using a boundary discontinuity design. Third, we note that because predominantly black, high-amenity neighborhoods are scarce in most U.S. cities, neighborhood race and neighborhood quality are often explicitly *bundled*: to choose high-amenity neighborhoods, households must typically live with a higher fraction of white neighbors. This bundling of neighborhood attributes is naturally captured using a discrete choice approach, which has an added attraction relative to hedonic demand models in that it lends itself to carrying out informative counterfactual simulations.

References

Bajari P, Benkard L (2005) Demand estimation with heterogeneous consumers and unobserved product characteristics: a hedonic approach. Journal of political economy 113: 1239–1276

Bajari P, Kahn ME (2005) Estimating housing demand with an application to explaining racial segregation in cities. Journal of business & economic statistics 23: 20–33

Bayer P, Ferreira F, McMillan R (2007) A unified framework for estimating preferences for schools and neighbors. Journal of political economy 115: 588–638

Bayer P, McMillan R (2006) Racial sorting and neighborhood quality. Working paper, NBER, Cambridge, United States

Bayer P, McMillan R, Rueben KS (2005) An equilibrium model of sorting in an urban housing market. Working paper 10865, NBER, Cambridge, United States

Black S (1999) Do better schools matter? Parental valuation of elementary education. Quarterly journal of economics 114(2): 577-599

Cropper M, Deck L, Kishor N, McConnell KE (1993) Valuing product attributes using single market data: a comparison of hedonic and discrete choice approaches. The review of economics and statistics 75: 225–232

Cutler DM, Glaeser EL, Vigdor JL (1999) The rise and decline of the american ghetto. Journal of political economy 107: 455–506

Ekeland I, Heckman JJ, Nesheim L (2002) Identification and estimation of hedonic models. Working paper CWP07/02, Centre for microdata methods and practice

Epple D (1987) Hedonic prices and implicit markets: estimating demand and supply functions for differentiated products. Journal of political economy 107: 645–81

Epple D, Filimon R, Romer T (1984) Equilibrium among local jurisdictions: towards an integrated approach of voting and residential choice. Journal of public economics 24: 281–304

Epple D, Filimon R, Romer T (1993) Existence of voting and housing equilibrium in a system of communities with property taxes. Regional science and urban economics 23: 585–610

Epple D, Sieg H (1999) Estimating equilibrium models of local jurisdictions. Journal of political economy 107: 645–681

Heckman JJ, Matzkin R, Nesheim L (2003) Simulation and estimation of hedonic models. IZA Discusion Paper 843; CESifo Working Paper Series 1014

McFadden D (1973) Conditional logit analysis of qualitative choice behavior. Frontiers in econometrics: 105–142

McFadden D (1978) Modeling the choice of residential location. In: Karlquist A, Lundqvist L, Snickars F, Weibull JW (eds) Spatial interaction theory and planning models. Elsevier, North-Holland, New-York

Nesheim L (2001) Equilibrium sorting of heterogeneous consumers across locations: theory and empirical implications. Ph. D. dissertation, University of Chicago

Rosen S (1974) Hedonic prices and implicit markets: product differentiation in pure competition. Journal of political economy 82: 34–55

Appendix

Appendix – Applying Hedonics in the Housing Market: An Illustration

Bengt Kriström

Swedish University of Agricultural Sciences, Umeå, Sweden

A.1 Introduction

This short chapter provides a basic introduction to the application of the hedonic approach. My aim is to provide the general reader with a roadmap to the estimation of the simplest possible hedonic model. I will use the freely available software R (see R Development Core Team 2007) so that the reader can follow step-by-step how the econometric model is specified and analyzed. I have in mind a student who wants a hands-on introduction to the method, where all the steps are explained, including the exact computer code. All the empirical analysis in this chapter is directly replicable. Because I am using a famous dataset, the student can explore further and compare his own analysis with what has been found in other literatures.

A.1.1 The Setting

I am interested in estimating a hedonic price function

$$p_i = f(x_i, y_i, z_i) \tag{1}$$

where p_i is the price of house $i = 1,2,...,n$, f is an unknown function, x_i is an M vector of house characteristics, y_i an S vector of locational characteristics and z_i an L vector of environmental characteristics (see Taylor, this Volume for a complete description of the theoretical foundations of the hedonic model). Thus, the dataset consists of n observations of prices on sold houses. Each house is described by its intrinsic properties, given by the x vector, the locational characteristics, portrayed by the vector y, its environmental quality characteristics (the $\mathbf{z}$ vector).

Let all characteristics be collected into $\boldsymbol{\Theta}_i = \{x_i, z_i, y_i\}$ and denote the dataset dat_n, $dat_n = \{e_1, e_2, e_3 ... e_n\}$, which has *n* observations on variables $e_i = \{p_i, \boldsymbol{\Theta}_i\}$.

A.1.2 The Conceptual Model

At the outset, it is important to note that there are several types of hedonic approaches even within the seemingly narrow set of hedonic models that we focus on here. In roughly chronological order, hedonic models (in environmental economics) started out with data based on tract averages. These were followed by applications using data on individual houses, after which the next natural step was to use repeated sales data. Several other variants have been introduced, including the more recent models using quasi-experimental data, spatial econometrics as well as discrete-choice models. The other chapters have details about these developments.

The first step of the analysis should, of course, be the conceptual model. I refer to the other chapters of the book for information about this and turn to the empirical analysis.

A.1.3 Initial Statistical Analysis

Space precludes a detailed discussion of sampling issues. Yet, the sense in which the sample can be regarded as random needs to be detailed, so that one can appreciate the possibilities of generalization as well as the validity of various econometric tests. Independently of which hedonic approach one selects to use, the second step of the analysis should include a detailed scrutiny of the variables in the obtained dataset dat_n.

We typically consider the prices p_i as values of independent random variables P_i. Let variables in $\boldsymbol{\Theta}$ be *uninformative* if the distribution of P_i is independent of those variables. Such variables will usually be deleted from the analysis. On the other hand, if we omit variables that are *informative*, the situation is considerably more problematic. In particular, the statistical inference can be erroneous when we are working with an incorrect statistical model. More on this below. Beyond the routine statistical analysis that will help reveal unusual observations, misrecordings and so on, it is imperative to provide a in-depth description of how the data were generated. It goes without saying that any published material should be easily replicable.

A.1.4 Data Issues

Theory posits that the prices are equilibrium prices and it is imperative that they can be so interpreted. While market imperfections may be irrelevant in many cases, or can be approximated away, there may be market idiosyncracies that suggest temporary disequilibria. It seems intuitively plausible that the hedonic relationship does not have to be stable in a "bubble" market see e.g. Case and Shiller (1988) for detailed analysis of "boom" and "post-boom" markets. For recent discussion about price formation in housing markets, see Gayer et al. (2007).

Turning then to the intrinsic characteristics of each house we first need to discuss the choice of variables used to describe the set of houses under scrutiny. Number of rooms, year the house was built, space are typical variables we would look at as buyers (as well as analysts). Because of the extensive literature and the expertise real estate agents can usefully provide, the choice of variables to describe the house can presumably be resolved quite easily. But as everyone who has ever bought a house knows, there usually are some hidden issues that surfaces after some time. The extent to which these issues were known to the seller (and his agent) at the time of the sale is a matter that sometimes end up in the courts. Markets with *imperfect information* have rather different welfare-properties compared to the perfect market paradigm underlying most of the hedonics literature. There is, of course, a very large literature on imperfect information in economics, which includes analysis of housing markets. For a recent theoretical analysis of welfare measurement in our context, see Konishi and Coggins (2007).

A similar set of issues surfaces when analyzing data needs for descriptors of location. In environmental economics application, we customarily divide these descriptors in vectors $\mathbf{z}$ (the environment) and $\mathbf{y}$ (the neighborhood). Suppose, for simplicity, that we are interested in the value of one environmental quality variable, so that $\mathbf{z}$ has one component. For concreteness, let this be the ambient level of nitrogen oxides (NOx). The basic hedonic model postulates that the market actors can properly understand the effects of NOx in the choice set. Indeed, the individual does make a choice about where to live, given the levels of environmental quality in all locations in the studied choice set[1]. The evidence we have today certainly indicates that the hedonic model works better when market participants are aware of the underlying issues.

At any rate, the analyst must make a decision about how the environmental indicator is to be included in the dataset; how is the environmental information to be aggregated? The sum of exposure (over a year, say) could be higher in tract A compared to tract B, while tract B experiences more frequent episodes, but less

[1] As an aside, the combination of NOx, volatile organic compounds and sunlight form photochemical smog with well-documented detrimental health impacts.

overall exposure. The analyst must then decide if the average exposure level, or some measure of incidence, is a better representation of the environmental data. Hedonic studies usually include community information on school quality and other public goods, as well as crime rates and so on. The question is whether useful proxies can be constructed. School quality is not easily measured and the scope for measurement error is significant. On top of these issues, the meta-analysis by Smith and Huang (1995) shows that the number of factors in the hedonic model does make a difference to the estimates. I will explore this in the illustration below.

A.2 A Worked-Out Example : The Harrison & Rubenfield (1978) Data

To put some meat to this discussion, let us consider the data used in the classic study by Harrison and Rubinfeld (1978), see Table 1. This dataset has been analyzed in a wide range of papers, because of its easy availability on the internet. Gilley and Pace (1996) published a correction of the data and re-analyzed the impact of the imposed censoring of the price variable (see below). Further corrections have been published as shown in the addendum.

Table A.1. The Harrison-Rubinfeld Data

Variable name	Description
cmedv	Median value of owner-occupied homes
room	Average number of rooms in owner units
older	Proportion of owner units built prior to 1940
B	Black proportion of the population[a]
lstat	Proportion of population that is of lower status[b]
crime	Crime rate by town/census tract
residential	Zoning variable[c]
industrial	Proportion of nonretail business acres per town
tax	Full property tax (USD 10,000)[d]
ptratio	Pupil-teacher ratio by town school district
riveryes	Charles River dummy variable
distance	Weighted distances to five Boston employment centers
highway	Index of accessibility to radial highways
nox	Nitrogen oxide concentrations in pphm[e]

[a] 1,000 $\times$(*blacks* -0.63)^2 where *blacks* is the proportion of blacks by town, [b] Proportion of adults without some high school education and proportion of male workers classified as laborers, [c] Proportion of town's residential land zoned for lots greater than 25,000 square feet,[d] Nominal tax rates were corrected by local assessment ratios to yield the full value tax rate for each town, [e] Annual average concentration in parts per hundred million. Data source : http://www.econ.ohio-state.edu/jhm/econ641/boston.txt.

The study uses data for census tracts in the Boston Standard Metropolitan Statistical Area (SMSA) in 1970, n=506. Thus, I am using for illustration what we today would consider an "old-fashioned" approach. In particular, the use of tract-data rather than data on individual units was initially considered to give much worse estimates (and the switch to using data on individual houses naturally followed); this view has now changed, as noted by Palmquist and Smith (2002). Still, we inevitably loose information when aggregating.

Let us now use the freely available software R (R Development Core Team 2007) to take a look at the data. Download the software at r-project.org and see the addendum for the code used here.

A.2.1 Price Variable

If we look at the price variable then, as noted, there is censoring at a maximum price of 50,000 USD, see Figure 1.

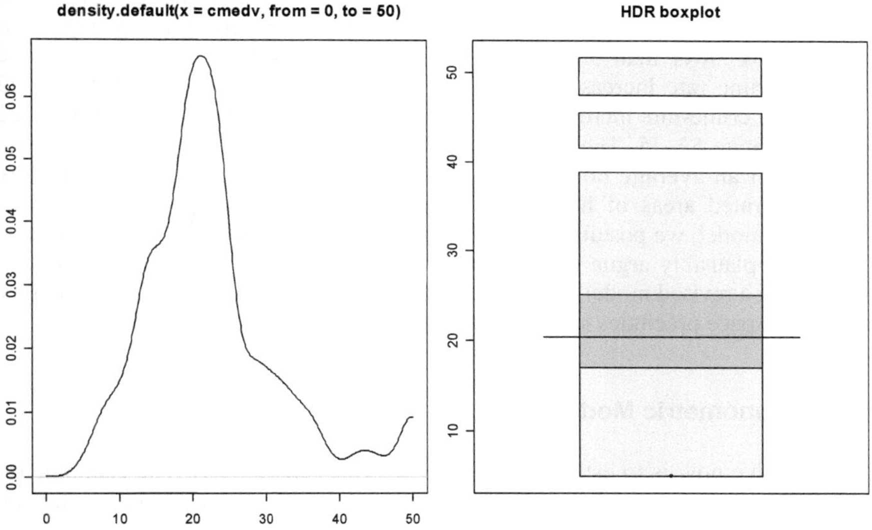

Fig. A.1. Estimated Density and the Highest Density Region Plot of the Price Variable. Data source : http://www.econ.ohio-state.edu/jhm/econ641/boston.txt.

I have plotted the estimated density and a HDR (Highest Density Region) plot. The figures show the slight bimodality of the distribution and the concentration of the density to the region 17,000 to 25,000 USD. Given the censoring, we know that the dependent variable cannot be normally distributed, so that classical regression does not apply. We can use Tobit regression or methods less sensitive to distributional assumption, as discussed below.

A.2.2 Air Pollution Variable

Air pollution (NOx) concentration was obtained from a meteorological model of the Boston air shed, the Transportation and Air Shed Simulation (TASSIM) Model developed by Ingram et al. (see e.g. Ingram and Fauth 1974). There are 81 unique observations on NOx. Given the way the variable is measured, a number of areas should have the same predicted level of NOx. The lowest value is 0.385 and the highest recorded observation of NOx is 0.871. A closer look at the data reveals that the low-pollution areas have relatively young houses, low criminality and a relatively large fraction of nonbusiness retail acres.

A.2.3 Other Variables

The variable measuring the crime rate is very interesting, in that the median is 0.25, while the mean is 3.6; it is thus highly skewed. The crime rate is very low, when nox is lower than 33.6 (about the 60th percentile). At nox levels beyond 33.6 the crime rate increases explosively. Curiously, at a nox-level between 45 and 51, the crime-rate increases dramatically after which it falls to about 6, in the pollution range 52–75. The crime rate is also strongly negatively correlated with the price of an average house. Thus, data seems to suggest that prices are low in concentrated areas of high criminality and high nox levels. In the hedonic regression model, we postulate that nox and crime are uncorrelated and exogenous. One could plausibly argue that this is not the case here. This would lead us into considering a revised model, in which we try to endogenize some of the explanatory variables. Space precludes such an exercise in this chapter.

A.2.4 Econometric Modelling

Our objective now is to estimate the hedonic price function $f(.)$. The econometric modelling should address, at least: functional form, multicollinearity, iden-tification issues, exogeneity and spatial issues. The usual way to estimate the hedonic price function is via regression methods and I will begin there.

A popular model is the semi-log,

$$log(p_j) = a + \sum b_i x_{ij} + \sum \beta_i y_{ij} + \sum \gamma_i z_{ij} + \varepsilon_j . \qquad (2)$$

We usually assume that ε_j is normally distributed, with constant variance. The modelling process can then be viewed as a set of procedures to ensure that our final empirical model produces "white noise" residuals. I will use this procedure here, because theory provides few restrictions on $f(.)$.

Choice of Functional Form

There are several ways to estimate *f*(.). Possible approaches include the usual parametric models, a family of parametric models, local regression (e.g. Cheng and Peng 2006), semi-parametric (e.g. Castillo et al. 2007) and non-parametric (Parmeter et al. 2007) methods, building upon different sets of assumptions. For dimension reduction problems, the so-called sliced regression has been used with these data, see Prendergast (2007). A Bayesian regression approach is reported in Yuan and Lin (2005). R includes a large variety of procedures, including an extensive set of robust regression procedures.

As a starting point, I suggest the following approach. Begin with the simplest regression model (a semi-log), explore the properties of the residuals using the q-q plot and other tests (to be detailed below) and use re-sampling methods to test for accuracy. Amend to these approaches what effectively entails different assumptions about ε, such as robust regression and quantile regression. I will illustrate this, but I will comment on some important econometric issues first.

Multicollinearity

Hedonic studies are plagued by correlations between the explanatory variables. For example, in a larger house, we expect to find more bathrooms. So-called help regressions, in which the independent variables are regressed against each other, provides one way of testing for multicollinearity, besides using conventional tests for multicollinearity that are explained in econometric textbooks. R offers several interesting approaches, including the `perturb` package, which adds random noise to the explanatory variables. If the parameters are sensitive towards perturbation, this is a warning sign. The standard variance inflation factors (see e.g. Fox (1997)) are directly available using the command `vif`.

Heteroscedasticity

When the residual variance is not constant, we have a deviation between what we usually assume about ε and the properties of the estimated residuals. In linear regression, heteroscedasticity affects the accuracy tests (such as t-values). In more complex models, the effect is more subtle; heteroscedasticity is a form of mis-specification. Handling this problem is routine in econometric modelling, although the particular "medicine" used varies. Here, I will only use re-sampling.

Accuracy

There are several ways that we can explore the accuracy of the estimators. I propose to use, as a complement to the usual t-values, re-sampling methods, because they are so easily available these days. In particular, R allows the use of re-sampling methods in a simple and powerful manner.

Spatial Econometrics

As illustrated in Taylor, this Volume and Geniaux and Napoléone, this Volume, spatial regression methods are becoming popular in the hedonics literature, see also e.g. Bivand (2002), Lesage and Pace (2004), Pace and Gilley (1997). There may be spatial linkages between the houses that we cannot easily pick up with conventional methods. It turns out that R has a set of powerful routines for doing spatial regression, but it will take us too far afield; see Bivand (2002) for an introduction.

A.2.5 Modelling Approach

Let us use the suggested strategy, and see where it leads us in the data at hand. To simplify our specification search, let us use the specification employed in the original paper by Harrison-Rubenfield. They used the model:

$$\begin{aligned} log(cmedv) = a + b_1 \times room2 + b_2 \times older + \beta_1 \times crime + \beta_2 \times residential \\ + \beta_3 \times industrial + \beta_4 \times river + \beta_5 \times log(distance) \\ + \beta_6 \times log(highway) + \beta_7 \times tax + \beta_8 \times ptratio + \gamma_1 \times nox2 \end{aligned} \quad (3)$$

The log of the median value is regressed against a number of variables in the dataset, where some of them have been transformed (after a specification search). nox2 and room2 are the squares of nox and room respectively, and distance and highway are introduced in log form. I am unable to exactly replicate their results, presumably because I am using a twice corrected dataset (see the addendum for details about the data). The differences are, however, not very large. The results are reported in Table 2.

Table A.2. Regression of log(Median Value of House)

Variables	Estimate	Std. Error	t value	Pr(>|t|)
(Intercept)	4.099	0.145	28.208	0.000
room2	0.009	0.001	7.179	0.000
older	-0.001	0.001	-0.973	0.331
log(distance)	-0.257	0.033	-7.708	0.000
log(highway)	0.100	0.019	5.211	0.000
tax	-0.001	0.000	-4.229	0.000

Table A.2. (cont.)

ptratio	-0.032	0.005	-6.469	0.000
B	0.000	0.000	3.662	0.000
stat	-0.029	0.002	-14.771	0.000
crime	-0.011	0.001	-8.484	0.000
residential	0.001	0.001	2.157	0.032
industrial	0.001	0.002	0.561	0.575
nox2	-0.666	0.113	-5.871	0.000
Residual standard error	0.184	on 493 degrees of freedom		
Multiple R-squared	0.803			
Adjusted R-squared	0.798			
F-statistic	167.100	on 12 and 493 degrees of freedom		
AIC	-264.739			
BIC	-205.568			

AIC and BIC are the Aikaike and the Bayesian information criteria for comparing different models.[2] Data source : http://www.econ.ohio-state.edu/jhm/econ641/boston.txt

The coefficients have the expected sign. For example, a lower status of the tract, a higher crime rate and higher NOx-emissions tend to lower the median price of a house. By differentiating equation (2) with respect to nox, the marginal willingness to pay for reducing NOx can be obtained. The interpretation of this derivative, and the caveats, is explained in more detail in Taylor's chapter, this Volume.

Removing the insignificant variables *older* and *industrial*, I get AIC = –267.45 and BIC = –216.73. Because these values are smaller, we can argue that the longer model that includes the insignificant variables should be retained. This seems inconsistent with what I said above about uninformative variables.

The explanation is that the parameters are correlated; we get an indirect signal of multicollinearity problems. A test for this is provided by the so-called variance-inflation-factors (VIFs)[3]. The VIF-statistics is reported in Table 3. A VIF statistic higher than four is often taken as a warning sign. See Judge et al. (1985), (pp. 868–870) for a useful discussion (including their suggested benchmark of a VIF greater than 5).

---

[2] The help file in R (R Development Core Team 2007) provides "AIC = –2×log-likelihood + k×npar, where npar represents the number of parameters in the fitted model, and k = 2 for the usual AIC, or k = log(n) (n the number of observations) for the so-called BIC or SBC (Schwarz's Bayesian criterion)".

[3] If the regressors are standardized, then the VIF-factors are the diagonal of the regression matrix (x'x)–1.

Table A.3. VIF-Statistics for the Model

Variables	VIF
room2	1.88
older	3.14
Log(distance)	4.85
log(highway)	4.21
tax	6.40
ptratio	1.77
B	1.34
lstat	2.90
crime	1.77
residential	2.11
industrial	3.96
nox_2	3.73

Data source : http://www.econ.ohio-state.edu/jhm/econ641/boston.txt.

The model fits the data rather well and now we will check the assumptions on the residual process. A convenient way is the quantile-quantile (QQ)-plot of the residuals against a normal distributed variable. The plot will be a straight line, if the residuals follow a normal distribution. See Figure 2.

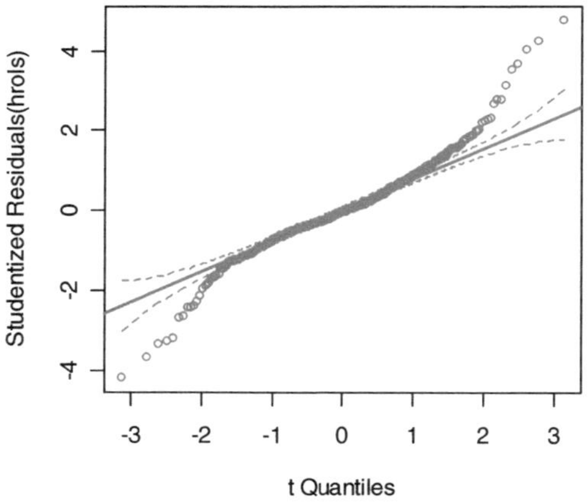

Fig. A.2. QQ-Plot of Residuals. Data source : http://www.econ.ohio-state.edu/jhm/econ641/boston.txt.

The plot shows that the model "works well" in the main body of the data; there is deviation from normality in the tails. This is a warning sign, in that many tests are based on assumptions of normality. Furthermore, it tells us that our model has difficulties predicting prices at the low and high ends of the market.

In order to allow for more general assumptions on the error process, I used robust regression (using the command `rlm` in R, see the addendum) but the differences compared to OLS were small. To further buttress the model, I also applied quantile regression (see e.g. Koenker and Hallock 2001) which can handle heterogeneity in a much more general way than OLS. It is available in the package `quantreg` in R. Ordinary regression gives us the conditional mean function, but quantile regression allows the analysis of the conditional quantile function. Therefore, it provides a more comprehensive view of how the market price of a house responds to the background variables. I found that most regression coefficients were stable, but that there is some heterogeneity in the response.

For the ordinary regression case, there are several other model checks that should be included, such as analysis of outliers, leverage and influential observations. These are available in the package `car` for direct use in R. If one saves the estimated regression model in a parameter called "M", then simply calling `plot(`M`)` in R provides a set of useful plots for analysis of the mentioned issues.

Accuracy

Re-sampling methods provide a computer-intensive approach to many statistical problems, including obtaining measures of accuracy. I have used the library `simpleboot` in R, which directly gives us standard errors of the estimates.

There are several ways of doing re-sampling, so here is just a simple illustration. The results are in Table 4.

Table A.4. Bootstrapped t-values for the Harrison-Rubinfeld Model

Variables	t-value
(Intercept)	16.29
room2	3.67
Older	−0.54
log(distance)	−51.36
log(highway)	34.18
Tax	−2.99
Ptratio	−3.29
B	1.84
Lstat	−7.69
Crime	−4.21
residential	1.14
industrial	0.31
nox_2	−3.15

Data source : http://www.econ.ohio-state.edu/jhm/econ641/boston.txt.

Thus, our conclusions regarding the accuracy of the parameter estimates are, on the whole, upheld.

A.3 Final notes

The availability of powerful and free software has extended our ability to carry out extensive econometric analysis of hedonic models. I have pointed to some ways in which one can use R to analyse hedonic data, barely scratching the surface of the program's capabilities and the ways data analysis can help us understand how the market maps the value consumers' place on environmental quality change.

References

Bivand R (2002) Spatial econometrics functions in R: classes and methods. Journal of geographical systems 4: 405–421

Castillo E, Hadi AS, Lacruz B, Pruneda RE (2007) Semiparametric nonlinear regression and transformation using functional networks. Computational statistics and data analysis 52: 2129–2157

Case KE, Shiller J (1988) The behavior of home buyers in boom and post-boom markets. New england economic review 29: 29–47

Cheng MY, Peng L (2006) Simple and efficient improvements of multivariate local linear regression. Journal of multivariate analysis 97: 1501–1524

Gayer G, Gilboa I, Lieberman O (2007) Rule-based and case-based reasoning in housing prices. Journal of theoretical economics 7:1. Available at: http://www.bepress.com/bejte/vol7/iss1/art10

Gilley OW, Pace RK (1996) On the Harrison and Rubinfeld data. Journal of environmental economics and management 31: 403–405

Harrison Jr D, Rubinfeld DL (1978) Hedonic housing prices and the demand for clean air. Journal of environmental economics and management 5: 81–102

Ingram GK, Fauth GR (1974) TASSIM: A transportation and air shed simulation model. Vol I. Case Study of the Boston Region Harvard University, Cambridge, Massachussets

Konishi Y, Coggins JS (2007) Environmental risk and welfare valuation under imperfect information. Forthcoming in Environmental & resource economics

Lesage JP, Pace RK (2004) Models for spatially dependent missing data. Journal of real estate finance and economics 29: 233–254

Fox J (1997) Applied regression, linear models, and related methods. Sage publications, New York

Judge OG, Griffith WE, Hill RC, Lee TC, Ltkepohl H (1985) The theory and practice of econometrics. 2nd edn, Wiley, New York

Koenker R, Hallock K (2001) Quantile regression. Journal of economic perspectives 15: 143–156

Pace RK, Gilley OW (1997) Using the spatial configuration of the data to improve estimation. Journal of real estate finance and economics 14: 333–340

Palmquist RB, Smith VK (2002) The use of hedonic property value techniques for policy and litigation. In: Tietenberg T, Folmer H (eds) The International yearbook of envi-

ronmental and resource economics 2002/2003. Edward Elgar, Cheltenham, UK, pp 115–164
Parmeter CF, Henderson DJ, Kumbhakar SC (2007) Nonparametric estimation of a hedonic price function. Journal of applied econometrics 22: 695–699
Prendergast LA (2007) Implications of influence function analysis forsliced inverse regression and sliced average variance estimation. Biometrika 94: 585–601
R Development Core Team (2007) R: A language and environment for statistical computing. R Foundation for statistical computing, Vienna, Austria, http://www.R-project.org
Smith VK, Huang JC (1995) Can markets value air quality? A meta-analysis of hedonic property value models. Journal of political economy 103: 209–227
Yuan M, Lin Y (2005) Efficient empirical bayes variable selection and estimation in linear models. Journal of the american statistical association 100 : 1215–1225

Addendum: R-code

This replicates the analysis in the paper. R is using "#"for commenting. I will use `this font` for R-commands.

Download and install the following packages from http://www.cran.r-project.org:

```
library(Hmisc)
library(car)
library(vioplot)
library(sm)
library(ineq)
library(lattice)
require(hdrcde)
library(MASS)
library(chplot)
library(xtable)
library(quantreg)
```

The following quote is an excerpt from http://www.econ.ohio-state.edu/jhm/econ641/boston.txt

"This data set was downloaded from the STATLIB data base site `http://lib.stat.cmu.edu/datasets/boston` and then corrected for OSU Econ641 per OW Gilley & RK Pace "On the Harrison and Rubinfeld Data", J. Env. Econ & Mgmt. 31: 403–5 (1996). I was unable to find the MEDV of 37.0 that they report should be 33.0 for observation 119, but have confirmed with Kelly Pace that this is itself a typo for observation 191, and have changed observation 191 accordingly. There are 35 header lines, counting the variable name line. There are 506 observations, representing Boston census tracts. Note that MEDV is top-coded at USD 50,000. Variables in order: CRIM per capita crime rate by town ZN proportion of residential land zoned for lots over 25,000 sq.ft. INDUS proportion of non-retail business acres per town CHAS Charles River dummy variable (= 1 if tract bounds river; 0 otherwise) NOX nitric oxides concentration (parts per 10 million) RM average number of rooms per dwelling AGE proportion of owner-occupied units built prior to 1940 DIS weighted distances to five Boston employment centres RAD index of accessibility to radial highways TAX full-value property-tax rate per USD10,000 PTRATIO pupil-teacher ratio by town, B = 1000 * $(Bk - 0.63)^2$, where Bk is the proportion of blacks by town LSTAT % lower status of the population MEDV Median value of owner-occupied homes in USD 1000's."

I will use the following variable names: `cmedv, crime, residential, industrial, river, nox, rooms, older, distance, highway, tax ,ptratio ,lstat, black`. Below is a transcript from the R-session.

Alternative ways of getting the data:
Alt 1. Getting it directly from the web

```
# load data after downloading the packages
boston<-read.table(url("http://www.econ.ohio-
state.edu/jhm/econ641/boston.txt"),skip=35,header=T)
```

Alt 2. Download the .sav file from my website www-sekon.slu.se\~bkr\boston.sav and save it in a local directory (I am using h:\arb\curres\baranzini). I will use this approach here (the results are very similar).

```
# load data after downloading from above address
load("h:\\arb\\curres\\baranzini\\boston.sav")

# If one prefers Alt 1, then change variable names
cmedv=MEDV
crime=CRIM
residential=ZN
industrial=INDUS
river=CHAS
nox=NOX
rooms=RM
older=AGE
distance=DIS
highway=RAD
tax=TAX
ptratio=PTRATIO
lstat=LSTAT
black=B

# DESCRIPTIVE STATISTICS OF THE VARIABLES
attach(boston)
```

```
describe(boston)

# SECTION ON THE PRICE VARIABLE
# figure 1
opar <- par(mfrow=c(1,2), mar=c(3,2,4,1))
plot(density(cmedv,from=0,to=50))
hdr.boxplot(cmedv, main="HDR boxplot")
savePlot("densities", "wmf")
# SECTION ON NOX
min(nox)
max(nox)

# Get the low and top % of nox
quantile(nox, probs=c(.1,.5,1,2,5,10,50,95,99)/100)

# SECTION ON OTHER VARIABLES
describe(crime)
x10=factor(cut2(nox, g=10))
c10=factor(cut2(crime, g=10))
# look at the crime rate in the top deciles!!
summary(crime~x10)

# SECTION ON MODELLING
# Transformations
nox2=nox*nox
room2=rooms*rooms

# OLS
hrols=lm(log(cmedv)~room2+older+log(distance)+log(highw
ay)+ tax +ptratio + black +lstat+crime+residential +
industrial +nox2)

# Make a nice looking table of the results
xtable(summary(hrols), caption="Regression of
log(median value of house)",label="tab ols", dig-
its=c(3), type="latex", file="hrols.tex", ta-
ble.placement = "tp", latex.environments=c("center",
"footnotesize"))

# Add some statistics by hand
summary(hrols)

# add AIC and BIC
AIC(hrols)

# A version of BIC or Schwarz' BC
AIC(hrols, k = log(nrow(boston)))
```

```
# Remove the insignificant variables and check the AIC,
BIC again
hrolsM=lm(log(cmedv)~crime+river+nox2+room2+older
+log(distance)+log(highway)+tax+ptratio)
# Add AIC and BIC
AIC(hrolsM)
# QQ-plot
qq.plot(hrolsM)

# Check the qq-plot and save it as a ps figure
windows()
myqqplotM=qq.plot(hrolsM)
savePlot("myqqplot", "ps")

# Multicollinearity
v1=as.matrix(vif(hrols))
xtable(v1)

# Bootstrapping
library(simpleboot)
set.seed(30)
lboot <- lm.boot(hrols, R = 1000)
summary(lboot)
b=coef(hrols)

# Collate the standard deviations
std=summary(lboot)[[6]]

# Compute t-statistics
tvalues=b/std
t=as.matrix(tvalues)
xtable(t)

# Robust regression
hrrlm=rlm(log(cmedv)~crime+residential+industrial+river
+nox2+room2+older+log(distance)+log(highway)+tax
+ptratio)

# Compare the coefficients in ols and robust
coefols=coef(hrols)
coefrlm=coef(hrrlm)
coefs=cbind(coefols,coefrlm)
coefs

# Quantile regression
rqbengt=plot(summary(rq(log(cmedv)~crime+residential+
```

```
industrial+river+nox2+room2+older+log(distance)+
log(highway)+tax+ptratio, tau = 1:10/11)))
```

General index

T

U

Author index

MIX
Papier aus verantwortungsvollen Quellen
Paper from responsible sources
FSC® C105338

If you have any concerns about our products,
you can contact us on
ProductSafety@springernature.com

In case Publisher is established outside the EU,
the EU authorized representative is:
Springer Nature Customer Service Center GmbH
Europaplatz 3, 69115 Heidelberg, Germany

Printed by Libri Plureos GmbH
in Hamburg, Germany